RELIGION, SCIENCE AND
MORAL PHILOSOPHY IN THE
HUGUENOT ENLIGHTENMENT
*JEAN HENRI SAMUEL FORMEY
AND THE BERLIN ACADEMY*

OXFORD UNIVERSITY STUDIES IN THE ENLIGHTENMENT
– formerly *Studies on Voltaire and the Eighteenth Century* (*SVEC*),
is dedicated to eighteenth-century research.

General Editor
Gregory S. Brown, University of Nevada, Las Vegas

Associate Editors
Jenny Mander, University of Cambridge
Alexis Tadié, Sorbonne Université

Ex-officio
Nicholas Cronk, University of Oxford

Editorial Board
Katherine Brading, Duke University
Jean-Luc Chappey, Université de Paris Panthéon-Sorbonne
Andrew Curran, Wesleyan University
Schmuel Feiner, Bar-Ilan University
Amy Freund, Southern Methodist University
Emily Friedman, Auburn University
Aurélia Gaillard, Université Bordeaux – Montaigne
Charlotte Guichard, Centre national de la recherche scientifique
Catherine M. Jaffe, Texas State University
Bela Kapossy, Université de Lausanne
Minchul Kim, Sungkyunkwan University
Avi Lifschitz, University of Oxford
Anton Matytsin, University of Florida
Pierre Musitelli, Ecole normale superieure
Nathalie Ferrand, Ecole normale superieure
Christy Pichichero, George Mason University
Siofra Pierce, University College Dublin
Glenn Roe, Sorbonne Université
Kelsey Rubin-Detlev, University of Southern California
Neil Safier, Brown University
Ayana O. Smith, Indiana University
Karen Stolley, Emory University
Geoffrey Turnovsky, University of Washington
Thomas Wallnig, University of Vienna
Masano Yamashita, Colorado University

Consultative Editors
Elisabeth Décultot, University of Halle
Andrew Jainchill, Queen's University
Andrew Kahn, University of Oxford
Lawrence Klein, University of Cambridge
Christophe Martin, Sorbonne Université
Kate Quinsey, University of Windsor

Religion, science and moral philosophy in the Huguenot Enlightenment
Jean Henri Samuel Formey and the Berlin Academy

ANNELIE GROßE

Published by Liverpool University Press on behalf of
© 2024 Voltaire Foundation, University of Oxford
ISBN 978 1 83764 403 2
Oxford University Studies in the Enlightenment 2024:02
ISSN 2634-8047 (Print)
ISSN 2634-8055 (Online)

Voltaire Foundation
99 Banbury Road
Oxford OX2 6JX, UK
www.voltaire.ox.ac.uk

A catalogue record for this book is available from the British Library

The correct style for citing this book is
Annelie Große, *Religion, science and moral philosophy in the Huguenot Enlightenment: Jean Henri Samuel Formey and the Berlin Academy*
Oxford University Studies in the Enlightenment
(Liverpool, Liverpool University Press, 2024)

Cover illustration 'Allegory of the agreement between religion and philosophy, or faith and reason'. Bernard Picart, Paris 1708.

Oxford University Studies in the Enlightenment

Religion, science and moral philosophy in the Huguenot Enlightenment
Jean Henri Samuel Formey and the Berlin Academy

Religion, science and moral philosophy in the Huguenot Enlightenment makes two significant contributions to existing scholarship on the Enlightenment. Firstly, as an author, journalist, translator and inexhaustible letter writer, the Huguenot pastor and secretary of the Berlin Academy of Sciences Samuel Formey was involved in most of the philosophical debates in the European Republic of Letters during the second half of the eighteenth century. This is the first monograph dedicated solely to Formey's multifaceted work. Secondly, the book recasts the concept of religious Enlightenment by considering Formey as a pastor-philosopher whose idea of philosophy included revealed religion instead of perpetuating the image of him as an 'enemy of Enlightenment' who opposed the philosophy of his time by referring to religion.

More precisely, the book explores the notion of the compatibility between reason and faith in Formey's thought on the existence of God, the freedom of will, divine providence and other questions relating to religion and metaphysics. It shows how Formey altered his portrayal of the relation between reason and faith depending on the genre and immediate context of his writings. The broader contextualisation of Formey's arguments in German rationalist philosophy and Calvinist theology not only unveils the overlaps between Wolffianism and eighteenth-century Calvinism but also gives an insight into the diversity of the thought of Huguenot pastors and philosophers during the Enlightenment.

Contents

Acknowledgements	xi
Abbreviations	xiii
Introduction	1
Reason and faith in the Enlightenment	2
The Huguenots and the Enlightenment	10
Religious Enlightenment	19
Method and structure of the book	28
Chapter 1: Formey's concept of philosophy and its relationship to religion	35
Philosophy as a universal science of reason	38
The epistemological foundations of Christian philosophy	42
The Christian philosopher in the French debate about the 'true' philosopher	49
Chapter 2: Formey in the Berlin Huguenot Enlightenment, or how to reconcile the pastor and the philosopher	55
Early Huguenot socialisation	56
Acquaintance with Wolffianism	66
Formey's transition from pastor to professor of philosophy	72

Chapter 3: Preaching like a philosopher and philosophising
like a preacher   83

    Philosophical preaching between Calvinist homiletic
        reform and Wolffianism   84

    Formey's transformation of philosophical sermons into
        moral philosophical essays   95

    Secularisation of morality   103

Chapter 4: The existence of God and the superiority
of metaphysics   109

    Rationalism against scepticism: Formey's dictionary entry
        for 'God'   110

    Metaphysics against physico-theology: Formey's revision of
        the teleological proof of God   121

    Formey and Maupertuis on metaphysics   131

    Newtonians against Wolffians: perception of the debate by
        two groups of contemporaries   141

Chapter 5: Pre-established harmony and fatalism   147

    Popularising Wolff's philosophy: Formey's *Belle wolfienne* 149

    Formey's multivocal criticism of pre-established harmony
        and the *nexus rerum*   154

    The origins of Formey's criticism   165

Chapter 6: The debate on free will   179

    An empirical science of the soul   180

    Free will between absolute necessity and liberty
        of indifference   189

    The free will debate at the Berlin Academy   199

Chapter 7: Providence, moral duties and optimism   213

    The Berlin Academy's 1751 prize essay competition on the
        theme of providence   218

    The 'real' theory of fortune: Formey and the winning essay   226

    The debate between Formey and Boullier about
        Leibnizian optimism   234

Chapter 8: Natural law, morality and science	249
Formey on Rousseau's *Discours sur les sciences et les arts*	251
Formey's scientific moral philosophy	258
Divine and natural law in Formey's moral philosophy	269
Conclusion: religious Enlightenment between Calvinism and Wolffianism	277
Bibliography	287
Archival material	287
Primary sources	288
Secondary sources	303
Index	325

Acknowledgements

This book is a significantly reworked version of my doctoral dissertation, which I wrote at the European University Institute (EUI) in Florence between September 2013 and October 2017. For me, preparing this volume has been a very exciting and inspiring time in an exceptional international research environment. In Florence and elsewhere I met many excellent scholars who generously shared their knowledge with me and shaped this book in many different ways. Here, I want to thank but a few of them, and I apologise to everyone I omit due to the attempt to keep these acknowledgements short.

I am most grateful to Ann Thomson, who, as my PhD supervisor, guided me with precious comments and enthusiasm through my doctoral research and beyond, and, most importantly, awakened my interest in the question of Enlightenment and religion. The nature and shape of this book owe a lot to the intellectual history that she practises with intelligence and passion. Moreover, I am very grateful to my second reader at the EUI, Stéphane Van Damme, whose expertise in a new history of science significantly broadened my approach to eighteenth-century ideas and learned culture.

I also want to thank Alexander Schmidt, who acquainted me with Formey in the first place when I was an MA student at the University of Jena, and has continued to advise me on eighteenth-century intellectual history and twenty-first-century academic life since then. I am grateful to Susanne Lachenicht, who invited me to discuss the role of Huguenot learned men in the early modern Republic of Letters in her doctoral seminar at Bernried, Germany, and who enabled a fruitful exchange with Jens Häseler at the ISECS congress in Rotterdam in 2015.

Richard Whatmore welcomed me in 2015 for three months at the Institute of Intellectual History in St Andrews, where I not only discovered different ways of doing intellectual history but was also able to discuss various subjects relating to my research. At the University of St Andrews Reformation Studies Institute, directed by Bridget Heal at the time, I received valuable comments on my thoughts concerning Formey's preaching practice. St Andrews was also the place where I first met Knud Haakonssen. I have benefited from his sound advice on a whole range of matters regarding eighteenth-century philosophy on many occasions ever since.

At the Institut d'histoire de la Réformation in Geneva, Maria-Cristina Pitassi enlightened me about Calvinist thought, especially on the Reformed replies to Bayle's scepticism, and kindly commented on an earlier version of chapter 4.

I am thankful to Daniel Fulda and Thomas Ahnert, with whom I was able to discuss Formey's role in eighteenth-century religious debates during my thesis defence in January 2018. I received very helpful suggestions and criticism from the two anonymous reviewers for Oxford University Studies in the Enlightenment, as well as from one anonymous member of the editorial board. Moreover, I want to thank the book series' general editor, Gregory S. Brown, for his assistance and his availability during the publication process.

This study has only been possible thanks to the financial support of the Deutsche Akademische Austauschdienst (DAAD) and the EUI, which have funded my doctoral research. My project supervisors at the Berlin-Brandenburg Academy of Sciences and Humanities – Wolfgang Neugebauer, Monika Wienfort and Bärbel Holtz – generously granted me paid leave that enabled me to write the manuscript for this book.

Finally, my most profound gratitude belongs to my husband Mikkel Jensen, for his selfless support and patience.

Berlin, January 2023

Abbreviations

BBAW	Berlin-Brandenburgische Akademie der Wissenschaften, Berlin
BCU	Bibliothèque cantonale et universitaire, Lausanne
CV	Collection Varnhagen von Ense (Biblioteka Jagiellońska, Krakow)
D	Collection Darmstädter (Staatsbibliothek zu Berlin – Preußischer Kulturbesitz)
FF	Fonds Formey (Staatsbibliothek zu Berlin – Preußischer Kulturbesitz)
GStA PK	Geheimes Staatsarchiv – Preußischer Kulturbesitz, Berlin-Dahlem
UBB	Universitätsbibliothek Basel
UBL	Universitätsbibliothek Leipzig

Introduction

During the eighteenth century, the idea that rational philosophy and religious faith were compatible was increasingly contested. Philosophy, and natural philosophy in particular, not only gained independence from theology after having been considered subordinate to it for centuries,[1] it also began to be measured against Christian dogma and theology – at least by some eighteenth-century thinkers.[2] Thus, the idea of a secular science that conflicted with religion – an idea that was consolidated in the nineteenth century and still holds strong in popular opinion today – took root.[3] However, this conceptual shift

1. See Werner Schneiders, 'Zwischen Welt und Weisheit: zur Verweltlichung der Philosophie in der Frühen Moderne', *Studia Leibnitiana* 15:1 (1983), p.2-18 (4 and 6). For the relationship between philosophy and theology in European institutions of higher education and the gradual emancipation of the faculty of philosophy, see Tim J. Hochstrasser, 'The institutionalisation of philosophy in continental Europe', in *The Cambridge history of eighteenth-century philosophy*, ed. Knud Haakonssen, 2 vols (Cambridge and New York, 2006), vol.1, p.69-96, and Notker Hammerstein, 'Vom Rang der Wissenschaften: zum Aufstieg der philosophischen Fakultät', in *Geschichte als Arsenal: ausgewählte Aufsätze zu Reich, Hof und Universitäten in der Frühen Neuzeit*, ed. Michael Maaser and Gerrit Walther (Göttingen, 2010), p.185-97.
2. Rational scrutiny of dogma was common in the deistic texts of the late seventeenth and early eighteenth centuries that circulated clandestinely. As the eighteenth century moved on, it became a crucial part of atheistic texts as well, for example, d'Holbach's *Christianisme dévoilé* (1766); see Winfried Schröder, *Ursprünge des Atheismus: Untersuchungen zur Metaphysik- und Religionskritik des 17. und 18. Jahrhunderts* (Stuttgart-Bad Cannstatt, 1998), p.305.
3. Emblematic for the conflict thesis: John William Draper, *History of the conflict between religion and science* (New York, 1875). Since the 1990s, historians of science have successfully challenged the conflict thesis by historicising the two categories of religion and science; see John Hedley Brooke, *Science and religion: some historical perspectives* (Cambridge and New York, 1991), and Peter

was a slow development, and it was anything but straightforward. The aim of this book is to demonstrate the impact this development had on different philosophical and theological debates that took place in the European Republic of Letters during the mid-eighteenth century. Through a case study of the Prussian Huguenot Jean Henri Samuel Formey, it examines the practices and thought of those who upheld the compatibility between philosophy and religion, and compares their beliefs with those of others who contested it. The volume analyses how the notion of a harmonious relationship between reason and faith was reflected in Protestant responses to central questions concerning religion and the human condition. The goal is to illustrate the strength of this notion during the Enlightenment as well as its context-related diversity.

Reason and faith in the Enlightenment

Since the late seventeenth century, treatises in defence of the compatibility between natural knowledge and divine revelation had been appearing across confessions, disciplines and geographical regions. In England, in the last decades of the seventeenth century, the experimental natural philosopher and member of the Royal Society Robert Boyle promoted the concept of the 'Christian virtuoso', that is, a natural philosopher committed to experience and reason as well as to Christian piety. As the title of his 1690 treatise suggests, Boyle believed that the practice of experimental philosophy helped the individual to excel in his Christian belief.[4] The Huguenot pastor Isaac Jaquelot in Berlin and the Lutheran polymath Gottfried Wilhelm Leibniz from Hanover

---

Harrison, *The Territories of science and religion* (Chicago, IL, and London, 2015). Peter Harrison, 'Myth 24: that religion has typically impeded the progress of science', in *Newton's apple and other myths about science*, ed. Ronald L. Numbers and Kostas Kampourakis (Cambridge and London, 2015), p.199-200, shows that the nineteenth-century narrative of a dichotomy between science and religion had its origins in the seventeenth-century Protestant polemics against Catholicism. This evolved into the eighteenth-century notion that, in general, religion impeded scientific progress.

4. Robert Boyle, *The Christian virtuoso: showing that by being addicted to experimental philosophy, a man is rather assisted, than indisposed to be a good Christian* (In the Savoy [London], n.n., 1690). Boyle's claim was rooted in his notion of 'right reason', that is, a human being's capacity to understand divine revelation; see Lotte Mulligan, 'Robert Boyle, the "Christian virtuoso" and the rhetoric of "reason"', in *Religion, reason and nature in early modern Europe*, ed. Robert Crocker (Dordrecht, 2001), p.97-116.

each published a demonstration of the conformity between reason and faith in 1705 and 1710, respectively. Jaquelot held that in most religious matters, such as God's nature, revelation taught only truths that were comprehensible through the human intellect;[5] he considered the few revealed truths that were above reason, such as the dogma of the Trinity, as not being contrary to reason.[6] This distinction between certain revealed truths being above but not contrary to reason was also embraced by Leibniz,[7] who added that Christian mysteries could not be contrary to the human intellect because this was, essentially, similar to God's infinite intellect, which had authored these mysteries.[8]

All the declarations of a harmonious relationship between reason and faith were meant to protect rationalism as much as revealed religion. In point of fact, late-seventeenth-century and early-eighteenth-century challenges to the compatibility between reason and faith were mostly grounded in scepticism with regard to the capacities of the human intellect and not in a reason-based rejection of dogma. On the contrary, these challenges were often inspired by religious concerns. For example, the scepticism of the Huguenot philosopher Pierre Bayle, against which both Jaquelot's and Leibniz's essays had been directed, went alongside his religious fideism.[9] As far as Robert Boyle was concerned, his invention of the Christian virtuoso was probably an answer to Francis Bacon's programme for the renewal of learning. Bacon proclaimed that natural philosophical enquiry should

---

5. See Isaac Jaquelot, *Conformité de la foi avec la raison, ou Défense de la religion, contre les principales difficultez répandues dans le Dictionaire historique et critique de Mr. Bayle* (Amsterdam, Desbordes & Pain, 1705), p.76.
6. See Jaquelot, *Conformité de la foi avec la raison*, p.90 and 111. See also Ruth Whelan, 'Reason and belief: the Bayle-Jacquelot debate', *Rivista di storia della filosofia* 48:1 (1993), p.101-10.
7. See Gottfried Wilhelm Leibniz, *Essais de théodicée, sur la bonté de Dieu, la liberté de l'homme et l'origine du mal*, 2nd edn (Amsterdam, Mortier, 1714), 'Discours de la conformité de la foy avec la raison', §23.
8. See Leibniz, 'Discours de la conformité de la foy avec la raison', §61. See also Maria Rosa Antognazza, 'Faith and reason', in *The Oxford handbook on Leibniz*, ed. Maria Rosa Antognazza (Oxford and New York, 2018), p.717-34.
9. This has been most famously argued by Elisabeth Labrousse, *Pierre Bayle*, 2 vols (Dordrecht, 1963-1964), and Richard H. Popkin, 'Pierre Bayle's place in 17th-century scepticism', in *Pierre Bayle: le philosophe de Rotterdam*, ed. Paul Dibon (Amsterdam, 1959), p.1-19. However, Bayle's contemporaries and today's scholars are not unanimous about the sincerity of Bayle's Calvinist fideism. In modern scholarship, for example, Gianluca Mori, *Bayle philosophe* (Paris, 1999) holds that Bayle's fideism was only a disguise for his atheism.

not interfere with matters of belief, a view that originated from his aim of keeping the integrity of both areas of knowledge.[10] Nevertheless, defenders of the compatibility between faith and reason such as Boyle, Jaquelot and Leibniz also revealed apologetic aims. They deplored the growing numbers of those who relied on philosophy and science to justify their anti-religious opinion. They considered this to be an abuse of philosophy.[11]

Whereas in the first half of the eighteenth century it was still relatively rare for contestations of the compatibility between natural and revealed knowledge to have anti-clerical and anti-religious motives, this did become common with the growth of deism and the rise of philosophical atheism in the second half of the century.[12] As a consequence, the reconciliation of reason and faith became a predominant trope of Christian apologetics. In France in particular, the numbers of such 'apologetics of reconciliation' exploded in the second half of the eighteenth century, just as did the number of publications considered heretical.[13] In the early 1780s, the French abbé Claude Yvon,

---

10. See Victor Nuovo, *John Locke: the philosopher as Christian virtuoso* (Oxford, 2017), p.9-15. See also Jerry Weinberger, 'Francis Bacon and the unity of knowledge: reason and revelation', in *Francis Bacon and the refiguring of early modern thought: essays to commemorate 'The Advancement of learning' (1605-2005)*, ed. Julie Robin Solomon and Catherine Gimelli Martin (Aldershot and Burlington, VT, 2005), p.109-27. Weinberger, however, suggests that Bacon's separation of knowledge about nature and knowledge about the divine was a result of his secret atheism.

11. See Boyle, 'The preface', in *Christian virtuoso*, sig.A, and Jaquelot, 'Préface', in *Conformité de la foi avec la raison*, sig.***v and p.265-66. Jaquelot believed that Bayle's claim that reason and faith were opposed to each other was a means of harming religion.

12. As Schröder, *Ursprünge des Atheismus*, p.77, argues, atheism, which is the denial of God's existence, only became relevant from the mid-eighteenth century onwards. However, in the seventeenth century, the term 'atheism' was used widely to refer to a myriad of heterodox opinions that could, potentially, lead to the denial of God's existence. Michael Hunter, 'Science and heterodoxy: an early modern problem reconsidered', in *Reappraisals of the scientific revolution*, ed. David C. Lindberg and Robert S. Westman (Cambridge, 1990), p.437-60 (445-46), emphasises that this was a response to the growing secularist and naturalistic tendencies of the new science as well as to the perception of increasing immoral behaviour in society.

13. See Didier Masseau, 'La position des apologistes conciliateurs', *Dix-huitième siècle* 34 (2002), p.121-30 (122), and Emmanuelle Brun, 'L'apologétique conciliatrice française et le dialogue de l'Aufklärung chrétienne avec le "parti philosophique"', doctoral dissertation, Université Nice Sophia Antipolis, 2014. Henri-Jean Martin, 'La tradition perpétuée', in *Histoire de l'édition française: le livre triomphant 1660-1830*, ed. Henri-Jean Martin and Roger Chartier (Paris,

who enjoyed an ambivalent reputation among the orthodox French Catholic clergy mainly because of his involvement in the Prades affair in 1752, published the apologetic *Accord de la philosophie avec la religion*.[14] He portrayed his claim for a 'confederation' between philosophy and religion as a reply to the usurpation of the title of philosopher by 'modern unbelievers' – an allusion to the so-called *parti des philosophes* that had dominated public discourse in France and beyond since the mid-eighteenth century. Moreover, Yvon held that the Christian religion was identical to true philosophy.[15] In the same decade, another French clergyman, the abbé Baudisson, defined the union between philosophy and Christian religion as a historical relationship of mutual support.[16] To back up his argument, he praised those philosophers of the seventeenth century in particular (for example, Descartes, Newton, Locke and Fénelon) who had combined philosophical excellence with piousness. Baudisson contrasted their merits with the undevout behaviour of the so-called philosophers of his own age.[17]

Therefore, in the period between the late seventeenth and the late eighteenth century, a variety of motives and arguments in defence of a harmonious relationship between philosophy and religion emerged. The philosophical and theological traditions on which the defenders of such a harmonious relationship drew were also very diverse: they ranged from scholastic philosophical theology through the Christian humanism of the Renaissance[18] and Cartesian and Malebranchean

---

1984), p.175-85, shows that in the mid-eighteenth-century French book market the increase in apologetic writings coincided with the increase in the number of heretical books.

14. Claude Yvon, *Accord de la philosophie avec la religion, ou Histoire de la religion, divisée en XII époques* (Paris, Valade, 1782). This work appeared in different editions and partly under different titles. Apparently, there had been a clandestine edition of the book as early as 1776. Moreover, it appeared in 1785 under the title *Histoire de la religion, où l'on accorde la philosophie avec le christianisme*, 2 vols (Paris, Valade, 1885). See Jeffrey D. Burson, *The Culture of enlightening: abbé Claude Yvon and the entangled emergence of the Enlightenment* (Notre Dame, IN, 2019), p.360-62.

15. See Yvon, *Accord de la philosophie avec la religion*, p.2.

16. See abbé Baudisson, *Essai sur l'union du christianisme avec la philosophie, ou l'on expose les progrès de la philosophie dans les siecles modernes, pour en conclure que les plus grands philosophes ont été soumis à la religion, & que la religion a rendu les plus grands services à la philosophie* (Paris, n.n., 1787), p.i-iv.

17. See Baudisson, *Essai sur l'union du christianisme avec la philosophie*, p.ix-xi.

18. See Brun, 'L'apologétique conciliatrice', p.548-49.

rationalist metaphysics[19] to Newtonian natural philosophy. This book concentrates on one such defender and self-declared Christian philosopher in particular: the Huguenot pastor and secretary of the Royal Academy of Sciences in Berlin during the second half of the eighteenth century Jean Henri Samuel Formey. His concept of the relationship between philosophy and religion combined influences of Calvinist theology with the ideas of the German philosophers Leibniz and Christian Wolff, and was shaped against the backdrop of the growing popularity of the French *philosophes*.

Formey was born in 1711 and was the son of a French Huguenot refugee who had settled in Berlin after the revocation of the Edict of Nantes. Formey first pursued the career of a pastor of the French Reformed Church; however, in 1739 he resigned from the pulpit and became a professor of philosophy at the Collège français, the French Huguenot colony's premier educational institution.[20] This prestigious position paved the way for his membership of the Academy. Formey became a member of this institution's philosophical class in 1744, and, from 1748 onwards, he also acted as its perpetual secretary, a position that enabled him to correspond with much of learned Europe. Formey was renowned among his contemporaries as he is among modern scholars for his critical and polemical engagement with the French *philosophes*.[21] He not only wrote refutations of Denis

19. See Laurence Devillairs, 'La voie d'une apologétique rationaliste: de Descartes à Fénelon', in *Apologétique 1650-1802: la nature et la grâce*, ed. Nicolas Brucker (Bern, 2010), p.85-105. See also Alan Charles Kors, *Atheism in France 1650-1729* (Princeton, NJ, 1990), p.323-40. Kors has shown that the opinion that Descartes's and Malebranche's philosophy was a truly Christian one was relatively widespread among French Catholics at the end of the seventeenth/beginning of the eighteenth century, despite the official rejection of this philosophy by the leading Jesuits and the universities.
20. On Formey's biography and thought, see his autobiographical book *Souvenirs d'un citoyen*, 2 vols (Berlin, La Garde, 1789), and the modern scholarship: Werner Krauss, 'Ein Akademiesekretär vor 200 Jahren: Samuel Formey', in *Studien zur deutschen und französischen Aufklärung*, ed. Werner Krauss (Berlin, 1963), p.53-62; Jens Häseler, 'Samuel Formey, pasteur huguenot entre Lumières françaises et *Aufklärung*', *Dix-huitième siècle* 34 (2002), p.239-47; and Martin Fontius, 'Zwischen "libertas philosophandi" und "siècle de la philosophie": zum geistesgeschichtlichen Standort Formeys und der zweiten Generation der réfugiés', in *L'Allemagne et la France des Lumières / Deutsche und französische Aufklärung: mélanges offerts à Jochen Schlobach par ses élèves et amis*, ed. Michel Delon and Jean Mondot (Paris, 2003), p.45-68.
21. See Jacques Voisine, 'J. Formey (1711-1797): vulgarisateur de l'œuvre de Rousseau en Allemagne', in *Mélanges d'histoire littéraire offerts à Daniel Mornet, professeur*

Diderot's deistic and atheistic writings,[22] but also repeatedly criticised Jean-Jacques Rousseau's bestselling books[23] and engaged in public polemics with Voltaire in the periodical press.[24]

Against this backdrop, a first wave of scholars interested in Formey evaluated his position within Enlightenment philosophy as conservative, anti-philosophical and insignificant.[25] However, this view has completely altered during the past twenty years; nowadays, scholars see in Formey a knowledge broker of the Enlightenment who contributed to the dissemination of information and ideas via learned journalism,[26] encyclopedias[27] and his European epistolary

---

honoraire à la Sorbonne, par ses anciens collègues et ses disciples français (Paris, 1951), p.141-53; Eva Marcu, 'Formey and the Enlightenment', doctoral dissertation, Columbia University, Ann Arbor, 1952; and Rolf Geissler, 'J.-H.-S. Formey critique des philosophes français: observations sur les rapports entre Wolffianisme et Lumières françaises', in *Transactions of the eighth international congress on the Enlightenment*, ed. H. T. Mason, 3 vols (1992), vol.1, p.507-11.

22. Formey, *Pensées raisonnables opposées aux Pensées philosophiques* (Berlin, Voss, 1749) and *Lettre de M. Gervaise Holmes à l'auteur de la Lettre sur les aveugles* (Cambridge [Berlin], n.n., 1750).
23. Formey, 'Examen philosophique de la liaison réelle qu'il y a entre les sciences et les mœurs', in *Histoire de l'Académie royale des sciences et belles lettres de Berlin* (1753; Berlin, Haude & Spener, 1755), p.397-416; *L'Esprit de Julie, ouvrage utile à la société et particulièrement à la jeunesse* (Berlin, Jasperd, 1762); *Anti-Emile* (Berlin, Pauli, 1763); and *Emile chrétien, consacré à l'utilité publique*, 4 vols (Berlin, Neaulme, 1764).
24. See Jacques Marx, 'Une liaison dangereuse au XVIIIe siècle: Voltaire et Jean-Henri Samuel Formey', *Neophilologus* 53:2 (1969), p.138-46.
25. See Christian Bartholmèss, *Histoire philosophique de l'Académie de Prusse depuis Leibniz jusqu'à Schelling, particul. sous Frédéric-le-Grand*, 2 vols (Paris, 1850), vol.1, p.365; Ludwig Geiger, *Berlin 1688-1840: Geschichte des geistigen Lebens der preußischen Hauptstadt*, 2 vols (Berlin, 1892), vol.1, p.361; Adolf Harnack, *Geschichte der Königlich Preussischen Akademie der Wissenschaften zu Berlin*, 3 vols (Berlin, 1900), vol.1, p.448-49; and Marcu, 'Formey and the Enlightenment', p.129-31.
26. For an overview of Formey's different journalistic enterprises, see Ann Thomson, 'Formey', in *Dictionnaire des journalistes (1600-1789)*, http://dictionnaire-journalistes.gazettes18e.fr/journaliste/310-jean-henri-formey (last accessed 11 July 2023), as well as the case studies by Rolf Geissler, 'Formey journaliste: observations sur la collaboration au *Journal encyclopédique* et d'autres journaux européens', in *La Vie intellectuelle aux refuges protestants*, ed. Jens Häseler and Antony McKenna (Paris, 1999), p.137-56, and Annett Volmer, 'Journalismus und Aufklärung: Jean Henri Samuel Formey und die Entwicklung der Zeitschrift zum Medium der Kritik', *Jahrbuch für Kommunikationsgeschichte* 9 (2007), p.101-29.
27. During his lifetime Formey conceived of, participated in and published

network.[28] This development in the scholarly evaluation of Formey has been the result of the diversification of the concept of Enlightenment and the cultural turn in history that not only allowed for a shift in focus – from the emblematic philosophers of the eighteenth century to minor figures – but also included the study of practices as well as ideas in research on the Enlightenment. Moreover, in the case of the scholarship on Formey in particular, in the 1960s, the German literature scholar Werner Krauss attempted to add a cultural–historical layer to what had previously been mainly philosophical–historical approaches to Formey. He pointed to the insights that the huge corpus of Formey's correspondence could offer in relation to research on eighteenth-century Francophone literary life[29] and, for the first time, emphasised Formey's merits as a cultural mediator between Germany and France, particularly with respect to his translation and popularisation of the philosophy of the German Christian Wolff.[30] Krauss' precursory claims sparked intense research on Formey that was mainly conducted at the Research Centre for the European Enlightenment at the University of Potsdam, which was active from 1992 until 2007. A large proportion of the results of this research has been published only recently in a collected volume.[31]

Another very valuable result of this earlier research on Formey has been to make his vast correspondence accessible. There are

---

several encyclopedic projects. See Rolf Geissler, 'Der Beitrag Formeys zum Enzyklopädismus im 18. Jahrhundert', in *Franzosen in Berlin: über Religion und Aufklärung in Preußen – Studien zum Nachlass des Akademiesekretärs Samuel Formey*, ed. Martin Fontius and Jens Häseler (Basel, 2019), p.293-373. This article contains the references to the different studies that deal with Formey's single encyclopedic projects.

28. See Jens Häseler, 'Jean Henri Samuel Formey – l'homme à Berlin', in *Les Grands Intermédiaires culturels de la République des Lettres: études et réseaux de correspondances du XVIe au XVIIIe siècle*, ed. Christiane Berkvens-Stevelinck, Hans Bots and Jens Häseler (Paris, 2005), p.413-34, and 'Entre république des lettres et république des sciences: les correspondances "scientifiques" de Formey', *Dix-huitième siècle* 40:1 (2008), p.93-103. The perception of Formey as a knowledge broker informed the engagement with him during a multidisciplinary conference on his work that took place at the University of Potsdam in 2013; for the conference proceedings, see *Jean Henri Samuel Formey: Wissensmultiplikator der Berliner Aufklärung*, ed. Jannis Götze and Martin Meiske (Erlangen, 2016).
29. See Werner Krauss, 'La correspondance de Formey', *Revue d'histoire littéraire de la France* 63 (1963), p.207-16.
30. See Krauss, 'Ein Akademiesekretär vor 200 Jahren', p.55.
31. See Fontius and Häseler, *Franzosen in Berlin*.

approximately 17,000 letters in the corpus, of which most are addressed to Formey and only a few are written by him. The largest number of letters is kept at the Berlin State Library, and a smaller but important number is kept at the Biblioteka Jagiellońska in Krakow.[32] They are easily traceable because there is a published inventory of all the known letters.[33] Moreover, nowadays, several single correspondence threads from the corpus exist as printed editions.

Formey's correspondence is not only useful for elucidating the learned practices and customs that characterised the culture of the Republic of Letters during the Enlightenment, it is also an invaluable source for contextualising his various publications. Between roughly 1740 and 1780, Formey published several hundred academic treatises, eulogies, sermons, popular philosophical essays, textbooks, abridgements, translations, reviews and so on.[34] However, studies that engage with this wide range of publications from the perspective of the history of philosophy or intellectual history are rare. To date, only a handful of scholars have looked at single thematic issues that Formey engaged with in his writings, that is his moral philosophical notion of beatitude,[35] his position concerning scientific progress,[36] and

---

32. During the forty years of the division of Germany, the largest part of Formey's correspondence was kept in the archives of the GDR (East Germany). In 1963, Krauss, who himself worked as a scholar in East Germany, indicated the existence of the vast corpus at the Berlin State Library (see 'La correspondance de Formey', p.207). However, at this point in time, he seems not to have been aware of the existence of that part of the correspondence that had been evacuated to Silesia during the Second World War and, therefore, ended up on Polish soil in Krakow afterwards. During the division of Germany, Western scholars could also gain access to Formey's correspondence as can be seen in the editions of Voltaire's correspondence by Theodore Bestermann and Rousseau's correspondence by Ralph Leigh. However, it was more difficult to do so then than it is nowadays.
33. See *La Correspondance de Jean Henri Samuel Formey (1711-1797): inventaire alphabétique*, ed. Jens Häseler (Paris, 2003). The introduction contains a detailed description of the conservation history of the correspondence.
34. For the list of all Formey's written works, see Rolf Geissler, 'Bibliographie des écrits de Jean Henri Samuel Formey', in *La Correspondance de Jean Henri Samuel Formey*, ed. J. Häseler, p.419-73.
35. See Sandra Pott, *Reformierte Morallehren und deutsche Literatur von Jean Barbeyrac bis Christoph Martin Wieland* (Tübingen, 2002).
36. See Alexander Schmidt, 'Scholarship, morals and government: Jean-Henri-Samuel Formey's and Johann Gottfried Herder's responses to Rousseau's first discourse', *Modern intellectual history* 9:2 (2012), p.249-74.

his views on the origin of language and cognition.[37] However, despite the various different advances in research on Formey, no monograph that engages with a significant part of his oeuvre has been published until the present day.

Moreover, the role of Formey's religious background in his oeuvre has not yet been analysed comprehensively, although previous studies have regularly referred to it as a constitutive element of his thought. How did Reformed teachings and different philosophical strands intersect in Formey's perception of the harmonious relationship between reason and faith? What was his position concerning central religious questions, and how did it reflect his concept of such a harmonious relationship between reason and faith? Finally, how did Formey's position differ from orthodox theology on the one hand and the anti-religious claims of freethinkers on the other, and how was his stance received among other Christian philosophers? The aim of this first monograph on Formey's thought is to provide answers to these questions as well as to evaluate the implications of an eighteenth-century Christian philosophy that assumed a harmonious relationship between reason and faith in Enlightenment debates more broadly.

The Huguenots and the Enlightenment

Having been a member of the Huguenot diaspora and an entire network of academies and learned societies, Formey not only embodied the union of religion and science, but he was also an integral part of the European culture of learning, which shaped the development of Enlightenment thought. Therefore, his case is a particularly revealing one. As has been emphasised repeatedly in scholarship, the religious refugees who fled France in large numbers after the revocation of the Edict of Nantes in 1685 established and maintained the infrastructure of the Republic of Letters, which allowed the circulation and discussion of ideas throughout Europe in the first half of the eighteenth century.[38] In Holland, England, Switzerland, Branden-

---

37. See Avi Lifschitz, *Language and Enlightenment: the Berlin debates of the eighteenth century* (Oxford and New York, 2012), p.138-39, and Cordula Neis, 'Formey's "Discours sur l'origine des sociétés et du langage et sur le système de la compensation" (1763) im Kontext der Berliner Debatte um den Sprachursprung', in *Jean Henri Samuel Formey: Wissensmultiplikator der Berliner Aufklärung*, ed. Jannis Götze and Martin Meiske (Erlangen, 2016), p.169-84.
38. See Erich Haase, *Einführung in die Literatur des Refuge: der Beitrag der französischen Protestanten zur Entwicklung analytischer Denkformen am Ende des 17. Jahrhunderts*

burg-Prussia and other places to which they emigrated, the refugees founded learned journals and publishing houses, and they translated, compiled and popularised the literary and scientific output of their host countries for a French-speaking audience. Conversely, they also brought French literature and scholarly culture to their host countries. Under the rule of the Calvinist elector Frederick William, Brandenburg-Prussia received approximately 20,000 French Huguenots and granted them legal, economic and ecclesiastical privileges.[39] In Berlin, Huguenot scholars were involved in the founding of the Academy in the last decades of the seventeenth and the beginning of the eighteenth century,[40] and they established the first learned periodicals.[41] As tutors of the local elite, they contributed to the development of eighteenth-century Prussian intellectual culture more broadly. Frederick II's affinity with French culture, which marked the Berlin Enlightenment during the second half of the eighteenth century, stemmed from the fact that he was educated by Huguenot tutors.[42]

(Berlin, 1959), p.401-17; Anne Goldgar, *Impolite learning: conduct and community in the Republic of Letters, 1680-1750* (New Haven, CT, and London, 1995), p.9; John Christian Laursen, 'Introduction', in *New essays on the political thought of the Huguenots of the Refuge*, ed. John Christian Laursen (Leiden, 1995), p.1-14 (6-11). Ann Thomson, *L'Ame des Lumières: le débat sur l'être humain entre religion et science: Angleterre-France (1690-1760)* (Seyssel, 2013), p.170-99, illustrates the role played by the Huguenot refugees in the processes of cultural transfer between England and France.

39. See Jürgen Wilke, 'Rechtsstellung und Rechtsprechung der Hugenotten in Brandenburg-Preußen (1685-1809)', in *Die Hugenotten 1685-1985*, ed. Rudolf von Thadden and Michelle Magdelaine (Munich, 1985), p.100-14, and Eckart Birnstiel, 'Asyl und Integration der Hugenotten in Brandenburg-Preußen', in *Hugenotten und deutsche Territorialstaaten: Immigrationspolitik und Integrationsprozesse*, ed. Guido Braun and Susanne Lachenicht (Munich, 2007), p.139-54.

40. See Conrad Grau, 'Die Berliner Akademie der Wissenschaften und die Hugenotten', in *Hugenotten in Berlin*, ed. Sibylle Badstübner-Gröger and Gottfried Bregulla (Berlin, 1988), p.327-62.

41. See Conrad Grau, 'Hugenotten in der Wissenschaft Brandenburg-Preußens Ende des 17. und im 18. Jahrhundert', *Zeitschrift für Geschichtswissenschaft* 34:6 (1986), p.508-22 (512). On the influence of the refugees on the development of German literature and literary criticism, see Volmer, 'Journalismus und Aufklärung', p.124, and Sandra Pott, '"Gentle, refined, cultivated, witty people": comments on the intellectual history of the Berlin Refuge and on relevant research', in *The Berlin Refuge 1680-1780: learning and science in European context*, ed. Sandra Pott, Martin Mulsow and Lutz Danneberg (Leiden and Boston, MA, 2003), p.3-24 (13-18).

42. See Rolf Geissler, 'Die Hugenotten im literarischen Leben Berlins', in *Hugenotten in Berlin*, ed. S. Badstübner-Gröger and G. Bregulla, p.363-91 (366-68).

The Huguenot refugees' role in the circulation of ideas in the Republic of Letters as well as their works of erudition are considered harbingers of the ideas commonly associated with the (French) Enlightenment. Several scholars have highlighted the fact that Huguenots were involved in the circulation of clandestine manuscripts during the early Enlightenment and, therefore, contributed to the spreading of heterodox ideas.[43] Erich Haase has underlined the role of Huguenot erudition in fostering analytical thinking that is characteristic of the 'philosophical age'.[44] Moreover, the Huguenots' experience of religious persecution and immigration stimulated political theories such as toleration and liberty of conscience, which can be subsumed under the concept of modern liberalism.[45] However, being Huguenot did not entail a coherent system of thought. On the contrary, there were fierce internal quarrels between the intellectuals in the Refuge, particularly with respect to theological issues that divided Arminians, Socinians and orthodox thinkers.[46]

The achievements of the first generation of refugees in the early Enlightenment until roughly 1730 are well documented, whereas the role played by their descendants during the second half of the eighteenth century is relatively underresearched.[47] In fact, because

43. See John Christian Laursen, 'Impostors and liars: clandestine manuscripts and the limits of freedom of the press in the Huguenot Netherlands', in *New essays*, ed. J. C. Laursen, p.73-100; Martin Mulsow, *Die drei Ringe: Toleranz und clandestine Gelehrsamkeit bei Mathurin Veyssière La Croze (1661-1739)* (Tübingen, 2001); Ann Thomson, 'Informal networks', in *The Cambridge history of eighteenth-century philosophy*, ed. K. Haakonssen, vol.1, p.121-36 (122-24).
44. See Haase, *Literatur des Refuge*, p.526-28.
45. See Georges Gusdorf, 'L'Europe protestante au siècle des Lumières', *Dix-huitième siècle* 17:1 (1985), p.13-40 (40); Elisabeth Labrousse, 'The political ideas of the Huguenot diaspora (Bayle and Jurieu)', in *Church, state, and society under the Bourbon kings*, ed. Richard M. Golden (Lawrence, KS, 1982), p.222-83; Laursen, 'Introduction', p.11-12, as well as the essays in this collective volume.
46. See Jonathan Israel, *Enlightenment contested: philosophy, modernity, and the emancipation of man 1670-1752* (Oxford and New York, 2006), p.387-92; Thomson, *L'Ame des Lumières*, p.174. In the Berlin Refuge, one of the most famous internal quarrels was about Jean Barbeyrac's presumed Socinianism at the beginning of the eighteenth century; see Fiammetta Palladini, *Die Berliner Hugenotten und der Fall Barbeyrac: Orthodoxe und 'Sozinianer' im Refuge (1685-1720)* (Leiden, 2011).
47. Haase's seminal *Literatur des Refuge* deals with the late seventeenth century only. As far as the intellectual history of the Berlin Refuge is concerned, the focus was also on its first generation; see Palladini, *Die Berliner Hugenotten*. Moreover, despite its relatively long chronology, the recent collective volume edited by Sandra Pott, Martin Mulsow and Lutz Danneberg, *The Berlin Refuge 1680-1780*,

of the processes of assimilation that took place in the course of the eighteenth century, it becomes difficult to discern a genuinely Huguenot aspect in the cultural and intellectual developments from 1750 onwards. In Prussia, from the mid-eighteenth century onwards, not only did the French language begin to disappear, several congregations began to dissolve and the number of interconfessional marriages started to increase.[48] In addition, Huguenot intellectuals adopted the local strands of thought more and more. As far as Formey and his peers were concerned, they became adepts of the philosophy of Christian Wolff, whose rationalism was both extremely influential and controversial among German philosophers during the first half of the eighteenth century. In the scholarship on the German Protestant Enlightenment, Wolff, as a follower of Leibniz, is traditionally considered a harbinger of Kant's idea of autonomous reason and transcendental self-clarification and rational self-governance of the human being,[49] as well as of the rational religion characteristic of the theological Enlightenment in Germany.[50]

Between *c.*1710 and his death in 1754, Wolff developed a complete philosophical system that ranged from logic to practical philosophy in two cycles: in the first period he approached all the aspects of his philosophy in German, and in the second he elaborated on his thought significantly and published it in Latin.[51] Wolff's theoretical

---

contains only one contribution that deals with the time after the 1730s (and this is about Formey). An exception from this focus on the early Refuge is Rosen Prest's study on Huguenot history writing at the end of the eighteenth century; see Viviane Rosen Prest, *L'Historiographie des huguenots en Prusse au temps des Lumières: entre mémoire, histoire et légende – J. P. Erman et P. C. F. Reclam, Mémoires pour servir à l'histoire des réfugiés français dans les Etats du roi* (Paris, 2002).

48. See Rosen Prest, *L'Historiographie des huguenots*, p.42-51, and, in more detail, Susanne Lachenicht, *Hugenotten in Europa und Nordamerika: Migration und Integration in der Frühen Neuzeit* (Frankfurt am Main, 2010), p.325-33, 377-83 and 405-15.
49. See Ian Hunter, *Rival enlightenments: civil and metaphysical philosophy in early modern Germany* (Cambridge and New York, 2001), p.15-16. He challenges this narrative, which presents the German Enlightenment as a uniform entity.
50. See Karl Aner, *Die Theologie der Lessingzeit* (Hildesheim, 1964), esp. p.3-4, and Walter Sparn, 'Vernünftiges Christentum: über die geschichtliche Aufgabe der theologischen Aufklärung im 18. Jahrhundert in Deutschland', in *Wissenschaften im Zeitalter der Aufklärung*, ed. Rudolf Vierhaus (Göttingen, 1985), p.18-57 (esp. 21-22).
51. All of Wolff's writings are accessible in a complete edition: *Christian Wolff: Gesammelte Werke*, ed. Jean Ecole *et al.* (Hildesheim, 1962-). However, most of its volumes lack a scholarly apparatus and critical introduction. For the history

philosophy, his metaphysics in particular, was much indebted to Leibniz's principle of sufficient reason, according to which nothing in the universe could occur without a cause, as well as to Leibniz's notion of the compatibility between reason and faith. In Wolff's view, the human intellect was able to account for even large parts of Christian dogma, except for a few revealed truths that were 'above reason', such as the Trinity or the virginity of Mary.[52]

The deterministic character of Leibniz's and Wolff's philosophies, which resulted from the principle of sufficient reason, and their leaning towards a rational religion were the origin of the controversies that Wolff and his disciples became involved in with regard to the different competing theological and philosophical strands of the German Protestant Enlightenment. From around 1680, Pietism, which was a reform movement within Lutheranism that emphasised individual piety and practical religiosity, emerged in Leipzig and, subsequently, spread to Halle. Around the same time, the jurist and philosopher Christian Thomasius, who was influenced by the natural lawyer Samuel Pufendorf and – as Ahnert has shown – by religious enthusiasm, developed a theory of natural law, which attempted to separate civil and religious governance. Although the Pietists and Thomasius diverged on many points,[53] they both contested the power of reason as a source of truth and opposed its interference in religious matters. This was the origin of their respective conflicts with Wolff

---

of Wolff's philosophy, see the recent excellent overview on Wolff's thought in relation to all philosophical disciplines: *Handbuch Christian Wolff*, ed. Robert Theis and Alexander Aichele (Wiesbaden, 2018). Apart from this, studies on Wolff's philosophy are piecemeal and have focused predominantly on his theoretical philosophy, that is to say, on logic and metaphysics instead of his practical philosophy. The most important contributions can be found in these edited volumes: *Christian Wolff 1679-1754: Interpretationen zu seiner Philosophie und deren Wirkung*, ed. Werner Schneiders, 2nd edn (Hamburg, 1986); *Christian Wolff und die europäische Aufklärung*, ed. Jürgen Stolzenberg, Oliver-Pierre Rudolph and Jean Ecole, 5 vols (Hildesheim and New York, 2007-2010). A popular biography on Wolff appeared recently: Hans-Joachim Kertscher, *'Er brachte Licht und Ordnung in die Welt': Christian Wolff – eine Biographie* (Halle, 2018).

52. See Mario Casula, 'Die theologia naturalis von Christian Wolff: Vernunft und Offenbarung', in *Christian Wolff 1679-1754*, ed. W. Schneiders, p.129-38.

53. On the relationship between the Pietists and Thomasius, particularly on Thomasius' early overlap with and later rupture from the Pietists, see Thomas Ahnert, *Religion and the origins of the German Enlightenment: faith and the reform of learning in the thought of Christian Thomasius* (Rochester, NY, 2006), p.27-42.

and his disciples.[54] Wolff's conflict with the Pietists in particular culminated in him being accused of heterodoxy and even led in 1723 to his suspension from the chair of philosophy at the University of Halle as well as his banishment from Prussia on royal order. This order was only withdrawn in 1740, and Wolff was allowed to return to Halle, where he taught until his death. Formey started to engage with Wolff's philosophy at the time the latter was repatriated to Prussia. For most of the time, however, this remained a long-distance engagement, that is to say, via Wolff's publications and indirectly via their common contact Ernst Christoph von Manteuffel.[55] Only after Manteuffel's death, from 1748 onwards, did Formey and Wolff maintain a personal epistolary exchange.[56] A central aim of the present work is to elaborate on Formey's oft-mentioned intellectual dependency on Wolff, and to compare it with other philosophical and theological traditions he appropriated.

The gradual intellectual and sociocultural assimilation of Formey's generation of Huguenots into Prussia went alongside the amplification of Berlin's intellectual culture. Whereas the first generation of refugees had dominated the intellectual landscape of the Prussian capital city, since 1740, their descendants had to 'share' it not only with exponents of the rising German literary scene but also with Swiss scholars and French *philosophes* who were attracted to Berlin during the reign of Frederick II. The king's liberal ideas – especially concerning religion – favoured a certain freedom of thought. During the final part of his reign, the educationalist Friedrich Gedike published a description of Berlin's cultural and intellectual atmosphere in his journal *Berlinische*

---

54. On the three-way conflict between the Pietists, Thomasius and Wolff in Halle in the first decades of the eighteenth century see Ian Hunter, 'Multiple enlightenments: rival Aufklärer at the University of Halle 1690-1730', in *The Enlightenment world*, ed. Martin Fitzpatrick *et al.* (New York, 2004), p.576-95.
55. A scholarly edition of the correspondence between Wolff and Manteuffel has been recently published: *Briefwechsel zwischen Christian Wolff und Ernst Christoph von Manteuffel 1738 bis 1748: historisch-kritische Edition in 3 Bänden*, ed. Jürgen Stolzenberg *et al.*, 3 vols (Hildesheim, 2019). This is an invaluable source of information on Formey's engagement with Wolff and Wolffianism. Based on this correspondence, Johannes Bronisch has provided a useful study of the Wolffian network that evolved around Manteuffel in the 1730s and 1740s: Johannes Bronisch, *Mäzen der Aufklärung: Ernst Christoph von Manteuffel und das Netzwerk des Wolffianismus* (Berlin, 2010).
56. From this correspondence, fifteen letters sent by Wolff to Formey between 1748 and 1753 have been preserved at the Biblioteka Jagiellońska in Krakow (Ms Berol. Varnhagen Sammlung 280).

Monatsschrift, which was a mouthpiece of the Enlightenment in Berlin. He stressed that it was because of Frederick that in Berlin, unlike the rest of Germany, a person would not be persecuted for defending natural religion instead of the Christian one (as Gedike himself did as a neologist) and, moreover, that Berlin was a place where a Church of natural religion could be founded.[57] In addition, Gedike also ascribed a rather liberal stance to the ecclesiastics in Berlin: in his view, the orthodox faction among them was quite weak and the majority of the clergy were, instead, enlightened and frank as well as possessing independent minds.[58] This portrayal of the legislators' progressive religious opinions and the state of the clergy coincided with the important reform of the Prussian judicial system that Frederick undertook at the beginning of his reign. This was based on the theory of natural law, and included the abolition of torture and the limitation of the death penalty.[59] As Ursula Goldenbaum emphasises, all of this and the relatively liberal censorship regulations contributed to the image of Frederick as 'enlightened' or *roi philosophe*. As a result, young innovative thinkers from the other German states and Europe were attracted to Berlin and contributed to the establishment of an enlightened sociability.[60] At the Berlin Academy, whose patron Frederick was, freedom of thought enabled an eclectic philosophy to flourish.[61] Moreover, Prussia became a safe haven for philosophers who had been persecuted for heresy in France, for example,

57. See Friedrich Gedike, 'Über Berlin, von einem Fremden', *Berlinische Monatsschrift* 3 (1784), p.268-81 (272-74).
58. See Friedrich Gedike, 'Über Berlin, von einem Fremden' (1784), p.278.
59. See Johannes Kunisch, *Friedrich der Grosse: der König und seine Zeit* (Munich, 2004), p.290-91.
60. See Ursula Goldenbaum, 'Der "Berolinismus": die preußische Hauptstadt als ein Zentrum geistiger Kommunikation in Deutschland', in *Aufklärung in Berlin*, ed. Wolfgang Förster (Berlin, 1989), p.339-62 (339-43).
61. This has been repeatedly emphasised by the Academy's president Pierre Louis Moreau de Maupertuis as well as by Johann Bernhard Merian, member of the philosophical class since 1750; see Maupertuis, 'Des devoirs de l'académicien', in *Histoire de l'Académie royale des sciences et belles lettres de Berlin* (1753; Berlin, Haude & Spener, 1755), p.511-21 (512-13), and Merian, 'Parallèle historique de nos deux philosophies nationales', in *Mémoires de l'Académie royale des sciences et belles-lettres* (1797; Berlin, Decker, 1800), p.53-96 (94-95). On Merian's conception of the academic spirit and eclecticism that reigned at the Berlin Academy, see Daniel Dumouchel, '"Hommes de nulle secte": éclectisme et refus des systèmes chez Jean Bernard Mérian', *Dialogue: Canadian philosophical review / Revue canadienne de philosophie* 57:4 (2018), p.745-65 (esp. 752-54 and 756-57).

the materialist Julien Offray de La Mettrie and the theologian Jean-Martin de Prades, whose doctoral thesis had caused scandal at the Sorbonne.

Frederick's obsession with French literature and philosophy led him to build a branch of Prussian Enlightenment with a decisively French tinge. Not only did he invite Voltaire, with whom he had corresponded since 1736, and the Italian populariser of Newton Francesco Algarotti to stay at his court, he was also successful in installing the French mathematician Pierre Louis Moreau de Maupertuis (1740) and the writer Jean-Baptiste de Boyer, marquis d'Argens (1742), as pillars of the renewed Academy (the former as its president and the latter as director of the class of literature). As well as these native Frenchmen, a significant number of Swiss scholars such as the famous mathematician Leonhard Euler, Nicolas de Béguelin, Johann Georg Sulzer, Johann Bernhard Merian, Henri de Catt and Jean III Bernoulli also became members of the Academy from the 1740s onwards. In contrast, the Prussian king despised German literature,[62] and excluded German intellectuals from the official institutions of learning, most prominently from the Academy, whose appointment policy he oversaw. However, this deliberate exclusion did not impede a German Enlightenment culture from developing; on the contrary, it fuelled it. The *Aufklärer* gathered in a non-state institutional environment, that is, in the enlightened societies such as the Mittwochsgesellschaft or the Montagsclub, and published their writings in journals, for example, the *Berliner Monatsschrift* and Friedrich Nicolai's *Allgemeine Deutsche Bibliothek*.[63]

From the mid-eighteenth century onwards, Huguenot scholars seem to have been almost intellectually marginalised within this complex configuration of the Enlightenment in Berlin. As Gedike insinuated in 1783, Berlin's German scholars did not find favour with

---

62. See Frederick II, *De la littérature allemande, des defauts qu'on peut lui reprocher, quelles en sont les causes, et par quels moyens on peut les corriger* (1780), in *Œuvres de Frédéric le Grand*, ed. Johann Preuss, vol.7 (Berlin, 1847), p.103-40, http://friedrich.uni-trier.de/fr/oeuvres/7/toc/ (last accessed 12 July 2023).
63. See Horst Möller, *Aufklärung in Preussen: der Verleger, Publizist und Geschichtsschreiber Friedrich Nicolai* (Berlin, 1974); H. Möller, 'Enlightened societies in the metropolis: the case of Berlin', in *The Transformation of political culture: England and Germany in the late eighteenth century*, ed. Eckart Hellmuth (London, 1990), p.219-33; and Hans Erich Bödeker, 'Journals and public opinion: the politicization of the German Enlightenment in the second half of the eighteenth century', in *The Transformation of political culture*, ed. E. Hellmuth, p.423-45.

the French – he seems to include the Huguenots here – because of their privileged status at the Academy and the court.[64] However, Huguenot scholars also avoided collaboration with the French *philosophes* who had come to Berlin at Frederick's invitation. Formey and his peers largely despised their materialistic, deistic and atheistic positions. As far as the Swiss members of the Academy were concerned, several of them (Euler, Béguelin, Merian) integrated themselves into the Berlin Huguenot colony, which had been open to everyone whatever their confession since 1751.[65] In terms of philosophy, however, they did not form a coherent group: Merian was an adept of British empiricism; Sulzer and Béguelin were more influenced by Wolffianism; and Euler was hostile to Wolff's philosophy. Moreover, compared with the time of the Academy's foundation in 1700 and its renewal in 1744 – in both instances Huguenots made up almost half of the ordinary members – the numbers of genuinely Huguenot members at the Academy dropped in the second half of the eighteenth century.[66]

Despite the Huguenots' ongoing assimilation into Prussian intellectual society and the diversification of French culture in Berlin, Formey's generation still felt a particular Huguenot identity. As Formey's correspondence reveals, he maintained close contact with the local and international places where the diaspora resided.[67] However, the Huguenot identity of Formey's generation is best described as a 'hybrid identity', which means that it combined the experiences of two cultures and allowed the holder to feel a member both of a minority and of the broader host society. As such, the Huguenots' 'hybrid identity' was the prerequisite for transcultural transmission and innovation.[68] This can be observed clearly in Formey's practices and thought as a philosopher: by merging Reformed theology with

64. See Friedrich Gedike, 'Über Berlin, von einem Fremden', *Berlinische Monatsschrift* 2 (1783), p.439-66 (455). On public aversion towards the French in general and particularly in Prussia, see *Gallophobie im 18. Jahrhundert*, ed. Jens Häseler and Albert Meier (Berlin, 2005).
65. See Rosen Prest, *L'Historiographie des huguenots*, p.46-47.
66. See Grau, 'Die Berliner Akademie der Wissenschaften', p.357.
67. See Jens Häseler, 'Introduction à l'inventaire de la correspondance de Jean Henri Samuel Formey', in *La Correspondance de Jean Henri Samuel Formey (1711-1797)*, ed. J. Häseler, p.9-35 (26-27).
68. See Katharina Middell, 'Hugenotten in Leipzig: Etappen der Konstruktion einer "hybriden" Identität', in *Réfugiés und Émigrés: Migration zwischen Frankreich und Deutschland im 18. Jahrhundert*, ed. Thomas Höpel and Katharina Middell (Leipzig, 1997), p.56-75 (75). This concept has also been applied by Pott, 'Gentle, refined, cultivated, witty people', p.8.

Wolffian philosophy, he drew on both his Calvinist heritage and Wolff's philosophy, and created a particular variation of philosophy within the Huguenot international scene. Another crucial aim of this book is to shed light on this alternative thought. In so doing, it compares Formey's standpoints with those of his Huguenot and Calvinist peers in Brandenburg-Prussia, Holland and Switzerland, and observes his engagement with Calvinist models of the past. As such, it is a contribution to the history of the Huguenot international scene during the second half of the eighteenth century.

Religious Enlightenment

With respect to the scholarship on the Enlightenment, this case study on the religious thought of a Huguenot scholar from Berlin situates itself in a branch of Enlightenment studies that surfaced roughly twenty years ago: research on religion and Enlightenment. By stressing the ongoing importance of religion in most areas of eighteenth-century culture as well as the theological roots of certain 'enlightened' ideas, studies on religion and Enlightenment have contributed to deconstructing the traditional concept of the Enlightenment as a genuinely French issue that was concerned exclusively with secular, rational and liberal ideas. However, despite this 'religious turn' in Enlightenment studies, the paradigm of the Enlightenment being the anti-religious and secular precursor to modernity still dominates historiography and public opinion.[69] This is why the present work is relevant.

The various efforts of scholars to 'reintroduce' religion to the intellectual history of the eighteenth century have produced an inspiring and very diverse field of research. There are two different branches in the history of religion and Enlightenment in particular:

---

69. See William J. Bulman, 'Introduction: Enlightenment for the culture wars', in *God in the Enlightenment*, ed. William J. Bulman and Robert G. Ingram (Oxford, 2016), p.1-41 (7). Typical examples of the renewed propagation of the traditional narrative of the Enlightenment as an anti-religious and secular movement are Jonathan Israel's three-volume work on the Enlightenment: Jonathan Israel, *Radical Enlightenment: philosophy and the making of modernity 1650-1750* (Oxford, 2001); *Enlightenment contested*; and *Democratic Enlightenment: philosophy, revolution, and human rights 1750-1790* (Oxford and New York, 2012), as well as Anthony Pagden, *The Enlightenment and why it still matters* (New York, 2013), and, more recently, Margaret C. Jacob, *The Secular Enlightenment* (Princeton, NJ, and Oxford, 2019).

the first includes studies that are usually concerned with the French context and deal with the historical actors who opposed the ideas of the French Enlightenment, whereas the second reveals the attempt to trace – depending on the phrasing – the application of 'enlightened' ideas to religion and theology or the religious roots of typical 'enlightened' ideas. Both research agendas have their merits and flaws. As exemplars of the first type of studies, Didier Masseau, Darrin McMahon, Olivier Ferret and, most recently, Mark Curran have analysed the polemical attacks of the so-called *anti-philosophes* against the French *philosophes* and/or their Christian apologetics during the second half of the eighteenth century.[70] Their research has the merit not only of rehabilitating French and Francophone second-tier authors who have been previously despised by scholars because of their literary mediocrity or presumed conservative intentions,[71] but also of revisiting the very definition of Enlightenment by portraying it as a dialectic process. By conceiving of the Enlightenment as a battle between force and counterforce, McMahon emphasises the non-linear emergence of Enlightenment thought.[72] Similarly, Ferret suggests that the pamphlet wars between the *philosophes* and the *anti-philosophes* between 1750 and 1770 contributed to the emergence of the 'esprit philosophique' characteristic of the Enlightenment.[73] As far as Masseau is concerned, he has underlined that it is almost impossible to draw a neat line between the *philosophes* and the *anti-philosophes*; not only were the two opposing camps ideologically and socially

---

70. See Didier Masseau, *Les Ennemis des philosophes: l'antiphilosophie au temps des Lumières* (Paris, 2000); Darrin M. McMahon, *Enemies of the Enlightenment: the French counter-Enlightenment and the making of modernity* (Oxford and New York, 2001); Olivier Ferret, *La Fureur de nuire: échanges pamphlétaires entre philosophes et antiphilosophes (1750-1770)*, SVEC 2007:03. Ferret scrutinises the debates between *philosophes* and *anti-philosophes* in terms of a literary quarrel and, therefore, excludes expressively apologetic pamphlets from his study. Mark Curran, *Atheism, religion and Enlightenment in pre-revolutionary Europe* (Woodbridge, 2012).
71. In her preface to a special issue of *Dix-huitième siècle* dedicated to religion and Enlightenment, Sylviane Albertan-Coppola highlighted that the interest in the so-called *anti-philosophes* had been preceded by an 'ideological' change among specialists of the Enlightenment who were biased towards Diderot, Voltaire and others; see Sylviane Albertan-Coppola, 'Présentation et état de recherche', *Dix-huitième siècle* 34 (2002), special issue: *Christianisme et Lumières*, ed. Sylviane Albertan-Coppola and Antony McKenna, p.5-9 (7).
72. See McMahon, *Enemies of the Enlightenment*, p.12 and 201, and, similarly, Masseau, *Les Ennemis des philosophes*, p.211.
73. See Ferret, *La Fureur de nuire*, p.9.

heterogeneous,[74] authors from the different camps also frequently shared the same literary practices[75] as well as philosophical positions.[76] Mark Curran's study on the international religious opposition to the atheistic works of Paul-Henri Thiry, baron d'Holbach, situates Christian apologists and *philosophes* under the common umbrella of the public sphere.[77]

However, despite their efforts to broaden the concept of Enlightenment and to blur the boundaries between 'champions' and 'enemies' of the Enlightenment, these studies on the conservative opposition to Voltaire, Diderot and the like tend to perpetuate the traditional paradigm that equates the Enlightenment with the ideas and style of the *philosophes*. They depict the moderate religious voices of the eighteenth century as being the result of a process of appropriating styles and modes of reasoning from the dominant group of French *philosophes* during the second half of the eighteenth century. For example, Masseau and Curran have established a teleological narrative of the *anti-philosophes*' rhetorical alignment with the *philosophes* or their adaptation to a public taste generated by the writings of the *philosophes*.[78] Ferret presents Voltaire's style of pamphlet writing as a role model that shaped the style of his contemporaries during the pamphlet wars, which took place between 1750 and 1770.[79] Moreover, Curran suggests that, beyond stylistic alignment, Christian apologists increasingly incorporated the core 'enlightened' ideas of the *philosophes* into their Christian worldview and became more critical towards religion themselves.[80] Moreover, the studies on the enemies of the Enlightenment hardly succeed in overthrowing the narrative established in the history of eighteenth-century apologetics, namely,

74. For the ideological heterogeneity of the group of *anti-philosophes*, see Masseau, *Les Ennemis des philosophes*, p.35-42. Ferret, *La Fureur de nuire*, p.427, also refers to the internal heterogeneity of the two camps; however, he claims that each of them had a strong group identity that resulted from their opposition to the enemy.
75. See Masseau, *Les Ennemis des philosophes*, p.318-19.
76. See Masseau, *Les Ennemis des philosophes*, p.377. A similar point is made by Geneviève Artigas-Menant, 'Perspectives', *Dix-huitième siècle* 34 (2002), special issue: *Christianisme et Lumières*, ed. Sylviane Albertan-Coppola and Antony McKenna, p.10-12 (10).
77. See Curran, *Atheism, religion and Enlightenment*, ch.7 and 8.
78. See Masseau, *Les Ennemis des philosophes*, p.312; Curran, *Atheism, religion and Enlightenment*, p.151-52.
79. See Ferret, *La Fureur de nuire*, p.12 and 425.
80. See Curran, *Atheism, religion and Enlightenment*, p.161-62.

that the apologists' attempts to beat the *philosophes* with their own weapons undermined the whole endeavour of the apologists because the rationalist defence of religion had already sown the seeds of doubt concerning dogma that would, ultimately, lead to the victory of secular Enlightenment.[81] Such a depiction of the role of religious actors within the Enlightenment points to the power of the traditional narrative of the Enlightenment as a process of progressive secularisation. Despite all attempts to pluralise the concept of Enlightenment, it seems to be extremely difficult to abandon this teleological narrative.[82] Therefore, studies on religion and Enlightenment often reveal an unintentional tendency to portray forms of religious Enlightenment as transitional moments within this process of secularisation.

Recently, Jeffrey Burson overcame the trend in French and Anglo-American scholarship to analyse the role of religion in the French Enlightenment within the framework of a struggle between two opposed ideological camps. In his study on one of the major arguments between *philosophes* and orthodox theologians in eighteenth-century France – the controversy about the censuring of Jean-Martin de Prades's doctoral thesis in 1751 – Burson rather looks at the theological origins of the so-called French Counter-Enlightenment and, thereby, sheds light on the theological Enlightenment that existed in France before the mid-century rise of the *philosophes*, something that is usually ignored.[83] He situates Prades's doctoral thesis, which was accused of containing deistic and sceptical implications by Jansenists and Jesuits alike, in the context of a Catholic Enlightenment, which in his view was characterised by a reasonable theology inspired by Lockean and Malebranchean ideas.[84] This enables him to point to the overlaps

81. See Masseau, *Les Ennemis des philosophes*, p.275-76. The point about this dilemma has also been made by Antony McKenna, 'Deus absconditus: quelques réflexions sur la crise du rationalisme chrétien entre 1670 et 1740', in *Apologétique 1680-1740: sauvetage ou naufrage de la théologie?*, ed. Maria Cristina Pitassi (Geneva, 1991), p.13-28, and Antony McKenna, 'Le dilemme de l'apologétique au XVIIIe siècle', in *Apologétique 1650-1802: la nature et la grâce*, ed. Nicolas Brucker (Bern, 2010), p.10-20.
82. This criticism is raised, for example, by Bulman, 'Introduction', p.11, and Knud Haakonssen, 'The historiographical vagaries of Enlightenment and religion', in *Enlightenments and religions: 14th C. Th. Dimaras lecture (2009)* (Athens, 2010), p.91-136 (103-104).
83. See Jeffrey D. Burson, *The Rise and fall of theological Enlightenment: Jean-Martin de Prades and ideological polarization in eighteenth-century France* (Notre Dame, IN, 2010), p.9.
84. See Burson, *Rise and fall*, p.43-54.

between theological, moderate and radical forms of Enlightenment that are illustrated by the Prades case.

As such, Burson's study is an example of the second branch of research on religion and the Enlightenment. This branch of research, which explores the religious roots of the Enlightenment, usually deals with non-French contexts, particularly Britain and Germany, where the eighteenth-century reform of thought was traditionally considered to have evolved within the Church and within theological discourse or conservatism at large and, hence, has not been recognised for a long time as belonging to *the* Enlightenment.[85] Brian Young's 1998 study demonstrates the clerical nature of the English Enlightenment by focusing on the intellectual controversies *within* the English clergy.[86] He analyses several chosen debates between orthodox and more heterodox English theologians and ecclesiastics about the texts of Locke, Newton and Hume, as well as about physico-theological apologetics and rational religion. This leads him to conclude that the English Enlightenment was dominated by an intellectual strand that lay in between religious conservatism and free thought,[87] and allows him to adjust the common depiction of the English legacy of the allegedly secular thought that was developed in eighteenth-century continental Europe.[88] A similar demonstration of the religious origins of supposedly 'enlightened' ideas has been achieved by Thomas Ahnert in the case of the early German Enlightenment and, more precisely, through one of its main figures, Christian Thomasius. Previous studies declared Thomasius to be an 'enlightened' thinker because he pursued a secular political and moral philosophy that was separated neatly from religious faith.[89] Ahnert reveals the inadequacy of this interpretation by showing that Thomasius' natural law and moral philosophy as well as the reform of learning he attempted were rooted in a concept of the relationship between reason and faith that was

---

85. See for Germany Joachim Whaley, 'The Protestant Enlightenment in Germany', in *The Enlightenment in national context*, ed. Roy Porter and Mikuláš Teich (Cambridge, 1981), p.106-17, and for Britain J. G. A. Pocock, 'Clergy and commerce: the conservative Enlightenment in England', in *L'età dei Lumi: studi storici sul settecento europeo in onore di Franco Venturi*, ed. Raffaele Ajello, E. Cortese and V. Piano Moratari, 2 vols (Naples, 1985), vol.1, p.523-62.
86. See B. W. Young, *Religion and Enlightenment in eighteenth-century England: theological debate from Locke to Burke* (Oxford, 1998), p.3.
87. See Young, *Religion and Enlightenment*, p.217.
88. See Young, *Religion and Enlightenment*, p.214-15.
89. See Ahnert, *Religion and the origins of the German Enlightenment*, p.1-2.

itself shaped by religious enthusiasm. In fact, Thomasius considered the human intellect to be too weak to comprehend religious truths, which is why he wanted philosophy and religion to be separated. Thus, Ahnert convincingly claims, Thomasius' secular philosophy cannot be part of the stereotypical picture of an Enlightenment that venerated reason and rationality.[90] More recently, Ahnert has provided a similar reevaluation of presumed eighteenth-century secular thought. In his study on the Scottish debates about morality during the eighteenth century, he challenges the common view that the increasing focus on moral conduct instead of doctrine in Scottish notions of religion was a sign of increasing secularisation during the Enlightenment. He argues that the shift from doctrine to moral conduct with regard to religion was not the result of a reconciliation between religious ideas and (rival) secular ideas that were based on rationality or ancient thought.[91] Rather, he shows that it emanated exclusively from an internal religious debate about the doctrine of solfideism between orthodox thinkers and enthusiasts in the Presbyterian Church.[92] Young's and Ahnert's accounts of regionally and intellectually different types of religious Enlightenment fruitfully question central principles such as secularism, rationality and liberalism, which are usually employed to characterise the Enlightenment. However, the accounts' revisions of the history of the Enlightenment come at the expense of a crystal-clear concept of Enlightenment; for example, Ahnert's attempt to include the Scottish theological debates about salvation in a history of the Scottish Enlightenment leads him to define the Enlightenment in a very loose way, namely, as 'the sum of the debates and ideas of the period from the late seventeenth to the early nineteenth centuries'.[93]

The recent reassessment of the Enlightenment in Geneva by scholar of theology Jennifer McNutt contains a similar flaw with respect to its definition of the Enlightenment, despite the many merits of her study. The accepted narrative of religious decline in eighteenth-century Geneva asserts that since the early eighteenth century the Genevan pastors had been developing a so-called 'enlightened orthodoxy', a type of Christian heterodoxy that was inspired by the teachings of Jean-Alphonse Turrettini and influenced by deism,

---

90. See Ahnert, *Religion and the origins of the German Enlightenment*, p.121-22.
91. See Thomas Ahnert, *The Moral culture of the Scottish Enlightenment, 1690-1805* (New Haven, CT, 2014), p.6.
92. See Ahnert, *The Moral culture*, p.12.
93. Ahnert, *The Moral culture*, p.13-14.

and that eventually led to the 'triumph of reason over revelation'.[94] This depiction of the Genevan clergy turning away from Calvin's teachings had already been suggested in the eighteenth century by Jean D'Alembert's article 'Genève' in the *Encyclopédie*, according to which all Genevan pastors were Socinian.[95] McNutt challenges this narrative by emphasising the continuities between sixteenth-century and eighteenth-century Calvinism in Geneva.[96] She describes the religious Enlightenment in Geneva as a convergence of Calvin's sixteenth-century teachings with Enlightenment thought. This allows her to attach importance to both continued adherence to Reformed tradition and acceptance of the theological and cultural changes provoked by the Enlightenment.[97] With respect to this, she stipulates an interesting but risky consideration, namely, that the appearance of an old idea in a new context should not automatically make it a novel idea.[98] It is certainly true that, in the past, Enlightenment studies have suffered from not relating eighteenth-century ideas to the philosophy and theology of previous centuries enough. As a result, certain eighteenth-century ideas and practices have been mistakenly considered to be innovative and secular in nature. However, McNutt's consideration could, potentially, evoke the image of the eighteenth century as a mere prolongation of the Reformation, just as her study as a whole could. This is an image that fails to acknowledge the particularity of eighteenth-century culture and, eventually, leads to the dissolution of the very concept of Enlightenment.

Another way of weakening the concept of Enlightenment is to conflate it with many different and even contradictory characteristics. This accusation has been made against research on the religious Enlightenment in particular, although, likewise, it can be applied to attempts to ideologically and geographically pluralise the hitherto unitary Enlightenment in general.[99] Indeed, David Sorkin's

---

94. See Jennifer Powell McNutt, *Calvin meets Voltaire: the clergy of Geneva in the age of Enlightenment, 1685-1798* (Farnham, 2013), p.3 and 6.
95. See McNutt, *Calvin meets Voltaire*, p.1.
96. Compare with Bulman, 'Introduction', p.15. He also underlines the close connection between the Enlightenment and the Reformation and the Renaissance.
97. See McNutt, *Calvin meets Voltaire*, p.17 and 21-22.
98. See McNutt, *Calvin meets Voltaire*, p.21.
99. See Bulman, 'Introduction', p.11; Simon Grote, 'Review-essay: religion and Enlightenment', *Journal of the history of ideas* 75:1 (2014), p.137-60 (145); and Jonathan Sheehan, 'Enlightenment, religion, and the enigma of secularization:

influential study on a transnational and multiconfessional religious Enlightenment makes a plea for considering the religious Enlightenment as an equally important element of an 'Enlightenment spectrum' alongside the radical and moderate enlightenments described by Jonathan Israel.[100] In addition to this, Sorkin's study is an example of the pluralisation of the religious Enlightenment itself. Through individual case studies he compares different variations of religious Enlightenment, including not only Catholicism, Protestantism and their respective dissenting sects, but also Judaism. Despite the confessional and local differences between these variations, they all reveal four intellectual and cultural–political characteristics, which, according to Sorkin, constituted the religious Enlightenment in eighteenth-century Europe: the embracing of a reasonable religion based on both reason and faith; adherence to a natural law-based concept of toleration; participation in a (secular) public sphere; and support for a moderate reform of the confessional state.[101] In addition to his strong synthesis of a transcultural religious Enlightenment, two of Sorkin's considerations in particular deserve attention. The first is his focus on the reasonable religion that was shared by the various 'religious enlighteners' he studied. This demonstrates that the perception of a harmonious relationship between revealed and natural truths was essential for eighteenth-century religious culture, although it drew on different sources and had slightly different emphases depending on the context. Second, Sorkin convincingly rejects the frequent narrative maintaining that the attempts of many religious enlighteners to reform orthodoxy by embracing a reasonable religion were doomed to failure from the beginning because they were nothing more than a step towards deism and the destruction of religion. Sorkin points out the ahistorical nature of such a claim by underlining that, as far as the historical

---

a review essay', *The American historical review* 108:4 (2003), p.1061-80 (1067). As far as the most influential attempts to pluralise the Enlightenment are concerned, see *The Enlightenment in national context*, ed. R. Porter and M. Teich, as well as J. G. A. Pocock, *Barbarism and religion*, vol.1: *The Enlightenments of Edward Gibbon, 1737-1764* (Cambridge, 1999), p.9.

100. See David Sorkin, *The Religious Enlightenment: Protestants, Jews, and Catholics from London to Vienna* (Princeton, NJ, 2008), p.19-20. A similar claim for a 'spectrum of thematic Enlightenment' has been made recently by Dale K. Van Kley, 'The varieties of enlightened experience', in *God in the Enlightenment*, ed. W. J. Bulman and R. G. Ingram, p.278-316 (289-90).

101. See Sorkin, *The Religious Enlightenment*, p.11-18.

actors were concerned, they perceived a reasonable religion to be a 'viable theological position'.[102]

These two considerations are reflected in the present work on the theological and philosophical debates in which Formey was involved. The book attempts to elucidate his version of religious Enlightenment, and takes the harmonious relationship between reason and faith to be the overarching principle that determined his thought and practices. This viewpoint is based on Formey's own perception of himself as a Christian philosopher. Unlike twenty-first-century convictions, Christian philosophy was anything but an oxymoron in the eyes of Formey and the majority of his eighteenth-century contemporaries. On the contrary, as a truly historical approach to past ideas is able to show, Christian philosophy was a mode of enquiry based on methodological and epistemological convictions that were deemed philosophical and that allowed their practitioners to account for all kinds of questions. At the same time, Christian philosophy also pursued apologetic aims. However, Formey's Christian opposition to the French *philosophes*, which he uttered in several refutations of their writings, was only one of the ways in which he applied this Christian philosophy in practice. To grasp fully the extent of his religious Enlightenment, it is necessary to analyse the debates that he led with Calvinist theologians, Huguenot pastors and his academic colleagues as well as his preaching and popular moral writings. Thematically, these debates were about fundamental issues of Christian religion such as the existence of God, free will, divine providence, the origin of evil and the relationship between natural and divine law. The main objects of enquiry in this book will, therefore, be these debates and writings, whereas Formey's opposition to the *philosophes* will be treated as the broader context in which they evolved. The perception that the *philosophes* dominated the public sphere with their anti-clerical and anti-religious claims was implicit in most of Formey's works, even when these were not explicit attacks against the *philosophes*. Moreover, his critical engagement with the *philosophes* sometimes inspired other publications or sparked discussions with his peers.

---

102. See Sorkin, *The Religious Enlightenment*, p.17. Haakonssen, 'The historiographical vagaries', p.134-35, makes the same point in a more general vein by criticising traditional studies on the Enlightenment for superimposing modern views of coherence and commensurability onto the historical actors' frames of reference.

Therefore, this book on Formey is situated at the intersection between the two different approaches to the study of religion and Enlightenment described above. Following the attempts of studies on the 'enemies of the Enlightenment', it reevaluates the thought of a second-tier author who, hitherto, has, in the main, only been appreciated for his *anti-philosophe* stance. The book wishes to show that Formey's philosophical method and style, and even certain of his arguments, overlapped in several respects with those of his apparent adversaries and other presumed exponents of a secular Enlightenment. However, it refrains from arguing that such overlaps were the result of Formey's adaptation to the ideas of these people or to a set of secular ideas that emerged for the first time in the eighteenth century. Rather, it makes a point in stressing that Formey's reasonable and non-dogmatic engagement with religious questions and revealed doctrine had a more conservative basis. In the same fashion as the above-mentioned studies on various religious enlightenments, this book traces Formey's rationalism and his often seemingly secular position to their religious roots by showing they resulted from a combination of Leibniz's and Wolff's compatibilist philosophy of the late seventeenth century and early eighteenth century and a liberal Calvinism. Moreover, the book wants to shed light on the internal discussions that took place in the religious realm and, therefore, compares Formey's perception of Christian philosophy and his arguments with those of other Calvinist or Huguenot pastor-philosophers.

Method and structure of the book

Formey's and his peers' perceptions and arguments have been significantly influenced by the eighteenth-century ways of acquiring, presenting and discussing knowledge and by the culture of enlightened institutions.[103] To account for the genuine interdependence between ideas and scholarly practices, this book is inspired by the traditional theories of intellectual history that described the interaction between the intention of a text and its context of emergence.[104] More than that,

---

103. This is inspired by Jonathan Sheehan's 'media-driven concept of the Enlightenment' by which he opposed the concept of the Enlightenment as a merely philosophical movement; see 'Enlightenment, religion, and the enigma of secularization', quote on p.1076-77.
104. Here I refer to Quentin Skinner's and J. G. A. Pocock's linguistic contextualism (see Quentin Skinner, 'Meaning and understanding in the history of ideas

it considers itself an example of the genuinely eclectic and interdisciplinary field that intellectual history has become in the past decade, one that enables its practitioners to analyse the kinds of ideas that are central to this book, that is to say, ideas that have previously been dealt with in the history of philosophy or in theology, as well as to combine methods from various different disciplines.[105] It particularly draws on two different theories of how to contextualise ideas in intellectual history and the history of philosophy: the persona approach and the analysis of historical debates.

The concept of the *persona* of the philosopher has been developed by Ian Hunter, Stephen Gaukroger and Conal Condren as a tool to pursue a non-presentist analysis of past philosophies. It attempts to consider philosophy from the past as an empirical, contingent and performative activity rather than a coherent and universal product of human reason.[106] The persona of the philosopher is defined as a self-image that is cultivated in a particular milieu and for a particular purpose, namely, to create knowledge 'deemed philosophical'. Philosophical problems are, thus, considered to emerge

---

(1969)', in *Visions of politics*, ed. Quentin Skinner, 3 vols, Cambridge, 2002, vol.1, p.57-89, and J. G. A. Pocock, 'The concept of language and the *métier d'historien*: some considerations on practice', in *The Languages of political theory in early modern Europe*, ed. Anthony Pagden, Cambridge, 1987, p.19-38) as well as to the considerations on the historicity of past thought put forward by the so-called 'Sussex school' of intellectual history (see Stefan Collini, Donald Winch and John Burrow, *That noble science of politics: a study in nineteenth-century intellectual history*, Cambridge, 1983, p.5-6).

105. For the genuinely interdisciplinary character of intellectual history, see Richard Whatmore, *What is intellectual history?* (Cambridge, 2016), p.14. For a critical opinion on the eclecticism in intellectual history, see Darrin M. McMahon and Samuel Moyn, 'Introduction: interim intellectual history', in *Rethinking modern European intellectual history*, ed. Darrin M. McMahon and Samuel Moyn (Oxford, 2014), p.3-12 (4 and 11). Recent examples with regard to the diversity of subjects dealt with in intellectual history are Thomson, *L'Ame des Lumières*; Dmitri Levitin, *Ancient wisdom in the age of the new science: histories of philosophy in England, c.1640-1700* (Cambridge, 2015), and Simon Grote, *The Emergence of modern aesthetic theory: religion and morality in Enlightenment Germany and Scotland* (Cambridge, 2017).

106. See Ian Hunter, Stephen Gaukroger and Conal Condren, 'Introduction', in *The Philosopher in early modern Europe: the nature of a contested identity*, ed. Conal Condren, Stephen Gaukroger and Ian Hunter (Cambridge and New York, 2006), p.1-16 (8), and Ian Hunter, 'The history of philosophy and the persona of the philosopher', *Modern intellectual history* 4:3 (2007), p.571-600 (574 and 583-84).

from particular intellectual practices and moral values embraced by the philosophical self and in accordance with a larger social and cultural context.[107] As well as linking philosophical claims of the past to perceptions of philosophy and to practices of elaborating and presenting such philosophical claims, the persona approach also broadens the study of an individual philosopher. By assuming that the individual's self-image is to a certain extent informed by the perception of their duties and role by others, the reconstruction of the persona of the philosopher needs to include accounts by the philosopher's peers and their reception of his/her writings.

These considerations are reflected in the approach to Formey's religious Enlightenment pursued in this book. Its first three chapters reconstruct Formey's self as a Christian philosopher and, thereby, build the background against which the content and presentation of his philosophical and theological claims are interpreted. Formey's and his contemporaries' perceptions of what he was doing as a Christian philosopher are described and compared with mid-eighteenth-century perceptions of what a philosopher and a theologian, respectively, ought to do. This allows us to apprehend the precarious nature of the concept of a harmonious relationship between reason and faith in the mid-eighteenth century with which Formey – as one of its defenders – had to cope. Chapter 1 traces the epistemological convictions characteristic of Formey's Christian philosophy, and situates his reflections on philosophy and on his own role as a philosopher within the mid-eighteenth-century French debate about what it meant to be a true philosopher. Chapter 2 portrays the milieu in which Formey first cultivated his practice as a Christian philosopher, namely, the Berlin Huguenot colony in the 1730s and 1740s, and elucidates his self-presentation in his local religious community. Chapter 3 illustrates one of Formey's central practices as a Christian philosopher, that is, providing moral instruction to an audience of common people; in searching for an answer to the perceived decline of religion and

---

107. See Hunter, Gaukroger and Condren, 'Introduction', p.7-8. The notion of the persona has also been employed in the history of science; see Lorraine Daston and H. Otto Sibum, 'Introduction: scientific personae and their histories', *Science in context* 16:1-2 (2003), p.1-8. Daston and Sibum defined the scientific persona as a context-bound cultural identity. More recently, the historian of humanities Herman Paul has shaped the concept of the 'scholarly self' based on the persona approach; see Herman Paul, 'What is a scholarly persona? Ten theses on virtues, skills, and desires', *History and theory* 53:3 (2014), p.348-71.

devoutness, he blurred the boundaries between sermons and popular philosophical writing.

This reconstruction of the persona of the Christian philosopher is followed by a demonstration of how the nature of Formey's self affected his responses to crucial theological and philosophical questions such as God's existence, pre-established harmony between soul and body, free will, providence and natural law, which are the subjects of chapters 4 to 8. The common factor between these issues is that they all touch upon crucial theological problems such as the conflict between God's omnipotence and His goodness, the tension between human beings' original sinfulness and the requirement to work for their salvation, and the difficulties faced by divine law because of the rise of natural law theories. Moreover, posed as philosophical problems, they lead to reflections on the epistemological differences and similarities between natural and revealed truths. Therefore, in Formey's engagement with these different thematic issues, the practical implications of his concept of a harmonious relationship between reason and faith become tangible. Methodologically, chapters 4 to 8 draw on the idea of contextualising past thought through the analysis of debates, which is an approach that has been promoted by Anthony La Vopa as well as Ann Thomson.[108] Through the analysis of debates, the focus of enquiry shifts from the author of an idea to its reception and, therefore, such an analysis allows a wide range of (opposing) positions as well as the tools and practices for disseminating these to a wider audience to be included. However, as Ann Thomson emphasises, the study of a debate not only broadens the scope of analysis by including the different contexts in which it has been situated, it narrows it at the same time because a debate usually

---

108. See Anthony La Vopa, 'A new intellectual history? Jonathan Israel's Enlightenment' (2009), in *Enlightenment past and present: essays in a social history of ideas*, Oxford University Studies in the Enlightenment (Liverpool, Liverpool University Press / Voltaire Foundation, 2022), p.99-125, and Ann Thomson, 'L'histoire intellectuelle: quelles idées, quel contexte?', *Revue d'histoire moderne et contemporaine* 59:4bis (2012), p.47-64. Both La Vopa's and Thomson's considerations resulted from a critical engagement with Jonathan Israel's 'controversialist method' in his *Enlightenment contested*, which, however, they qualify as being unhistorical. With regard to the history of philosophy, Sarah Hutton has suggested an approach similar to La Vopa's and Thomson's. She makes a plea for conceiving of philosophical practice as consisting of conversations that philosophers from the past maintained with their predecessors and contemporaries; see Sarah Hutton, 'Intellectual history and the history of philosophy', *History of European ideas* 40:7 (2014), p.925-37 (935-37).

concentrates on one specific thematic question at a particular time and in a particular place. This narrow focus allows the complexity of the question at stake to be grasped.[109] In the case of Formey in particular, the debates about metaphysical, theological and moral questions in which he was involved reveal differences in opinion among apparently like-minded figures as well as overlaps between presumed opponents. The scrutiny of these debates, therefore, has the potential to challenge accepted narratives of a coherent religious Enlightenment that was ideologically opposed to the ideas of the *philosophes*. Moreover, the analysis of debates not only shows the diversity of existing positions on a particular question, it also discloses the impact of external factors on the way in which philosophical positions were defended by the historical actors, for example, the affiliation to a perceived national or ideological group.[110]

Chapter 4 examines Formey's thoughts about the provability of God's existence by presenting two different debates: first, his debate with Pierre Bayle, in which Formey opposes the former's scepticism concerning the rational provability of God's existence by putting forward arguments inspired by the Huguenot rationalists Jean Le Clerc, Jacques Bernard and Isaac Jaquelot, and, second, the debate with Maupertuis, the Newtonian president of the Academy, about the nature of metaphysics and its usefulness in proving the existence of God. Chapter 5 traces how Formey revived the debate about Leibniz's theory of pre-established harmony between soul and body that had been subjected to charges of fatalism from various sides since the early eighteenth century. Formey adopted the criticism of the Calvinist philosopher Jean Pierre de Crousaz in particular and, in combination with Pietist and other criticism of this allegedly deterministic theory, used it to attack Christian Wolff, whom he was supposed to defend. Although Formey's critical stance in relation to pre-established harmony in this debate came as a surprise to his Wolffian friends, it conveyed the ambivalent attitude concerning this theory that had prevailed among German scholars since the first half of the eighteenth century, other Wolffians included. Only a few years later, however, Formey took a completely different position

---

109. See Thomson, *L'Ame des Lumières*, p.19.
110. As Thomson, 'L'histoire intellectuelle', p.59-60, emphasises, sociological factors are, however, only one aspect that needs to be taken into consideration in the analysis of debates. Political and religious factors too, as well as many other aspects, determined the thinking of actors from the past.

with respect to the presumed determinism of Leibniz's and Wolff's philosophical theories. Chapter 6 shows that since the 1740s several members of the Academy had engaged in a debate about free will, which touched on similar issues covered by the debate about pre-established harmony. However, in this debate, Formey defended the compatibility between predetermination and freedom that had been promoted by Leibniz. As a result, he was opposed by his colleagues Merian and Prémontval, who advocated a liberty of indifference and denigrated Leibniz. Formey's main claim that distinguished him from his colleagues was epistemological and was inspired by Wolff's science of the soul: he claimed that human liberty relied on unshakeable empirical evidence. The question of the role of providence in the world, which is the subject of Chapter 7, also sparked controversy at the Academy. Formey, who adopted an optimist concept of providence in his moral philosophical writings, defended it against the criticism of D'Alembert in an argument about one of the Academy's prize questions that was released in 1749. Shortly after this, he led a public debate about the same question with another Huguenot theologian that was sparked by Formey's refutation of Diderot's rebuttal of optimism. The last chapter deals with one of the most famous controversies in mid-eighteenth-century Europe, namely, the controversy in relation to Rousseau's claim that the progress of science had a detrimental effect on morals. Formey entered the public debate about this subject at several different times and by using different genres of writing. Most importantly, it affected his theory of moral philosophy, which was mainly inspired by Wolff's ethics based on natural law.

The different thematic debates in which Formey was involved not only provide insights into the meaning of certain theological and philosophical questions for him as a Christian philosopher, they also illustrate how Formey adapted his position concerning these questions and the emphasis he put on the compatibility between reason and faith according to context. La Vopa, who seems to have a slightly narrower approach to the study of debates than Thomson, emphasises in particular the rhetorical dimension of a philosophical debate. In his view, the agency of past authors can be retrieved not only from the content of their arguments, but also from the reception of their arguments and from their rhetorical choices in a particular text. By arguing that an author's rhetorical choices were able to shape the reception of their ideas, La Vopa draws attention to the importance of studying an author's use of different genres and styles of writing.[111] Moreover, to recover the historical meaning of an argument, he believes the analysis of public debate must be supplemented by the analysis of an author's subjectivity as it is articulated in correspondence, journals or autobiographical writing.[112]

The analysis of Formey's involvement in the above-mentioned debates relies on a broad concept of reception inspired by La Vopa's considerations on the rhetorical dimension of a debate. First, attention is paid to the various different genres of writing that Formey employed. In addressing different audiences – academic colleagues, amateur philosophers, members of the congregation, French *philosophes* or the European scholarly public at large – Formey's choices of genre disclose his intentions in considering and emphasising particular aspects of a question. Genre-related choices were also strategic in situations of conflict; Formey uttered his criticism of the theory of pre-established harmony in a novelistic narrative, and he conveyed his opinion with regard to the Academy's essay competition on providence via a translation of the winning piece for good reasons. Second, the analysis of the different thematic debates is informed by a survey of the reactions to his arguments that Formey received. For this reason, mainly, his correspondence with his Calvinist and Huguenot peers in Prussia and Europe has been consulted because it offers valuable insights into the acceptance of Formey's thought among other Christian philosophers. By elucidating Formey's contributions to eighteenth-century philosophical and theological thought from various perspectives – thematically, rhetorically and through their reception – this book tries to reveal both the ongoing high relevance and the contested nature of Christian philosophy in the mid-eighteenth century.

---

111. See La Vopa, 'A new intellectual history?', p.116.
112. See La Vopa, 'A new intellectual history?', p.122-24.

1. Formey's concept of philosophy and its relationship to religion

In 1750, Formey published the first volume of his *Philosophe chrétien*, a collection of popular moral philosophical essays that became one of his most successful books, as he fully expected it would.[1] For modern critics, *Le Philosophe chrétien* is a key publication for understanding how actors such as Formey saw the world in which they lived and what role they attributed to themselves in it. The book appeared in four successive volumes, the last being published in 1757. There were also several French and German editions.[2] In addition, it led to two later follow-up works, the *Discours moraux* in 1764 and the *Consolations raisonnables et religieuses* in 1768, both of which Formey advertised with explicit reference to *Le Philosophe chrétien*.[3] These numerous volumes were filled with reworked versions of Formey's sermons, which, stripped of most of their pastoral rhetoric, were supposed to attribute a 'sane philosophy' to Christian doctrines, as Johann Bernhard Merian in his 'Eloge de Formey' claimed retrospectively.[4] As such, *Le Philosophe chrétien* could be defined nowadays as a kind of

---

1. See Formey, 'Notice de mes ouvrages', in *Conseils pour former une bibliothèque peu nombreuse mais choisie*, 3rd edn (Berlin, Haude & Spener, 1755), p.104-22 (118).
2. The different editions of *Le Philosophe chrétien, ou Discours moraux* are: 1st edn: 4 vols (Leiden, E. Luzac, 1750-1757); 2nd expanded edn: 3 vols (Leiden, E. Luzac, 1752-1755); 3rd edn: 4 vols (Leiden, E. Luzac, 1755-1758). Formey, in his 'Notice de mes ouvrages', p.119, spoke of two more editions produced in Lausanne and Lyon. Furthermore, there are two German editions, translated by Osterländer.
3. Formey, *Discours moraux pour servir de suite au Philosophe chrétien*, 2 vols (Leiden, Jasperd, 1764-1765), and *Consolations raisonnables et religieuses* (Yverdon, [Felice], 1768).
4. Johann Bernhard Merian, 'Eloge de Monsieur Formey', in *Mémoires de l'Académie royale des sciences et belles-lettres* (1797; Berlin, Decker, 1800), p.49-82 (55).

secularised sermon collection; Formey's contemporaries classified the work under theology and, more precisely, under the genre of so-called 'literature of edification'.[5] This genre implies the book's relatively easy intellectual and practical accessibility to wide groups of readers, many of them women.[6] In general, the book seems to have been read mostly by readers of the Reformed confession, not only in the German lands, but also in Geneva[7] and in France.[8] The widespread success of *Le Philosophe chrétien* made it a perfect vehicle for self-fashioning.

Many of Formey's contemporaries characterised him with reference to the title of his book and, thus, it shaped their visions and expectations with regard to Formey's work and his merit as a Christian philosopher. For example, in 1751, the Genevan professor of literature (and later of theology) Jacob Vernet, after having praised Formey's two moral philosophical writings *Le Système du vrai bonheur* and *Le Philosophe chrétien*, described him as someone who held the torch of religion in one hand and that of philosophy in the other.[9] The author of the review of *Le Philosophe chrétien*'s German translation in the *Freymüthige Nachrichten von neuen Büchern* from Zürich called Formey a Christian philosopher because he used his philosophical qualities in

---

5. See Merian, 'Eloge de Formey', p.54.
6. The dedications of the different volumes and editions show that a female readership was targeted: the first volume of *Le Philosophe chrétien* was dedicated to 'La Reine mère', who was Sophie Dorothea von Hannover, the wife of Frederick William I of Prussia and the mother of Frederick II; and the dedication in the second edition of the same volume was to Philippine Charlotte of Prussia, the daughter of the former and, thus, sister of Frederick II. The *Discours moraux* and the *Consolations raisonnables et religieuses* had no such royal 'patrons'; instead, they were dedicated to Prussian noblewomen. The first was dedicated to the dowager countess of Golowkin and the second to Friedericke Charlotte of Brandenburg-Schwedt. It can be seen from Formey's correspondence that women actually enjoyed reading *Le Philosophe chrétien*, for example, in Abraham Bocquet to Formey (30.12.1750), FF.
7. See Jacob Vernet to Formey (18.6.1753), in *Lettres de Genève (1741-1793) à Jean Henri Samuel Formey*, ed. André Bandelier and Frédéric Eigeldinger (Paris, 2010), p.368, and François de Roches to Formey (29.11.1753), in *Lettres de Genève*, p.383. In general, Formey's works have been well received in Geneva; see André Bandelier and Christian Sester, 'Science et religion chez quelques correspondants genevois de l'Académie de Berlin', in *L'Encyclopédie d'Yverdon et sa résonance européenne: contextes, contenus, continuités*, ed. Jean-Daniel Candaux *et al.* (Geneva, 2005), p.31-54 (49).
8. See Merian, 'Eloge de Formey', p.55.
9. Vernet to Formey (28.1.1751), in *Lettres de Genève*, p.296.

the service of Christian religion;[10] in this reviewer's opinion, Formey's work contributed to the advancement of reasonable piety.[11]

Furthermore, Formey's contemporaries detected in Formey's work as a Christian philosopher the aim of offering a counterbalance to the superficiality and lightheartedness that were considered to dominate the literature of the time. Jean-Laurent Garcin, who was a Huguenot pastor and preceptor in Holland, collaborated with Formey on the publication of the *Emile chrétien*, and held such a view with reference to Formey's *Discours moraux*, the follow-up book to his *Philosophe chrétien* that was published in 1764, claiming that Formey's writings served to censor the works of other authors in this, a 'frivolous age'.[12] The task of opposing the decline in standards of contemporary literature and philosophy was most often linked to the apology of religion. In the eyes of Formey's Calvinist readers, he was the best person to carry out the task of defending religion precisely because he combined philosophy and theology in his work and person. As Vernet put it, this provided him with more authority in the public debate. Therefore, on the publication of Formey's refutation of Diderot's *Pensées philosophiques*, his *Pensées raisonnables*, Vernet stressed that he considered the Christian philosopher to hold a position in between irreligion and superstition:

> Il est tres à propos que des savans bien reconnus par [les] philosophes defendent la cause de la religion; ils le font avec plus de succès, parce qu'ils ont un système de theologie plus raisonnable, & que leur autorité frappe plus que celle d'un theologien titré. Ainsi, Monsieur, vous etes l'homme qu'il nous faut, & je vous sai tout le gré possible de vous mettre si courageusement à la tâche. [...] Il y a une mode en cela comme en autre chose, & le beau rolle sera toujours de ceux qui savent tenir un milieu entre l'impieté & la superstition.[13]

Vernet was not alone in ascribing a liberal religious attitude to Formey; the Genevan natural philosopher Charles Bonnet also emphasised that he expected Formey to judge his *Essai analytique sur les facultés de l'ame* as a 'theologien philosophe'. By this, Bonnet meant that Formey would have a more moderate opinion on his mechanical

---

10. See *Freymüthige Nachrichten von neuen Büchern, und andern zur Gelehrtheit gehörigen Sachen* 11 (1754), p.234.
11. See *Freymüthige Nachrichten von neuen Büchern*, p.235.
12. See Jean-Laurent Garcin to Formey (11.8.1764), FF.
13. See Jacob Vernet to Formey (25.5.1749), in *Lettres de Genève*, p.235.

description of the human being than orthodox Swiss theologians.[14] Even among German Lutheran scholars, Formey's reputation as a Christian philosopher took hold. By the end of 1749, the professor of physics at the University of Wittenberg, Georg Matthias Bose, was accused of unorthodoxy by the university's theological faculty. In this situation, Bose appealed to his correspondent Formey to vouch for him in front of the Lutheran theologians. He justified his appeal to Formey first and foremost by saying that he was under the impression that Formey was a moderate and fair theologian who would willingly defend him against his orthodox adversaries.[15] The manifold expectations of Formey's diverse contemporaries were, thus, all linked with the combination of philosophy and Christian theology that his *Philosophe chrétien* promoted so symbolically.

Le Philosophe chrétien became an important pillar of Formey's self-representation and the perception of this by others because of the programmatic claims concerning the concept of Christian philosophy that it contained. Formey's central claim in the work was that philosophy and Christian religion needed to be reunited to preserve Christian dogma and the happiness that people would find in recognising it – a task that he wanted to fulfil in his book.[16] This claim will be dissected in the chapter that follows through an analysis of the concept of philosophy on which it relied as well as the mid-eighteenth-century debate about the nature of the 'true' philosopher by which it was most likely fuelled.

Philosophy as a universal science of reason

The foundation of Formey's concept of Christian philosophy was his view that philosophy naturally embraced religion. This view relied

---

14. Charles Bonnet, *Essai analytique sur les facultés de l'ame* (Copenhagen, Philibert, 1760). See Bonnet to Formey (17.6.1761), in *Lettres de Genève*, p.546-47.
15. See Georg Matthias Bose to Formey (26.3.1750), FF. In turn, Formey apparently helped Bose by writing a letter in his defence to present at Bose's trial; see Bose to Formey (20.5.1751), FF. Another aspect that seems to have motivated Bose was Formey's writings against the Catholic Cardinal Quirini, in which he defended Luther, despite being of the Reformed confession; see Formey, *Sendschreiben an S. Eminenz den hochwürdigsten Herrn, Herrn Angelus Maria Quirini [...] in welchem erwiesen wird, daß D. Luther gelehrter und tugendhafter und folglich zur Besserung der Kirche tüchtiger gewesen sei, als die Kardinäle seiner Zeit* (Berlin, Voss, 1749).
16. See Formey, *Philosophe chrétien*, 1st edn, vol.1, sig.[*3r-v], 'Dédicace à la reine mère'.

on his definition of philosophy as a universal science that comprised all particular sciences or forms of human knowledge, as he held in the introduction to a short history of philosophy that he published in 1760, his *Histoire abrégée de la philosophie*.[17]

Such a concept of philosophy as a universal science was common in eighteenth-century Europe and can be traced in different sources. In the *Système des connoissances humaines* at the beginning of the Parisian *Encyclopédie*, philosophy was defined as the 'science of reason', or as the part of human knowledge related to human reason.[18] In this classification of the sciences or different branches of knowledge, which was to a certain extent inspired by Francis Bacon's *Advancement and proficiencie of learning* (1603), reason was understood as the centremost of three cognitive faculties based on human understanding, the other two being memory and imagination.[19] According to the 'Explication détaillée', memory, which was the object of history, was the simple reproduction of the human being's sensory perceptions. Reason had the task of forming clear ideas of these perceptions through reflection, whereas imagination imitated and falsified these perceptions and, hence, was the object of poetry.[20] Philosophy was considered to be all encompassing because it consisted of all sciences, or the subcategories of human knowledge that could be formed on the basis of each of the manifold human perceptions. In this sense, philosophy fulfilled the role of a foundational and almost universal science that embraced three main objects of investigation: God, humankind and nature, which in turn were subdivided into other distinct sciences.[21]

The German philosopher Christian Wolff established a concept of philosophy that had significant similarities with that of the *Encyclopédie* because he also defined philosophy as a science that explained different phenomena, and he established a similar conceptual link between history as factual knowledge and philosophy as causal knowledge.[22]

17. See Formey, *Histoire abrégée de la philosophie* (Amsterdam, Schneider, 1760), p.9.
18. See 'Explication détaillée du système des connoissances humaines', in *Encyclopédie, ou Dictionnaire raisonné des sciences, des arts et des métiers, etc.*, ed. Denis Diderot and Jean D'Alembert, vol.1 (Paris, Briasson *et al.*, 1751), p.xlvii-li (including 'Système figuré des connoissances humaines', without pagination).
19. See Robert Darnton, 'Epistemological angst: from encyclopedism to advertising', in *The Structure of knowledge: classifications of science and learning since the Renaissance*, ed. Tore Frängsmyr (Berkeley, CA, 2001), p.53-75 (57-58).
20. See 'Explication détaillée', p.xlvii.
21. See 'Explication détaillée', p.xlviii.
22. See Christian Wolff, *Discurus praeliminaris de philosophia in genere / Einleitende*

Like the *encyclopédistes*, Wolff also distinguished between three different types of knowledge (*Erkenntnis*), but with one difference. In addition to historical and philosophical knowledge, he cited mathematical knowledge (instead of imagination, as was the case in the *Encyclopédie*). For Wolff, philosophical knowledge was the knowledge of causes, and it dominated the two other types of knowledge – history as the knowledge of facts and mathematics as the knowledge of quantities – on which it drew for a source and methodological role model, respectively.[23] Wolff's concept of philosophy was also the basis of Johann Jakob Brucker's critical history of philosophy that appeared in Latin in the early 1740s. Brucker was a German theologian and historian and an exponent of philosophical eclecticism as well as being a supporter of Wolff's philosophical ideas.[24] His *Historia critica* proved to be very influential in mid-eighteenth-century Europe, and Diderot drew heavily on it for most of the *Encyclopédie*'s philosophical articles.[25] Formey's above-mentioned *Histoire abrégée de la philosophie* was also based on it.

Therefore, it is not surprising that Formey articulated the idea of philosophy as a universal science and reflected on a division between memory and reason or history and philosophy that resembled Wolff's as well as the concepts developed by the French *encyclopédistes*. More precisely, Formey defined philosophy as the science that provided intelligible explanations of and reasons for simple facts that relied on human perception: 'Ainsi toutes les connoissances humaines, dès que ce ne sont plus de simples connoissances de fait, mais qu'elles s'élèvent aux raisons des faits, & en donnent de valables, rentrent dans la Philosophie.'[26] Hence, as far as its eighteenth-century practitioners

---

Abhandlung über Philosophie im Allgemeinen: historisch-kritische Ausgabe (1728), ed. Günter Gawlick and Lothar Kreimendahl (Stuttgart-Bad Cannstatt, 1996), §6, 7, 10.

23. See Wolff, *Discursus praeliminaris*, §17, 26 and 27; Werner Schneiders, 'Deus est philosophus absolute summus: über Christian Wolffs Philosophie und Philosophiebegriff', in *Christian Wolff 1679-1754*, ed. W. Schneiders, p.9-30 (15).

24. Johann Jakob Brucker, *Historia critica philosophiae a mundi incunabulis ad nostram usque aetatem deducta*, 5 vols (Leipzig, Breitkopf, 1742-1744). On Brucker and his history of philosophy see Mario Longo, 'A "critical" history of philosophy and the early Enlightenment: Johann Jakob Brucker', in *Models of the history of philosophy*, vol.2: *From the Cartesian age to Brucker*, ed. Gregorio Piaia and Giovanni Santinello (Dordrecht, 2011), p.477-577. For the Wolffian influence on Brucker, see especially p.486.

25. See Longo, '"Critical" history of philosophy', p.557-58.

26. See Formey, *Histoire abrégée*, p.10.

understood it, Formey included, philosophy was a type of knowledge that was characterised less by its subjects – basically, everything observable was the subject of philosophy – than by its method, which was based on the natural cognitive capacities of the human being.

In addition to this generally accepted basic definition of philosophy, each 'philosophical school' had its own viewpoint. In comparison with the definition of philosophy in the *Système des connoissances humaines*, Wolff enlarged the method and scope of philosophy in his *Discursus praeliminaris de philosophia in genere*. As far as he was concerned, it was the science that explained the existing *and* the possible.[27] Hence, philosophy not only explained historical facts or experiences and, therefore, did not rely exclusively on sensory experience as the *Encyclopédie* suggested, it also accounted for things that only potentially existed and, as such, used purely rationalist methods. Moreover, extending the scope of philosophy to include potentially existing phenomena caused it to become the science of virtually everything; hence, the universality of Wolff's definition of philosophy was emphasised far more strongly compared with the *Encyclopédie*.[28] Formey adopted Wolff's formulation of the science of the possible in his *Histoire abrégée*: '[la Philosophie] tend en général à donner une explication solide & intelligible de tout ce qui est, & de tout ce qui peut être.'[29] Another distinctive feature of a particularly Wolffian concept of philosophy, which can be found in Formey's works, is the strong emphasis on the rational and systematic character of the philosophical method. This could be used with the same scientific certainty as the mathematical method,[30] and had the purpose of making philosophical knowledge appear as absolutely certain knowledge that used its fundamental principles to serve other

---

27. See Wolff, *Discursus praeliminaris*, §29 and 46.
28. See Schneiders, 'Deus est philosophus', p.18. Schneiders uses the term 'Gesamtwissenschaft'.
29. See Formey, *Histoire abrégée*, p.9-10.
30. Wolff saw analogies between the mathematical and demonstrative method in methaphysics, yet did not argue that mathematics should be applied to philosophy: see Giorgio Tonelli, 'La disputa sul metodo matematico nella filosofia della prima metà del settecento e la genesi dello scritto kantiano sull'evidenza', in *Da Leibniz a Kant: saggi sul pensiero del settecento*, ed. Claudio Cesa (Naples, 1987), p.81-107 (87); Stefanie Buchenau, 'Notions directrices et architechtonique de la métaphysique: la critique kantienne de Wolff en 1763', *Astérion* 9 (2011), https://doi.org/10.4000/asterion.2136 (last accessed 12 July 2023), §6.

sciences.[31] Wolff's presentation of this method was itself characterised by the reference to original universally evident notions from which philosophical knowledge was to be deduced.[32] In Formey's account of philosophy in his *Histoire abrégée*, this Wolffian method of certainty clearly resonated: 'C'est une Science solide, puisée dans les plus pures sources de la raison & de l'expérience; un assemblage de principes évidens par eux-mêmes, ou évidemment prouvés, & de conséquences qui en sont légitimement déduites.'[33]

Consequently, Formey's concept of philosophy corresponded to the general eighteenth-century view that philosophy was a science linked to the human capacity for reason, this being represented symbolically in the *Encyclopédie*. At the same time, his concept was very much informed by the particularities of Christian Wolff's understanding of philosophy as being universal and rational, and possessing scientific certainty.

The epistemological foundations of Christian philosophy

According to both the common and the particularly Wolffian understanding of philosophy as a universal science of reason, this did not exclude religion. In the 'Système figuré des connoissances humaines', both natural and revealed theology appeared as subcategories of the 'science de Dieu' that was part of philosophy; however, the *encyclopédistes* remained vague with regard to how the acquisition of knowledge about God should function. Moreover, as Véronique Le Ru has suggested, the schematic depiction of theology in the *Encyclopédie*'s system of knowledge, according to which an abuse of religion led to superstition, could be seen as a subversive means of discrediting revealed religion. Furthermore, she pointed out that in most of the *Encyclopédie*'s articles that dealt with religion, revealed truths were excluded.[34] Wolff's classification of philosophy clearly stated that God's nature and existence were part of philosophy as far as they could be apprehended by natural reason; as such, God was the

---

31. See Schneiders, 'Deus est philosophus', p.13.
32. See Wolff, *Discursus praeliminaris*, §30.
33. See Formey, *Histoire abrégée*, p.11.
34. See Véronique Le Ru, 'De la science de Dieu à la superstition: un enchaînement de l'arbre encyclopédique qui donne à penser', *Recherches sur Diderot et sur l'Encyclopédie* 40-41 (2006), p.67-76, https://doi.org/10.4000/rde.346 (last accessed 12 July 2023).

subject of natural theology. Wolff also made it clear that, according to this definition, revealed religion could not be part of philosophy.[35] The particularity of Wolff's philosophy compared with the *Encyclopédie* was that he constantly emphasised the compatibility between natural and revealed religion, hence of philosophy and the Bible's teachings.[36] In his German *Metaphysik*, he claimed the truths that can be recognised through use of reason were as much inspired by God as the truths directly revealed by Him and, hence, reason and revelation existed next to one another.[37] Similarly, Leibniz argued against Bayle in his famous essays on theodicy that the truths of revelation and the truths of nature did not contradict one another.[38]

The Leibnizian and Wolffian concept of the compatibility between reason and faith was at the centre of Formey's Christian philosophy and, thus, shaped the way in which he evaluated natural and revealed truths as epistemic categories in his writings. Human reason or natural knowledge indicated a particular source of knowledge rooted in nature, which was, therefore, given to every human being by God. In contrast, divine revelation, or faith, was provided by God to only a few. Although Formey generally considered these two sources of knowledge to be compatible, they were not usually comfortable bedfellows. Depending on context, he assessed the role of each differently.

Formey's considerations of reason and faith as epistemic categories were rooted in the Christian dogma of original sin. Since the time of Saint Augustine, the idea of original sin has shaped not only the understanding of morality but, likewise, that of human knowledge. However, in the eighteenth century, the idea was in permanent decline.[39] Based on Genesis 1.3, the dogma of original sin divided

---

35. See Wolff, *Discursus praeliminaris*, §57, and *Theologia naturalis, methodo scientifica pertractata: pars prior, integrum systema complectens, qua existentia et attributa Dei a posteriori demonstrantur* (2nd edn, 1739), ed. Jean Ecole, in *Christian Wolff: Gesammelte Werke*, ed. J. Ecole *et al.*, section 2, vol.7.1 (Hildesheim, 1978), §1.
36. See Robert Theis, 'Theologie', in *Handbuch Christian Wolff*, ed. R. Theis and A. Aichele, p.219-50 (221 and 244-47).
37. See Christian Wolff, *Der Vernünfftigen Gedancken von Gott, der Welt und der Seele des Menschen, auch allen Dingen überhaupt, anderer Theil, bestehend in ausführlichen Anmerckungen* (4th edn, 1740), ed. Charles A. Corr, in *Christian Wolff: Gesammelte Werke*, ed. J. Ecole *et al.*, section 1, vol.3 (Hildesheim, 1983), §363 (referred to subsequently as *Anmerckungen*).
38. See Leibniz, 'Discours de la conformité de la foy avec la raison'.
39. See Ernst Cassirer, *Die Philosophie der Aufklärung*, in *Gesammelte Werke, Hamburger Ausgabe*, vol.15 (Hamburg, 2003), p.148; with particular focus on Leibniz's

human existence into two states: an innocent, naturally knowing pre-lapsarian state; and a guilty, ignorant lapsarian state. According to this belief, human beings' natural reason has been flawed since the Fall, and nothing but faith in revealed knowledge is able to provide them with knowledge and salvation. By despising human natural reason so strongly, the dogma of original sin implied a strong distrust of the human capacity for cognition, which was the basis of the concept of philosophy as a universal method able to explain the world. Luther in particular opposed this concept of philosophy,[40] but early Calvinism also adhered quite strictly to the Augustinian idea of original sin, which was explained in the Reformed *confession de foi* that was still the basis of the dogma to which the Reformed congregations of the Refuge adhered in Formey's day:

> Nous croyons que l'homme, ayant été créé pur & entier, & à l'image de Dieu, il est déchû par sa propre faute, de la grace qu'il avoit reçûë; & qu'ainsi, il s'est éloigné de Dieu, qui est la source de la justice & de tout bien: ce qui fait que la nature de l'homme est tout à fait corrompuë, son esprit aveuglé, son coeur dépravé.[41]

Nevertheless, the original Calvinist dogma and Calvin's teachings left some room for interpretation. Only one line below in the same article of the *confession de foi*, the complete intellectual and moral corruptness of human beings was relativised: 'Et quoiqu'il ait encore quelque discernement du bien & du mal, nous ne laissons pas de dire, que ce qu'il a de clarté se change en ténébres, quand il s'agit de chercher Dieu.' According to this, some elements of reason remained in human beings after the Fall, although not enough for them to understand God. This concession not only allowed the Reformed doctrine to maintain human responsibility for sin,[42] but also constituted a

---

Théodicée: Wilhelm Schmidt-Biggemann, 'Mutmaßungen über die Vorstellung vom Ende der Erbsünde', in *Deutschlands kulturelle Entfaltung: die Neubestimmung des Menschen*, ed. Bernhard Fabian, Wilhelm Schmidt-Biggemann and Rudolf Vierhaus (Hamburg, 1980), p.171-92.

40. See Michael Albrecht, 'Die Tugend und die Chinesen: Antworten von Christian Wolff auf die Frage zum Verhältnis von Religion und Moral', in *Nuovi studi sul pensiero di Christian Wolff*, ed. Sonia Carboncini (Hildesheim, 1992), p.239-62 (249-50).
41. See *Das Recht der Französisch-Reformierten Kirche in Preußen: urkundliche Denkschrift*, ed. Ernst Mengin (Berlin, 1929), 'Confession de foi, fait d'un commun accord par les Eglises réformées de France', §IX, p.45.
42. See McNutt, *Calvin meets Voltaire*, p.197.

1. Formey's concept of philosophy and its relationship to religion

prerequisite for the concept of philosophy as a science able to explain the world. However, certain aspects of the tradition of original sin remained strong within this concept of philosophy, and this can usually be observed in the way theologians and philosophers of the Reformed confession regarded revelation as being more important than natural reason.[43] This was also the case with regard to most of Formey's writings, in particular his popular philosophical works such as *Le Philosophe chrétien*.

In the eleventh essay in the second volume of *Le Philosophe chrétien* entitled 'Sur la connoissance de la vérité', Formey claimed the intellectual corruption of the human being that was caused by Adam's sin and, hence, portrayed revelation as the unique, valuable means to human Enlightenment. More precisely, he depicted revelation as a gift from God that enabled human beings to overcome the state of obscure and confused knowledge in which they had been trapped since the Fall:

> La Révélation est un moyen extraordinaire & surnaturel, dont Dieu se sert pour instruire les Hommes des Vérités qui échapent aux lumières naturelles, & qui sont néanmoins essentielles au salut. La nécessité de ce moyen, comme nous venons de l'insinuer, procède uniquement du changement de situation que le péché a causé dans l'Homme. Innocent, la Raison lui suffisoit; elle éclairoit sa gloire & sa félicité. Pécheur, cette même Raison l'accable d'humiliantes refléxions; & les tristes lueurs qu'elle jette encore, ne servent qu'à lui découvrir le précipice entr'ouvert sous ses pas.[44]

As in the biblical dogma, Formey presented the divine gift of revelation as absolutely necessary for human beings' salvation in eternal life and for their earthly happiness. Moreover, towards the end of this essay, he slightly extended this fundamental function of revelation and introduced its additional assets: it was able to enhance human beings' natural knowledge of God; it provided people with a more distinct idea of the afterlife; and it gave them motives for being virtuous.[45] This passage betrays a detachment from the historical narrative of original

---

43. See McNutt, *Calvin meets Voltaire*, p.193-94 and 201-202, who describes this way of conceiving of the relationship between reason and revelation as characteristic for the Genevan clergy in the eighteenth century. In her view, only the Genevan pastor Jacob Vernes constituted an exception from this mainstream attitude by holding that there was no article of faith that could not be explained by reason.
44. Formey, *Philosophe chrétien*, 3rd edn, vol.2, p.151.
45. See Formey, *Philosophe chrétien*, 3rd edn, vol.2, p.154.

sin according to which revelation necessarily superseded natural knowledge. Instead, revealed knowledge appeared as a supplementary epistemological category to natural knowledge; however, it was still considered superior to the latter because it brought human beings closer to God.

Formey's different assessment of reason and revelation was not always linked to their ability to bring salvation or closeness to God. On the contrary, in another essay in *Le Philosophe chrétien* that dealt with the question of how human beings could gain reassurance about the immortality of their soul, Formey judged the two categories by their probative force. Moreover, in this essay, Formey distinguished not only between natural and revealed knowledge, but between three different forms of knowledge that differed in the degree of certainty with which they could answer the aforementioned question: natural reason, natural religion and revelation. He developed the arguments each of them had in support of the soul's immortality, but maintained that only the last – revelation – was able to provide absolute certainty: 'il n'y a que la Démonstration de la Foi, qui puisse entraîner notre consentement d'une manière victorieuse, & bannir pour jamais les doutes, les agitations, les allarmes.'[46] Applying natural reason instead left too many doubts and did not prove the soul's immortality exclusively and directly,[47] and the explanation of natural religion, which was based on the assumption of the existence of a Creator God and His resemblance to human beings, was more persuasive than the first but could still only be considered a conjecture rather than a demonstration of certainty.[48] Only the existence of revelation itself and the message it contained were able to assure human beings of their immortality.[49] This discussion about degrees of probative force shows very clearly how the dogma of original sin was integrated into the concept of philosophy as a method of acquiring causal knowledge of existing and possible phenomena. Revealed knowledge had the same function as any other kind of knowledge, and was judged by its ability to work within philosophy's demonstrative method. At the same time, the dogma of original sin seems to have lingered on in the background in the sense that it allowed revelation to maintain the status of being the most certain knowledge.

46. Formey, *Philosophe chrétien*, 1st edn, vol.1, p.180.
47. See Formey, *Philosophe chrétien*, 1st edn, vol.1, p.183.
48. See Formey, *Philosophe chrétien*, 1st edn, vol.1, p.189-90.
49. See Formey, *Philosophe chrétien*, 1st edn, vol.1, p.193.

Therefore, the particularity of Formey's Christian philosophy seems to lie precisely in this integration of dogma into philosophical method. Epistemologically, his Christian philosophy can, therefore, be characterised as involving not only natural knowledge as a source of truth, but also revealed knowledge. As such, Formey's view on philosophy differs from that of the *encyclopédistes* or Wolff who made God the subject but not the source of philosophy. Moreover, Formey's tendency to stress the superiority of divine knowledge appears to diverge from the Wolffian and Leibnizian claim about the compatibility between natural and revealed truths, which implies epistemological parity between the two categories. However, there are moments in which Formey's vision of Christian philosophy seems more reminiscent of the Wolffian idea of the compatibility between reason and faith than the tradition of original sin, in the sense that he attributed the same epistemological status to both sources of knowledge. In his three-volume work entitled *Le Philosophe payen*, an annotated edition of letters written by Pliny the Younger published in 1759, nine years after the first appearance of *Le Philosophe chrétien*, he remained to a certain extent committed to the historical narrative of original sin because he referred to Christian philosophy as the state of philosophy after the birth of Christianity rather than pagan philosophy.[50] However, he did not include the usual account of the superiority of revelation over nature. In the dedication to *Le Philosophe payen*, Formey established the link to *Le Philosophe chrétien* as follows. He claimed that his edition of Pliny the Younger presented the 'sagesse payenne', whereas his own moral philosophical essays contained the 'sagesse chrêtienne', whereupon he stated: 'En reünissant *Le Philosophe Payen* & *Le Philosophe Chrêtien*, je me persuade qu'on aura une idée assez juste des devoirs de la Morale, déduits des notions fondamentales de la Raison & de la Religion.'[51] This comparison reveals a vision of natural and revealed knowledge as complementary and *equally valuable* means of establishing a moral theory. Compared with Formey's above-mentioned two essays in *Le Philosophe chrétien*, this depiction of natural (pagan) knowledge and revealed (Christian) knowledge making an equal contribution to morality appears exceptional. This can be explained by the different setting of the two books: *Le Philosophe payen* is a scholarly book, whereas *Le Philosophe chrétien* is a popular philosophical book that

50. Formey, *Le Philosophe payen, ou Pensées de Pline, avec un commentaire littéraire et moral*, 3 vols (Leiden, E. Luzac, 1759).
51. Formey, *Philosophe payen*, vol.1, p.iii.

relied on sermons and, hence, presumably had to stick to a more orthodox interpretation of the dogma.

The idea of the compatibility between philosophy and religion also resonated in the *Histoire abrégée de la philosophie*. This, too, is a scholarly book. A particular version of this idea is contained in Formey's assessment of the goal of philosophy as being to provide human beings with happiness. According to Formey, the philosophical method allowed human beings to know themselves, the world in which they existed and God as the author of it all.[52] On the basis of this knowledge, and through the observance of the teachings that it contained, human beings could achieve happiness: 'elle [la philosophie] lui [à l'homme] fait sentir que le bonheur doit être le but unique & invariable de ses démarches, qu'il ne peut attendre ce bonheur que de l'Auteur de son existence, & que pour l'obtenir, il doit lui plaire, se conformer à ses intentions, & exécuter ses volontés, autant qu'il est à portée de les connoître.'[53] According to this, the function of philosophy was to support religious doctrine because the former could fuel the recognition of the latter.

Therefore, it seems that Formey's concept of the relationship between natural and revealed knowledge that constituted his Christian philosophy was informed by at least two sources: the Reformed dogma of original sin that allowed reason and revelation as sources of knowledge to be integrated into one universal philosophy, yet considered revealed truths to be superior; and the Leibnizian and Wolffian understanding of philosophy according to which reason and revelation were compatible. It is important to note that the Leibnizian and Wolffian concept of the relationship between reason and revelation also had a confessional background that contained a 'softened version' of original sin similar to the Calvinist one. Some scholars even argue that, at the end of the seventeenth century, German Lutheran theology in general and the dogma of original sin in particular had adopted influences of Reformed theology or, to put it more precisely, Covenant theology.[54] However, from early on, trends to loosen the rigidity of the Augustinian concept of original sin were also present within Lutheran orthodoxy; these trends are attributed to Philipp Melanchthon, and Wolff is said to have developed his moral

---

52. See Formey, *Histoire abrégée*, p.11.
53. Formey, *Histoire abrégée*, p.12-13.
54. See Anselm Schubert, *Das Ende der Sünde: Anthropologie und Erbsünde zwischen Reformation und Aufklärung* (Göttingen, 2002), p.125-26.

philosophy partly according to this tradition.[55] Consequently, the two main sources of Formey's Christian philosophy are similar to a certain extent, although they could result in slightly different evaluations of philosophy and its sources. Drawing on these two sources, Formey was able to be either less or more orthodox with regard to his concept of reason and revelation depending on the context.

The Christian philosopher in the French debate about the 'true' philosopher

Formey's Christian philosophy was not only a philosophical concept that embraced certain epistemological convictions, it was also a vehicle for self-representation with the help of which he positioned himself in an important public debate that had been taking place in the Francophone Republic of Letters since the 1750s: that of determining who, exactly, was a 'true philosopher'. This debate was fuelled by a paradigm shift in the early modern definition of philosophy, mainly with respect to the question of philosophy's relationship to religion. In the debate, this question was linked to the definition of the practitioner of philosophy, the *philosophe*.

As Rolf Reichardt and Hans Ulrich Gumbrecht have shown in their history of the concept of the *philosophe* in France, the idea of the philosopher's role underwent a significant change between the late seventeenth and the late eighteenth century: from being the reclusive self-reflecting thinker within the court structure of the *Ancien Régime*, the *philosophe* became the prototype of the Enlightenment thinker who combined reflection with the criticism of authority and, as such, became the victim of polemics from more conservative societal and religious groups in the middle of the eighteenth century. During the French Revolution, the *philosophe* eventually became a rather radical figure.[56] According to Reichardt and Gumbrecht's account, the consolidation of the term *philosophe* to mean a reflective and critical writer in France in the 1730s and 1740s went hand in hand with the dispute about who had the right to call themselves a philosopher. In particular, the treatise entitled *Le Philosophe*, which was attributed to César Chesneau Du Marsais, and which to a large extent was later

55. See Albrecht, 'Die Tugend und die Chinesen', p.250-51.
56. See Hans Ulrich Gumbrecht and Rolf Reichardt, 'Philosophe, Philosophie', in *Handbuch politisch-sozialer Grundbegriffe in Frankreich 1680-1820*, ed. Rolf Reichardt and Eberhard Schmitt, vol.3 (Munich, 1985), p.7-89.

reproduced in the *Encyclopédie*'s article 'Philosophe',[57] contributed to the consolidation of this concept. In Du Marsais's depiction, a *philosophe* was someone who, through unbiased empirical thinking and refusal of the passions, worked for the good of society and humanity at large.[58] Although he emphasised that this task carried out on behalf of society had nothing to do with the anti-clericalism and irreligion of freethinkers, which actually destroyed the foundations of society,[59] it was precisely this point that constituted the main criticism from those who, like Formey, opposed this new type of philosopher.[60]

This criticism evolved into a public debate about who had the right to call themselves a *philosophe*, and, fuelled by the appearance of the *Encyclopédie* and its programmatic view on philosophy as being an emancipation from scientific and religious dogma, this debate reached its peak in the 1750s and 1760s.[61] More and more writers (often with religious backgrounds) commonly became known as *anti-philosophes* (they are the protagonists of the above-mentioned studies on the 'enemies of the Enlightenment' by Masseau and others), because they opposed the new *philosophes* in treatises and pamphlets and, most famously and influentially, in a theatre play entitled *Les Philosophes* that was presented at the Comédie-Française in May 1760.[62] In the 1760s, the writings of the *anti-philosophes* had, in fact, become the majority in the debate and, thus, the *anti-philosophes*' negative perception of the *philosophes* was more easily adopted by the wider public.[63] As well as blaming the *philosophes* for immoral behaviour and the destruction of religion, the *anti-philosophes* accused them of

57. See Herbert Dieckmann, *Le Philosophe: texts and interpretation* (St Louis, MO, 1948).
58. See Gumbrecht and Reichardt, 'Philosophe', p.18-19; compare with 'Philosophe', in *Encyclopédie*, ed. D. Diderot and J. D'Alembert, vol.12 (Neuchâtel, Faulche, 1765), p.509-11 (510).
59. See 'Philosophe', in *Encyclopédie*, p.509.
60. See Gumbrecht and Reichardt, 'Philosophe', p.20-21.
61. See Gumbrecht and Reichardt, 'Philosophe', p.22. Compare with Stéphane Van Damme, '"Philosophe"/Philosopher', in *The Cambridge companion to the French Enlightenment*, ed. Daniel Brewer (Cambridge, 2014), p.153-66 (155-56). Van Damme also describes the *philosophe* as an 'Enlightenment invention' and sees an example of the breadth and diversity of philosophy in the eighteenth century in the coexistence of the traditional role of the philosopher as an erudite and the new role of the *philosophe* as a man of letters.
62. Charles Palissot de Montenoy, *Les Philosophes: comédie, en trois actes, en vers* (Paris, Duchesne, 1760).
63. See Gumbrecht and Reichardt, 'Philosophe', p.28 and 37-38.

1. Formey's concept of philosophy and its relationship to religion

defending materialism and atheism, of being fanatical and intolerant, and of forming a sect.[64] As Gumbrecht and Reichardt stressed, the particularity of this polemic debate was that each of the two groups claimed the title of philosopher for itself and, therefore, the arguments of one group were mostly negations of the other's, which themselves were often negations.[65]

One important point in this debate, which was also the origin of Formey's claim to be a Christian philosopher, was the question of philosophy's (and the philosopher's) relationship to revealed religion. In the *Encyclopédie*, the possibility that reason and revelation could both be a part of philosophy was denied – 'La raison est à l'égard du philosophe, ce que la grace est à l'égard du chretien. La grace détermine le chrétien à agir; la raison détermine le philosophe.'[66] Formey, however, was convinced of it. In a broad sense, Formey's *Philosophe chrétien* was a contribution to the mid-eighteenth-century French public debate between *philosophes* and *anti-philosophes* about what it meant to be a 'true philosopher'. By arguing that philosophy and Christianity needed to be united, Formey attempted to safeguard philosophy as a universal science that allowed a harmonious relationship between natural and revealed knowledge. In the dedication to the book, he accused the *philosophes* of deliberately establishing themselves in opposition to Christians or, more precisely, of spreading the idea that philosophy and the Christian faith mutually excluded one another: 'mais par un travers bien déplorable, & qui suffit pour faire éclipser les plus brillans avantages, on sépare le titre de PHILOSOPHE de celui de CHRÉTIEN, & l'on s'imagine que la possession décidée du prémier ne sauroit s'établir que sur la ruïne de l'autre.' From this criticism, Formey extrapolated the task he had chosen for himself, namely, to unite the philosopher and Christian into one person and, in so doing, made reparation for this misapprehension of philosophy.[67] In this way, Formey also contributed to shaping the increasingly dominant public perception of the *philosophe* as an atheist and freethinker.

Equally important in this debate was the question of using the right philosophical method, and, with respect to this, both the *philosophes* and their critics – or at least Formey – used largely the same arguments for characterising their own positions: both laid

---

64. See Gumbrecht and Reichardt, 'Philosophe', p.28-34.
65. See Gumbrecht and Reichardt, 'Philosophe', p.37-38.
66. 'Philosophe', in *Encyclopédie*, p.509.
67. Formey, *Philosophe chrétien*, 1st edn, vol.1, sig.[*3*r*], 'Dédicace à la reine mère'.

claim to the so-called *esprit philosophique*, an empiricist and logical way of reasoning.[68] In 1754, the Académie française held an essay contest that asked for the meaning of the *esprit philosophique*, but posed the question in such a way as to ensure a conservative response: the contestants were asked to define the *esprit philosophique* with respect to the biblical saying that one should not know more than one needed to know.[69] The winner was a Jesuit priest who emphasised that philosophy's task was to inspire faith. Formey also participated in the essay competition, underlining how important the debate about the 'true' philosopher was to him. As far as he was concerned, the *esprit philosophique* was simply to reason on the basis of good logic.[70] Similarly to what Du Marsais claimed in *Le Philosophe* and what was later reproduced in the *Encyclopédie*,[71] Formey held that the 'true' *esprit philosophique* was having a particular mindset, one that formed judgements on the basis of facts and that proceeded without bias or haste and without the interference of the passions.[72] As a consequence, the picture that Formey drew of the philosopher who possessed such capacities was the following:

> Un Esprit philosophe ne juge point par orgueil, par hauteur, par envie de faire sentir sa supériorité; mais il juge parce qu'il ne peut s'empêcher de le faire, par ce que ce jugement n'est chez lui qu'une simple intuition, qu'un effet des idées nettes & distinctes qu'il possede, & qu'il est dans le cas d'un homme qui, ayant la vuë excellente, ne peut s'empêcher d'appercevoir les objets placés à la portée de l'organe.[73]

This depiction of the *esprit philosophique* contained the idea of philosophy as a universal method linked to cognition.[74] Formey embedded his

---

68. See Gumbrecht and Reichardt, 'Philosophe', p.34.
69. See Gumbrecht and Reichardt, 'Philosophe', p.30, n.57. The prize question was: 'En quoi consiste l'Esprit philosophique conformément à ces paroles de l'Ecriture: "Non plus sapere, quam oportet sapere"?'
70. See Formey, 'Discours sur l'esprit philosophique', in *Le Triomphe de l'évidence*, 2 vols (Berlin, Lange, 1756), vol.2, p.iii-xxiv (xx). This work was the main source for Fontius' analysis of Formey's concept of philosophy (see 'Zwischen "libertas philosophandi" und "siècle de la philosophie"'). However, he ignored the text's origin in the Académie française's essay competition.
71. See 'Philosophe', in *Encyclopédie*, p.510.
72. See Formey, 'Discours sur l'esprit philosophique', p.xix.
73. Formey, 'Discours sur l'esprit philosophique', p.xix-xx.
74. The 'Discours sur l'esprit philosophique', p.ix, also contained the definition of

description of the *esprit philosophique* in a polemical rhetoric, similar to the one he had put forward in *Le Philosophe chrétien* with respect to the role of religion in philosophy. He claimed that many of those who professed to be philosophers in his day spread paradoxical opinions that lacked any logic and only served as a means for gaining personal glory.[75] It was against the backdrop of this alleged abuse that he fashioned his concept of the *esprit philosophique* as the true one, which was capable – if joined with due respect to religion – of chasing away its disgraceful rival.[76] Hence, Formey's essay shows that the argument against the *philosophes* also functioned with reference to the supposedly legitimate way of reasoning, and only with a minor reference to the apology of religion, which was his broader purpose.

This strategy can also be observed in Formey's refutation of Diderot's *Pensées philosophiques*, which appeared only a year before the first volume of *Le Philosophe chrétien*. It, too, was published by Elie Luzac in Leiden. Likewise, in this, Formey drew heavily on the topos of defending the 'true' philosophy.[77] He disputed Diderot's right to use the term *philosophique* in the title of his work by declaring that it was far from being truly philosophical.[78] In his view, Diderot had argued indefensible things, claimed principles that were devoid of any connection to reality and drawn conclusions that could never result from any principles and, thus, did not follow the rules of logic.[79]

In Formey's refutation of Diderot, just as in his essay on the *esprit philosophique*, the character of philosophy as a science of reason was highlighted in his definition of 'true' philosophy, whereas Christian dogma, which as far as Formey was concerned was always linked to it to a greater or lesser degree, was only mentioned in passing here, and religious rhetoric was diminished.[80] This was completely different from *Le Philosophe chrétien*, in which Formey dispensed with an overly strong reference to logic and emphasised religion

---

philosophy as the knowledge of causes deduced from observable facts, as in Formey's *Histoire abrégée de la philosophie*.
75. See Formey, 'Discours sur l'esprit philosophique', p.xxi.
76. See Formey, 'Discours sur l'esprit philosophique', p.xxii.
77. Formey, *Pensées raisonnables*. The title page of the book indicates Berlin to be the place of publication. However, it was revealed in Luzac's correspondence with Formey and by Formey himself in his 'Notice de mes ouvrages', p.117, that the book was published by Luzac.
78. See Formey, *Pensées raisonnables*, p.v.
79. See Formey, *Pensées raisonnables*, p.x.
80. See Formey, *Pensées raisonnables*, p.xi.

instead. This difference between the two works was because of the different audiences Formey directed his writing at: *Le Philosophe chrétien* was addressed to a popular and religious public, whereas the *Discours sur l'esprit philosophique* was rooted in the learned professional context of the French Academy and the *Pensées raisonnables* in the learned, half-professional and half-popular context of the Republic of Letters more broadly. The different target audiences and contexts corresponded to the different socioprofessional roles that Formey assumed as a practitioner of philosophy: he could be the traditional philosopher, who through erudite writing postulated the pursuit of certainty, as well as the writer-philosopher, who through the use of more appealing and accessible literary forms reached a more popular public, just like the *philosophes*.[81] In both roles, however, the core of his Christian philosophy remained the same: it consisted of a reasonable way of accounting for the phenomena in the world that relied on natural and revealed sources of truth.

---

81. For the distinction between these roles see Van Damme, '"Philosophe"/philosopher', p.155 and 158-59. He described them as being opposed to one another.

2. Formey in the Berlin Huguenot Enlightenment, or how to reconcile the pastor and the philosopher

Formey's concept of Christian philosophy and his practices as a pastor-philosopher had their roots in the Berlin Huguenot Enlightenment, which was the context of his socialisation. In this context, the tradition of Calvinist learning was combined with German academic philosophy. Formey's early career was exemplary with regard to the practices and thought of the Berlin Huguenot Enlightenment in the 1730s and 1740s because he took part in the learned culture that developed among the young Huguenot pastors and amateur philosophers of his generation who were very enthusiastic about Wolffian philosophy. However, Formey's career soon became outstanding compared with the other members of his cohort because he was able to extend his intellectual network to different circles of the Republic of Letters by becoming affiliated to the Berlin Academy.[1] His transition from holding a pastoral office to becoming a professor of philosophy during his early career was the beginning of his development. At the same time, this transition constituted an early key moment for portraying himself as a Christian philosopher (much earlier than the *Philosophe chrétien*), in which he put forward his claims with regard to the relationship between religion and philosophical education to his Reformed congregation. The chapter that follows analyses his claims and situates them within the intellectual culture of the Huguenot Enlightenment in Berlin in the 1730s and 1740s.

---

1. See Häseler, 'Formey – l'homme à Berlin', p.421. Häseler divides Formey's epistolary network into three overlapping parts: chronologically, the earliest part is comprised of the pastors and amateur men of letters who belonged to the Huguenot Refuge; later, the academic and journalistic subnetworks developed and partly intersected with the first one.

Early Huguenot socialisation

By the mid-eighteenth century, the French Huguenot colony in Berlin was comprised of about 6500 people.[2] As a result, the Prussian elite developed an appreciation of French culture, particularly from 1740 onwards during the reign of Frederick II, and this led not only to the installation of the Huguenots in high positions in the state administration but also to their increasing prestige in the Prussian cultural sphere.[3] However, these positions were only available to the upper and better-educated ranks of the French colony, the Huguenot elite described by Susanne Lachenicht as the 'gate-keepers' who created and defended the identity of the colony.[4] Formey became part of this group of people very early on in his life because of his attendance at the Collège français, the French colony's own institution of higher education that was founded in 1689 and was under the direct control of the French Reformed Church and the Prussian sovereign.[5] This institution was, traditionally, the gateway to a career in the

---

2. See Rosen Prest, *L'Historiographie des huguenots*, p.575, and Martin Fontius, 'Privilegierte Minderheiten als Instrument königlicher Kulturpolitik?', in *Französische Kultur: Aufklärung in Preußen*, ed. Martin Fontius and Jean Mondot (Berlin, 2001), p.17-30 (18). Fontius speaks of 9000 members of the French colony shortly before the beginning of the reign of Frederick II. According to him, this corresponded to 15 per cent of the entire population of Berlin.
3. See Fontius, 'Privilegierte Minderheiten', p.22 and 24.
4. See Susanne Lachenicht, 'Etude comparée de la création et de la survie d'une identité huguenote en Angleterre et dans le Brandenbourg au XVIIIe siècle', in *L'Identité huguenote: faire mémoire et écrire l'histoire (XVIe-XXIe siècle)*, ed. Philip Benedict, Hugues Daussy and Pierre-Olivier Léchot (Geneva, 2014), p.279-94 (279-80).
5. For the history of the Collège français see the different *Festschriften* on the occasion of the anniversary of its founding: Jean-Pierre Erman, *Mémoire historique sur la fondation du Collège royal françois de Berlin* (Berlin, Starcke, 1789); G. Schulze, *Festschrift zur Feier des 200jährigen Bestehens des kgl. Französischen Gymnasiums* (Berlin, 1890); Werner Pohlmeyer, *250 Jahre Staatliches Französisches Gymnasium 1689-1939* (Berlin, 1939); and Christian Velder, *300 Jahre Französisches Gymnasium Berlin / 300 ans au Collège français* (Berlin, 1989). See, furthermore, more recent works by Agnes Winter, 'Die Hugenotten und das höhere Bildungswesen in Brandenburg-Preußen', in *Im Spannungsfeld von Staat und Kirche: 'Minderheiten' und 'Erziehung' im deutsch-französischen Gesellschaftsvergleich, 16.-18. Jahrhundert*, ed. Heinz Schilling and Marie-Antoinette Gross (Berlin, 2003), p.271-95, and Franziska Roosen, *Soutenir notre Eglise: hugenottische Erziehungskonzepte und Bildungseinrichtungen im Berlin des 18. Jahrhunderts* (Bad Karlshafen, 2008).

ecclesiastical, juridical and educational institutions of the Refuge and the Prussian state.[6]

Modelled on the French Protestant academies, the Collège français was an institution that functioned both as a grammar school and as a place of academic learning.[7] With regard to their education, the students had to complete two different components, one of which depended on the other: first, they passed through five classes of classical education including lessons in Latin, Greek, French literature and grammar, elocution, mathematics and Bible studies and, following this, they undertook a two-year course of philosophy that was mandatory for those who wanted to become ministers or study at university.[8] The philosophy course thus constituted the academic element of the Collège; as at universities, philosophical disputations were held twice a year and the teaching was undertaken by a professor, who was also the school's director, rather than a teacher.[9] As Agnes Winter stresses, in terms of philosophical teaching, the Collège was in the vanguard of Berlin grammar schools at the end of the seventeenth and beginning of the eighteenth century because it renounced Aristotelian scholastics and embraced Cartesianism instead; the emerging disciplines of natural law and natural philosophy were taught in its philosophy classes.[10]

Formey began attending the Collège in 1720, and between 1725 and 1727 he followed the course of philosophy taught by Mathurin Veyssière de La Croze. On completion of the course, he did not go on to study at a university – Berlin did not have a university at this time – but, instead, undertook the education required for an ecclesiastical career

6. See Christian Decker, *Vom Höfling zum städtischen Handwerker: soziale Beziehungen hugenottischer Eliten und 'gemeiner' Kolonisten in Preußen 1740 bis 1813* (Frankfurt am Main, 2012), p.48.
7. See Winter, 'Hugenotten und das höhere Bildungswesen', p.281.
8. See the statutes of the Collège of 1 December 1689, in Erman, *Mémoire historique*, p.8-12 (esp. 10). For the curriculum for five years of humanistic education in 1703 see Erman, *Mémoire historique*, p.159-67, and Schulze, *Festschrift*, p.26-28. See also Velder, *300 Jahre*, p.127.
9. See Winter, 'Hugenotten und das höhere Bildungswesen', p.286-87, and *Disciplina seu Leges Gymnasii Gallici a serenissimo ac potentissimo Electore Brandenburgico Friderico Tertio Berolini fundati & erecti anno 1689. Coloniae ad Spream Typis Ulrici Liebperti Electoral. Brandenb. Typogr*, printed in Erman, *Mémoire historique*, p.158. The preservation of the chair of philosophy and, thus, of the Collège's academic character was very important to the members of the colony; see Palladini, *Die Berliner Hugenotten*, p.286-87.
10. See Winter, 'Hugenotten und das höhere Bildungswesen', p.288.

within the colony: first he was a *proposant* for two years, then a *candidat* for another two years before, finally, becoming a minister in 1731.[11] This two-step educational path for ministers included practical training through preaching as well as lectures in theology and Church history that were held in private by renowned theologians and preachers belonging to the colony such as Simon Pelloutier, Jacques Lenfant and Isaac de Beausobre.[12] Following his education in theology, Formey left the Prussian capital for a few months in 1731 to work as a pastor in Brandenburg before eventually obtaining an appointment as assistant preacher to Philippe Forneret at the Friedrichstadt church in Berlin.[13]

Formey's education was, thus, overseen by first-generation Huguenot refugees who – except for Pelloutier, who was born in Leipzig – had been born in France and experienced persecution and emigration. La Croze was, in fact, originally of the Catholic creed; he had been a Benedictine monk in Saint-Germain-des-Prés in Paris before he fled the monastery and converted to Calvinism in 1696 in Basle.[14] As a scholar, La Croze was still deeply rooted in scholasticism.[15] Before they arrived in Berlin, Lenfant and Beausobre had been educated at the Protestant Academy of Saumur, the most liberal Protestant institution of higher education in seventeenth-century France, in which Cartesian philosophy had taken hold.[16] Lenfant had also been trained at the traditionally more orthodox Academy of Geneva, which he was forced to leave in 1683 because of his strong disagreement with François Turrettini, the orthodox professor of theology.[17] When Pelloutier, who had first studied in

11. Formey described his route through education, and emphasised in 'Notice de mes ouvrages', p.105, that the only education he received was theological. See also Velder, *300 Jahre*, p.103.
12. See Merian, 'Eloge de Formey', p.50.
13. See Formey, *Souvenirs*, vol.1, p.74-75 and 90.
14. See Formey, 'Eloge de M. La Croze', in *Eloges des académiciens de Berlin et de divers autres savans*, 2 vols (Berlin, Bourdeaux, 1757), vol.2, p.63-79 (64-65).
15. See Formey, *Souvenirs*, vol.1, p.68, and Erman, *Mémoire historique*, p.26.
16. See Frédéric Hartweg, 'Le grand Beausobre: Aspekte des intellektuellen und kirchlichen Lebens der ersten Generation des Berliner Refuge', in *Geschichte als Aufgabe: Festschrift für Otto Büsch*, ed. Wilhelm Treue (Berlin, 1988), p.55-82 (64). On the role of the Academy of Saumur in the seventeenth century, see Haase, *Literatur des Refuge*, p.66, and, more extensively, Frans P. Stam, *The Controversy over the theology of Saumur, 1635-1650: disrupting debates among the Huguenots in complicated circumstances* (Amsterdam, 1988).
17. See Maria-Cristina Pitassi, '"Des explications de l'Ecriture plus raisonnables que dans les sermons": autour du Nouveau Testament de Jacques Lenfant

Halle, attended the Academy of Geneva between 1712 and 1713, the theological climate was much more liberal, with Turrettini's son, Jean-Alphonse, defending a reasonable Christian religion.[18] Forneret himself had studied at the Reformed University in Frankfurt an der Oder (Prussia), and in Lausanne, and served as a pastor in the Prussian province and in Berlin from then on.[19]

Formey's teachers belonged to a generation that did not personally witness the internal dogmatic crises that changed Calvinism profoundly during the seventeenth century – the 'Arminian crisis' and the application of Cartesian rationalism to theology – and that eventually led to what Pocock calls liberal Protestantism or Arminian Enlightenment.[20] However, the new openness in Calvinism marked Formey's teachers' approach to theology and belief. Furthermore, they were affected by the debates concerning orthodoxy that arose in the aftermath of these changes to Calvinism. In particular, in Berlin at the end of the seventeenth and beginning of the eighteenth century, the aim of safeguarding orthodoxy was very pronounced. For example, in 1691, the pastors of the Berlin Refuge penned a declaration in which they openly condemned any new teachings, as well as heresies such as Arianism, Socinianism and Pelagianism that had begun to flourish, especially in the Dutch Refuge, and in which they confirmed their absolute commitment to the Reformed Church's confession of faith.[21] This declaration was followed by an act of orthodoxy in October 1694 that all new ministers had to sign in addition to the Reformed confession of faith and the Church discipline ('Discipline ecclésiastique') before they were allowed to preach in Berlin.[22] The

---

et Isaac de Beausobre', in *Refuge et désert: l'évolution théologique des huguenots de la révocation à la Révolution française*, ed. Hubert Bost and Claude Lauriol (Paris, 2003), p.143-56 (p.144, n.2). With regard to the history of the Academy of Geneva where Cartesianism had been introduced in 1669 by Jean-Robert Chouet who had previously taught at Saumur, see Michael Heyd, *Between orthodoxy and the Enlightenment: Jean-Robert Chouet and the introduction of Cartesian science in the Academy of Geneva* (The Hague, 1982).

18. See Formey, 'Eloge de Monsieur Pelloutier', in *Histoire de l'Académie royale des sciences et belles lettres de Berlin* (1757; Berlin, Haude & Spener, 1759), p.439-47.
19. See Formey, *Souvenirs*, vol.1, p.70-71.
20. See Pocock, *The Enlightenments of Edward Gibbon*, ch.2, esp. p.66.
21. See Frédéric Hartweg, 'Frühaufklärung und Orthodoxie im Widerstreit: Dokumente aus der Frühphase der französisch-reformierten Kirche in Berlin', *Recherches germaniques* 16 (1986), p.225-48, in which the declaration and its accompanying documents are printed.
22. See Palladini, *Die Berliner Hugenotten*, p.187-91.

purpose of this was to prevent ministers who held heterodox opinions – Arminianism and Socinianism were cited in the act of orthodoxy – from preaching in Berlin. Even in Formey's day, young pastors were required to sign this act of orthodoxy; this led Formey's Genevan correspondents in particular to consider the Berlin Reformed Church as being especially orthodox.[23] Moreover, at the beginning of the eighteenth century, trials of pastors who spread supposedly heterodox ideas to their congregations were fairly common in the Berlin Refuge; the most startling of these cases was that of Jean Barbeyrac, later to be the translator of Pufendorf's natural law, who between 1699 and 1700 was accused of heterodoxy (in particular his not believing in the Trinity) and lost his right to catechise and to instruct his congregation. This eventually caused him to leave Berlin.[24]

Formey's teachers played an ambivalent role here. As pastors they professed their orthodoxy – Lenfant was among those to sign the declaration of 1691 – whereas at the same time they (i.e. Forneret, Lenfant and Beausobre) judged the above-mentioned act of orthodoxy to be not only superfluous but also theologically incorrect.[25] Moreover, they had themselves been accused of heterodoxy by members of the Berlin Church, particularly by the orthodox and quarrelsome pastor Gabriel d'Artis, but also by the former Catholic monk La Croze. Lenfant and Forneret, in particular, had been suspected several times of secretly being Socinian, yet without being convicted by the consistory.[26]

Except for La Croze, who never became a minister in Berlin, all of Formey's teachers fulfilled simultaneously the role of pastor and scholar. They engaged in historical, biblical and philological scholarship: Pelloutier published a history of the Celts,[27] and La

---

23. See the reservations of Formey's correspondent Jean Peschier with regard to moving to Berlin to become a pastor because of the severe orthodoxy he believed existed there: Peschier to Formey (20.2.1742 and 17.4.1742), in *Lettres de Genève*, p.18 and 33-34. However, in the last letter, Peschier stated that another Berlin pastor, Isaac Théodore Cabrit, had told him that the act of orthodoxy was not implemented so rigorously as it had been at the end of the seventeenth century.
24. For the detailed reconstruction of Barbeyrac's case and the analysis of the theological and philosophical debates that took place during the first generation of the Berlin Refuge, see Palladini, *Die Berliner Hugenotten*.
25. See Palladini, *Die Berliner Hugenotten*, p.191-96.
26. See Palladini, *Die Berliner Hugenotten*, p.51-56.
27. Simon Pelloutier, *Histoire des Celtes, et particulièrement des Gaulois et des Germains,*

Croze was the author of several dictionaries of oriental languages and of histories of Christian missions and heresies in India (1724) as well as in Ethiopia and Armenia (1739) that were characterised by their impartial and undogmatic treatment of the subject matter.[28] In addition, Beausobre's main work was a historical investigation into an early Christian heresy – Manicheism – that was inspired methodologically by critical histories of philosophy such as Brucker's.[29] Among others, Lenfant published histories of the councils of Constance and Pisa. Together, Lenfant and Beausobre became famous for their translation of the New Testament in which they intended to apply a historical–critical method to Scripture to help its readers recognise the conditions of salvation.[30] Their aim was to provide 'reasonable explanations' of the sacred authors' texts while recognising the limits of reason in the explanation of certain mysteries. In so doing, they wanted to oppose both the freethinkers who ridiculed religion for its mysteries and the scholastics who made these mysteries even more obscure by trying to explain them metaphysically.[31] As Maria-Cristina Pitassi believes, these claims betray the apologetic motives of the two scholars.[32] Be that as it may, the pastor d'Artis, who was Lenfant's and Beausobre's contemporary, judged their translation of the New Testament that appeared in 1718 to be an example of Socinianism.[33]

Pocock generally regards the historical–critical approach in biblical and ecclesiastic scholarship practised by Formey's teachers as an

---

depuis les tems fabuleux, jusqu'à la prise de Rome par les Gaulois, 2 vols (The Hague, Beauregard, 1740-1750).

28. See Mulsow, *Die drei Ringe*, p.45-54. For a commentary on La Croze's works, see Formey, 'Eloge de La Croze', p.63-79.
29. See J. G. A. Pocock, *Barbarism and religion*, vol.5: *Religion: the first triumph* (Cambridge, 2011), p.140-43.
30. Isaac de Beausobre and Jacques Lenfant, *Le Nouveau Testament de notre seigneur Jesus-Christ, traduit en françois sur l'original grec, avec des notes literales pour éclaircir le texte*, 2 vols (Amsterdam, Humbert, 1718), vol.1, p.i-iii.
31. See Beausobre and Lenfant, *Nouveau Testament*, vol.1, p.cl.
32. See Pitassi, 'Des explications de l'Ecriture', p.155.
33. Gabriel d'Artis, *Lettre pastorale du plus ancien et plus légitime pasteur de l'eglise françoise de Berlin, à son troupeau, écrite de Londres, à l'occasion et au sujet de la traduction et des notes sur le Nouveau Testament, publiées par M.M. de Beausobre et Lenfant* (Amsterdam, Aux dépens de l'auteur, 1719). D'Artis's accusations dealt explicitly not with the methodological and epistemological considerations of Lenfant and Beausobre's introduction but with single passages of the translation, which according to him challenged certain dogma.

expression of their Arminianism or liberal Protestantism.[34] In terms of doctrine, Arminians believed that predestination existed not by absolute decree but due to humans being able to acquire grace through their own works. On a methodological level, this greater appreciation of human beings and their capacities favoured the explanation of Christian belief and history through the human intellect and rationality.[35] In contrast, Laursen sees a Baylian heritage in Beausobre's critical–historical scholarship because he set a limit on reason with regard to it being able to explain faith, and rejected the union of philosophy and theology.[36] The above-mentioned first-generation Huguenot intellectuals in Berlin seemed to have observed this conceptual separation of philosophy and theology in their learned sociability, which was characterised by the neat separation of their pastoral duties and scholarly work. Since 1707 or 1709, the pastors and learned men of Berlin – among others Beausobre, Etienne Chauvin, Alphonse Des Vignobles, Paul-Emile Mauclerc, Pelloutier and La Croze – had met weekly in Lenfant's house to discuss new literary publications and to present their own scholarly work. They called themselves the Société anonyme, and in 1720 they established the Francophone learned journal *Bibliothèque germanique*, whose editor Formey also later became.[37] According to the Société anonyme's members' own description of their practices, they rarely discussed matters of faith during their gatherings and, if they did, they did so only 'soberly'.[38] This suggests that the religious and scholarly

---

34. Pocock, *Religion: the first triumph*, ch.5, establishes this argument particularly with regard to the case of Beausobre's history of Manicheism (see esp. p.153-54).
35. See Pocock, *The Enlightenments of Edward Gibbon*, ch.2, esp. p.51-52.
36. See John Christian Laursen, 'Temporizing after Bayle: Isaac de Beausobre and the Manicheans', in *The Berlin Refuge 1680-1780: learning and science in European context*, ed. Sandra Pott, Martin Mulsow and Lutz Danneberg (Leiden and Boston, MA, 2003), p.89-110 (esp. 103). Frédéric Hartweg, 'Le grand Beausobre', p.59-60, and 'Toleranz, Naturrecht und Aufklärung / Lumières im Berliner Refuge', in *Hugenotten und deutsche Territorialstaaten: Immigrationspolitik und Integrationsprozesse*, ed. Guido Braun and Susanne Lachenicht (Munich, 2007), p.211-29 (220), has emphasised that the Huguenot scholars in Berlin were less eager to believe that reason and faith were fully compatible than their colleagues in the Netherlands such as Jacques Abbadie and Isaac Jaquelot.
37. See Jens Häseler, 'Société anonyme [San]', in *Handbuch der Berliner Vereine und Gesellschaften 1786-1815*, ed. Uta Motschmann (Berlin, 2015), p.5-6. Palladini, *Die Berliner Hugenotten*, p.71-75.
38. 'Article XIV. Nouvelles litteraires', *Bibliothèque germanique* 5 (1723), p.203-41 (238-40).

duties of the Berlin Huguenot intellectuals barely interfered with one another.

The intellectual culture of the Huguenot community in Berlin during the first decades of the eighteenth century was, thus, characterised by the coexistence of a strong commitment to Calvinist orthodoxy and an engagement with critical–historical scholarship that had an Arminian tinge. Growing up in this culture, Formey followed in the footsteps of his teachers and became a minister and scholar.

Merian suggested in his 'Eloge de Formey' that, after the first part of his education, Formey completely turned away from the teachings he had received in the Huguenot context to adopt a 'new' genre of philosophy (by which he meant Wolffianism).[39] However, such a neat rupture between Formey's Calvinist and Wolffian training is unlikely. On an ideological level, eighteenth-century 'reasonable' Calvinism was not contradictory with Wolff's natural theology, which was based on a 'softened version' of the dogma of original sin. On the contrary, Formey himself stressed his teacher Beausobre's agreement with Christian Wolff's natural theology: in the introduction to the sixth volume of his *Belle wolfienne* in 1753, Formey quoted an anecdote according to which Beausobre, on one occasion, that is, shortly before his death and after having read Wolff's *Theologia naturalis*, had claimed Wolff was even more orthodox than he was himself, and, on another occasion, had stated that he would have liked to have known Wolff's teachings earlier in his life.[40] Moreover, Beausobre shared with Wolff the apologetic purpose of revealing the truth of Christian religion through the use of reason. This was a motive not only of Lenfant and Beausobre's critical translation of the Bible but also of Wolff's *Theologia naturalis*, in which he claimed that natural reason was able to demonstrate what was stated in Scripture about God and, therefore, helped to confirm the true and divine nature of revelation.[41] In addition, on a methodological level, several similarities existed between the critical biblical and ecclesiastical scholarship of Formey's Huguenot teachers and the rationalist philosophy of Christian Wolff. It seems, thus, that the Huguenot intellectual culture

39. See Merian, 'Eloge de Formey', p.49.
40. See Formey, *La Belle wolfienne, tome 6: contenant l'abrégé de la Theologie naturelle* (The Hague, Neaulme, 1753), p.xxv-xxvi.
41. See Wolff, *Theologia naturalis: pars prior*, §18. Compare with Jean Ecole, 'Introduction de l'éditeur', in Wolff, *Theologia naturalis: pars prior*, p.v-cxvi (xii).

in which he grew up facilitated Formey's acquaintance with Wolff's philosophy.

An important part of this intellectual culture was the learned infrastructure and sociability through which Formey acquired the practices of the Republic of Letters. During Formey's everyday life in the early 1730s, after he had been appointed minister in Berlin, clerical and erudite practices converged, as did young and old members of the colony. His days were marked by his pastoral duties, conversations with friends and parish members, dinner parties and similar events. Formey seems to have spent time mainly with friends from his school and college days such as the brothers Alexandre-Auguste and Jacques de Campagne, Guillaume Pelet[42] and the pastors of the two other French churches in Berlin, Paul Loriol d'Anières and Pierre Des Combles, as well as with his former professors Beausobre and La Croze.[43] As an associate of Beausobre, Formey had been involved in the publication of the Francophone literature journal *Bibliothèque germanique* since 1733.[44] Because of Beausobre's illness and, thus, his reduced work capacity, Formey became even more closely involved in this enterprise towards the end of 1737 and, eventually, replaced Beausobre as the editor of the journal, a role he shared with another first-generation Huguenot refugee, Paul-Emile Mauclerc from Stettin. As far as Formey was concerned, having such a role in relation to an influential instrument of learned journalism was very useful later in his career as a philosopher and secretary of the Academy, because it helped him to promote both his own opinions and the work of the Academy.[45] In 1733, it presumably helped him to practise writing book reviews, the production of which was one of the central tasks of the Republic of Letters.

---

42. See Guillaume Pelet to Formey (3.7.1731), FF.
43. See Formey to Suzanne Bonafous (9.7.1734), CV. Compare with Häseler, 'Formey – l'homme à Berlin', p.421. Häseler emphasises the heterogeneity of Formey's social network within the Huguenot colony, combining as it did people from his own generation and the preceding one.
44. See Jan Schillings, 'Elargissement de la République des Lettres vers les "pays du Nord": la *Bibliothèque germanique* et ses suites – profil thématique et géographique du journal', in *Journalisme et République des Lettres: l'élargissement vers les 'pays du Nord' au dix-huitième siècle*, ed. Christiane Berkvens-Stevelinck and Hans Bots (Amsterdam, 2009), p.15-82.
45. See Jens Häseler, 'Journaux savants et l'Académie de Berlin: deux acteurs sur le marché de l'information scientifique en Prusse', *Archives internationales d'histoire de science* 63 (2013), p.199-214 (esp. 210 and 214).

In addition to all his other activities, since September 1731[46] the young pastor Formey had also been a member of a private learned society, the Société amusante, which was founded by Jean Des Champs, another young Huguenot pastoral candidate,[47] and was modelled on the Société anonyme established by the previous generation of Huguenot pastors and scholars. Its purpose was private self-education in literature and the sciences. During the weekly meetings, the members, whom Des Champs recruited among his friends – almost always young pastoral candidates from the colony – read and commented on each other's writings. Moreover, they presented *extraits* of books they had read, and exchanged *nouvelles littéraires*. Like the renowned public learned societies, the Société amusante had clear rules with regard to the terms of membership and structure of its meetings, and it was also meticulous about keeping minutes and copies of its discourses.[48] Through his membership of such a private learned society, Formey not only became involved in the practices of a man of letters, but was also probably first introduced to Wolff's philosophy.[49] The society's founder, Des Champs, had been fond of Wolff's philosophy since the late 1720s because he had studied under Wolff in Marburg from 1727 to 1729, and had translated his *Logik*.[50]

46. See Jean Des Champs to Formey (25.9.1731), in *Lettres de l'Angleterre à Jean Henri Samuel Formey à Berlin: de Jean Des Champs, David Durand, Matthieu Maty et d'autres correspondants (1737-1788)*, ed. Uta Janssens and Jan Schillings (Paris, 2006), p.329-30; and Alexandre-Auguste de Campagne to Formey (26.6.1731 and 24.9.1731), FF.
47. On Des Champs see Uta Janssens-Knorsch, 'Jean Deschamps, Wolff-Übersetzer und "Aléthophile français" am Hofe Friedrichs des Großen', in *Christian Wolff 1679-1754*, ed. W. Schneiders, p.254-65. Janssens-Knorsch also published Des Champs's autobiography, his *Mémoires secrets*: Uta Janssens-Knorsch, *The Life and 'Mémoires secrets' of Jean Des Champs, 1707-1767: journalist, minister, and man of feeling* (Amsterdam, 1990).
48. See Janssens-Knorsch, *The Life and 'Mémoires secrets'*, p.99-100. According to Janssens-Knorsch, the members of the Société amusante were MM. de Félix, d'Esperon, Peloux, Pinault, Beausobre, Campagne, Formey, Sauveterre and himself. Furthermore, there were three associates who had fewer obligations towards the society: MM. Des Champs, Milsoneau and Gobin. Another description of the Société can be found in a letter from one of its members, Jacques de Campagne, to Formey (n.d.), FF.
49. According to Janssens-Knorsch, *The Life and 'Mémoires secrets'*, p.291, n.36, the Société amusante ceased to exist in 1736 because of Des Champs's and Formey's admission to the Wolffian Société des aléthophiles.
50. See Janssens-Knorsch, 'Jean Deschamps', p.255-56.

Acquaintance with Wolffianism

Formey's education and early learned life inside the Berlin Refuge favoured and paved the way for his introduction to Wolffianism. The central figure in the development and pursuit of Wolffianism in Prussia during the 1730s and 1740s was Count Ernst Christoph von Manteuffel, a former Saxon minister and patron of the arts and sciences. Since 1733, in Berlin, Manteuffel had created a meeting point in his house for intellectual exchange, the Palais Kameke.[51] Jean Des Champs described this 'institution' in 1740 as follows: 'La Maison de ce Seigneur [Manteuffel] étoit depuis 7 à 8 ans le *Rendez-vous* de tous les *savans*, et de tous les *Gens d'Esprit* de *Berlin*. Jamais *Homme de Lettres* ne trouva nulle part autant de protection et de secours, que chés ce digne *Fils d'Apollon*.'[52] It seems there were several learned Huguenot men present at these gatherings; this is probably unsurprising because Manteuffel's house was in the Dorotheenstadt, a neighbourhood with a strong Huguenot population.[53] According to his own testimony, Formey became acquainted with Manteuffel in early 1732 on the occasion of a translation job that Manteuffel offered him. Formey's translation of some political writings about the crisis of the Polish succession to the throne constituted his first two publications.[54]

Formey benefited in several ways from his close acquaintance with Manteuffel, who had good connections to the court of Frederick William I and to the future King Frederick II, whose political values he tried to influence.[55] First, through the gatherings at Manteuffel's house, Formey was able to extend his acquaintances beyond the relatively closed Huguenot circle by meeting state officials and German noblemen.[56] Second, Manteuffel contributed significantly to the development of Formey's career. He not only inspired and supported Formey's first publications, he also guaranteed the advancement of Formey's institutional career by lobbying on his behalf at the court

---

51. Bronisch, *Mäzen der Aufklärung*, p.76, indicates 1733 as the date of Manteuffel's installation in Berlin, whereas Formey, *Souvenirs*, vol.1, p.40, dated it as 1731.
52. Janssens-Knorsch, *The Life and 'Mémoires secrets'*, p.180 (emphasis in the original).
53. See Bronisch, *Mäzen der Aufklärung*, p.76, esp. n.13. In a letter to his future wife Suzanne Bonafous (9.7.1734), CV, Formey states that La Croze had also been invited to dinner at Manteuffel's house.
54. See Formey, 'Notice de mes ouvrages', p.106.
55. For the circumstances of Manteuffel's stay in Prussia see Bronisch, *Mäzen der Aufklärung*, ch.1 and 2.
56. See, for example, Formey to Suzanne Bonafous (28.5.1734), CV.

on at least two occasions: first, in the spring of 1736 Manteuffel arranged for Formey to stay longer in the capital;[57] and second (more importantly), in 1739, he obtained the king's approval of Formey's application for the chair of philosophy at the Collège français, which had become vacant after the death of La Croze.[58]

However, in addition to Manteuffel's crucial role in extending Formey's network and career, the noble patron also created the context in which Formey, together with his entire cohort of young Huguenot pastors, became deeply engaged with the philosophy of Christian Wolff. In 1736, Manteuffel founded the Société des aléthophiles, a secret society that attempted to defend and promote Christian Wolff's philosophy in Germany and abroad.[59] The immediate motive for

57. See Manteuffel to Formey (2.3.1736), CV: 'Je prens tant de part a ce qui est arrivé avec votre chef, que je n'ai pas vacancé un moment d'ecrire la lettre que vous m'avez demandée. [...] La justice et vos merites parlant pour vous, j'ai appuié uniquement sur ces deux argumens, et j'ai representé, que ce seroit une perte pour Berlin, que de vous forcer par une injustice manifeste, a chercher fortune ailleurs.' With regard to this letter, see also Bronisch, *Mäzen der Aufklärung*, p.131, n.2. Bronisch attributes this comment to Formey's appointment to the Collège, which is unlikely at this point. It is more likely that Formey encountered problems in keeping his job as an assistant pastor at the Friedrichstadt church because Forneret, his supervisor, had died just one week earlier. Manteuffel's next letter on 12 March 1736 indicates that Formey's problem had been resolved thanks to Crown Prince Frederick. In a letter from Frederick to Manteuffel dated 8 April 1736, the prince states that Formey would replace a certain Saurin with regard to preaching on Sundays (this is a reference to Manteuffel's letter to Frederick dated 5 April 1736, together with which he had sent Formey's *Sermons sur le contentement*; see also Bronisch, *Mäzen der Aufklärung*, p.60).

58. More precisely, it was the Lutheran preacher Gustav Reinbeck who prepared Formey's request to be released from his clerical functions; see the two letters from Reinbeck to Formey ([5.1739] and 31.5.1739), CV. Reinbeck was one of Manteuffel's intimate acquaintances in Berlin and was influential at the Prussian court. Formey became acquainted with him through Manteuffel.

59. On the Société des aléthophiles, see [Carl Günther Ludovici], 'Wahrheitliebende Gesellschafft', in *Grosses vollständiges Universal-Lexicon aller Wissenschafften und Künste, welche bisher durch menschlichen Verstand und Witz erfunden und verbessert worden*, ed. Johann Heinrich Zedler, 64 vols (Leipzig and Halle, Zedler, 1731-1754), vol.52 (1747), p.947-54. For recent research on the subject, see Detlef Döring, 'Beiträge zur Geschichte der Gesellschaft der Alethophilen in Leipzig', in *Gelehrte Gesellschaften im mitteldeutschen Raum (1650-1820)*, ed. Detlef Döring and Kurt Nowak, vol.1 (Stuttgart, 2000), p.95-150, and the aforementioned Bronisch, *Mäzen der Aufklärung*. For the circumstances that led to the founding of the society, see Döring, 'Beiträge', p.100-101.

founding this organisation had been to ensure Wolff's repatriation to Prussia after he had been expelled for heterodoxy in 1723.[60] Wolff's main enemy, who had caused his expulsion and wanted to prevent his repatriation, was the Pietist theologian and professor of theology at Halle University Joachim Lange, who accused Wolff of embracing atheism and fatalism. In his own defence, Wolff emphasised that the purpose of his philosophy was to fight atheism, and that his philosophy did not preclude human liberty.[61] Since 1736, when people at the Prussian court had begun to consider repatriating Wolff, the dispute between Wolff and the Halle Pietists had been reignited. The Société des aléthophiles's main activity from its founding until 1740 was, therefore, to publish pro-Wolffian pamphlets on this theological debate between Wolff and Lange, the aim of which was to demonstrate that Wolff's teachings were compatible with Christian doctrine.[62] The society's patron, Manteuffel, who orchestrated the Wolffian participation in this public debate, also pursued political motives alongside this, because lobbying on behalf of Wolff was meant to assure the latter that he had the confidence of the future King Frederick II, who in his early years had admired Wolff's philosophy.[63]

60. See Döring, 'Beiträge', p.99-104. For the circumstances of Wolff's expulsion from Prussia in 1723 because of his dispute with the Halle Pietists, see Bruno Bianco, 'Freiheit gegen Fatalismus: zu Joachim Langes Kritik an Wolff', in *Zentren der Aufklärung*, vol.1: *Halle: Aufklärung und Pietismus*, ed. Norbert Hinske (Heidelberg, 1989), p.111-55; Hunter, 'Multiple enlightenments'; Albrecht Beutel, 'Causa Wolffiana: die Vertreibung Christian Wolffs aus Preußen 1723 als Kulminationspunkt des theologisch-politischen Konflikts zwischen Halleschem Pietismus und Aufklärungsphilosophie', in *Reflektierte Religion: Beiträge zur Geschichte des Protestantismus*, ed. Albrecht Beutel (Tübingen, 2007), p.125-69; and, most recently, Anna Szyrwińska, 'Die Pietisten', in *Handbuch Christian Wolff*, ed. R. Theis and A. Aichele, p.383-403.
61. See *Recueil de nouvelles pieces philosophiques, concernant le different renouvellè entre Messieurs Joachim Lange [...] et Chretien Wolf [...]: seconde edition augmentee considerablement* (n.p., n.n., 1737), p.208 and 205.
62. See Bronisch, *Mäzen der Aufklärung*, p.165-66. The principal publications of the *aléthophiles* against Wolff's Pietist critics were assembled in *Nouvelles pieces sur les erreurs pretendues de la philosophie de Mons. Wolf. Contenant I. Memoire de Mons. Lange, contre cette philosophie. II. Reponse preliminaire d'un auteur anonime a ce memoire. III. Sommaire de la reponse de Mr. Wolf meme avec un avis au lecteur de l'histoire de ce nouveau differend* (n.p., n.n., 1736), and *Recueil de nouvelles pieces philosophiques*. For the whole list of twenty-one pro-Wolffian publications that appeared under Manteuffel's supervision between 1736 and 1748, see Bronisch, *Mäzen der Aufklärung*, p.388-90.
63. See Bronisch, *Mäzen der Aufklärung*, p.84.

2. Formey in the Berlin Huguenot Enlightenment

The actions taken in defence of Wolff's philosophy were, eventually, successful, because he was repatriated to Prussia in 1740 and regained his chair in mathematics and philosophy at the University of Halle. However, the political influence that Manteuffel had hoped for never transpired. Manteuffel himself had to leave Berlin in 1740 after being accused of treason. He moved to Leipzig, where his Société des aléthophiles found a new but less influential home than in Berlin. Moreover, Frederick's II philosophical interest turned fully towards French sceptical and materialist philosophers such as Voltaire and La Mettrie.[64] In the subsequent period until the society's dissolution after Manteuffel's death in 1749, Wolff's partisans were, thus, increasingly involved in defending his philosophical rationalism and natural theology against the doctrines of French freethinkers and the Newtonian philosophers who settled in the revamped Berlin Academy.

The core members of the Société des aléthophiles were Germans active in the Church and publishing market. The cofounder of the society was Johann Gustav Reinbeck, a pastor and councillor from the Lutheran Church consistory in Berlin and a close confidant of King Frederick William I; he played an important role in the theological debates in connection with Wolff's repatriation, and his sermons and theological treatises betray a reasonable faith inspired by Wolff's natural theology.[65] Other members were the Berlin bookseller Ambrosius Haude and the court preacher August Friedrich Wilhelm Sack, as well as the journalist Johann Christoph Gottsched and his wife Luise Adelgunde, and the university professors Carl Günther Ludovici, Romanus Teller and Christian Gottlieb Jöcher from Leipzig. In addition, Manteuffel made his young Huguenot acquaintances in Berlin members of his society. Formey and Jean Des Champs were affiliated as early as 1736, and Jacques Pérard, who was a French pastor in Stettin, in 1745. As official members of the Société des aléthophiles, they also involved their Huguenot friends in Manteuffel's Wolffian endeavours.

Manteuffel had a strong interest in involving the Huguenots in his society because they were able to spread the Wolffian message to the

---

64. See Döring, 'Beiträge', p.105-106 and 128-29, and Bronisch, *Mäzen der Aufklärung*, p.114-17.
65. See Bronisch, *Mäzen der Aufklärung*, p.166. For more details on Reinbeck's moderate Wolffian theology, see Stefan Lorenz, 'Theologischer Wolffianismus: das Beispiel Johann Gustav Reinbeck', in *Christian Wolff und die europäische Aufklärung*, ed. J. Stolzenberg, O.-P. Rudolph and J. Ecole, vol.5, p.103-21.

French refugees in Berlin and Prussia, and through them further afield to the rest of the Francophone Republic of Letters. Moreover, given that the Prussian political elite at the time also spoke French, French versions of Wolff's philosophy were certainly also targeted at Crown Prince Frederick.[66] In a letter to Wolff in 1741, Manteuffel described how he used the young Huguenots as promoters of Wolffianism by assigning them educational and literary tasks:

> Mais enfin, quoique j'aie toujours douté, que ces deux hommes [Des Champs and Formey], devinrent jamais de grands arcsboutans de la Verité, je me suis servis très utilement d'eux, pour faire gouter vôtre Philosophie à leurs compatriotes réfugiez, qui en avoient, il y a quelques années, des idées très confuses et fausses. [...] j'ai animé et presque forcé Formey, à etudier vôtre Philosophie, et a l'enseigner publiquement à ses auditeurs; j'ai même poussé le même Formey, a écrire sa Belle Wolfienne, et je ne cesse pas de l'exhorter à en donner la continuation.[67]

Given the two men's profession – both were pastors, and since 1739 Formey had also been a professor of philosophy – they were able to reach the popular public, which was a large audience.[68]

Moreover, during the first period of the society's existence, Manteuffel commissioned the Huguenot members to translate several of Johann Gustav Reinbeck's sermons, which betrayed a new Wolffian homiletics. As such, these translations also served as contributions to the theological debate between Wolff and his Pietist opponents. This becomes particularly clear in Pérard's and Formey's translations of Reinbeck's two sermons on the mystery of the birth of Christ that he preached during the Christmas of 1737. The translation was embedded in an extended paratext by Manteuffel himself, in which he polemicised against Wolff's Pietist critic Lange and pleaded the compatibility between Wolff's philosophy and revealed doctrine.[69] The same was true in relation to the collection of five of Reinbeck's

---

66. See Bronisch, *Mäzen der Aufklärung*, p.89-90.
67. Manteuffel to Wolff (10.2.1741), in *Briefwechsel zwischen Wolff und Manteuffel*, vol.1, p.406-407. Formey's *Belle Wolfienne* and its role in promoting Wolffianism, as mentioned here by Manteuffel, will be discussed in chapter 5.
68. See Manteuffel to Luise Adelgunde Gottsched (24.11.1739), in Johann Christoph Gottsched, *Briefwechsel unter Einschluß des Briefwechsels von Luise Adelgunde Victorie Gottsched*, ed. Detlef Döring *et al.*, vol.6 (Berlin, 2012), p.211-12.
69. Johann Gustav Reinbeck, *Sermons sur le mystere de la naissance de J.-C., prononcez le premier & le second jour de Noël 1737*, [...]; *traduits par un anonyme, & Messrs.*

sermons that Des Champs translated a year later,[70] and the translation of a further four sermons, in which task, in addition to Des Champs, two provincial pastors, Abraham Bocquet and Isaac Théodore Cabrit, were involved.[71] The collaboration of the latter two had been arranged partly through Formey.[72] The young Huguenots' translations on behalf of the *aléthophiles* boosted their involvement with Wolffian philosophy, something that had probably been underway since their attendance at Des Champs's Société amusante meetings.

There is evidence that, since the late 1730s, the young men had mutually urged each other on to practise what they called 'philosopher à la wolffienne'. At the beginning, it was mainly Des Champs who fuelled the perception of Wolff as the Huguenots' 'héro de la philosophie' and supported his friends' engagement with Wolff's ideas. After Formey published something in favour of Wolff's ideas in his literary journal *Mercure et Minerve*, Des Champs did not hide his enthusiasm and promised to send Formey's works to their idol personally:

> Je ne manquerai pas de communiquer à notre 'Héros de philosophie' toutes vos pièces qui le concernent dès que j'en trouverai l'occasion. Je suis au reste extrêmement aise que vous ayez enfin pris goût aux ouvrages de M. Wolff; mon zêle pour cet excellent homme acquiert un nouveau degré de vivacité depuis qu'il se sent autorisé et appuïé du vôtre.[73]

In addition to Formey, Des Champs inspired their common friends Cabrit and Achard with Wolff's philosophy, and regularly discussed the philosopher's ideas with them. With respect to his exchange with Cabrit, Des Champs even suggested that Formey join the discussion so the three of them could share their views.[74] However, in 1739, Formey still had some reservations about adopting Wolff's philosophy

---

S. Formey & J. Perard, *ministres de l'Eglise françoise* (Berlin and Leipzig, Haude, 1738). See Bronisch, *Mäzen der Aufklärung*, p.398-400.

70. *Recueil de cinq sermons, prononcez par Monsieur Jean Gustave Reinbeck [...]; traduits par un anonyme, & par Mons. Jean Des-Champs* (Berlin, Haude, 1739). See Bronisch, *Mäzen der Aufklärung*, p.400-401.
71. *Nouveau recueil de quatre sermons, prononcez par Monsieur Reinbeck [...], traduits de l'allemand, avec un ajouté de quelques pieces interessantes* (Berlin and Leipzig, Haude, 1741). See Bronisch, *Mäzen der Aufklärung*, p.410-12.
72. See Théodore Cabrit to Formey (21.9.1738 and 26.9.1738), FF.
73. Des Champs to Formey (23.4.1738), in *Lettres de l'Angleterre*, p.330-31.
74. See Des Champs to Formey (22.10.1739), in *Lettres de l'Angleterre*, p.340, with

entirely, and did not prefer it to that of Leibniz. To overcome these reservations, Des Champs praised Wolff's philosophical system and the genius it betrayed.[75] Only shortly afterwards, in 1740, did Formey, in fact, become a point of reference for Wolffianism in the colony and promote Wolff's philosophy among his fellow Huguenots. In his letters to Formey, the pastor Abraham Bocquet of Prenzlau regularly testified to their mutual affinity for Wolff's thought.[76]

It can be seen that, in the generation of the Berlin Huguenot Enlightenment to which Formey belonged, Wolffianism constituted the intellectual culture that determined the social and intellectual exchanges of the young pastors. However, in terms of their intellectual sociability and practices, Formey, Des Champs and their friends followed in the footsteps of the previous generation. Like their teachers, the young Huguenots simultaneously carried out the duties of pastors and those of learned men. However, unlike Lenfant and Beausobre and others, the boundaries between their religious and scholarly practices seem to have been much more blurred. Whereas the previous generation had tried to ensure their critical–historical scholarship did not interfere with doctrine, Formey's cohort engaged in a theological dispute initiated by the Wolffians that took place in both a religious and a scholarly setting: from the pulpit and via scholarly works. Furthermore, by participating in the *aléthophiles'* pamphlet war against the Pietists, they defended a person of a different confession – the Lutheran Wolff – against the charge of heterodoxy. However, there is no evidence that this earned the criticism of the young Huguenots' confessional community.

Formey's transition from pastor to professor of philosophy

Although the simultaneous execution of the duties of a pastor and those of a scholar was common practice in the Berlin Huguenot community for a time at the start of Formey's career, it was condemned theoretically by the legal rules of the Reformed Church. According to the 'Discipline ecclésiastique' of the French Reformed Church (1666), which had been adopted as a legal framework by the Huguenot churches in Berlin, the pastoral office was a lifelong

---

regard to the exchange with Cabrit and (8.11.1739), *Lettres de l'Angleterre*, p.342, with regard to the same with Achard.
75. See Des Champs to Formey (8.11.1739), in *Lettres de l'Angleterre*, p.342.
76. See Bocquet to Formey (5.7.1740 and 26.8.1740), FF.

exclusive commitment to perform the tasks of evangelising and proclaiming God's word to the people. Moreover, it prohibited the promulgation of any form of learning that was unconventional and not appropriate for edification.[77] To guarantee the exclusive exercise of pastoral duties, the 'Discipline ecclésiastique' forbade its pastors from carrying out any other professional duties, such as those relating to medicine or law, or from spending an undue amount of time educating young people.[78] However, the rules of the Church did allow those pastors who possessed literary skills to use them modestly in the honour of God, but with a caveat: the pastors' literary output, especially when it dealt with theological controversy, had to be controlled by the council of each provincial church.[79] Thus, it would appear it was not the general rule that pastors should perform the tasks of learned men.

In Formey's day, the implementation of the rules of the 'Discipline ecclésiastique' had become less rigorous. However, remnants of these rules still shone through in the Berlin Huguenots' conceptualisations of their role as pastors. Formey himself, in one of his moral discourses in *Le Philosophe chrétien*, pointed out the inappropriate behaviour of a pastor who indulged in literary criticism and the investigation of nature. He acknowledged that a pastor had to be educated to fulfil his office with dignity, but he should not pursue these studies beyond the needs of his office:

> Mais ses [du ministre] prémières études lui ayant laissé un goût vif & dominant pour les sciences, il s'y jette à corps perdu, il s'enfonce dans le vaste Ocean de la Litterature & de la Critique, il étudie d'un oeil curieux les secrets de la Nature, c'est un savant distingué, il va prendre sa place au Temple de Mémoire, & son nom sera préservé de l'oubli, auquel le Tombeau condamne les hommes vulgaires. Mais son tems étoit-il à lui pour en disposer de la sorte? Non, sans contredit; & malgré la Renommée qui publie ses talens, je m'écrie encore; Occupation déplacée, tems mal employé.[80]

---

77. See *Das Recht der Französisch-Reformierten Kirche in Preußen: urkundliche Denkschrift*, ed. E. Mengin, 'Discipline ecclésiastique des églises réformées de France, imprimée selon l'édition faite en Hollande en 1710 sur celle donnée par M. d'Huisseau ministre & par luy dediée de Saumur le 30. avril 1666 a tous les pasteurs des eglises réformées de France', ch.1, §XI and §XII, p.64-185 (71).
78. See 'Discipline ecclésiastique', ch.1, §XIX, p.75.
79. See 'Discipline ecclésiastique', ch.1, §XV, p.73.
80. Formey, *Philosophe chrétien*, 1st edn, vol.1, p.11-12.

It is important to note that Formey did not consider that the pursuit of learned practices or philosophy was as dangerous per se; on the contrary, he said it was, potentially, even praiseworthy. What was detrimental was rather the preacher's misbehaviour in allowing himself to be distracted from his duty by other work.[81]

Furthermore, in addition to the potential neglect of their pastoral duties, there was a strong moral motive behind the criticism of pastors who engaged in literary and scholarly work. The best example with regard to this could be Abraham Bocquet, who was a pastor in several Brandenburgian towns and later in Magdeburg. In his letters to Formey, he pronounced enthusiastically his weakness for philosophy in general, and Wolff's philosophy in particular,[82] and he described his practices as being characteristic of a learned man: he corresponded with various people;[83] he had built up a multifarious library containing not only theological writings but also the libertine ones typical of the century;[84] he wrote reviews for journals;[85] and he had founded an amateur learned society in Magdeburg, the Société impartiale.[86] Nonetheless, it appears that he did not wish to admit the authorship of his own writings. In 1741, Manteuffel revealed that Bocquet had been the translator of one of Reinbeck's sermons, apparently without his consent. Bocquet was somewhat angry about this, because he feared other people would mock him for aspiring to fame in the Republic of Letters through the translation of a sermon.[87] Bocquet's concern was clearly motivated by questions of modesty and decency, which were important moral characteristics for a pastor to exemplify. He had similar concerns in 1754 when he appeared as the author of a discourse he had contributed to the third volume of Formey's *Philosophe chrétien*.[88] As he reported to Formey, people

---

81. See Formey's general considerations with regard to the relationship between duty and conduct, *Philosophe chrétien*, 1st edn, vol.1, p.10.
82. See Bocquet to Formey (5.7.1740), FF.
83. See Bocquet to Formey (21.11.1740), FF.
84. See Bocquet to Formey (23.10.1741), FF.
85. See Bocquet to Formey (3.10.1740), FF.
86. See Bocquet to Formey (18.1.1742), FF.
87. See Bocquet to Formey (23.10.1741), FF: 'Me voila bien payé des railleries que j'ai faites sur ceux qui courent après les occasions de lire leur nom imprimé. J'endeve quand je pense qu'il y aura des gens qui me croiront asses sot que de prétendre quelque rang dans la Rep. des lettres à cause que j'ai traduit un sermon allemand en françois.'
88. See Bocquet to Formey (17.10.1754), FF.

mocked him because they assumed he longed to be published and because they did not believe his writing deserved literary glory.[89]

In addition to the traditional rules of the Church having a lasting effect on the concept of a pastor's commitment to the pulpit and good moral conduct, since the second quarter of the eighteenth century the perception of pastor–philosophers had been influenced by a growing reservation about the use of philosophy. Bayle's and Spinoza's rationalist critiques of dogma as well as the French public debate about the true philosopher made many clergymen question the beneficial effect of philosophical research on society and religion. Even Bocquet, who was so enthusiastic about the sociability of the philosopher, voiced his concerns in this respect. In 1742, when Formey told Bocquet about his project to write a philosophical dictionary based on the model of Pierre Bayle's famous but controversial *Dictionnaire historique et critique* (this will be discussed in more detail in chapter 4), Bocquet was worried that philosophical reflection would automatically lead its practitioners to become sceptics. As far as he himself was concerned, he claimed to prefer the study of theology:

> Au reste je ne doute pas que l'ouvrage en question [Formey's *Dictionnaire*] ne soit pour vous une occupation très agréable: mais vous me permettrez de ne pas avouer aussi facilement que les Meditations auxquelles il vous engage, soient les seules dont on puisse tirer des usages satisfaisans. 1. Y a t'il une seule partie de la Philosophie qui soit entierement audessus des atteintes du Scepticisme? 2. Si mon experience peut entrer en ligne de compte, je vous assure que je n'ai gueres gouté de plus grande satisfaction que dans l'Etude de certaines matieres de Théologie.[90]

Such fears about the genuine sceptical character of philosophy probably increased with the creation of the image of the heretic and immoral *philosophes* in the mid-eighteenth century, to which Formey's critical writings also contributed.

Moreover, there seems to have been a fear that pastors in particular could turn into freethinkers or *philosophes*. A fictional description of such a scenario appeared in another of Formey's moral philosophical essays in *Le Philosophe chrétien*. According to this, a pastor turned away from his duties and became an enemy of God because he was appointed to his office too early in life without a proper grounding in

89. See Bocquet to Formey (8.4.1755), FF.
90. Bocquet to Formey (21.5.1742), FF.

what it entailed. As Formey stated, such a conversion had the most terrible effect on the believers:

> Mais de bonne foi, que veut-on que réponde à un Libertin, un Ecclésiastique qui ne vaut pas mieux que lui, ou plutôt beaucoup moins, puisqu'au libertinage il joint l'oubli de son caractère, & la violation de ses engagemens? Que veut-on que pense un Troupeau, s'il lui arrive de voir ses Conducteurs, après avoir prêché trente ou quarante ans l'Evangile, en liaison intime avec les plus profanes Ennemis du Sauveur, des gens qui ne savent dire que des blasphêmes ou des ordures?[91]

It seems that the concern with renegade pastors expressed in Formey's essay had not been provoked by one particular event in his immediate context as such. However, it is likely that it was influenced by the memory of the frequent trials against supposedly heterodox pastors in the Berlin Reformed Church at the beginning of the eighteenth century. In particular, the persecution of Barbeyrac must have been strongly rooted in the memory of the Refuge, because Formey still recalled it in his *Souvenirs d'un citoyen* in 1789, although he did not personally witness it.[92] In addition to such memories, in Formey's day, the pastors experienced the alteration of the concept of philosophy through the deist and atheist publications of the self-declared French *philosophes* such as Voltaire and Diderot. It is, therefore, likely that any association between the philosopher and the freethinker also affected the image of the pastor who undertook any occupation deemed to be philosophical; he could have been viewed as potentially heterodox.

Against this backdrop, Formey's resignation from pastoral office in 1739 to take over the chair of philosophy at the Collège français was, potentially, problematic and needed to be justified to the Huguenot community: why would somebody who was destined to serve the Church for life quit this job to pursue an activity that in the opinion of the congregation had ambiguous connotations? Formey's main argument for quitting his pastoral duties was his ill health, which required him to carry out a less physically tiring job than his role as pastor. This argument appears in all documents, from his official request to the king to be released

---

91. Formey, *Philosophe chrétien*, 3rd edn, vol.2, p.383-84.
92. See Formey, *Souvenirs*, vol.2, p.262-63.

from the pastoral office,[93] to his farewell sermon,[94] through to his autobiographical writings.[95] This argument facilitated the idea that Formey's resignation from the pastoral office for which he had been destined was involuntary.[96] In addition to emphasising his regret at leaving the pulpit, Formey tried to justify the utmost usefulness of his new office as a professor of philosophy for the Church with respect to both doctrinal issues and the structure of the colony. In other words, when Formey exchanged the pulpit for the lectern in 1739, he developed his concept of the Christian philosopher in front of his congregation. Whereas in the debate with the *philosophes* on true philosophy he had focused on the constituents of philosophical method, among his co-confessionals he emphasised the practical assets of the union of religion and philosophy.

In his 1739 farewell sermon, Formey also established his concept of the Christian philosopher as being based first and foremost on considerations regarding the tangled relationship between natural reason and revealed religion. In this respect, it is interesting to observe his line of argument, in which the balance between reason and faith shifted throughout. At the beginning of the sermon, he highlighted the predominant role of the Christian faith, without which everything else – and in particular the pursuit of reason – would be destructive: 'La Religion, c'est la connoissance & le culte de la Divinité. Et que seroit l'homme, s'il en etoit denué? Plus malheureux mille fois que les Bêtes, le flambeau de la Raison ne seroit qu'une lumiere trompeuse qui le conduiroit au précipice.'[97] Conversely, towards the end of the sermon, Formey presented the reverse concept of the relationship between the two entities of reason and revelation. At this point, he did not suggest that reason would lead to the downfall of mankind if it were not supported by religion, but he did state that religion would collapse without the foundations of philosophical research. This statement, according to which reason was the prerequisite and guarantee of faith, resulted from Formey's announcement that he

---

93. See the request Formey made to King Frederick William I (21.5.1739), GStA PK, I. HA Rep. 122, 7 a II, Nr. 1, vol.1, f.256-57.
94. See Formey, *Sermons sur divers textes de l'écriture sainte* (Berlin, Michaelis, 1739), p.144.
95. See Formey, 'Notice de mes ouvrages', p.108.
96. Formey drew this colourful image in his farewell sermon: *Sermons sur divers textes de l'écriture sainte*, p.143-44.
97. Formey, *Sermons sur divers textes de l'écriture sainte*, p.133.

was going to quit the pulpit to become a professor of philosophy and, therefore, was used by him as a strategy of legitimisation:

> j'ai sujet de benir l'Auteur de toute bonne donation, [...], de ce qu'il ne m'a fait descendre de cette Chaire de Verité, que pour monter dans une autre, où la Verité est objet constant de toutes les recherches, où il s'agit de poser des fondemens, sans lesquels la Religion elle même crouleroit, & de former la plupart de ceux qui conduiront dans la suite nos Troupeaux, de les former, dis-je, à allier les lumieres de la Raison à celle de la Revelation.[98]

Formey's metaphorical depiction of the dependency that existed between the pulpit and the lectern contained the concept of a philosophy that explored the gospel and that taught the coexistence of natural and revealed knowledge. This dependency, as Formey's sermon illustrated, functioned both ways – philosophy depended on revealed truths and the comprehension of revealed truths depended on philosophy – and, thus, could be considered mutual. As such, it implied a concept of philosophy that merged into theology and vice versa.

In addition to considering the conceptual relationship between reason and faith, Formey's assessment of this relationship highlighted its practical consequences by referring to his duty of educating the colony's pastoral offspring. This task was as important as preaching with regard to safeguarding religion within the religious community. By teaching philosophy, Formey would supply the parish with well-trained pastors who, in turn, were able to ensure the devoutness of the congregation. This depiction corresponded to the traditional Calvinist view of education according to which school and Church were intertwined with one another[99] and philosophy was seen as propaedeutic to theology.[100] In practice, this meant that Reformed teachers were subject to Church discipline and the confession of faith,[101] and, as was particularly the case with regard to the Collège français in Berlin, Church officials decided on the institution's curriculum and personnel.[102] Education in philosophy was particularly important for

---

98. See Formey, *Sermons sur divers textes de l'écriture sainte*, p.144-49 (NB: there is a mistake in the pagination; it should be p.145 instead of p.149).
99. See Roosen, *Soutenir notre Eglise*, p.43.
100. See Haase, *Literatur des Refuge*, p.61.
101. See 'Discipline ecclésiastique', ch.2, §II, p.91.
102. See Decker, *Vom Höfling zum städtischen Handwerker*, p.344. Formey, *Philosophe payen*, vol.1, p.xv, also emphasised that since its establishment the chair of philosophy at the Collège had always been occupied by former clergymen.

the Church because Reformed pastors had to pass an examination in the essentials of philosophy before being ordained.[103] Until 1770 – the date of the founding of the Séminaire de théologie – the French Church in Berlin did not possess a separate institution for the education of pastors and, therefore, pastoral candidates received their theoretical training mainly from the professor of philosophy at the Collège français.[104]

Therefore, the trope of enhancing devoutness through education had its origins in early Calvinism, and remained common in the communities of the Refuge during the whole of the eighteenth century. Jean-Pierre Erman, the headmaster of the Collège français in the later eighteenth century, developed this trope in much more detail than Formey had done before him. In a sermon that Erman preached at the hundredth anniversary of the Collège français in 1789, he used the concept of *sagesse humaine*, understood as the knowledge of Creation, which was acquired through observation and reasoning. For Erman, the benefit of *sagesse humaine* was threefold: first, it would make pupils susceptible to the divine word and, therefore, lead them to the practice of religion; second, it would show them the limits of natural knowledge that could only be overcome by the Bible; and third, it would encourage pupils to acquire the necessary intellectual qualities for spreading the divine word efficiently among the people through scientific education.[105] Consequently, (philosophical) education served the devoutness of both the individual and the masses. Furthermore, as Erman's sermon suggests, the crux of the Huguenot pedagogical doctrine – the utilitarian reconciliation of human reason and Christian faith – remained quite stable during the eighteenth century.

With regard to the content of lessons delivered by Formey as a professor of philosophy, his farewell sermon betrayed yet again his concept of Christian philosophy, that is to say, an enquiry into the world that drew on both natural and revealed truths. According to Formey's understanding, his lessons served not to introduce students

---

103. See 'Discipline ecclésiastique', ch.1, §V, p.67.
104. See Velder, *300 Jahre*, p.132; Roosen, *Soutenir notre Eglise*, p.197. In contrast, Erman *Mémoire historique*, p.82, indicated that the Séminaire de théologie had been founded in 1772. Despite the founding of this separate institution, Formey's classes on philosophy also seem to have been attended by the students of the Séminaire.
105. Jean-Pierre Erman, *Sermon pour le premier jubilé du centénaire de la fondation du Collège royal françois* (Berlin, Starcke, 1789). See Roosen, *Soutenir notre Eglise*, p.61-67.

to the doctrines of particular philosophical schools but to teach them an appropriate and thorough way of reasoning.[106] As he claimed in 1766, this methodological purpose caused him to lecture as follows on Leibniz's and Wolff's philosophy:

> je me suis en même tems affermi dans l'idée que je conçus de la Philosophie que j'enseigne dès le premier Cours que j'en fis il y a vingt-sept ans: c'est qu'en ne décidant point sur les dogmes qui font porter à cette Philosophie le nom de Leibnitienne, ou de Wolfienne, en mettant à l'écart toutes les Controverses auxquelles ses dogmes peuvent donner lieu, elle a du moin ce mérite, elle possede incontestablement cette prérogative, qu'elle forme l'esprit humain à la justesse & à l'ordre, qu'elle l'accoutume à cette méthode qui ouvre & applanit toutes les routes, qui apprend à penser & à raisonner conséquemment, à n'admettre aucun terme sans l'entendre, aucune proposition à moins qu'elle ne soit bien prouvée, aucun raisonnement si des prémisses évidentes ne menent à une conclusion légitimement déduite.[107]

In 1746, Formey wrote his own textbook, which was an extremely shortened version of all of Wolff's Latin works, comprising logic, ontology, cosmology, psychology, practical philosophy and natural theology: the *Elementa philosophiae seu medulla wolfiana*.[108] Formey lectured four times a week in Latin, and on the fifth day he summarised his lectures in French. As was tradition at the Collège français, these lectures in French were open to interested members of the public,[109] such as members of the Prussian state administration and amateur philosophers, who, according to Manteuffel, attended Formey's speeches in considerable numbers and were all enthused by Wolff's ideas.[110]

---

106. Compare with Ian Hunter, 'The university philosopher in early modern Germany', in *The Philosopher in early modern Europe*, ed. C. Condren, S. Gaukroger and I. Hunter, p.35-65 (51), who claims that no fixed curriculum for teaching philosophy existed in Calvinist German universities and, therefore, it depended on regional and/or personal customs as to which philosophical doctrines were taught.
107. Formey, 'Discours préliminaire', in *Tableau du bonheur domestique, suivi de quelques discours sur des vérités intéressantes de la religion et de la morale* (Leiden, Jacqueau, 1766), p.i-lxxii (xv-xvi).
108. Formey, *Elementa philosophiae seu medulla wolfiana in usum auditorum* (Berlin, Haude & Spener, 1746). Compare with Formey's own review of this work, 'Article XVI. Elementa', *Nouvelle bibliothèque germanique* 2 (1746), p.186-89.
109. See Erman, *Mémoire historique*, p.17-18.
110. Manteuffel to Luise Adelgunde Gottsched (17.10.1739), in Gottsched, *Briefwechsel*, vol.6, p.139-40.

With the decision to teach Wolff's philosophy at the Collège français, Formey institutionalised the intellectual culture that determined his generation of Huguenot pastors and became the mouthpiece of a new phase of the Huguenot Enlightenment in Berlin. Compared with the beginning of the eighteenth century, the climate in the Berlin Refuge had changed significantly in the sense that the strong concern with orthodoxy had vanished and the intertwinement of pastoral and scholarly duties had become almost the rule, despite the fact that the 'Discipline ecclésiastique' contained reservations about it. This change had not occurred abruptly. Up to a certain extent, the Calvinist tradition and the colony's institutional structures allowed people such as Formey to promote Christian philosophy from the pulpit, at the lectern and via publications. Moreover, the education Formey had received from Lenfant, Beausobre and others, who were Cartesian and probably influenced by Arminianism, certainly prepared him for an engagement with natural theology in general and Wolff's rationalist metaphysics in particular.

Nevertheless, Formey's transition from pastor to professor of philosophy required a certain sort of justification for him to be able to emphasise the beneficial interlinking of the two offices. The growing assaults against the Church and religion by men who called themselves philosophers led Formey to assure the congregation that he himself would use philosophy in the service of religion. In the context of the Church, therefore, his depiction of Christian philosophy was a means of preventing the potential suspicions of heterodoxy.

3. Preaching like a philosopher and philosophising like a preacher

Although Formey officially quit his position as a pastor in the French Church in 1739 to become a professor of philosophy at the Collège français, he continued preaching on a regular basis throughout his life.[1] This double function as a pastor and professor of philosophy entailed an increasing convergence of pastoral and philosophical practices that can be best observed in Formey's different writings for popular audiences; he broke down the boundaries that separated the specific genres, which were associated with preaching on the one hand and philosophy on the other. He not only applied philosophy to his sermons, he also turned them into popular philosophical essays that he published in the numerous volumes of his famous *Philosophe chrétien*.

As far as Formey was concerned, transforming his sermons into 'secular' philosophical essays was often the only means by which he could publish them; most of the sermons in *Le Philosophe chrétien* had an exclusively oral origin, such as *Sur la joye*, which he preached in 1741 and which appeared in the first volume of *Le Philosophe chrétien* in 1750.[2] By publishing his sermons in *Le Philosophe chrétien*, he was also able to reach an audience that went beyond his congregation. In addition to this, Formey still published sermons in the classical way: his list of publications contains about twenty sermons and collections

---

1. See Merian, 'Eloge de Formey', p.50. A letter by Jean-Pierre Erman to Formey (27.2.1758), D, suggests that he preached as much as an ordinary pastor, and in a letter to Charles Bonnet (6.4.1765) in *Lettres de Genève*, p.660, Formey also claimed that he preached almost every week.
2. See Formey, *Philosophe chrétien*, 1st edn, vol.1, p.249-62. Manteuffel's letters to Formey (22.3.1741), FF, and to Reinbeck (25.3.1741), UBL, Ms 0344, indicate the essay was originally presented as a sermon.

of sermons.[3] Moreover – and this is the most interesting point – under the cover of *Le Philosophe chrétien* Formey actually republished some of the sermons that had already been published. His 1739 sermon collection *Sermons sur divers textes de l'écriture sainte* contained three different thematic series of sermons delivered in 1736 and 1739 in the Friedrichstadt church in Berlin. The first three sermons, *Sur la nature et les sources du vrai contentement*, reappeared in the first volume of *Le Philosophe chrétien* (1750), the subsequent two sermons, *Le Fidèle fortifié par la grace*, in the second volume of *Le Philosophe chrétien* (1752) and the last three sermons, which dealt with the biblical story of Martha and Mary, eventually reappeared in the third volume of the same book (1755).

The following comparison of Formey's different published sermons with their respective moral philosophical essays shows that his 'sacred' and 'secular' texts were extremely similar in form and content. This was largely because the sermons themselves relied on content and methods borrowed from philosophy and, thus, were secularised to a large extent before they were even transformed into another genre. As such, Formey's sermons reflected a dominant trend in eighteenth-century Protestant preaching that was aimed at plainer and more comprehensive sermons as well as the attempts of Wolffian theologians to devise philosophical sermons. The motives that lay behind such a secularisation of sermons shed light on the complexity of Formey's apologetic mission as a Christian philosopher. The following chapter first contextualises the transformation of Formey's sermons within the multiple attempts to reform preaching from the beginning of the eighteenth century onwards, and then reconstructs his strategies for defending religion among a popular audience, something that he pursued alongside the modification of his writings.

Philosophical preaching between Calvinist homiletic reform and Wolffianism

Since the late seventeenth century, Catholic and Protestant preaching had undergone significant changes. So that an 'enlightened' audience could appreciate religious teachings, sermons of all confessions and religious movements became plainer in style and based on the

---

3. See Geissler, 'Bibliographie des écrits de Jean Henri Samuel Formey', p.427-48. There might be a few double entries because several sermons were first published individually before being reissued together with others in a collection.

believers' experiences.[4] Such changes also included preaching in the Huguenot Refuge. As Christiane Berkvens-Stevelinck has shown, the sermons of the exiled Huguenot ministers in Prussia had significantly altered in tone, subject and sources during the first half of the eighteenth century.[5] Moreover, the preaching of Formey and of the other Huguenot pastors of his cohort in particular was influenced by a (temporary) homiletic trend that evolved among Lutheran preachers in the 1730s and 1740s, that is, adopting the principles of Wolff's logic for sermons. According to the historian of theology Andres Strassberger, this so-called genre of 'philosophical sermon' emerged out of the attempt to oppose Lutheran orthodoxy and Pietism alike.[6] Central to this was the application of a different concept of edification that was based on the close link Wolff had established between psychology and morality. In line with this, the 'philosophical sermon' was meant to speak to the believers' understanding and will instead of particularly appealing to their feelings as practised in Pietist preaching. Defenders of Wolffian philosophical preaching were convinced that, if the believer understood doctrine properly, then he would be guided naturally towards good moral behaviour.[7]

The inventors and promoters of Wolffian philosophical preaching were the Prussian court preacher Johann Gustav Reinbeck and the Leipzig professor of philosophy and literature Johann Christoph Gottsched, who were both members of Manteuffel's Société des aléthophiles. The latter, at the suggestion of Manteuffel and in close collaboration with Reinbeck, published an anonymous homiletic

---

4. See Joris van Eijnatten, 'Reaching audiences: sermons and oratory in Europe', in *The Cambridge history of Christianity*, ed. Stewart J. Brown and Timothy Tackett, vol.7: *Enlightenment, reawakening and revolution 1660-1815* (Cambridge, 2006), p.128-46 (141-44). Explicitly on Protestant preaching see Albrecht Beutel, 'Evangelische Predigt vom 16. bis 18. Jahrhundert', *TRE* 27 (1997), p.296-311 (304-307).
5. See Christiane Berkvens-Stevelinck, 'Entre ferveur et scepticisme: une enquête huguenote', in *Scepticisme, clandestinité et libre pensée / Scepticism, clandestinity and free-thinking*, ed. Gianni Paganini, Miguel Benítez and James Dybikowski (Paris, 2002), p.195-212 (200 and 212), and Christiane Berkvens-Stevelinck, 'Prediger der französischen Kirche in Berlin', in *Franzosen in Berlin*, ed. M. Fontius and J. Häseler (Basel, 2019), p.97-124 (105).
6. See Andres Strassberger, *Johann Christoph Gottsched und die 'philosophische' Predigt: Studien zur aufklärerischen Transformation der protestantischen Homiletik im Spannungsfeld von Theologie, Philosophie, Rhetorik und Politik* (Tübingen, 2010), p.245.
7. See Strassberger, *'Philosophische' Predigt*, p.251-54.

manual in 1740, the *Grund-Riß einer Lehr-Arth ordentlich und erbaulich zu predigen*, which presented the rules that characterised his and Reinbeck's practice of preaching.[8] In his introduction to this manual, Reinbeck argued for forming clear and understandable notions of revealed truths to convince believers of the necessity of these truths,[9] as well as for presenting sermon content, including Bible passages, using logical reasoning.[10] In addition to these formal requirements for a good sermon, Reinbeck also stressed that preachers should explain certain Christian doctrines through both natural reason and divine revelation, because in his view such doctrines that were clearly intelligible through reason did exist. He implied, too, that revealed religion built upon natural religion.[11] These characteristics can also be found in the sermons of Huguenot preachers, particularly in Formey's sermons and in single essays in his *Philosophe chrétien*, providing evidence that the young Huguenot pastors in Prussia had read Gottsched and Reinbeck's homiletic manual.[12]

Moreover, Gottsched and Reinbeck's new homiletics also met with political approval in Prussia; Reinbeck promoted it at court and it became a crucial element of Frederick William I's Church reform.[13] On 7 March 1739, the king issued an order to the consistory of the German Reformed Church in Prussia, the aim of which was to make preaching easier to understand; sermons were to become more 'reasonable, clear and convincing', and less 'oblique, artificial and forced'.[14] For this purpose, the order's second article suggested

---

8. [Johann Christoph Gottsched], *Grund-Riß einer Lehr-Arth ordentlich und erbaulich zu predigen nach dem Inhalt der Königlichen Preussischen allergnädigsten Cabinets-Ordre vom 7. Martii 1739 entworffen* (Berlin, Haude, 1740). For the genesis of the book and Manteuffel's role in it, see particularly Strassberger, *'Philosophische' Predigt*, p.367-78.
9. See Johann Gustav Reinbeck, 'Vorbericht und Einleitung zu einer ordentlichen und erbaulichen Lehr-Art im predigen', in [Gottsched], *Grund-Riß einer Lehr-Arth*, sig.d7r.
10. See Reinbeck, 'Vorbericht', sig.g3r.
11. See Reinbeck, 'Vorbericht', sig.b4v.
12. See Bocquet to Formey (26.8.1740), FF, who claimed to currently read Gottsched's homiletic manual.
13. For the context of the law see Strassberger, *'Philosophische' Predigt*, p.344-66.
14. See *Allergnädigste Verordnung wegen der Prediger und Candidaten deutlichen Lehr=Art, vom 8. Febr. 1740 nebst Beylage sub A. B. & C.*, printed in Strassberger, *'Philosophische' Predigt*, p.553. On 8 February 1740, the *Kabinettsorder* was introduced in the Lutheran Church; in the cited version, supplement A contains the original text that was intended for the Reformed Church.

explicitly that future pastors should be instructed in the logic of Christian Wolff. This point not only constituted a political victory for the Wolffian party over its Pietist adversaries within the above-mentioned debate on Wolff's potential repatriation to Prussia, it also meant that the more comprehensible form of preaching being attempted was equated with the adoption of Wolffian philosophy for sermons. The reform of preaching also reached the French Reformed clergy in Prussia because the royal order was immediately translated into French and communicated to the French supreme consistory.[15]

In addition to the official introduction of Gottsched and Reinbeck's Wolffian homiletics via a royal order, the young Huguenot pastors in Formey's entourage had been adherents since the late 1730s. Through their translations of Reinbeck's sermons, which were commissioned by Manteuffel, they became familiar with the implementation of these homiletics in Lutheran sermons and, furthermore, they approved of the change. In a review of Reinbeck's Christmas sermons of 1737 and his five sermons translated by Des Champs in 1739 in the *Bibliothèque germanique*, Formey judged that Reinbeck's method was excellent for convincing the faithful, and that it was much more effective in this respect than the common preaching style that consisted of senseless and light-hearted declamations.[16]

Most importantly, the young Huguenots also employed themselves in writing Wolffian sermons based on Reinbeck's homiletics. In 1740, Jean Des Champs published *Cinq sermons sur divers textes, expliqués selon la méthode du célèbre Mr. Wolff* after he had delivered them at the court of the Prussian queen Elisabeth Christine. As he claimed in the dedication, the purpose of his sermons was to address as a preacher the same subjects as Wolff had addressed as a philosopher.[17] Indeed, the subjects of Des Champs's sermons were inspired by Wolff's *Horae subsecivae marburgenses*, a three-volume collection of short philosophical treatises on various topics that he had addressed while lecturing at the University of Marburg.[18] Wolff himself had stressed that the natural

---

15. For the whole administrative process see GStA PK, I. HA Rep. 244, Nr. 82, f.158r-162r. The royal letter to the consistory is from 19 March 1739.
16. See 'Article VI. Sermons sur le mystère de la naissance de J. Christ', *Bibliothèque germanique* 45 (1739), p.125-43 (135).
17. See Des Champs, *Cinq sermons sur divers textes, expliqués selon la méthode du célèbre Mr. Wolff prononcés devant Sa Majesté la reine de Prusse* (Berlin, Haude, 1740), 'Epitre dédicatoire à Sa Majesté la reine', sig.*4v-*5r.
18. Christian Wolff, *Horae subsecivae marburgenses, quibus philosophia ad publicam privatamque utilitatem aptatur* (1729-1741), ed. Jean Ecole, 3 vols, in *Christian*

moral theory developed by him in some of these treatises could be used effectively in sermons to facilitate the interpretation of doctrine.[19] As a result, Des Champs had written sermons that dealt with such moral philosophical topics as forgiveness, arrogance, charity, perfection and Christian servitude. In addition, these sermons were still a contribution to the *aléthophiles*' campaign to defend and popularise Wolff's philosophy in Prussia:[20] Manteuffel wrote the 'Avertissement' to the volume, and he made it clear the sermons were supposed to prove the purity and orthodoxy of Wolff's thought.[21]

In 1747, several years after the height of the *aléthophiles*' pamphlet war against the Pietists, Formey also drew on one of Wolff's treatises in the *Horae subsecivae marburgenses* to practise writing 'Wolffian sermons'. His three sermons *L'Idée, les règles et le modèle de la perfection* engaged with Wolff's core principle of natural law – human perfectibility – and earned him the appreciation of Manteuffel and Gottsched.[22] As he did with many of his other sermons, Formey later republished these three Wolffian sermons as a philosophical essay entitled *Essai sur la perfection*, which was first published in France in 1751 and presented as a follow-up work to his *Système du vrai bonheur*, a free translation of Johann Joachim Spalding's moral theological essay *Die Bestimmung des Menschen*, a key text of the German Protestant Enlightenment.[23] Three

---

Wolff: Gesammelte Werke, ed. J. Ecole et al., section 2, vol.34:1-3 (Hildesheim, 1983).

19. See Christian Wolff, 'De principio juris naturalis ex doctrina Christi, Matth. V, 48', in *Horae subsecivae marburgenses anni MDCCXXX, quibus philosophia ad publicam privatamque utilitatem aptatur* (1731), ed. Jean Ecole, in *Christian Wolff: Gesammelte Werke*, ed. J. Ecole et al., section 2, vol.34:2 (Hildesheim, 1983), p.343-67 (354).
20. See Bronisch, *Mäzen der Aufklärung*, p.407-409.
21. See [Manteuffel], 'Avertissement de l'éditeur', in Des Champs, *Cinq sermons sur divers textes*, sig.**2r.
22. See Manteuffel to Wolff (25.11.1746), in *Briefwechsel zwischen Wolff und Manteuffel*, vol.2, p.405-406, and Manteuffel to Formey (26.11.1746 and 20.12.1746), CV.
23. Formey, *Systesme du vrai bonheur* (Utrecht [Paris], [Briasson], 1751) and *Essai sur la perfection pour servir de suite au Système du vrai bonheur* (Utrecht [Paris], [Briasson], 1751). Both were under a *fausse adresse* chosen by Briasson to circumvent the censorship in France; see Briasson to Formey (28.5.1751 and 20.9.1751), in *Correspondance passive de Formey, Antoine-Claude Briasson et Nicolas-Charles-Joseph Trublet: lettres adressées à Jean-Henri-Samuel Formey (1739-1770)*, ed. Martin Fontius, Rolf Geissler and Jens Häseler (Paris, 1996), p.67 and 69. On the history of Formey's translation of Spalding's *Bestimmung des Menschen*, see Martin Fontius, '"Libertas philosophandi" und "siècle de la philosophie": zum

years later, the *Essai sur la perfection* also appeared in a collection of Formey's philosophical treatises, the *Mélanges philosophiques*.

In addition to their engagement with the *aléthophiles*' cause, Huguenot pastors like Des Champs and Formey had other motives for implementing the genre of 'philosophical sermon' that were linked to the protection of religion and devoutness in their confessional community. They were concerned with the effect that preaching had on the perception of the Church in general and on the faith of believers, an issue that had already been discussed among Reformed theologians and pastors before Formey and his peers encountered Wolffianism. Since the beginning of the eighteenth century there had been attempts to reform Calvinist preaching that focused on similar issues to Reinbeck's Wolffian homiletics.[24] In 1708, the Huguenot pastor Jean Barbeyrac translated the sermons of the Latitudinarian minister and archbishop of Canterbury John Tillotson, who had been a forerunner in the reform of Protestant preaching in the Enlightenment.[25] In his introduction to Tillotson's sermons, Barbeyrac pleaded for a more reasonable type of preaching.[26] A few years later, in 1723, the Huguenot theologian Pierre Roques from Basle published his reflections on the history and current state of the Protestant ministry, *Le Pasteur évangélique*, in which he criticised the state of preaching in his day and advocated rhetorically simpler and more logical sermons.[27]

---

geistesgeschichtlichen Standort Formeys', in *Franzosen in Berlin*, ed. M. Fontius and J. Häseler, p.125-252.

24. See Beutel, 'Evangelische Predigt', p.304-305. He states that complaints about the diminishing effect of preaching already existed in the Protestant Church more generally during the seventeenth century, and that they had always been linked to claims for a reform of homiletics.

25. On Tillotson's role see Eijnatten, 'Reaching audiences', p.141.

26. See Jean Barbeyrac, 'Préface du traducteur telle qu'elle étoit dans la première édition MDCCVIII', in *Sermons sur diverses matieres importantes, par Mr Tillotson archevêque de Cantorberi, traduit de l'anglois par Jean Barbeyrac*, 6 vols (Amsterdam, Humbert, 1744), vol.2, p.v-xlviii.

27. See Pierre Roques, *Le Pasteur évangélique, ou Essais sur l'excellence et la nature du St. Ministère, sur ce qu'il éxige de ceux qui en sont revêtus, & sur les sources du peu de progrès que fait, aujourd'hui, la prédication de l'Evangile* (Basle, König, 1723). See especially the seventh essay, in which he outlined the characteristics of good preaching, p.355-476. On Roques, see Jean-Daniel Candaux, 'Roques', in *Dictionnaire des journalistes (1600-1789)*, http://dictionnaire-journalistes.gazettes18e.fr/journaliste/704-pierre-roques (last accessed 17 July 2023). See Formey, *Lettres sur la prédication* (Berlin, Bourdeaux, 1753), p.91.

The predominant purpose behind these Calvinist claims for a new style of preaching was first and foremost to protect the Church from the external threats it had faced since the late seventeenth century because of growing irreligious and anti-clerical discourses. According to Roques, clear and logical preaching that included natural theology and moral philosophy should prove the truth and utility of the duties that God required believers to undertake as well as counteract the *esprits forts* who discredited Christianity.[28] This claim was based on Roques's conviction that God had revealed Himself through both nature and Scripture. Formey, who in 1753 published his own homiletic manual entitled *Lettres sur la prédication*, claimed similar purposes for philosophical sermons as Roques had done thirty years earlier. He explained that his attempt to explain the truth of religion clearly in sermons was to make religious dogma appealing to the congregation, even though this dogma was depicted as being scandalous or ridiculous by many people at that time.[29] In his view, the prevailing type of preaching, which he described as mediocre, helped the growth of unbelief in society[30] because it confused the knowledge of believers and gave credibility to unbelievers who considered religion to be charlatanistic.[31]

Both Roques and Formey wanted preaching to react against the external threat to religion, but this was only one part of the problem. Formey's description of the mediocre preaching of his day reveals his perception of an existing moral decline in preachers and congregations. According to him, most preachers were driven by low moral incentives because they saw preaching either as a mere livelihood or as a means by which to improve their reputation:

> Il est rare que la Prédication soit autre chose qu'un spectacle ou un mêtier; & dès-qu'elle est l'un ou l'autre, il n'y a plus de fruit à en attendre. Elle est un spectacle pour ceux qui s'y devoüent dans l'intention de briller, & de se faire une réputation de Prédicateur. [...] Dès qu'il est question surtout de paroître devant une Cour, on [*sic*] dans un Auditoire fort brillant, on ne pense guères qu'à plaire.[32]

---

28. See Roques, *Pasteur évangélique*, p.365-66. For a similar argument in Barbeyrac, see 'Préface du traducteur', p.xl-xli.
29. See Formey, *Lettres sur la prédication*, p.91.
30. See Formey, *Lettres sur la prédication*, p.40.
31. See Formey, *Lettres sur la prédication*, p.41-42.
32. Formey, *Lettres sur la prédication*, p.42-43.

He attributed this craving for admiration predominantly to the very young preachers who were prone to the vice of vanity and, as a result, he made a plea for appointing older ministers to pastoral office.[33] In 1708, Barbeyrac had already linked bad preaching to the vanity and lack of education of young pastors.[34] Roques's *Pasteur évangélique* also contained similar criticism to the work of Formey. Roques held some pastors' lack of piety responsible for the decreasing impact of preaching on the community of believers.[35]

In addition, in 1753, Formey referred to the role played by the congregation in the debate that was raging around them. In his view, the pastors' immoral incentives for preaching were supplemented and enhanced by the immoral behaviour of the congregation. Formey accused churchgoers of attending the Sunday service only out of curiosity because they wanted to see a new or foreign minister who was supposed to be preaching: 'J'ai en vérité honte pour l'Auditoire, quand je vois cette affluence de monde dans un Temple pour l'ordinaire vuide, & cet empressement pour voir en Chaire une figure qu'on n'y a pas encore vüe; car voilà au fonds à quoi tout se réduit.' When the initial curiosity had passed, people stopped coming to listen to this particular minister.[36] Formey's unfavourable description of the congregation was also reflected in the complaints of his pastoral colleagues about churchgoers' lack of interest in sermons and in religion in general. Antoine Achard dedicated a whole sermon to this subject, in which he bemoaned that people only went to church out of habit and the need to safeguard the external image of their morality because they had lost the original religious zeal, or even their faith.[37] In addition, Balthasar Catel complained in a letter to Formey in 1764 that his congregation showed an increasing reluctance to listen to someone preaching.[38]

The consistency with which Huguenot pastors criticised preaching and congregations' religious practices from the beginning of the eighteenth century until the time of Formey emphasised the depth of the perceived crisis facing practical religion and devoutness.

33. See Formey, *Lettres sur la prédication*, p.43.
34. See Barbeyrac, 'Préface du traducteur', p.xxxi-xxxii.
35. See Roques, *Pasteur évangélique*, p.490-91.
36. Formey, *Lettres sur la prédication*, p.48-49.
37. See Antoine Achard, 'Le peu de fruit des prédications', in *Sermons*, 2 vols (Berlin, Decker, 1774), vol.2, p.153-78 (esp. 159).
38. See Balthasar Catel to Formey (30.12.1764), FF.

Moreover, in Formey's case, this perception of crisis had certainly been increased, in particular by the start of the dissolution of the Huguenot community in Prussian exile. In studies on the Huguenot diaspora, the dissolution of the exiled community and of its identity is usually equated with the assimilation of the migrant population into the host country on different levels.[39] In addition to linguistic assimilation[40] and the intermingling of French and German people through marriage,[41] there was significant religious assimilation. According to Lachenicht, in Berlin, the number of communicants in the French Church had already decreased by the 1720s, and the membership of the colony also decreased from the 1740s onwards. This was mostly a result of the believers moving over to other confessions in the host country.[42]

It can be seen, therefore, that Formey's philosophical sermons emerged from the broad and continuing concern of eighteenth-century clerics that the rise of irreligion in society and popular culture would affect the devoutness of believers negatively, as well as from his own particular and acute fear of the dissolution of his confessional community in exile. Secularising preaching by borrowing from philosophy was, thus, conceived of as a means of counteracting these developments from inside the religious community. The secularisation of preaching had existed among Calvinist pastors since the beginning of the eighteenth century, and, in the case of Formey's preaching, the influence of Wolffian homiletics supplemented and enhanced reflections on this.

Nevertheless, the effect of philosophical preaching did not entirely correspond with its aims, as shown by its ambivalent reception by the public. In relation to Formey's more strictly Wolffian preaching in particular, a clear division existed between the professionals and the common people in the Huguenot congregation. This division is

---

39. See Myriam Yardeni, *Le Refuge huguenot: assimilation et culture* (Paris, 2002), and *Hugenotten zwischen Migration und Integration: neue Forschungen zum Refuge in Berlin und Brandenburg*, ed. Manuela Böhm, Jens Häseler and Robert Violet (Berlin, 2005).
40. See Lachenicht, 'Etude comparée', p.292. For a more detailed analysis from a linguistic perspective, which also includes a comparison between Berlin and the Prussian province, see Manuela Böhm, *Sprachenwechsel: Akkulturation und Mehrsprachigkeit der Brandenburger Hugenotten vom 17. bis 19. Jahrhundert* (Berlin and New York, 2010).
41. For mixed marriages see Lachenicht, 'Etude comparée', p.290-91.
42. See Lachenicht, *Hugenotten in Europa und Nordamerika*, p.327.

illustrated in a letter by Ernst Christoph Manteuffel to Luise Adelgunde Gottsched in November 1740, in which Manteuffel reported on the reaction to one of Formey's Sunday services in Berlin. Instead of a sermon, Formey had presented a lecture containing Leibnizian concepts such as sufficient reason and metaphysical optimism that he had previously prepared for his philosophy class. Hence, he had, literally, transferred philosophy teaching to the pulpit. According to Manteuffel, the reactions of the audience were mixed: the 'gens du métier' praised his sermon, whereas the ordinary people remained puzzled because they were not familiar with these concepts.[43]

Commentators on Formey's Wolffian sermons on perfection published in 1747 held similar views in the sense that they appreciated the sermons' content although they doubted their comprehensibility for an audience of common people. The Huguenot philosopher, friend of Formey and author of the *Law of nations* Emer de Vattel appreciated how Formey presented Wolff's philosophy with clarity and eloquence. However, he found that his prose was too abstract and too charged with metaphysical terms for the majority of the audience.[44] A German reviewer, who was writing for the Hamburg-based *Freye Urtheile*, claimed that only 'thoughtful philosophers' would be able to read these sermons, although they would not need them for their edification as such because they were already able to form the thoughts expressed therein.[45] In general, criticism of the Wolffian 'philosophical' sermons increased in Germany after the mid-eighteenth century.[46] Moreover, Wolff himself, in a private letter to Manteuffel, criticised Formey's sermons on perfection for similar reasons to Vattel and the German reviewer. He claimed that sermons should be grounded in Scripture to incite the devotion of listeners.[47] These reactions to Formey's sermons indicate a mismatch between the genre and their content:

---

43. See Manteuffel to Luise Adelgunde Gottsched (2.11.1740), in Gottsched, *Briefwechsel unter Einschluß des Briefwechsels von Luise Adelgunde Victorie Gottsched*, ed. Detlef Döring *et al.*, vol.7 (Berlin, 2013), p.201-202.
44. Emer de Vattel to Formey (28.4.1747), in *Emer de Vattel à Jean Henri Samuel Formey: correspondances autour du droit des gens*, ed. André Bandelier (Paris, 2012), p.79-80.
45. *Freye Urtheile und Nachrichten zum Aufnehmen der Wissenschaften und der Historie überhaupt. XVI. Stück, Hamburg, Freytags, den 24. Februar 1747*, p.123-24.
46. See Strassberger, *'Philosophische' Predigt*, p.483-534.
47. See Wolff to Manteuffel (7.12.1746) and Manteuffel to Wolff (9.12.1746), in *Briefwechsel zwischen Wolff und Manteuffel*, vol.2, p.428 and 431.

the sermon was a form of popular writing, whereas Wolff's academic philosophy was targeted at an audience of professional philosophers.

In actual fact, only a few years after the publication of his Wolffian sermons, Formey himself reflected on their inadequacy for the common believer. In his 1753 homiletic handbook, he emphasised the need to accommodate preaching to the taste and intellectual capacities of the majority of the audience.[48] In addition, in 1766, in some homiletic reflections that he published in a collection of religious and moral philosophical essays, Formey eventually argued against transmitting philosophy directly from the pulpit, while at the same time he strongly defended its guiding role for theology:

> Il est incontestable que la Philosophie a une union si étroite, non seulement avec la Théologie, mais avec toutes les Sciences qu'on ne sçauroit en traiter aucune méthodiquement & utilement, à moins qu'on ne soit guidé par le flambeau philosophique [...] L'Orateur Philosophe dévient un vain discoureur, s'il porte en Chaire des leçons de Philosophie proprement dites, s'il se sert, soit par ostentation, soit par inadvertance, de termes inconnus au vulgaire, s'il fait des raisonnemens trop abstraits pour être saisis, surtout en aussi peu de tems qu'on en met à les écouter, s'il s'enfonce dans des spéculations où il n'y a que des Philosophes qui peuvent le suivre. Quand même ce ne seroit pas là cette fausse Philosophie que l'Apôtre rejette, c'est toujours une Philosophie déplacée, faite pour une autre Chaire que celle de J.C.[49]

From the 1760s at the latest, Formey was, thus, aware of the limits of combining philosophy and religion in the context of preaching. These limits resulted not from the fundamental qualities of philosophy that supported religion, but from its complexity, which was inappropriate for a popular audience. The extent to which context mattered in this case is emphasised by the fact that Formey's sermons, once they had been transformed into the genre of the moral philosophical essay, were very much appreciated publicly. In the eyes of the reviewer of Formey's *Essai sur la perfection* in the *Journal des sçavans*, it was a 'traité refléchi et divisé' that contained excellent considerations on morality.[50] Similarly, when the *Essai sur la perfection* was assessed by the Dutch bookseller Elie Luzac, he apparently did not realise it was a reworked

---

48. See Formey, *Lettres sur la prédication*, p.69-70. For a more precise description of the rhetoric mentioned, see p.95.
49. Formey, 'Discours préliminaire', in *Tableau du bonheur domestique*, p.lviii-lx.
50. See *Journal des sçavans* (July 1752), p.488 and 493.

version of Formey's sermons because he stated that in his opinion it was a positive counterexample to *Le Philosophe chrétien*, which he considered to be too sermon-like.[51]

Formey's transformation of philosophical sermons into moral philosophical essays

The main difference between Formey's philosophical sermons and his moral philosophical essays was the context of their publication. Apart from this, they were virtually identical in content and form. In terms of their content, Formey only had to make minor adjustments when he transformed his sermons into philosophical essays. As was generally the case in eighteenth-century Protestant preaching,[52] Formey's and the other Huguenot pastors' sermons dealt only rarely with the core doctrines of Christian religion. Rather, they considered moral philosophical topics that usually appealed to believers' life experiences,[53] such as the nature and achievement of human satisfaction, how to be joyful and attain 'true' happiness and perfection, as well as friendship, modesty and such practical things as rules for a good marriage. Most of these topics were linked to questions of self-governance, which was an increasingly popular moral philosophical concept in the eighteenth century.[54]

With this shift in sermon topics, the importance of Scripture as a textual foundation for sermons decreased in Germany in the first half of the eighteenth century.[55] However, Calvin's premise of the absolute authority of Scripture resonated in Reformed preaching until the late seventeenth century. The 'Discipline ecclésiastique' of the French

---

51. See Elie Luzac to Formey (12.10.1754), in *Lettres d'Elie Luzac à Jean Henri Samuel Formey (1748-1770): regard sur les coulisses de la librairie hollandaise du XVIIIe siècle*, ed. Hans Bots and Jan Schillings (Paris, 2001), p.257.
52. For the German case, see Beutel, 'Evangelische Predigt', p.305.
53. See Berkvens-Stevelinck, 'Entre ferveur et scepticisme', p.205.
54. See J. B. Schneewind, *The Invention of autonomy: a history of modern moral philosophy* (Cambridge and New York, 1998), p.5.
55. See Pasi Ihalainen, 'The Enlightenment sermon: towards practical religion and a sacred national community', in *Preaching, sermons and cultural change in the long eighteenth century*, ed. Joris van Eijnatten (Leiden and Boston, MA, 2009), p.219-60 (242), and Hans Martin Müller, 'Homiletik', *TRE* 15 (1986), p.526-65 (537). Both refer to the German lands and, more precisely, to the so-called neologists Spalding and Mosheim who published influential homiletics in the second half of the eighteenth century.

churches in exile still claimed the necessity of basing each sermon on a biblical text, although, equally, it prohibited the unjustified overuse of biblical quotations.[56] About a hundred quotations from the Bible could still be found in Genevan Calvinist sermons from the 1660s and 1670s.[57] By contrast, Formey's three sermons on satisfaction only contained approximately a dozen (referenced) biblical quotations. When he republished the sermons in *Le Philosophe chrétien*, he either deleted the quotations[58] or did not identify them as such.[59]

Nevertheless, exegetical sermons centred on one particular Bible passage continued to exist and were more difficult to transform into 'secular' forms of writing, an issue that Formey and his publisher, Elie Luzac, were aware of. For example, Formey instructed his friend Abraham Bocquet, who was supposed to contribute a piece to his *Philosophe chrétien*, to choose a sermon that was not too closely based on Scripture.[60] Luzac noted that stories from the life of Christ fitted the purpose of *Le Philosophe chrétien* less well than texts on morality.[61] Despite these reservations, Formey included some exegetical sermons in his *Philosophe chrétien*: his sermons on Martha and Mary that he had preached in 1739 and then reissued in the book's third volume in 1755. The changes were minimal because he delivered, as in the sermon, a text-based explanation of the biblical story. The only real change he made was to swap round the position of the corresponding passage from the Bible. Whereas the sermon started with the passage from the gospel and then made remarks on the general application of the text, the essay began with the remarks and quoted the biblical text later.[62]

---

56. See 'Discipline ecclésiastique', ch.1, §XII, p.73.
57. See Nicholas Must, *Preaching a dual identity: Huguenot sermons and the shaping of confessional identity, 1629-1685* (Leiden and Boston, MA, 2017), p.36-37. He quotes the examples of two Genevan sermons from the 1660s and 1670s.
58. See, for example, Formey, *Sermons sur divers textes de l'écriture sainte*, p.11, and compare with *Philosophe chrétien*, 1st edn, vol.1, p.216.
59. See, for example, Formey, *Sermons sur divers textes de l'écriture sainte*, p.14, and compare with *Philosophe chrétien*, 1st edn, vol.1, p.219.
60. See Bocquet to Formey (29.1.1751), FF, in which Bocquet enumerated several reasons why his sermons would not be suitable for the next volume of *Le Philosophe chrétien*, among others: 'D'un autre coté presque tous mes sermons sont des explications de Textes, tellement liées avec les Termes du Texte sur lequel ils roulent, qu'il ne seroit guere possible de les ajuster même à quelque parallele, bien loin d'y trouver une suite indépendamment de tout Texte.'
61. See Luzac to Formey (13.8.1754), in *Lettres d'Elie Luzac*, p.252.
62. See Formey, *Philosophe chrétien*, 1st edn, vol.3, p.203.

Usually, however, in Formey's sermons, the exegesis of passages from the Bible was diminished. Instead, he used biblical quotations only as sources of inspiration for addressing general human problems. For example, when he preached on satisfaction, Formey quoted one single sentence by Paul to the Philippians at the beginning of his series of three sermons: 'J'ai appris d'être content de l'état où je me trouve' (Philippians 4.11). He then skipped the usual explanation and contextualisation of the quotation within the Bible and went directly to its application by stating that these few biblical words represented a universally applicable art – that of being satisfied with what one had.[63] Formally, Formey's arguments were still strongly tied to Scripture; the reference to the one Bible passage on Paul reappeared throughout the whole sermon. However, this reference betrayed Formey's understanding of Scripture as historical rather than doctrinal because he allowed his audience to identify with Saint Paul by presenting him as both a contemporary model of conduct[64] and a historical witness for his arguments.[65] Moreover, Formey was careful to avoid using the image of the apostle imposing (divine) laws on the congregation.[66] Subsequently, when Formey republished these sermons as moral essays in *Le Philosophe chrétien*, he retained all the instances in which he referred to Saint Paul as a role model and witness,[67] and he emphasised these functions more than he had done in the sermon. In *Le Philosophe chrétien* he called Paul 'cet Apôtre' instead of 'notre Apôtre' as he did in the sermons. This reinforced the apostle's role as a historical figure rather than him being part of a confessional identity.[68] In addition, Formey dispensed with the excessive praise for Paul that had been present in the sermons.[69]

Formey often inserted biblical quotations at the head of his sermons, a practice that emphasises the function of the quotations as sources of inspiration. When he transformed his sermons into essays in *Le Philosophe chrétien*, he changed these headline biblical quotations

63. See Formey, *Sermons sur divers textes de l'écriture sainte*, p.5.
64. See Formey, *Sermons sur divers textes de l'écriture sainte*, p.16.
65. See Formey, *Sermons sur divers textes de l'écriture sainte*, p.12.
66. See Formey, *Sermons sur divers textes de l'écriture sainte*, p.22.
67. See Formey, *Sermons sur divers textes de l'écriture sainte*, p.12 and 22, and compare with *Philosophe chrétien*, 1st edn, vol.1, p.217 and 227.
68. See Formey, *Sermons sur divers textes de l'écriture sainte*, p.13, and compare with *Philosophe chrétien*, 1st edn, vol.1, p.218.
69. See Formey, *Sermons sur divers textes de l'écriture sainte*, p.22, and compare with *Philosophe chrétien*, 1st edn, vol.1, p.227.

to non-biblical ones. Whereas he used quotations from ancient philosophers and poets in the first two and the fourth volumes of the book, he chose quotations from the *Anti-Lucretius*, which was an apologetic and anti-materialist poem by the French Catholic cardinal Melchior de Polignac, for the third volume.[70]

Because sermons were dealing less with Christian doctrine and more with morality, non-sacred knowledge such as natural theology and natural law was incorporated into the sermon alongside biblical and theological teachings. In his 'Wolffian sermons' of 1747, *L'Idée, les règles et le modèle de la perfection*, Formey developed the core concept of Wolff's natural law, namely that human morality resulted from human beings' natural striving for perfection.[71] This included preaching about metaphysical notions such as the harmonic connection between soul and body and the state of the human will.[72] Formey's three sermons on perfection constituted a particular case because their very purpose had been to present one of Wolff's philosophical treatises from the *Horae subsecivae marburgenses*. However, other sermons of Formey's also contained philosophical concepts that were mostly inspired by Wolff and Leibniz. For example, in Formey's sermon on joy, Wolff's notion of human perfectibility also resonated,[73] and, in others, his notion of the *nexus rerum*[74] and Leibniz's theory of monads were exposed.[75]

Both Formey's sermons and his moral philosophical essays reflected explicitly on the qualities of the different sources of truth on which they drew – natural and divine knowledge – and conceptualised their relationship to one another. Usually, the arguments resulting from God's word were presented as superior to those that relied on nature and human experience. In terms of sermon structure, this hierarchy often resulted in a two- or three-part exposition according to which the teachings of human reason and/or experience were explored before the sermon culminated in an appraisal of the arguments drawn from revelation. In his sermons on satisfaction, as well as in

70. Melchior de Polignac, *Anti-Lucretius sive de deo et natura libri novem: opus posthumum*, 2 vols (Amsterdam, Rey, 1748). See Wolfgang Bernard Fleischmann, 'Zum Anti-Lucretius des Kardinals de Polignac', *Romanische Forschungen* 77 (1965), p.42-63.
71. See Formey, *L'Idée, les règles et le modèle de la perfection en trois sermons sur St. Matth. Ch. V. v. 48* (Berlin, Jasperd, 1747), p.17 and 24.
72. See Formey, *L'Idée, les règles et le modèle*, p.11 and 13.
73. See Formey, *Philosophe chrétien*, 1st edn, vol.1, p.259.
74. See Formey, *Philosophe chrétien*, 1st edn, vol.1, p.18.
75. See Formey, *Philosophe chrétien*, 1st edn, vol.1, p.181.

the corresponding discourse in *Le Philosophe chrétien*, Formey claimed to draw inspiration from three different sources – nature, experience and religion[76] – to explain how satisfaction could be reached. Religion was regarded as being superior to the other two.[77] The only difference between the sermon and the corresponding moral philosophical essay was that, in the sermon, the statement about the superiority of religion was amplified and embellished significantly.[78] A similar tendency can be observed in Formey's three sermons on perfection, *L'Idée, les règles et le modèle de la perfection*, and his corresponding 'secular' *Essai sur la perfection*. In the sermons, he first stated the equality of natural law and divine revelation and, thereby, adopted Wolff's argument in the *Horae subsecivae marburgenses*.[79] Thus, in the first of the three sermons, he provided an analysis of perfection that was based solely on natural law. However, at the end of this first sermon, he corrected his previous assumption and stated that revealed religion was still superior to nature alone because it was more powerful in inciting and guiding the human pursuit of perfection.[80] The third and last sermon was then dedicated completely to the teachings of revelation. There were two instances in the sermon collection in which the superiority of religion was emphasised, that is, at the end of the first sermon and in the entire last sermon, and these were bridged by a sermon that was based on theories of natural law. The *Essai sur la perfection* differed from the original sermon text only in the arrangement of its parts. The final passage of the first sermon, in which Formey emphasised the superiority of revealed religion as a source of perfection, was moved to the end of the essay. Hence, in the *Essai sur la perfection*, the authority of revealed knowledge was not anticipated as in the sermons, but was rather shaped as a punchline at the end.[81] In addition, Formey curtailed the original conclusion of the sermon in which he had enthusiastically exhorted people to lead a pious life by following the example of God ('Vous imiterez votre Père qui est aux Cieux').[82] In general, when transforming his sermons into 'secular' essays, Formey maintained the hierarchical relationship between

---

76. See Formey, *Sermons sur divers textes de l'écriture sainte*, p.22.
77. See Formey, *Philosophe chrétien*, 1st edn, vol.1, p.238.
78. See Formey, *Sermons sur divers textes de l'écriture sainte*, p.40.
79. See Formey, *L'Idée, les règles et le modèle*, p.7 and 18-19.
80. See Formey, *L'Idée, les règles et le modèle*, p.19-20.
81. See Formey, *Essai sur la perfection*, p.85-90 (esp. 89).
82. See Formey, *L'Idée, les règles et le modèle*, p.52-54 (esp. 53).

reason and revelation; however, in the essays, he usually softened the statement about the superiority of religion.

However, if pushed to the limit, the epistemological superimposition of revelation onto natural reason potentially came at the expense of philosophy. For example, in Formey's moral philosophical essay *Sur la joye*, which, as the correspondence with Manteuffel reveals, he originally delivered as a sermon in 1741, Formey discredited philosophy as a 'school of vanity' in which people sought vainly to learn the principles of their happiness, principles that only religion was able to teach.[83] In fact, the whole sermon/essay reveals that Formey had difficulties in conforming with the usual hierarchy that placed revelation above natural law. Right at the beginning of the sermon, Formey gave much weight to theories of natural law by claiming that the feeling of joy, like all other moral feelings, depended on human freedom alone and not on directions given to the individual by somebody else. He then recognised that this contrasted with the biblical tradition according to which the apostle Paul commanded the people to 'be always joyful', just as if they were not free to be so.[84] To overcome this contradiction between natural law and the apostle's word, Formey stated that the apostle's word ought to be interpreted not as a simple obligation but as a way of saying that religion facilitated people's recognition of their natural motives.[85] It seems, however, that Formey sensed the weakness of his claim and, therefore, also decided to attack the integrity of philosophy to restore the power of revelation. This example shows that the combination of natural law and revealed truths in Formey's sermons was not always free of tensions, and that the introduction of arguments from natural law was a challenge to the authority of Scripture. Furthermore, in his secular moral philosophical publications, Formey argued in the same way as in his sermons and, thus, maintained his claim against philosophy. Manteuffel and Wolff, who read Formey's manuscript before it was published as *Le Philosophe chrétien*, condemned his attack against philosophy as an expression of Augustinian orthodoxy.[86]

In terms of style and form, however, it was philosophy that imposed its rule on the sermons of Formey and his colleagues. More precisely,

---

83. See Formey, *Philosophe chrétien*, 1st edn, vol.1, p.260.
84. See Formey, *Philosophe chrétien*, 1st edn, vol.1, p.249-50.
85. See Formey, *Philosophe chrétien*, 1st edn, vol.1, p.250.
86. See Manteuffel to Formey (10.8.1748), D, and Wolff to Manteuffel (22.8.1748), *Briefwechsel zwischen Wolff und Manteuffel*, vol.3, p.453-54.

they adopted the concepts of clarity and probability that were shaped by the discipline of philosophy and to which every argument in a sermon was subjected. As such, they emphasised that persuasion was the main purpose of a sermon because those who listened to sermons were only incited to act if they felt persuaded by what they heard. The highest degree of persuasion, however, was still attributed to revelation or faith. As Des Champs put it in his *Cinq sermons*, faith entailed a much greater persuasion than natural truths and, therefore, people would execute the revealed word with greater ardour:

> Tant que vôtre Esprit n'est pas persuadé, tant que vous êtes en suspens, vous ne vous sentez point porté à agir. Mais vôtre empressement à mettre la main à l'œuvre, ira toujours en croissant, à mesure que la certitude de vôtre foi, prendra de nouvelles forces. Plus les vérités qui vous sont proposées, vous paroitront évidentes, & plus vous les persuaderez vous [*sic*]; & plus aussi vous presserez vous d'en tirer l'usage, auquel elles sont destinées. Et comme la persuasion que produit la foi, est beaucoup plus vive, que celle qui naît des vérités naturelles; l'ardeur, l'activité avec laquelle nous nous appliquons les vérités Révélées, est aussi bien plus grande, & bien plus forte![87]

A similar connection between the persuasiveness of Christian religion and action can also be found in Formey's sermons on perfection.[88] Equally, in his sermons on satisfaction, he justified the particular persuasiveness of religion with reference to the concepts of clarity and probability. He claimed that religion, unlike nature and human experience, provided more than just speculation when it came to proving the existence of providence; rather, religion 'stated positively' and 'proved clearly' the truth of providence.[89] Therefore, the superiority of the divine revelation that Formey and others propagated in their sermons became an epistemological superiority.

Linked to the adoption of epistemological notions from philosophy was the application of a logical structure and demonstrative method to sermons to create persuasiveness. The Huguenot pastors' sermons were full of deductive reasoning that usually comprised the definition of certain concepts central to the sermon's topic or biblical quotation, the collection of evidence, the establishment of proof and the drawing of conclusions. Although the Reformed Church traditionally

---

87. Des Champs, *Cinq sermons sur divers textes*, p.42.
88. See Formey, *L'Idée, les règles et le modèle*, p.19-20.
89. See Formey, *Sermons sur divers textes de l'écriture sainte*, p.40-41.

propagated a rather simple and plain homiletics,[90] eighteenth-century homiletics added a new, strong focus on logic. However, whereas Barbeyrac and Roques referred to the logical coherence of a text taught by the ancient rhetorician Quintilian,[91] Formey's homiletics and sermons bore the imprint of Wolff's demonstrative method. As in his metaphysical treatises presented at the Academy – for example, his two essays on the proof of the existence God in 1747 – Formey advocated deducing every argument from clear notions.[92] He even applied this philosophical method in his exegetical sermon on the two sisters Martha and Mary. In this, he set out to prove the necessity and utility of reaching salvation, two aspects he called 'deux grandes veritez', and which required a demonstration to be proved: 'Pour proceder avec quelque ordre, & pour former une espece de Démonstration, (car il ne faut pas moins qu'une Démonstration, pour engager les Hommes à quitter le présent pour l'avenir, le [sic] Terre pour le Ciel,) commençons par définir le mot de nécessaire, & en fixer l'idée.'[93] The demonstration had to begin with two steps, and it needed to start with a definition of the subject matter – 'necessity' in this context – and then determine its meaning. Following on from this, by employing a large body of elaboration that was informed by several everyday examples, Formey eventually concluded his discourse by stating: 'telles sont enfin les principales preuves, dont je voulois former une Démonstration abrégée de la Verité de mon Texte: c'est que l'Ouvrage du salut, plus nécessaire que tous les autres, lorsqu'il va de concert avec eux, le devient uniquement quand ils ne peuvent plus s'accorder ensemble.'[94]

It is likely that a preaching style marked to such an extent by philosophical epistemology and methods would cause a general shift in the perception of religious doctrine. God's revelation increasingly lost its traditional authority when it was evaluated according to the thelogical coherence and clarity of its arguments, despite the Huguenot pastors' strong claims for the indispensable and superior character of revelation compared with philosophy.

90. See James Thomas Ford, 'Preaching in the Reformed tradition', in *Preachers and people in the reformations and early modern period*, ed. Larissa Taylor (Leiden and Boston, MA, 2001), p.65-88 (73-74).
91. See Barbeyrac, 'Préface du traducteur', p.xxxi, and Roques, *Pasteur évangélique*, p.453-54.
92. See Formey, *Lettres sur la prédication*, p.68.
93. Formey, *Sermons sur divers textes de l'écriture sainte*, p.118-19.
94. Formey, *Sermons sur divers textes de l'écriture sainte*, p.121.

Secularisation of morality

Not only were the form and content of Formey's philosophical sermons and moral philosophical essays identical, but the aims he pursued with the two genres of writing were also very similar. As mentioned above, the aim of Formey's *Philosophe chrétien* was to defend and promote a philosophy that supported religion in times of growing unbelief and anti-clericalism with regard to popular philosophy. In terms of content, the moral philosophical essays assembled in *Le Philosophe chrétien* should, thus, indicate an 'enlightened piety', that is to say, a piety that relied on clear knowledge of God.[95] In the introductory essay that Formey published at the beginning of the second edition of *Le Philosophe chrétien* in 1752, this claim was, however, not targeted directly at unbelievers as had been the case in the dedication letter written for the first volume. Rather, in the introductory essay of the second edition, Formey opposed those inside the Church who – as he claimed – facilitated the denunciation of religion by unbelievers by obscuring it and propagating blind fideism or fanaticism.[96]

However, in the market for popular philosophical literature, Formey's moral philosophical essays were meant to compete directly with anti-religious and materialist popular literature by philosophers such as Voltaire and Diderot. Sermons sold very badly in Formey's day, and publishers were reluctant to publish them because the amount of popular literature more generally and readers' reservations about sermons were both growing.[97] To publicise his sermons and their predominantly moral message despite readers' reservations, Formey disguised them, as he claimed in the third volume of his *Philosophe chrétien*.[98] The driving force behind this camouflage was Formey's publisher from Leiden, Elie Luzac, who urged Formey to purge his *Philosophe chrétien* manuscript of all sermon-like elements in order to attract a public that went beyond 'les personnes pieuses et

---

95. See Formey, 'Discours préliminaire sur la vraie piété', in *Philosophe chrétien*, 2nd edn, vol.1, p.v-xxviii (vii-viii).
96. See Formey, 'Discours préliminaire sur la vraie piété', p.xxiii-xxiv.
97. See 'Article VIII. Sermons sur divers textes de l'écriture sainte par Samuel Formey', *Bibliothèque germanique* 47 (1740), p.189-208 (189). The new competition between sermons and a secular 'moral-aesthetic edification literature' that arose in the seventeenth and eighteenth centuries is also mentioned by Beutel, 'Evangelische Predigt', p.304-305.
98. See Formey, 'Avertissement', in *Philosophe chrétien*, 1st edn, vol.3, sig.*3r.

vouées au christianisme'.[99] Luzac's demands must have been motivated mainly by economic considerations; however, they also revealed his undogmatic view on how to counteract irreligion and immorality in society. With respect to Formey's refutation of Diderot's *Pensées philosophiques* – the *Pensées raisonnables* that had also been published by Luzac in 1749 – the latter claimed it was not necessary to use the whole repertoire of biblical expressions to sell 'sane philosophy', as opposed to the 'wrong philosophy' of the French *philosophes*. On the contrary, in Luzac's view, the use of biblical quotations and the like could even harm a book's reputation because they were badly used by other (orthodox) authors.[100] With regard to moral literature in particular, Luzac defended a very pragmatic approach because he considered that (secular) moral philosophy was as good as revealed religion as a means of inspiring virtue in people. He claimed that, because contemporary readers were less attracted to revealed religion, it was only realistic to resort to moral philosophy instead for the sake of raising morality.[101] Animated by such an opinion, Luzac had tried since 1754 to persuade Formey to write moral philosophical essays that neglected Christian doctrine completely.[102]

In a very similar vein to Luzac's argument, another bookseller called Fortunato Bartolomeo de Felice, who was a Neapolitan convert to Calvinism and had established an influential printing house in Yverdon in 1762, put forward his own. Between 1770 and 1780, he edited and published the Protestant reply to the Parisian *Encyclopédie*, the *Encyclopédie d'Yverdon*, to which Formey also contributed.[103] In 1768, Felice published Formey's *Consolations raisonnables et religieuses*, one of the follow-up-books to *Le Philosophe chrétien*. Like Luzac before him, he too exhorted Formey to delete the traces of his sermons in the manuscript.[104] He seems to have considered this to be the best

---

99. Luzac to Formey (2.6.1749), in *Lettres d'Elie Luzac*, p.64-66.
100. See Luzac to Formey (11.2.1749), in *Lettres d'Elie Luzac*, p.42.
101. See Luzac to Formey (23.10.1754), in *Lettres d'Elie Luzac*, p.260.
102. See Luzac to Formey (12.10.1754), in *Lettres d'Elie Luzac*, p.257.
103. On Felice's life and thought, see the essays in *Fortunato Bartolomeo de Felice: un intellettuale cosmopolita nell'Europa dei lumi* (Milan, 2017), ed. Stefano Ferrari; on his encyclopedia see *L'Encyclopédie d'Yverdon et sa résonance européenne*, ed. Jean-Daniel Candaux *et al.*, and on Formey's contribution to it see Clorinda Donato, 'Jean Henri Samuel Formey's contribution to the *Encyclopédie d'Yverdon*', in *Schweizer im Berlin des 18. Jahrhunderts*, ed. Martin Fontius and Helmut Holzhey (Berlin, 1996), p.87-98.
104. See Fortunato Bartolomeo de Felice to Formey (2.12.1767), CV.

3. Preaching like a philosopher and philosophising like a preacher 105

strategy for making Formey's Christian moral philosophy competitive with the works of Rousseau, Voltaire and the like, which were much more in demand with the public.[105] Like Luzac, Felice acknowledged that the truth of religion had to be defended continuously in the light of growing deism in society, and he considered Formey the right person to do this. However, in contrast to Luzac, Felice considered it important that apologetic writings promote the necessity of revealed religion and make clear the insufficiency of natural religion.[106]

Finally, it was not only the publishers and booksellers who embraced the strategy of camouflaging sermons to guarantee them public success. Formey's Genevan correspondents were also supportive of this strategy and praised the good that Formey had done for religion with such publications. As the pastor Jean Peschier put it, Formey with his moral philosophical essays had reached people who would never have read sermons.[107] Moreover, on the eve of the publication of the third volume of *Le Philosophe chrétien*, the Genevan theologian Jacob Vernet asked Formey, on behalf of the Swiss friends they had in common, to return to the style characteristic of its first volume, namely, a style that did not resemble sermons. The second volume had been far too sermon-like for the taste of Vernet and his friends.[108] It is, therefore, safe to say that many of Formey's Calvinist contacts from publishers to theologians supported his practice of transforming sermons into a more secular genre of popular philosophy. They shared the idea of liberal apologetics, that is, a defence of religion that intentionally omitted its formal characteristics and – in parts – its core content.

However, it seems that Formey's own idea of these liberal apologetics differed slightly from that of his Genevan co-confessionals and from that of Jacob Vernet in particular. Moreover, he never seems to have fully endorsed his publishers' strategy of hiding the pastoral origin of his writings. After the publication of the first volume of *Le Philosophe chrétien*, not only did Formey take less care to camouflage the sermons behind his moral philosophical essays in the book's later volumes, but in 1764, when he published the *Discours moraux*, the

---

105. See Felice to Formey (21.5.1765), FF. Felice wanted to publish a new edition of the *Philosophe Chrétien* but he eventually abandoned this plan because he had heard that not all copies from the book's third edition in Leiden had yet been sold; see Felice to Formey (2.7.1765), D.
106. Felice to Formey (19.11.1765), FF.
107. See Peschier to Formey (11.3.1755), in *Lettres de Genève*, p.429.
108. See Vernet to Formey (18.6.1753), in *Lettres de Genève*, p.371.

follow-up book to *Le Philosophe chrétien*, he also stated explicitly that he no longer wanted to purge his essays of pastoral style and religious content. Rather, he emphasised that the moral rules contained in his essays were deduced uniquely from Christian doctrine.[109] Therefore, he presented his *Discours moraux* as a reply to the defenders of an 'essential religion', that is to say, a religion that excluded dogma and consisted of evangelical morality alone. Although he acknowledged that these people thought to act for the benefit of religion, he accused them of being, in reality, the internal enemies of religion.[110] In 1764, Formey considered that religion would lose its power if it was deprived of revealed doctrines, as some of his correspondents had suggested, and that a morality not based on these doctrines was insufficient because it did not lead to salvation.

The difference between the Genevan theologians' and Formey's view with regard to liberal apologetics became clear as early as 1756, when Formey publicly condemned a work by his correspondent Jacob Vernet because it oversimplified or omitted Christian dogma for the sake of popular accessibility. Here, he was referring to Vernet's *Instruction chrétienne* (1751-1754), an introduction to Christian theology and morals that was situated between a catechism and an academic course. In his review of the book in his *Nouvelle bibliothèque germanique*, Formey suggested that the slightest neglect of doctrinal content would support all those who had argued against religion for a long time. He particularly deplored the practice of some theologians who considered certain Christian doctrines as being above human reason and excluded them from religion on these grounds. Strangely enough, this had been one of Roques's suggestions in his *Pasteur évangélique*.[111] As far as Formey was concerned, he was convinced of the capacity of human understanding to explain every revealed doctrine, no matter how obscure it appeared. He had already stated in his introductory essay to the second edition of his *Philosophe chrétien* in 1752 that the only reason certain Christian doctrines still could not be explained was the limitations imposed by human understanding. He was, however, confident that revealed religion would become less obscure the more human reason progressed.[112]

---

109. See Formey, 'Discours sur la dépendance necessaire, où la morale se trouve à l'égard de la foi', in *Discours moraux*, vol.1, sig.B10v-b11r.
110. See Formey, 'Discours sur la dépendance necessaire', sig.a9r-v.
111. See 'Article IX. Instruction chrétienne', *Nouvelle bibliothèque germanique* 18 (1756), p.153-82 (154-55), and compare with Roques, *Pasteur évangélique*, p.506.
112. See Formey, 'Discours préliminaire sur la vraie piété', p.xxiv-xxv.

Vernet, who considered Formey's criticism of his *Instruction chrétienne* to be an accusation of heterodoxy, defended the opposite view.[113] He was against explaining every dogma rationally, especially in non-theological popular religious writings. In general, he found that the original simplicity of the Christian religion had been disfigured by scholastic theologians who wanted to explain every little bit of it, and that it was precisely because of them that religion was under attack at the time of Vernet and Formey.[114] Therefore, he argued for silently removing these logically unsustainable and, thus, harmful explanations of dogma – he cited the scholastic hypotheses concerning original sin and the Trinity – from contemporary religion.[115] Although Formey publicly withdrew his accusation of heterodoxy against Vernet and shared his claim concerning the harm done by scholastic theologians to the comprehensibility of dogma, nevertheless, he insisted on demonstrating morality's dependence on dogma in order to uphold the sacred character of religion.[116]

Formey's claims in his *Discours moraux* in 1764 and his earlier dispute with Vernet demonstrate not only the multiple and, sometimes, contradictory motives of eighteenth-century Calvinist religious apologetics but also the ambivalence of Formey's own position within it. Although Formey contributed to a certain extent to the secularisation of sermons by introducing philosophical concepts and methods and by transforming them into a popular philosophical genre, his main purpose was to counteract the secularisation of religion. Philosophy was meant to help him keep dogma relevant, not render it obsolete. To do so, he employed philosophical reasoning against two opposing enemies: the fanatics who obscured religion for fideistic reasons, and the progressive theologians who abandoned dogma voluntarily for the sake of an essential religion. According to his Genevan peers, this position did not match the expectations they had of Formey; during their debate about the role of dogma in moral philosophy,

---

113. Vernet's position was also defended by the Genevan pastor Jean Peschier; see Peschier to Formey (7.3.1757), in *Lettres de Genève*, p.454.
114. See Vernet to Formey (13.3.1757 and 2.6.1757), in *Lettres de Genève*, p.456 and 464.
115. See Vernet to Formey (2.6.1757), in *Lettres de Genève*, p.463-64. Compare with Vernet to Formey (3.5.1758), in *Lettres de Genève*, p.477.
116. See 'Article VII. Oratio dicta à Jacobo Verneti', *Nouvelle bibliothèque germanique* 21 (1757), p.97-111 (99-100).

Vernet claimed that he did not recognise the Christian philosopher in Formey anymore.[117]

Formey's practice of transforming sermons into moral philosophical essays reveals different layers of his role as a Christian philosopher. First, it shows the complexity of his aim to safeguard religion that was targeted not only at the external enemies of religion but also at extreme positions – orthodox and heterodox – in the religious community itself. Second, on a formal level, his practice illustrates his contribution to the creation of a genre of popular religious writing that was facilitated by his double affiliation as a pastor and a professor of philosophy. His *Philosophe chrétien*, therefore, not only expressed his concept of Christian philosophy, it also promoted a practical philosophy that was tinged with religion. Third, Formey's practice of preaching like a philosopher and philosophising like a preacher demonstrates yet again that he merged the Wolffian influences contained in Gottsched and Reinbeck's philosophical homiletics with considerations and needs that were inherent in his Calvinist culture.

These insights into Formey's behaviour, practices and self-representation as well as into his intellectual and cultural affiliations more broadly provide the basis for the analyses of the philosophical controversies that will appear in the following five chapters. Here, the focus is on Formey's ideas and claims concerning fundamental theoretical questions relevant to religion and morality, namely, those questions relating to God's existence, divine providence and human liberty. Formey's ideas concerning these questions were in many respects the metaphysical foundation of the popular philosophy that he developed in his sermons and moral philosophical essays. However, the way he presented his claims in the context of scholarly debates was different from his method with a popular audience. He particularly stressed his strictly rationalist approach in his contributions to the Academy, an approach that had been judged inadequate for his sermons, as has been shown.

---

117. See Vernet to Formey (13.3.1757), in *Lettres de Genève*, p.456.

4. The existence of God and the superiority of metaphysics

In his contributions to the class of speculative philosophy at the Berlin Academy, a member of which he was from 1744, Formey almost entirely neglected revelation and Scripture as accounting for religious and moral teachings and, instead, relied on an epistemology based on natural reason alone. Nevertheless, the subjects he dealt with in his academic writings all had an impact on religion and morality and, usually, a more or less strong apologetic purpose as well. Among his academic writings, his two essays on the existence of God, which he presented in the spring and autumn of 1747 to his colleagues and which were published in the 1749 Academy yearbook, were of great significance because they disclosed Formey's perception of the relationship between religion and science. In addition to containing a natural theological demonstration of God's existence, the two essays reflected on the most adequate method of 'scientifically' proving the existence of God. More precisely, Formey judged the physico-theological (also teleological) or design proof of the existence of God, according to which His existence is based on the observation of nature's regularity and purposiveness,[1] to be vulnerable to attacks by unbelievers and, thus, pleaded for its revision. In this respect, Formey criticised one of the most popular eighteenth-century proofs of the existence of God, a proof that had blossomed with the development of the hybrid discipline of physico-theology by English natural philosophers such as Newton and Robert Boyle who combined natural philosophical and biblical knowledge to account for God's purpose with regard to nature.[2] Since

1. See Maria Rosa Antognazza, 'Arguments for the existence of God: the continental European debate', in *The Cambridge history of eighteenth-century philosophy*, ed. K. Haakonssen, vol.2, p.731-48 (738).
2. See Peter Harrison, 'Physico-theology and the mixed sciences: the role of theology in early modern natural philosophy', in *The Science of nature in the*

the beginning of the eighteenth century, theologians such as William Derham and Samuel Clarke had popularised physico-theological considerations of God's existence and nature through the famous Boyle Lectures.[3]

As will be shown in the present chapter, Formey's criticism of the physico-theological or design argument relied on Wolff's natural theology in particular. However, his general conviction of the rationality of theological teachings dated back to before he became familiar with Wolff's work, emerging out of his critical engagement with Pierre Bayle's philosophical and religious scepticism against which Formey upheld Cartesian rationalism. In this respect, Formey's argument with Bayle about the comprehensibility of God's existence that appeared in the article entitled 'Dieu' in the Parisian *Encyclopédie* deserves attention because it was Formey's first engagement with natural theology.[4] His Cartesian background in natural theology was still very evident in his two academic essays in 1747, although they were imbued with Leibnizan and Wolffian metaphysics.

Moreover, with their strong focus on metaphysical method, Formey's two essays were part of his dispute with Maupertuis about the nature and use of metaphysics, reflecting the ideological and methodological divide between Wolffian and anti-Wolffian scholars at the Berlin Academy and beyond. By elaborating on this context, the present chapter sets the scene for Formey's further activities as a Christian philosopher at the Berlin Academy before they are discussed in more detail in chapters 6 and 7.

Rationalism against scepticism: Formey's dictionary entry for 'God'

Between 1742 and 1747, Formey worked on a philosophical dictionary that was methodologically inspired by Pierre Bayle's *Dictionnaire historique et philosophique* and also relied in part for its content on the

---

seventeenth century: patterns of changes in early modern natural philosophy, ed. Peter R. Anstey and John A. Schuster (Dordrecht, 2005), p.165-83, and M. A. Stewart, 'Arguments for the existence of God: the British debate', in *The Cambridge history of eighteenth-century philosophy*, ed. K. Haakonssen, vol.2, p.711-30 (717-20).

3. On the context of the early Boyle Lectures see Ann Thomson, 'Les premières "Boyle Lectures" et les verités au-dessus de la raison', *Revue de la Société d'études anglo-américaines des XVIIe et XVIIIe siècles* 68 (2011), p.97-110.
4. See 'Dieu, (Métaph. & Théol.)', in *Encyclopédie*, ed. D. Diderot and J. D'Alembert, vol.4 (Paris, Briasson *et al.*, 1754), p.976-83.

German *Philosophisches Lexicon* by the Lutheran professor of theology Johann Georg Walch.[5] Although it was never published, it served as a source for more than a hundred articles for Diderot and D'Alembert's famous *Encyclopédie* that appeared from 1751 onwards.[6] In April 1747, Formey sold the manuscript of his so-called *Dictionnaire philosophique* to the *Encyclopédie*'s editors, who subsequently used it to enrich their translation of Chambers' *Cyclopaedia*.[7] At the time it was sold, Formey's dictionary consisted of about 1900 folio pages. In return for his contribution, Formey was acknowledged as a source in each article that had relied on his manuscript in one way or another (at least for the first volumes). The *Encyclopédie*'s article on God, entitled simply 'Dieu', which appeared in the fourth volume in 1754, is one of these articles that was taken (probably in its entirety) from Formey's manuscript. Therefore, it has to be considered as one of Formey's earliest engagements with the proofs of God's existence.

'Dieu' consists of two different parts: first, a refutation of Bayle's scepticism concerning the provability of God's existence; and second, an almost faithful reproduction of three different proofs of God from the end of the seventeenth and beginning of the eighteenth century. The three proofs are as follows: the metaphysical proof by the

5. On Formey's *Dictionnaire philosophique* see Eva Marcu, 'Un encyclopédiste oublié: Formey', *Revue d'histoire littéraire de la France* 53:3 (1953), p.296-305; François Moureau, 'L'*Encyclopédie* d'après les correspondants de Formey', *Recherches sur Diderot et l'Encyclopédie* 3 (1987), p.125-45; André Bandelier, 'L'encyclopédisme avant l'*Encyclopédie*: attentes genevoises et projet de "Dictionnaire philosophique" de J. H. S. Formey', in *L'Encyclopédie d'Yverdon et sa résonance européenne*, ed. J.-D. Candaux *et al.*, p.55-68, and, most recently, my own 'Stranding in the *Encyclopédie*: the case of Samuel Formey's philosophical dictionary, 1742-1747', in *Stranded encyclopedias, 1700-2000: exploring unfinished, unpublished, unsuccessful encyclopedic projects*, ed. Linn Holmberg and Maria Simonsen (Cham, 2021), p.37-71. It can be seen from his correspondence with Abraham Bocquet that Formey relied on translations of Walch's *Philosophisches Lexicon* for some of his articles; see Bocquet to Formey (21.5.1742 and 26.2.1745), FF.
6. See *Inventory of Diderot's Encyclopédie*, ed. Richard N. Schwab, Walter E. Rex and John Lough, vol.6, *SVEC* 93 (1972), p.100-101. The *Edition Numérique Collaborative et CRitique de l'Encyclopédie (ENCCRE)*, http://enccre.academie-sciences.fr/encyclopedie/ (last accessed 18 July 2023), lists 114 articles that quote Formey as a source.
7. See Louis-Philippe May, 'Histoire et sources de l'*Encyclopédie*: d'après le registre de délibérations et de comptes des éditeurs et un mémoire inédit', *Revue de synthèse* 58 (1938), p.5-30 (21), and the *Encyclopédie*'s editor's (Jean-Paul de Gua de Malves's) letter to Formey (29.4.1747), printed in Elisabeth Badinter, *Les Passions intellectuelles*, 2 vols (Paris, 2010), vol.1, p.401-402, n.1.

English theologian Samuel Clarke;[8] the historical proof by Calvinist pastor Isaac Jaquelot;[9] and the physical proof by the secretary of the Parisian Academy of Sciences Bernard de Fontenelle.[10] This thematic three-part division of the argument relied on the traditional early modern taxonomy of proofs of God's existence that can be found in the article entitled 'Gott' in Walch's *Philosophisches Lexicon*.[11] In the overarching narrative of 'Dieu', these three different proofs of God served as positive counterexamples to Bayle's scepticism and, thus, as argumentative support for Formey. However, in terms of Formey's view on natural theology, the article's first part – the refutation of Bayle – is of particular interest because it contains the central points of his vision concerning the rationality of God's existence. As such, it discloses his indebtedness to Cartesian metaphysics.

In contrast, Bayle's scepticism and related fideism resulted from the denial of Descartes's rationalism and its absolute trust in evidence.[12] Applied to religion, Bayle's doubt with regard to the capacities of human understanding led to his conviction that philosophy and Christian religion were not compatible. As far as he was concerned, faith could only emerge from a strict adherence to revelation and the authority of God because a rational proof of God's existence was not possible. Moreover, reason would be somewhat destructive to faith.[13] Most of Bayle's contemporary critics considered this fideist

8. Based on Samuel Clarke, *Traités de l'existence et des attributs de Dieu: des devoirs de la religion naturelle et des verités de la religion chrétienne, traduit de l'anglois par M. Ricotier* (1717), 2nd edn, 3 vols (Amsterdam, Bernard, 1727-1728). This was the translation of two of Clarke's Boyle Lectures from 1704 and 1705 that appeared under the title *A Discourse concerning the being and attributes of God, the obligations of natural religion, and the truth and certainty of the Christian revelation* (London, Botham & Knapton, 1705).
9. Based on Isaac Jaquelot, *Dissertations sur l'existence de Dieu, où l'on démontre cette verité par l'histoire universelle de la première antiquité du monde, par la refutation du systeme d'Epicure et de Spinosa, par les characteres de divinité qui se remarquent dans la religion des Juifs, et dans l'etablissement du christianisme* (The Hague, Foulque, 1697), 'Que le monde n'est pas de toute éternité; et que sa durée est conforme à la cronologie de Moïse', p.1-314.
10. Based on Bernard de Fontenelle's 'De l'existence de Dieu', in *Œuvres diverses de M. de Fontenelle* (1714), 3rd edn, 3 vols (The Hague, Gosse & Neaulme, 1728), vol.1, p.363-68.
11. See Johann Georg Walch, *Philosophisches Lexicon* (Leipzig, Gleditsch, 1726), 'Gott', p.1339-55 (1340).
12. See Popkin, 'Pierre Bayle's place in 17th-century scepticism', p.3.
13. See Stefano Brogi, *Teologia senza verità: Bayle contro i 'rationaux'* (Milan, 1998), p.26, 30-31 and 57, and Maria Rosa Antognazza, 'Reason, revelation and

claim to be hypocritical and accused him of atheism. Moreover, they regarded his dictionary in particular, with its complex entanglement of notes and references containing seemingly random discussions of the most important dogma, as a means of sowing sceptical and heterodox thought into its readers' minds.[14] Within the milieu of Huguenot erudition, Bayle's most famous critics were Jacques Bernard, Jean Le Clerc and Isaac Jaquelot, who were educated in Cartesian philosophy and belonged to the liberal strand of Calvinism; Le Clerc was Arminian, and the other two were influenced by Arminianism.[15] They defended the congruency of faith and reason and considered that reason supported the authority of religion, although they were also aware of the limits of reason.[16] Leibniz argued similarly against Bayle. His defence of the compatibility between faith and reason at the beginning of his famous *Essais de théodicée* was a reply to Bayle's *Dictionnaire historique et critique.*[17] In Formey's own lifetime, a lot of this criticism against Bayle was renewed and expanded by the Swiss philosopher Jean-Pierre de Crousaz, who in 1733 published his lengthy *Examen du pyrrhonisme ancien et moderne*, in which he attacked Bayle's pyrrhonism on all levels.[18] Like his Calvinist forebears, Crousaz upheld Cartesian epistemology and ontology as well as a rational religion.[19]

---

arguments for the deity', in *The Routledge companion to eighteenth-century philosophy*, ed. Aaron Garrett (London and New York, 2014), p.145-66 (146).

14. The intelligent composition of Bayle's *Dictionnaire historique et critique* has just recently been perfectly portrayed by Mara van der Lugt, *Bayle, Jurieu, and the Dictionnaire historique et critique* (Oxford, 2016), especially ch.1.
15. For a brief summary of the criticism of these authors see Anton Matytsin, *The Specter of skepticism in the age of Enlightenment* (Baltimore, MD, 2016), p.54-65. For a more in-depth analysis see Brogi, *Teologia senza verità*.
16. See Brogi, *Teologia senza verità*, p.28-29.
17. See Paul Rateau, 'Sur la conformité de la foi avec la raison: Leibniz contre Bayle', *Revue philosophique de la France et de l'étranger* 136:4 (2011), p.467-85.
18. Jean-Pierre de Crousaz, *Examen du pyrrhonisme ancien et moderne* (The Hague, Hondt, 1733). Crousaz's arguments are summarised in Antony McKenna, 'Les critiques de Bayle au 18e siècle: l'exemple de Jean-Pierre de Crousaz', in *Aufklärung und Aufklärungskritik in Frankreich: Selbstdeutungen des 18. Jahrhunderts im Spiegel der Zeitgenossen*, ed. Johannes Rohbeck and Sonia Asval (Berlin, 2003), p.35-62, and Anton Matytsin, 'The Protestant critics of Bayle at the dawn of the Enlightenment', in *Scepticism in the eighteenth century: Enlightenment, Lumières, Aufklärung*, ed. Sébastien Charles and Plinio J. Smith (Dordrecht, 2013), p.63-76.
19. With respect to the rejection of Bayle's religious viewpoints in particular, Crousaz followed in the footsteps of Le Clerc and Jaquelot; see Pierre Rétat, *Le 'Dictionnaire' de Bayle et la lutte philosophique au XVIIIe siècle* (Paris, 1971), p.159.

Formey was familiar with Crousaz's arguments against Bayle before he had, presumably, even read the *Dictionnaire historique et critique* himself.[20] Between 1733 and 1740 he worked through and shortened Crousaz's entire *Examen du pyrrhonisme*, a work that Formey himself said was the 'premier enfant de [s]a plume' and which eventually resulted in the publication of his *Triomphe de l'évidence* in 1756.[21] In the introduction to this abridgement, Formey joined Crousaz's harsh rejection of Bayle, and called the *Dictionnaire historique et critique* the most dangerous book that existed.[22]

Formey's own philosophical dictionary, the remnants of which are to be found in the published *Encyclopédie*, was in a number of respects a reply to Bayle's. On the one hand, he applied a critical method that was inspired by the alternation of text and comments in Bayle's *Dictionnaire historique et critique* and, on the other hand, in some of his articles, he also engaged critically with pyrrhonism and Bayle's sceptical arguments. Formey's article on God – 'Dieu' in the *Encyclopédie* – illustrates very well this formal and content-related engagement with Bayle.[23] In this, Formey discussed two core arguments that formed the basis of Bayle's critical position with regard to natural theology: the irrationality and the non-innate character of human beings' idea of God. Bayle addressed these issues in the article entitled 'Simonides' in his *Dictionnaire historique et critique*[24] as well as in his *Continuation des pensées diverses sur la comète*,[25] the two main sources to which Formey referred in 'Dieu'. The arguments developed

20. Formey only obtained a copy of the 1730 edition of the *Dictionnaire historique et critique* in late 1740; see Formey to Prosper Marchand (30.12.1740), in Jan Schillings, 'La correspondance entre Formey et Marchand (1736-1749)', *Lias* 39:2 (2012), p.231-320 (247).
21. See Formey, *Le Triomphe de l'évidence*, 2 vols (Berlin, Lange, 1756). For the history of the work's genesis see the preface to its first volume.
22. Formey, 'Introduction', in *Triomphe de l'évidence*, vol.1, p.lxviii-lxix. For a similar viewpoint on Bayle and his method see also Formey, *Histoire abrégée*, p.247-48.
23. Other examples are 'Dialéle, (Logique)', in *Encyclopédie*, vol.4 (Paris, Briasson et al., 1754), p.935, and 'Epoque, (Logiq.)', in *Encyclopédie*, vol.5 (Paris, Briasson et al., 1755), p.831-33.
24. Pierre Bayle, 'Simonides', in *Dictionnaire historique et critique*, 5th edn, 4 vols (Amsterdam, Compagnie des libraires, 1740), vol.4, p.208-15, The ARTFL Project, https://artfl-project.uchicago.edu/content/dictionnaire-de-bayle (last accessed 18 July 2023).
25. Pierre Bayle, *Continuation des pensées diverses, écrites à un docteur de Sorbonne à l'occasion de la comète qui parut au mois de decembre 1680, ou Réponse à plusieurs dificultez que Monsieur *** a proposées à l'auteur*, 2 vols (Rotterdam, Leers, 1705).

by Bayle in these two instances relied on Cicero's *De natura deo*[26] and touched upon the question of whether human beings in general and common people in particular were able to comprehend the existence of God. Contrary to Bayle, Formey answered this question positively by claiming the notion of God's existence was instilled in the human mind by nature: 'Je dis donc & je soûtiens que l'existence de Dieu est une vérité que la nature a mise dans l'esprit de tous les hommes, qui ne se sont point étudiés à en démentir les sentimens.'[27] Moreover, he emphasised the exclusively rational character of this knowledge because it resulted from the rationality of human nature.[28]

Formey's assertion that the knowledge of God's existence was innate was a common stance in (orthodox) theology and scholastic philosophy, and was defended by Calvin as well as by Descartes. In fact, the demonstration that the notion of God was innate was an essential element of Descartes's famous ontological proof that he developed in his fifth meditation. This allowed him to claim that God's essence was real instead of only imagined, and his proof depended on this being recognised.[29] However, since the appearance of Locke's empiricist approach to human understanding at the latest, innatism had been in decline. This decline was also reflected in the article 'Gott' in Walch's *Philosophisches Lexicon*, in which Descartes's ontological proof was said to be logically insufficient, mainly because its core assumption, the innate idea of God, could not be proved.[30] Formey actually upheld innatism in his philosophical dictionary, and this betrays a rather conservative approach. Moreover, a few lines further in 'Dieu', he confirmed his plea for innatism in his discussion of Bayle's refutation of the proof of God via the *consensus omnium*, that is, the universal agreement that there was a God.[31] This traditional

---

26. In his *Continuation des pensées diverses*, vol.1, p.82, Bayle referred to the anterior article 'Simonides' to demonstrate how difficult it was to define God.
27. 'Dieu', p.976 (§10).
28. See 'Dieu', p.977 (§17).
29. See Emanuela Scribano, *L'Existence de Dieu: histoire de la preuve ontologique de Descartes à Kant* (Paris, 2002), p.73-74, and Emanuela Scribano, 'Ontological argument', in *The Cambridge Descartes lexicon*, ed. Lawrence Nolan (Cambridge, 2015), p.544-49 (545).
30. See Walch, 'Gott', p.1340-41.
31. Bayle's refutation was based on three arguments exhibited in his *Continuation des pensées diverses*, vol.1, p.55, 60, 63, 109 and 111: the existence of atheism; the difficulty of discerning how human beings obtained the idea of God; and the epistemological weakness of the proof from the *consensus omnium*.

moral argument lost its persuasiveness during the seventeenth century,[32] and its capacity to prove that human knowledge of God's existence was innate has been particularly challenged.[33] Formey, however, held that there existed universal and stable knowledge about God that had not been inculcated in human beings through education and therefore was innate.[34]

Formey's objection to Bayle's claim of the irrationality of knowledge about God also resonated with traditional Cartesian assumptions. 'Dieu' begins with anecdotes about two ancient philosophers, Thales and Simonides, who were asked by their sovereigns to define God but were not able to give a satisfactory reply. Bayle used these same anecdotes in his *Dictionnaire historique et critique* to emphasise that there was a difference between believing in God, as every unsophisticated Christian did, and having evident knowledge of God's existence and attributes, as the pagan philosophers Simonides and Thales tried to gain. In Bayle's view, the latter was simply not possible, and this was why the two philosophers refrained from giving an answer to their sovereigns.[35] In a fideist reading, this ancient anecdote exemplified the fundamental impossibility of explaining God philosophically.

In contrast, Formey suggested a different interpretation of this anecdote. He argued that the nature of God remained incomprehensible to a large extent, but that there were, nevertheless, several things that human beings were able to comprehend about Him, namely, His existence, intelligence, wisdom and power.[36] A similar claim was also contained in the fictional answer that Formey suggested to Simonides in the *Triomphe de l'évidence*, his abridgement of Crousaz's treatise against pyrrhonism. Here, Formey argued that Simonides, when asked to define God, could have easily cited God's existence, His perfections and His creations, all of which were 'verités capitales'.[37] Moreover, in 'Dieu', Formey also accounted for the origin of this knowledge; it resulted from the similarity between God and His creatures. According to Formey, all of God's attributes were also contained in His creatures, although to a considerably different degree.[38] The argument that God's intelligence,

---

32. See Brogi, *Teologia senza verità*, p.89-90.
33. See Brogi, *Teologia senza verità*, p.87.
34. See 'Dieu', p.977 (§18-19).
35. See Bayle, 'Simonides', p.211. See Brogi, *Teologia senza verità*, p.32.
36. See 'Dieu', p.976 (§1).
37. See Formey, *Triomphe de l'évidence*, vol.2, p.114.
38. 'Dieu', p.976 (§1 and 9).

4. The existence of God and the superiority of metaphysics

omniscience, goodness and omnipotence were intelligible if He was assumed to be the Creator of the world was also maintained by Jaquelot in his *Conformité de la foi avec la raison*, in which he had opposed Bayle in 1705.[39]

Furthermore, according to Formey, God's eternal existence in particular was comprehensible to human beings because it emerged from the human perception of a first cause, a cause that was responsible for the existence of human beings and for all the marvels of nature.[40] Bayle also recognised the fact that everything had a first cause, yet did not consider that this could account for God's existence. In his view, to be certain that this first cause was identical to God, its nature had to be properly defined, something that all philosophers had as yet failed to do.[41] Crousaz replied to Bayle's criticism of the argument in relation to the first cause, and Formey replicated this in his *Triomphe de l'évidence* by saying that human beings were able to apprehend the intelligence and liberty of the first cause through observation of the harmonious order of nature.[42] By contrast, Jaquelot's reply to Bayle's criticism was slightly different. The former admitted that the notion of God could not simply be deduced from the acknowledgement of a first cause; rather, it had to result from the persuasion that an infinitely perfect being existed.[43]

Finally, Formey also emphasised his conviction that the recognition of God's existence was bound to human understanding in his reply to Bayle's view on atheism that is also contained in the article 'Dieu'. In order to refute the proof of God via the *consensus omnium*, Bayle referred to the existence of atheism. Formey, however, argued that atheism was an acquired habit that resulted from the deliberate misuse (or rather absence of use) of human understanding.[44] Moreover, he underlined that only the intellect could be the origin of the idea of God's existence, whereas the passions, by which humans could potentially be corrupted, inevitably led to error.[45] The obligation to

---

39. See Jaquelot, *Conformité de la foi avec la raison*, p.11-14.
40. See 'Dieu', p.976 (§2 and 9).
41. See Bayle, *Continuation des pensées diverses*, vol.1, p.80. Compare with Brogi, *Teologia senza verità*, p.137-38.
42. See Formey, *Triomphe de l'évidence*, vol.2, p.88-89.
43. See Jaquelot, *Conformité de la foi avec la raison*, p.6-7.
44. See 'Dieu', p.977 (§17). To express his vision that reason was a universal human capacity Formey stated: 'Les hommes, des qu'ils sont hommes, c'est-à-dire capables de société & de raisonnement, reconnoissent un Dieu.'
45. See 'Dieu', p.977-78 (§20).

apprehend God via reason instead of the senses was also emphasised by Jaquelot; in his *Dissertations sur l'existence de Dieu* he similarly exhorted his readers not to let their heart and their passions interfere with reason in this matter.[46]

Consequently, in 'Dieu', Formey developed the foundations of a natural theology that relied on Cartesian rationalism in general and on Descartes's ontological proof in particular, according to which God's existence could be deduced from human beings' innate notion of the divine with the help of reason. The second part of 'Dieu', in which three different proofs of God's existence were noted, shows, however, that Formey had already gone partly beyond the Cartesian tradition that he had probably adopted from Crousaz and the seventeenth-century rationalist Calvinist theologians. In addition to referring to the justification of the biblical chronology by Isaac Jaquelot, who belonged to this tradition, Formey engaged with the above-mentioned English theologian and famous Boyle lecturer Samuel Clarke, whose cosmological or a posteriori proof of God's existence resembled to a certain extent the Leibnizian notion of an independent, necessary and free God in a contingent universe, but also contained visible traces of Newtonian physico-theology. Moreover, in 'Dieu', Formey quoted the attempt of Bernard de Fontenelle, the secretary of the Parisian Academy of Sciences, to prove the existence of God through the observation of the generation of animals. Fontenelle, who was suspected of criticising religion covertly, also developed a proof that bore elements of physico-theology but went further than Clarke's because Fontenelle's proof contained a naturalist description of the universe and expressed the notion of God as the organiser of nature's order.[47] Interestingly, Formey's early engagement with the proofs of God in his philosophical dictionary contained no overt traces of Wolff's Latin natural theology that had been published in two volumes in 1736 and 1737.

In point of fact, Formey's engagement with Wolff's natural theology[48]

---

46. See Jaquelot, 'Préface', in *Dissertations sur l'existence de Dieu*, sig.**4v.
47. For the detailed interpretation of the different proofs of God that were contained in the second part of 'Dieu', see my 'Dossier critique de l'article DIEU, (Métaph. & Théol.) (*Encyclopédie*, t.IV, p.976a-983a)' (2019), in *Edition Numérique Collaborative et CRitique de l'Encyclopédie (ENCCRE)*, http://enccre.academie-sciences.fr/encyclopedie/article/v4-2500-0/ (last accessed 18 July 2023).
48. For an analysis of Wolff's natural theology, see Ecole, 'Introduction de l'éditeur', in Wolff, *Theologia naturalis: pars prior*, p.v-cxvi, and 'Introduction de l'éditeur', in Wolff, *Theologia naturalis, methodo scientifica pertractata: pars posterior qua existentia et attributa Dei ex notione entis perfectissimi et natura animae demonstrantur*

dated back to 1747 when he presented two essays on the existence of God at the Academy.[49] In these essays, he distanced himself from Cartesian natural theology, although remaining indebted to the essential premises of Cartesian rationalism. Like Leibniz and Wolff, Formey criticised Descartes's ontological proof for its incompleteness[50] and weak evidence. As Formey claimed, all the attributes of God that resulted from Descartes's notion of the perfect being were only hypothetical because the notion itself lacked proof.[51] To make Descartes's proof valid, Formey was convinced that the Wolffian method of common notions had to be applied to it, a claim that he tried to demonstrate in his first essay. Moreover, Formey overcame Descartes's notion of human beings' idea of God being innate and, instead, portrayed – in line with Wolff – the notion of God's essence as an act of comprehension. More precisely, in his first essay, 'Les preuves de l'existence de Dieu, ramenées aux notions communes', he

---

(2nd edn, 1741), ed. Jean Ecole, in *Christian Wolff: Gesammelte Werke*, ed. J. Ecole et al., section 2, vol.8 (Hildesheim, 1980), p.v-lxxix. More recently, Robert Theis, '"Ut & scias, & credas, quae simul sciri & credi possunt" Aspekte der Wolffschen Theologie', in *Die natürliche Theologie bei Christian Wolff*, ed. Michael Albrecht (Hamburg, 2011), p.17-39, and Theis, 'Theologie'.

49. Formey, 'Les preuves de l'existence de Dieu, ramenées aux notions communes', in *Histoire de l'Académie royale des sciences et belles lettres de Berlin* (1747; Berlin, Haude, 1749), p.341-64, and 'Examen de la preuve qu'on tire des fins de la nature, pour établir l'existence de Dieu', in *Histoire de l'Académie royale des sciences et belles lettres de Berlin* (1747; Berlin, Haude, 1749), p.365-84. Formey presented each of the two discourses in two parts at the Academy's assembly, the first on 27 April and 29 June 1747 and the second on 14 September and 2 November 1747. The two essays were later republished, again successively, in Formey, *Mélanges philosophiques*, 2 vols (Leiden, E. Luzac, 1754), vol.1, p.1-42 and 43-76.

50. Formey mentioned this aspect in particular in 'Preuves de l'existence', p.363-64. Compare with Wolff, *Theologia naturalis: pars posterior*, 'Dedicatio': 'Cartesius, fulgens istud Galliae sidus, ex notione entis perfectissimi existentiam Numinis supremi demonstrare aggressus est; sed foetum in partu destituit' ('Descartes was close to proving the existence of the supreme being from the notion of the perfect being, but his argument died almost before it was made'; my translation). In Formey's manuscript of his essay, he made a reference to this sentence; see 'Discours sur les preuves de l'existence de Dieu', in BBAW, I. Historische Abteilung, PAW (1700-1811), Ms C5, vol.1 (1747), I-M 345, f.113r.

51. Formey, 'Examen de la preuve', p.366. Compare with Leibniz's criticism according to which Descartes had not succeeded in proving the reality of God's possible existence; see Antognazza, 'Arguments for the existence of God', p.736, and Robert Merrihew Adams, *Leibniz: determinist, theist, idealist* (New York, 1994), p.135.

demonstrated how the notion of God was obtained by deducing His essential attributes from the essential attributes observed in human beings. The attributes of an infinite being like God had to be the diametrical opposite of those of finite beings like humans:

> La notion de l'Etre réellement infini s'acquiert d'une toute autre maniere, & bien loin que ce soit en ajoutant continuellement, & en amplifiant à perte de vuë, les proprietés que nous remarquons en nous mêmes, & dans les objets qui nous environnent, il faut au contraire prendre le contrepied, & attribuer à l'Etre indépendant des proprietés, diamétralement opposées à celles que nous présentent les choses dépendantes.[52]

This method had its foundation in the assumption that God's essence was similar to the essence of the human soul, despite the latter's limitations as compared with the infinite God, an assumption that Wolff had already put forward in his *Metaphysik*.[53] In the second part of his *Theologia naturalis* in 1737, Wolff relied on this method for his a priori proof that started with the notion of the perfect being.[54] However, Formey slightly modified Wolff's description of this method; whereas the latter argued that the idea of divine attributes was obtained if a person imagined their own attributes stripped of their limitations, Formey held that a person had to conceive of opposite attributes. Wolff used the metaphor of the 'world as a mirror' to portray being able to infer God's attributes via the observation of His creatures,[55] a metaphor that Formey also cited at the end of his first essay.[56]

Despite his criticism of Descartes's ontological proof and his shift in thought to align with Wolff's natural theology, Formey considered Wolff's deduction of God's attributes, which was based on

---

52. Formey, 'Preuves de l'existence', p.350.
53. See Christian Wolff, *Vernünfftige Gedancken von Gott, der Welt und der Seele des Menschen, auch allen Dingen überhaupt* (11th edn, 1751), ed. Charles A. Corr, in *Christian Wolff: Gesammelte Werke*, ed. Jean Ecole *et al.*, section 1, vol.2 (Hildesheim, 1983) (subsequently quoted as *Metaphysik*), §1067 and 1076-77. See Matteo Favaretti Camposampiero, 'Der psychotheologische Weg: Wolffs Rechtfertigung der Gotteserkenntnis', in *Die natürliche Theologie bei Christian Wolff*, ed. M. Albrecht, p.71-96 (72-75).
54. See Ecole, 'Introduction de l'éditeur', in Wolff, *Theologia naturalis: pars posterior*, p.vi-vii, and Theis, 'Theologie', p.228-31.
55. See Wolff, *Metaphysik*, §1046 and 1079.
56. See Formey, 'Preuves de l'existence', p.363.

the similarity between God and humans, to be based on Descartes's rationalism. More precisely, he equated the Cartesian notion of the rational human being – as contained in the famous *cogito ergo sum* – with Wolff's fundamental notion that the comprehension of God's existence resulted from human beings' own existence.[57] Furthermore, Formey showed that he clearly perceived a Cartesian legacy in the principle of sufficient reason that was central to Leibniz's and Wolff's metaphysics in general and Wolff's a posteriori proof of God in particular. According to Formey, Descartes gave the impetus for this principle of causality that Leibniz further elaborated on and that finally obtained demonstrative force through Wolff.[58] Finally, the whole purpose of Formey's two essays in 1747 was to put forward 'full evidence' in support of the argument for God's existence, a purpose that corresponded to his Cartesian-inspired rejection of Bayle's scepticism. Hence, although Formey changed his philosophical preference from Cartesian to Wolffian natural theology in 1747, his fundamental aim to protect religion against scepticism remained unchanged.

Metaphysics against physico-theology: Formey's revision of the teleological proof of God

Nevertheless, the immediate target of Formey's two essays in 1747 was not the sceptics or unbelievers. Instead, he was critical of other proofs of the existence of God that in his view were vulnerable to attack from sceptics and unbelievers. In particular, his focus was on the physico-theological proof and its epistemological insufficiency.

Formey's epistemological criticism of the physico-theological proof was fully developed in his second essay, entitled 'Examen de la preuve qu'on tire des fins de la nature, pour établir l'existence de Dieu', whereas his first essay, 'Les preuves de l'existence de Dieu, ramenées aux notions communes', contained more general claims with regard to the right method of establishing proofs of the existence of God. The manuscripts of both essays still exist in the Academy's archives. A comparison between the manuscripts and the printed versions reveals that Formey originally intended them to appear in reverse order. Moreover, he probably wrote the 'Examen de la preuve' as an introduction to a different work and modified it later to fit the format of an academic

---

57. See Formey, 'Preuves de l'existence', p.363.
58. See Formey, 'Examen de la preuve', p.372.

essay. The handwritten version of the 'Examen de la preuve' contains a more elaborate introduction as well as a substantial second part in which Formey underlined his general support for natural philosophical research on God's purposes. In the printed version, this second part has been cut, and the essay has been infused with the defence of metaphysics that was contained in the 'Preuves de l'existence'. In this version, it appears rather as if Formey's discussion of God's existence in 1747 endorsed the subjugation of natural philosophy to the supremacy of metaphysics. Moreover, the manuscript of the 'Examen de la preuve' betrays the fact that Formey's original intention had not been to engage in a debate with the Academy's president Maupertuis over the role of metaphysics. This meaning was added to the text only for publication. Thus, before analysing the difference of opinion between Formey and Maupertuis, light needs to be shed on the origins and intentions of Formey's criticism of the physico-theological argument by also taking into account the second essay's unpublished parts.

What the handwritten and printed versions of the two essays have in common is their plea for the cosmological or a posteriori proof of God's existence, which was stated initially by Leibniz and then elaborated on by Wolff. Basically, this proof relied on the observation of a contingent world order from which the necessary existence of God was inferred. As Formey outlined in his first essay, this proof was established with the help of two interconnected basic notions: the principle of contradiction, which says that two contradictory things cannot both be true at the same time; and the principle of sufficient reason, which says that everything that exists must have a sufficient reason for doing so. From these two notions he inferred another central concept according to which only the essence of a being is absolutely necessary, while every externally induced modification of it is not absolutely necessary. The proof started from the observation that the universe consisted of a chain of finite interdependent beings. Because the existence of those beings was not contained in their essences and because nothing could emerge out of nothing, these beings must have developed for an external reason. This external reason must itself be an absolutely necessary and self-existent being because it contains the reason for its own existence in its essence. As Formey concluded: 'Puisque toutes ces choses existent, & que le néant ne sauroit rien produire, il existe nécessairement un Etre, qui ne tient son existence que de lui-même.'[59]

59. Formey, 'Preuves de l'existence', p.355-57; compare with 'Examen de la preuve', p.379.

4. The existence of God and the superiority of metaphysics

In Wolff's view, the cosmological argument from contingency was the only relevant and necessary proof for establishing the truth of God's existence.[60] In 1718, in his *Ratio praelectionum*, he rejected all other existing proofs because of their formal mistakes and because of their inability to prove categorically what they assumed.[61] This rejection also included the physico-theological or teleological argument, according to which the order observed in nature allowed the existence of the author of this order to be inferred. In Wolff's view, the flaw of this argument was that it lacked proof that the order in nature was not necessary but contingent and, thus, failed to justify the necessary existence of the world's creator.[62] Wolff's rejection of the physico-theological argument resulted in criticism from his Pietist and Lutheran orthodox adversaries, who accused him of blasphemy and of destroying one of the most understandable proofs of God's existence.[63] In 1730, Wolff replied to such criticism in one of his essays in the *Horae subsecivae marburgenses*[64] by emphasising the importance of reducing the physico-theological proof to the proof from contingency to protect it from the attacks of Spinozists and fatalists who assumed a necessary world order.[65] Wolff's demonstration of a corrected version of the physico-theological proof had, thus, two different targets: unbelievers and critics of religion on the one side and orthodox theologians on the other.

In contrast, Formey, who drew on Wolff's essay in the *Horae subsecivae marburgenses* for his own 'Examen de la preuve' in 1747, fashioned his criticism of the physico-theological proof first and

---

60. See Michael Albrecht, 'Einleitung', in *Die natürliche Theologie bei Christian Wolff*, ed. M. Albrecht, p.9-16 (10), and Theis, 'Ut & scias, & credas', p.27-28.
61. See Theis, 'Theologie', p.221-23.
62. See Fernando Luigi Marcolungo, 'Christian Wolff und der physiko-theologische Beweis', in *Die natürliche Theologie bei Christian Wolff*, ed. M. Albrecht, p.147-61 (151).
63. The criticism against Wolff and his early replies to it were also sketched out in Walch, 'Gott', p.1348-49. Walch focused on the criticism made by his father-in-law, the Lutheran theologian Johann Franz Budde.
64. See Christian Wolff, 'De methodo existentiam Dei ex ordine naturae demonstrandi', in *Horae subsecivae*, vol.34:2, p.660-83. The following reference is from a German translation: 'Wie fern man aus der Ordnung der Natur beweisen könne, daß ein Gott seye', in *Gesammelte kleine philosophische Schriften, welche meistens aus dem Lateinischen übersezt, vierter Theil* (1739), in *Christian Wolff: Gesammelte Werke*, ed. Jean Ecole *et al.*, section 1, vol.21:4 (Hildesheim, 1981), p.233-75.
65. See Wolff, 'Wie fern man aus der Ordnung der Natur', p.234 and 240-41.

foremost as a criticism of natural philosophers' superficiality. More precisely, he began his essay (i.e. its manuscript version) by citing the pioneers of physico-theology in seventeenth-century England and Holland: the theologian and naturalist John Ray,[66] the Boyle lecturer William Derham[67] and the physician and experimental philosopher Bernard Nieuwentijt,[68] as well as their more recent German followers, the classical philologist Johann Albert Fabricius, who had written a theology of water in 1730,[69] and the Lutheran pastor Friedrich Christian Lesser, who had published a theology of insects in 1738.[70] Formey declared their works to be excellent, yet too vague in terms of the teleological proof of the existence of God.[71] Furthermore, Formey aimed a subtle attack at Newton, who as a physicist had glorified the physico-theological proof despite its philosophical vagueness. In the manuscript of Formey's essay, which at the beginning contains two additional handwritten pages that the printed version does not have, he first showed his understanding of the impression the marvels of nature had made on Newton:

> Je ne suis point surpris que de toutes les preuves de l'Existence de Dieu, celles des causes finales ait fait les plus vives impressions sur l'Esprit de divers Philosophes distingués, et en particulier sur celui de Newton. [...] Ses connoissances sublimes dans la Geometrie et dans

66. See John Ray, *The Wisdom of God manifested in the works of the Creation* (London, Smith, 1691).
67. See William Derham, *Physico-theology, or a Demonstration of the being and attributes of God from his works of Creation* (London, Innys, 1713).
68. See Bernard Nieuwentijt, *The Religious philosopher, or the Right way of contemplating the works of the creator*, 3 vols (London, Senex & Taylor, 1718-1719). This was a translation from the 1715 Dutch original by Johan Chamberlayne. On Nieuwentijt, see Riek Vermij, 'Nature in defence of Scripture: physico-theology and experimental philosophy in the work of Bernard Nieuwentijt', in *The Book of nature in early modern and modern history*, ed. Klaas van Berkel and Arjo Vanderjagt (Leuven, 2006), p.83-96.
69. See Johann Albert Fabricius, *Hydrotheologie, oder Versuch durch aufmercksame Betrachtung der Wasser, die Menschen zur Liebe und Bewunderung ihres gütigsten, weisesten, mächtigsten Schöpfers zu ermuntern* (Hamburg, König & Richter, 1730).
70. See Friedrich Christian Lesser, *Insecto-Theologia, oder Vernunfft- und schrifftmäßiger Versuch wie ein Mensch durch aufmercksame Betrachtung derer sonst wenig geachteten Insecten zu lebendiger Erkänntniß und Bewunderung der Allmacht, Weißheit, der Güte und Gerechtigkeit des grossen Gottes gelangen könnte* (Frankfurt am Main and Leipzig, Blochberger, 1738).
71. See Formey, 'Discours sur les fins de la nature', in BBAW, I. Historische Abteilung, PAW (1700-1811), Ms C5, vol.1 (1747), I-M 346, f.192r.

4. The existence of God and the superiority of metaphysics 125

cette partie de la Physique sur laquelle les Mathematiques répandent de si grandes clartés, lui avoient découvert des beautés, des marques evidentes d'ordre et de regularité, qui echappent à des yeux moins clairvoyans.

As emerges from the footnotes in the handwritten version of the second essay, Formey's engagement with Newton's natural philosophy was inspired by Voltaire, who in his *Métaphysique de Newton* had argued that Newton's physico-theological proof of God's existence had previously been rejected because it was based on sensory experience.[72] However, as far as Formey was concerned, the reliance on sensory experience was not the crux of the problem with Newton's proof. Rather, it was that Newton and others had not traced their empirical observations back to the most simple metaphysical notions and Newton had, thus, failed to give his proof the strength of a solid scientific base.

> Ce n'est point l'evidence de cette Demonstration, qui l'a fait tomber dans le mépris [...]; c'est que la plupart des Philosophes, qui ont exalté cette preuve par dessus toutes les autres, se sont jettés dans une espece de déclamation, c'est qu'ils se sont hatés d'édifier, avant que d'avoir posé des fondemens assès solides, c'est qu'ils ont negligé de remonter aux premieres notions evidentes, sur lesquelles cette preuve s'appuye et qui seules en font une démonstration invincible. Par ce moyen les causes finales sont devenuës suspectes, je l'avoue, à quelques Génies, dont la pénétration assès étendue pour demeler des défauts dans la maniere dont on les mettoit en œuvre, n'a pas suffi pour redresser ces défauts, et rendre à ce bel argument sa véritable force. Mais heureusement, il s'en est trouvé d'autres, qui se sont bien gardés d'abandonner à la légère un principe de conviction aussi efficace; sentant au contraire toute son importance, ils ont fait leurs efforts pour le mettre désormais au dessus de toute exception; et ce sont aussi nos vuës.[73]

Formey's appraisal of the Newtonian physico-theological argument was, therefore, not absolute; he acknowledged its importance, yet called for it to be grounded in metaphysical principles to make it

---

72. From 1741 onwards, Voltaire's *Métaphysique de Newton* was published as an introduction to his *Elémens de la philosophie de Newton* (Paris, Prault). See *Eléments de la philosophie de Newton*, ed. Robert L. Walters and William H. Barber, in *The Complete works of Voltaire*, vol.15 (Oxford, 1992), p.197.
73. Formey, 'Discours sur les fins de la nature', f.192r-v. Compare with 'Examen de la preuve', p.365, from which this entire passage, including the mention of Newton, is omitted.

more convincing. Actually, Formey followed here a common trend in German philosophy in which, since the days of Leibniz, Newton's natural philosophy in general had been criticised for its lack of a metaphysical foundation.[74] With respect to the physico-theological argument, Formey saw himself as inheriting the legacy of those scholars who, in his view, had reworked the argument to elevate it above all doubt, and by this he certainly meant Wolff. Therefore, in his essay, Formey portrayed the Wolffian proof through contingency as the only legitimate one. The key element in his account was the Leibnizian principle of sufficient reason, which he considered to be the most general and self-evident principle, and it was on this principle that every a posteriori proof of God's existence was, eventually, based.[75] Hence, in his view, those who defended the physico-theological proof were mistaken when they denied its dependency on this metaphysical root.[76] Having stated this, Formey then went on to 'correct' the physico-theological proof by applying the principle of sufficient reason to it, as Wolff had done before him in his *Horae subsecivae marburgenses*. His crucial claim here was to state that an observable order in nature was not sufficient for inferring the existence of an author of this order.[77] To be able to infer such an existence, a precise notion of this order had to be established and, more importantly, it had to be shown that this order was contingent by nature because only the contingency of the order made it possible to conceive of the necessity of its author:

> Tout ce qui résulteroit de la notion d'un semblable Ordre [un ordre unique qui ne peut pas être substitué par un autre], c'est que l'Existence de Dieu y seroit possible, mais qu'elle ne seroit pas nécessaire, & que par conséquent on n'auroit aucun droit d'argumenter de l'Ordre à l'Auteur de l'Ordre. Cet Auteur ne devient nécessaire, & son existence ne se démontre, qu'après qu'on a mis en évidence la contingence de l'Ordre & des Fins, qui s'observent dans l'Univers.[78]

In turn, Formey argued that the contingency of the world's order could only be accomplished if the laws of movement were contingent

---

74. See Thomas Ahnert, 'Newton in the German-speaking lands', in *The Reception of Isaac Newton in Europe*, ed. Helmut Pulte and Scott Mandelbrote, 3 vols (London, 2019), vol.1, p.41-58 (49-50).
75. See Formey, 'Examen de la preuve', p.369.
76. See Formey, 'Examen de la preuve', p.373.
77. See Formey, 'Examen de la preuve', p.377. Compare with Wolff, 'Wie fern man aus der Ordnung der Natur', p.237.
78. Formey, 'Examen de la preuve', p.378-79.

4. The existence of God and the superiority of metaphysics

too, and this was only the case if they were rooted in the principle of sufficient reason (instead of the principle of least action, as will be shown below).[79] The reason he provided for this was that the principle of sufficient reason naturally and always accounted for hypothetical necessities or contingency.[80] This statement relied on the Leibnizian theory of existence, according to which sufficient reason was what made potential existence, which was contained in the essence of each thing, become real existence. In Leibnizian logic, this meant that everything that could be explained through sufficient reason was only hypothetically and not absolutely necessary. Therefore, Formey's revision of the physico-theological argument corresponded to Wolff's undertaking to demonstrate the contingency of the order in nature, an undertaking that itself relied on Leibnizian notions. Like Wolff, Formey claimed this undertaking was meant to prevent the proof's denigration by Spinozists and fatalists, who would abuse the physico-theological argument by pretending that it demonstrated a determinate world order and, thus, the non-existence of an omnipotent and independent creator.[81] The final step of the proof, namely, the demonstration that the author of this contingent order was the Christian God, consisted in showing that the attributes of the natural theologically proved God were identical with the characteristics that Scripture ascribed to God.[82] Formey also adopted this element from Wolff's *Horae subsecivae marburgenses* and, thus, he followed Wolff in assuming compatibility between natural theological and revealed knowledge about God.

Although the printed version of the 'Examen de la preuve' ended after the demonstration of God's necessary existence was accomplished – as did Wolff's *Horae subsecivae marburgenses* – the manuscript went on for a further seventeen pages. Here, Formey continued to defend the order in nature, which he described in terms of Leibniz's universal harmony, countering accusations of fatalism.[83]

In addition, the second, handwritten, part of Formey's essay provides important insights into his perception of the role of

---

79. See Formey, 'Examen de la preuve', p.379. Compare with Wolff, 'Wie fern man aus der Ordnung der Natur', p.259.
80. See Formey, 'Examen de la preuve', p.379 and 380.
81. See Formey, 'Examen de la preuve', p.376.
82. See Formey, 'Examen de la preuve', p.383. Compare with Wolff, 'Wie fern man aus der Ordnung der Natur', p.270-72.
83. See Formey, 'Discours sur les fins de la nature', f.205*v*-207*r*.

the natural theologian and of the relationship between natural philosophy and religion. More precisely, Formey defended the legitimacy of natural theology in general and physico-theology in particular. First, he distinguished between the popular and the philosophical recognition of God's existence via the observation of the marvels of nature, acknowledging that everybody was able to perceive God's wisdom in nature. However, compared with the ordinary people, philosophers would have a different kind of admiration for God because of their more profound and clear insights into nature:

> Nous appercevons au premier coup d'œil assès de merveilles dans l'Univers, pour etre disposés à recevoir cette verité [que l'univers soit l'ouvrage d'une sagesse et d'une puissance sans bornes]; mais une etude suivie et approfondie des œuvres de la Nature la met dans une toute autre evidence. Chaque decouverte d'Astronomie, de Physique, chaque pas dans le Sanctuaire de la Nature decouvre des rapports et des usages nouveaux, qui nous etonnent et nous ravissent d'admiration et de reconnoissance. Ainsi quoique cette admiration et cette reconnoissance s'excitent naturellement dans tous les hommes, les plus grossiers memes et les plus ignorans, à la vue de ce soleil, de cette Terre, de tous ces biens qu'une main liberale a repandue dans le Monde, il est pourtant vrai qu'un Philosophe, a proportion de ses lumieres, admire tout autrement la Divinité que le vulgaire, que c'est à lui proprement qu'il appartient de la celebrer dignement, et qu'il peut seul entonner un hymne à la gloire de ces perfections, dont il se forme des idées egalement distinctes & satisfaisantes.[84]

Thus, in Formey's view, the obligation to worship God and praise His perfections arose from the philosopher's extraordinary ability to discover God in a philosophical sense. With this claim, Formey gave legitimacy to natural theological research.

Formey then strengthened this legitimacy against potential objections. One crucial objection to physico-theology was that the philosophical attempt to explain divine wisdom, which appeared in the Creation, ran contrary to accepting what was taught in the Bible, namely, the enigmatic character of God's purposes and their unintelligibility for human beings. Would the pursuit of physico-theological research, therefore, be a denial of the Bible? Formey acknowledged the limitations of human beings' understanding in

---

84. Formey, 'Discours sur les fins de la nature', f.204r.

general and the inability of natural philosophical research to ever fully penetrate God's unlimited wisdom.[85] However, he denied that these limits of the human capacity to comprehend God meant prohibiting the further scrutiny of God's purposes in the world. On the contrary, prohibiting the scrutiny of the order in nature would contradict God's aim of revealing His perfection through Creation:

> Disons donc que tous les details de la Sagesse Divine, l'assemblage de toutes ses fins et de tous ses moyens, sont et seront à jamais imperscrutables pour nous. Leur etude suffira pour nous occuper dans toute l'eternité et nous ne l'espuiserons jamais. Mais disons en meme tems que ce n'est point une raison qui doive nous détourner d'en faire l'objet de nos recherches et de notre Meditation. Si cette occupation nous etoit interdite, ou qu'il fut impossible d'y vaquer, il en resulteroit l'absurde consequence que Dieu a manqué son but, puisque nous avons vu qu'il n'a pu s'en proposer d'autre dans la Creation de l'Univers, que la manifestation de ses perfections et de sa gloire. Or cette manifestation ne sçauroit consister que dans la connoissance des fins que Dieu a eu en vüe, et des moyens dont-il s'est servi pour y arriver, entant que des Etres intelligens peuvent aquerir cette connoissance.[86]

Formey concluded his essay (the handwritten version) with an appraisal of natural philosophy and of the engagement of the philosophers who constantly enhanced knowledge about nature with the purpose of inciting devoutness in the population.[87]

The target of Formey's claims was Descartes, who like Francis Bacon had excluded the study of God's purposes from (natural) philosophy.[88] In contrast, Wolff gave teleology, that is, the science of (God's) purposes in the world, a prominent place in his physics and, thus, reduced the unique authority of natural theology to account for God.[89] Hence, Formey's appraisal of the contribution of natural philosophy to religion was another sign of his distancing himself from Cartesian natural theology due to the influence of Wolffianism.

---

85. See Formey, 'Discours sur les fins de la nature', f.209*v*.
86. Formey, 'Discours sur les fins de la nature', f.210*r*.
87. See Formey, 'Discours sur les fins de la nature', f.211*r*.
88. See René Descartes, *Les Méditations métaphysiques touchant la première philosophie, nouvelle édition revûê & corigée*, 2 vols (Paris, Huart, 1724), 'Méditation IV', vol.1, p.lxxix-lxxx. See Harrison, 'Physico-theology and the mixed sciences', p.170.
89. See Stefanie Buchenau, 'Die Teleologie zwischen Physik und Theologie', in *Die natürliche Theologie bei Christian Wolff*, ed. M. Albrecht, p.163-74.

Formey's appraisal of physico-theology, however, almost disappeared in the versions of his essays on God in the 1747 Academy yearbook. The two essays rather focus on the above-mentioned metaphysical revision of the physico-theological proof of God and, therefore, emphasised the superior role of metaphysics among the philosophical disciplines. Formey's first essay in particular, the 'Preuves de l'existence', was a testimony of a staunch metaphysician who denied the independence of the other sciences. More precisely, Formey argued against multiplying the proofs of God's existence but spoke out in favour of enhancing the persuasiveness of existing proofs by instilling in them a solid metaphysical foundation. This meant linking each argument in favour of God back to self-evident common notions or first principles.[90] These common notions not only led to stronger persuasion,[91] but they could also be understood by anybody regardless of their education.[92] The concept of common notions was essential to Wolff's metaphysics, and he had developed it in a Latin treatise in 1729 in particular. Formey translated this treatise into French and published it as an introduction to the fourth volume of his *Belle wolfienne* in 1746.[93] Formey's unconditional plea for metaphysical proofs of God's existence in his 'Preuves de l'existence' came at the expense of all the other sciences that had formed such proofs – physico-theology probably included. Formey disparaged all sciences that did not base their claims on common notions because, in his view, they served no purpose.[94] Moreover, he denigrated all philosophers who neglected metaphysics because they preferred mystery and spectacle to clear but dull notions, and also criticised them for their lack of scientific effort.[95] Hence, although Formey's purpose with his two essays on God was not to dismiss the physico-theological

90. See Formey, 'Preuves de l'existence', p.347.
91. See Formey, 'Preuves de l'existence', p.342.
92. See Formey, 'Preuves de l'existence', p.355.
93. See Christian Wolff, 'De notionibus directricibus & genuino usu philosophiae primae', in *Horae subsecivae marburgenses anni MDCCXXIX, quibus philosophia ad publicam privatamque utilitatem aptatur* (1729), ed. Jean Ecole, *Christian Wolff: Gesammelte Werke*, ed. Jean Ecole *et al.*, section 2, vol.34:1 (Hildesheim, 1983), p.310-50, and Formey's translation of this text: 'Introduction à la métaphysique, ou dissertation préliminaire sur les notions directrices & sur le véritable usage de l'ontologie', in *La Belle wolfienne*, vol.4 (The Hague, Neaulme, 1746), p.i-xxiii (full bibliographical details for *La Belle wolfienne* are given in chapter 5, note 6). See also Buchenau, 'Notions directrices et architechtonique de la métaphysique'.
94. See Formey, 'Preuves de l'existence', p.343.
95. See Formey, 'Preuves de l'existence', p.348.

4. The existence of God and the superiority of metaphysics

proof but to improve it by adding a metaphysical foundation to it, he nevertheless made it appear weak if not superfluous. By pleading for the unique legitimacy of metaphysics and reducing the physico-theological argument to the cosmological argument from contingency, Formey seems to implicitly suggest that the physico-theological argument was unnecessary to prove God's existence. The reason for Formey's unconditional plea for metaphysics lay in the context in which he presented it.

Formey and Maupertuis on metaphysics

The context in which Formey delivered his two essays on the existence of God at the Berlin Academy was marked by tensions that arose from divergent philosophical opinions as well as personal animosities between Wolffian and supposedly Newtonian philosophers. At the centre of these tensions were the Academy's new president, the French mathematician Pierre Louis Moreau de Maupertuis, who was installed in office on 1 February 1746,[96] and the famous Swiss mathematician Leonhard Euler, who had already joined the Berlin Academy in 1741 before its definitive renewal.[97] Throughout scholarly Europe, both men were considered to be Newtonians, although they would not have described themselves as such.[98] More importantly, in terms of the content of their philosophies this label did not completely fit.[99] Wolff and his disciples in Germany had a rather negative attitude towards Newtonianism in general and Maupertuis and Euler in particular. Wolff discredited Newton's science as being not philosophical but

---

96. See Harnack, *Geschichte der Königlich Preussischen Akademie*, vol.1:1, p.293-99. One of Maupertuis's first acts as president was to revise the Academy's statutes, these being confirmed by Frederic II on 10 May 1746. See also Mary Terrall, *The Man who flattened the earth: Maupertuis and the sciences in the Enlightenment* (Chicago, IL, 2002), p.236-43, and Hans Aarsleff, 'The Berlin Academy under Frederick the Great', *History of the human sciences* 2:2 (1989), p.193-207.
97. See Eduard Winter, *Die Registres der Berliner Akademie der Wissenschaften 1746-1766* (Berlin, 1957), p.16-19.
98. See Ahnert, 'Newton in the German-speaking lands', p.47.
99. With regard to Maupertuis, Terrall, *The Man who flattened the earth*, p.173-98, points to the possibility that he had overcome his predilection for Newtonianism shortly before he arrived in Berlin, namely, through the invention of his principle of least action. With regard to Euler's limited adoption of Newton's ideas, see Thomas Ahnert, 'Newtonianism in early Enlightenment Germany, c. 1720 to 1750: metaphysics and the critique of dogmatic philosophy', *Studies in history and philosophy of science* 35:3 (2004), p.471-91 (483-85).

merely geometrical.[100] He believed Maupertuis to be an arrogant Newtonian,[101] and considered Euler as rude and lacking in intelligence.[102] Wolff's and the Wolffians' aversion to Maupertuis and Euler was also reflected in their negative view of the renewed Berlin Academy. In a polemical account of the new Academy in the review of its 1746 yearbook in Gottsched's *Neuer Büchersaal*, Maupertuis was mocked for ostensibly having claimed that English and French science was superior to German science,[103] and the way the Academy had been divided into four classes was criticised.[104] On the other side, it was mostly Euler who polemicised against Wolff and attacked his traditional metaphysics.[105] It is, thus, not entirely wrong to speak of a Newtonian–Wolffian divide at the Berlin Academy during Maupertuis's presidency.[106] However, it appears that this divide resulted very much from the subjective perceptions of the contemporaries involved that were shaped by prejudice and personal animosity. Philosophically, the positions of alleged Wolffians and Newtonians were not always diametrically opposed to one another. Thomas Ahnert has, in fact, shown this with respect to the criticism of Wolff's philosophy by German and Swiss academicians.[107]

As far as Formey's role at the Academy was concerned, however, the perceived Newtonian–Wolffian divide put him in a difficult position. As a Wolffian and *aléthophile* he was supposed to defend Wolff's philosophy at the Academy, whereas his career prospects required him to maintain a good relationship with the Academy's president. At the time when Formey presented his two essays on

100. See Wolff to Manteuffel (1.10.1740 and 19.10.1740), in *Briefwechsel zwischen Wolff und Manteuffel*, vol.1, p.375 and 379.
101. See Wolff to Manteuffel (6.1.1741), in *Briefwechsel zwischen Wolff und Manteuffel*, vol.1, p.399.
102. See Wolff to Formey (7.5.1748), CV.
103. See 'I. Histoire de l'Académie royale', *Neuer Büchersaal der schönen Wissenschaften und freyen Künste* 7:2 (1748), p.99-117 (104-105).
104. See 'I. Histoire de l'Académie royale', p.110. For a detailed account of Wolff's opinion on the renewed Berlin Academy and its members, see Bronisch, *Mäzen der Aufklärung*, p.197-201.
105. See Eberhard Knobloch, 'Leonhard Euler als Theoretiker', *Berichte und Abhandlungen der Berlin-Brandenburgischen Akademie der Wissenschaften* 13 (2007), p.241-60 (243-45).
106. See Harnack, *Geschichte der Königlich Preussischen Akademie*, vol.1:1, p.432-33, and Ronald S. Calinger, 'The Newtonian–Wolffian controversy: 1740-1759', *Journal of the history of ideas* 30:3 (1969), p.319-30.
107. See Ahnert, 'Newtonianism in early Enlightenment Germany'.

4. The existence of God and the superiority of metaphysics

God's existence, the hostility between Wolffians and anti-Wolffians in Germany had just openly broken out over the philosophical prize essay competition concerning Leibniz's monadology.

To explain, the question of the Academy's essay competition of 1747 concerned the validity of Leibniz's monadology.[108] As the correspondence between Wolff, Manteuffel, Gottsched and Formey shows, the mere proposition of such a question and, furthermore, the conduct of certain of the Academy's members – in particular that of the mathematician Leonhard Euler – in relation to it was considered by the *aléthophiles* to be a direct assault on the foundations of Leibnizian and Wolffian metaphysics. Immediately after the public announcement of the prize question in 1746, Euler tried to influence the opinion of the competition's participants by publishing a piece in which he refuted Leibniz's theory of monads. To oppose Euler and to inculcate the scholarly public with a pro-monad point of view, Formey wrote a reply to Euler's work, the *Recherches sur les elemens de la matière*.[109] The content of this anonymous work of Formey's and the process of its publication were controlled and organised by both the *aléthophiles* in Leipzig and Wolff himself, and they made the *Recherches sur les elemens de la matière* an integral part of their campaign against the enemies of Leibnizian monadology.[110] Moreover, throughout the two years of the running and aftermath of the essay competition, Formey provided Manteuffel in Leipzig with insider information on the Academy's internal proceedings and struggles in relation to this issue.[111]

Even after an anti-monad piece was awarded the Academy's prize in June 1747, the public debate on the subject continued. In September 1747, Manteuffel was still encouraging Formey to influence the opinions of his academic colleagues on the subject of monads,

---

108. See Terrall, *The Man who flattened the earth*, p.257-65, and Cornelia Buschmann, 'Die philosophischen Preisfragen und Preisschriften der Berliner Akademie der Wissenschaften im 18. Jahrhundert', in *Aufklärung in Berlin*, ed. W. Förster, p.165-228 (183-86).
109. Formey, *Recherches sur les elémens de la matière* (n.p., n.n., 1747).
110. See Bronisch, *Mäzen der Aufklärung*, p.280-85.
111. See, for example, Manteuffel's request for information on the Academy members in charge of deciding the winner, Manteuffel to Formey (10.6.1747), CV: 'L'ami [...] me charge de vous prier, cher Gr. Aumonier, de nous apprendre les noms des membres du committé, qui a examiné et jugé les pièces monadieres, et de nous procurer confidemment une copie de celle, qui a été si liberalement couronnée.'

particularly the opinion of the president, Maupertuis, to whom Formey was supposed to send all publications that opposed Euler and the winner of the essay contest, Johann Heinrich Gottlob von Justi.[112] In general, Manteuffel and Wolff were inclined to believe that Maupertuis secretly supported the anti-Leibnizians and anti-Wolffians.[113] In contrast, some of Formey's colleagues at the Academy seem to have suspected him of being biased towards Wolffianism because they accused him of having intercepted the anti-monad piece that was eventually awarded the essay prize.[114] Consequently, it seems that the events in relation to the 1747 competition placed Formey in a difficult position: in between those who agreed with his ideological role model and a certain part of his academic colleagues who did not. Throughout this entire situation, however, Formey continuously emphasised Maupertuis's impartiality and seems to have maintained a good relationship with him. This could also have been because of Formey's ambition to attain the position of secretary to the Academy; if he was to realise this, he needed the president's support.[115] Nevertheless, in his philosophical contributions to the Academy, Formey continuously put forward Wolffian

---

112. See Manteuffel to Formey (29.9.1747), CV: 'Ne pourriez vous pas faire en sorte, que cette brochure de Halle [against Euler] fut bien traduite en françois, en omettant ou en adoucissant un peu les traits caustiques, dont elle est remplie? Ce seroit peutètre le moyen de rectifier vòtre president et celuy d'empecher, par luy, la Societé, de se prèter au dessein insensé du Rabuliste antimonadier, supposé que mes nouvelles de Halle disent vrai.' Maupertuis did not read German and, therefore, depended mainly on his secretary's translations of the various pieces circulating in the German sphere concerning the debate on monads.

113. See Manteuffel to Formey (10.6.1747), CV: 'Il y en a, qui soupçonnent vòtre President, de se chauffer du mème bois, que le grand anti-monadier [Euler], quoiqu'il ait trop d'esprit et savoir-vivre, pour le declarer aussi grossierement que son collegue.' In contrast, as Terrall, *The Man who flattened the earth*, p.258, n.100, rightly says, there is no evidence that Maupertuis took an openly anti-Leibnizian or anti-Wolffian position at any time during the entire debate. On the contrary, he even made an effort to ensure any assaults on Wolff in the winning essay were deleted before its publication (Terrall, *The Man who flattened the earth*, p.263).

114. See Formey to Manteuffel (3.6.1747), UBL, Ms 0347.

115. Since June 1746, Formey had been acting as deputy to Jariges, the Academy's secretary (see Formey, 'Eloge du Grand-Chancelier de Jariges', in *Nouveaux mémoires de l'Académie royale des sciences et belles-lettres*, 1771; Berlin, Voss, 1773, p.41-45, 45). Apparently, it was expected that he would officially be promoted to the latter's position in November 1746 when Jariges went to Pomerania

4. The existence of God and the superiority of metaphysics

ideas. His first academic essay, which dealt with a psychological theory of dreaming, developed ideas taken from Wolff's empirical psychology.[116] The two essays on God's existence that appeared in 1747 and their strong plea for Wolff's metaphysics were, thus, part of Formey's attempt to uphold Wolff's ideas in a period of anti-Wolffianism at the Academy.

Nevertheless, Formey took a conciliatory approach in his own two essays because he declared them to be linked with an essay Maupertuis had presented the previous year in which he had demonstrated God's existence through a principle derived from the laws of motion.[117] The manuscript of Formey's second essay, which was entitled the 'Examen de la preuve', reveals that he fashioned it only retroactively as a reply to Maupertuis's essay. Moreover, Formey formulated his reply to Maupertuis not in opposition to but in line with the latter's opinion. As Formey stated at the beginning of his essay, his reflections on God were meant to lead to the same result as Maupertuis's, although he applied different measures to achieve it.[118] In fact, the common purpose of Maupertuis's and Formey's essays was to strengthen the truth of God's existence by dismissing weak proofs of it, more

---

to reform the juridical system there; see Wolff to Manteuffel (29.10.1746), in *Briefwechsel zwischen Wolff und Manteuffel*, vol.2, p.358-59.

116. Formey, 'Essai sur les songes', in *Histoire de l'Académie royale des sciences et belles lettres de Berlin* (1746; Berlin, Haude, 1748), p.317-34. Formey mentioned the source of his essay in a letter to Manteuffel (27.1.1748), UBL, Ms 0347.

117. Maupertuis, 'Les loix du mouvement et du repos déduites d'un principe métaphysique', in *Histoire de l'Académie royale des sciences et belles lettres de Berlin* (1746; Berlin, Haude, 1748), p.267-94. The essay was presented at the Academy on 6 October 1746. See Terrall, *The Man who flattened the earth*, p.270-79. Terrall suggests that this discourse served to present Maupertuis as a man of science in his new institution for the first time and that, likewise, it was supposed to 'set a new standard for the metaphysics class', p.270. In 1751 Maupertuis published an extended version of his 'Loix du mouvement' under the title *Essai de cosmologie* (n.p., n.n., 1751), which became one of his most famous works.

118. See Formey, 'Examen de la preuve', p.365. Compare with 'Discours sur les fins de la nature', f.192r. The manuscript version of the reference to Maupertuis is slightly longer and more explanatory than the one in the printed version: '(*) C'est ce que Mr. de Maupertuis a mis dans une pleine evidence dans ses Loix du Mouvement et du Repos etc. An. 1746 p.267 etc. Il y porte sur l'argument tiré des fins de la Nature le jugement, auquel nos Refléxions vont aboutir. Seulement nous tendons au même but par des routes différentes. Mr. de Maupertuis résout cet argument dans celui qui est tiré de la consideration des Loix générales de la Nature; au lieu que le but de notre analyse est de remonter aux notions communes, sur lesquelles cet argument est fondé, et qui en font toute la force.'

precisely, the physico-theological proof.[119] Interestingly, Maupertuis, like Formey in his manuscript, criticised Newton and the famous physico-theologians Derham, Fabricius and Lesser for their naïve use of physical proofs for the existence of God.[120] Apparently, they were both convinced that the better alternative to these weak proofs, which were based on empirical observation alone, was the application of universal metaphysical principles.[121] Therefore, Maupertuis's and Formey's essays both engaged in the question of the role of metaphysics in proving the existence of God and they both attempted to provide natural philosophical arguments with a metaphysical foundation.

As such, their essays were part of a broader debate on the role of metaphysics as compared with that of the other philosophical disciplines that occupied the Academy for several decades after its renewal in 1746.[122] This debate was fuelled not only by such programmatic contributions by its members as Maupertuis's 'Discours sur les devoirs de l'académicien' (1750) and Merian's 'Discours sur la métaphysique' (1765),[123] but also by the essay contests on metaphysical subjects. For example, in 1763, the prize question was about whether metaphysical truths were as evident as mathematical ones, and in 1795 it was still about the progress that metaphysics had made in Germany since the time of Leibniz and Wolff.[124] In 1744, at the start of all these discussions about metaphysics, a class of speculative philosophy, which was the equivalent of metaphysics, was established

---

119. See Formey, 'Examen de la preuve', p.367-68, and Maupertuis, 'Loix du mouvement', p.270.
120. See Formey, 'Discours sur les fins de la nature', f.192r-v.
121. See Maupertuis, 'Loix du mouvement', p.277-78: 'Ce n'est donc point dans les petits détails, dans ces parties de l'Univers dont nous connoissons trop peu les rapports, qu'il faut chercher l'Etre suprême, c'est dans les Phenomênes dont l'universalité ne souffre aucune exception, & que leur simplicité expose entierement à notre vuë.' See also a similar statement on p.279.
122. See Annelie Große, '"Mother of all sciences" or mere speculation? The justification of metaphysics at the Berlin Academy between 1746 and 1765', in *The Berlin Academy in the reign of Frederick the Great: philosophy and science*, ed. Tinca Prunea-Bretonnet and Peter R. Anstey, Oxford University Studies in the Enlightenment (Liverpool, Liverpool University Press / Voltaire Foundation, 2022), p.39-69.
123. See Maupertuis, 'Des devoirs de l'académicien', and Merian, 'Discours sur la métaphysique', in *Histoire de l'Académie royale des sciences et belles lettres de Berlin* (1765; Berlin, Haude & Spener, 1767), p.450-74. Maupertuis's discourse had already been presented on 18 June 1750.
124. See Buschmann, 'Die philosophischen Preisfragen'.

4. The existence of God and the superiority of metaphysics   137

at the Academy. This was very unusual for an institution such as the renewed Berlin Academy that saw itself as competing with the big centres of science in London and Paris and, therefore, attached great importance to mathematics and the emerging experimental sciences.[125]

Moreover, in the preface to the first volume of the 1745 Academy yearbook, it was strongly emphasised that metaphysics was seen as a foundational science that – as Wolff described in his general introduction to philosophy – contained the principles on which all other sciences were based.[126] Formey himself wrote this statement of the Academy's self-concept in his role as the institution's historian; however, Maupertuis, who arrived in Berlin in the autumn of 1745, most likely confirmed or perhaps even contributed to it.[127] In the statement, the pursuit of a modern metaphysics in the Academy's new class of speculative philosophy was propagated, a metaphysics that had distanced itself from its scholastic predecessor and would, instead, be a foundational science that provided the most general and certain principles:

> La Metaphysique est sans contredit la Mére des autres Sciences, la Theorie qui fournit les principes les plus généraux, la source de l'evidence, & le fondement de la certitude de nos connoissances. Ces beaux caractéres ne convenoient pas à la verité à la Metaphysique des Scolastiques, terre ingrate, qui ne produisoit gueres que des ronces et des épines. [...] De grands Genies, en donnant une nouvelle culture à cette portion de l'Empire des Sciences, lui ont fait revêtir une toute autre face. Au lieu d'un Dictionnaire de termes barbares, nous commençons à avoir une pépiniere, où chaque Science trouve, pour ainsi dire, sa semence, et d'où naissent tous les principes, toutes

---

125. See Harnack, *Geschichte der Königlich Preussischen Akademie*, vol.1:1, p.309-10, and Terrall, *The Man who flattened the earth*, p.265.
126. See Wolff, 'Vorbericht von der Welt-Weisheit', in *Vernünfftige Gedancken von den Kräften des menschlichen Verstandes und ihrem richtigen Gebrauche in Erkäntniss der Wahrheit* (14th edn, 1754), ed. Hans Werner Arndt, in *Christian Wolff: Gesammelte Werke*, ed. Jean Ecole *et al.*, 4th edn, section 1, vol.1 (Hildesheim, 2006), p.115-22, §14, and Wolff, *Discursus praeliminaris*, §73.
127. See 'Actum 22.9.1745', in BBAW, I. Historische Abteilung, PAW (1700-1811), Abt. IV, Nr. 12: 'Protokolle bei der Errichtung der neuen Akademie der Wissenschaften 1744-1746', f.119. In this document, the assembly was instructed to provide Maupertuis with all the material that had been written to date for the yearbook so that it could be revised. This was also, supposedly, the reason why the publication of the first yearbook was delayed until 1746, although it had initially been planned for 1745.

les notions directrices qui nous guident, de quelque coté que nous tournions nos pas.[128]

Furthermore, as Formey specified in the short history of the Academy that followed his preface, it was not intended that this modern form of metaphysics would carry out a fanciful ('chimérique') sort of system building any more, but that it would rely on experience and observation of nature and, in so doing, would incorporate the achievements of modern science.[129] Theoretically, all members of the Berlin Academy adhered to this understanding of metaphysics as the one science in which all other sciences, especially natural philosophy, were grounded. This general understanding underlay Formey's and Maupertuis's respective attempts to fruitfully enhance the physico-theological proof of God's existence in particular.

However, Maupertuis's and Formey's considerations of the proofs of the existence of God differed a great deal with regard to the particular character of their metaphysics and the universal principles they used. Formey's metaphysics was ontologically inspired, whereas Maupertuis's was physico-mathematically inspired. Formey made a plea for the principle of sufficient reason, whereas Maupertuis relied on the principle of least action, which said that changes in nature were stimulated by the smallest amount of power possible. As far as Maupertuis was concerned, this principle was the most universal because all the laws of motion and inactivity that could be observed in nature depended on it. As such, it correlated with the wisdom and dignity of a supreme being.[130] In contrast, Formey, in reference to Leibniz, regarded the laws of motion as a demonstration of the contingent world order because they were contingent too and, hence, grounded in the principle of sufficient reason.[131]

Maupertuis's and Formey's different choices of metaphysical principles went alongside their different perceptions of the epistemological nature of metaphysical principles in general. Maupertuis even introduced a fundamental challenge to the vision of the superior role

---

128. [Formey], 'Préface', in *Histoire de l'Académie royale des sciences et des belles lettres de Berlin* (1745; Berlin, Haude, 1746), sig.)()(2r-v.
129. See Formey, 'Histoire du renouvellement de l'Académie en MDCCXLIV', in *Histoire de l'Académie royale des sciences et des belles lettres de Berlin* (1745; Berlin, Haude, 1746), p.1-9 (2).
130. See Maupertuis, 'Loix du mouvement', p.286.
131. See Formey, 'Examen de la preuve', p.379-80. For Leibniz's support for Formey's argument, see the footnote on p.380-81.

played by metaphysics among the sciences. He did not consider his metaphysical a priori principle of least action as self-sufficient in the establishment of the laws of motion, whereas Formey was convinced of the standalone quality of a simple metaphysical notion such as the principle of sufficient reason. Maupertuis constructed his proof of God's existence on the basis of two sources of knowledge that confirmed one another and, as such, reinforced that proof: he declared that the laws of motion he had deduced from the principle of least action were the same as could be induced through the observation of nature. It was precisely the compatibility between the results of the two epistemic procedures (deduction and induction) that convinced Maupertuis of the truth of his principle and, as a consequence, of God's existence.[132] In terms of the relationship between the disciplines of metaphysics (more precisely, cosmology) and physics (more precisely, mathematical mechanics), Maupertuis's epistemological approach implied their mutual dependence. Christian Leduc recently described Maupertuis's concept of the metaphysics of nature, or cosmology, as follows: Maupertuis considered metaphysics to be a foundational science that received its legitimation only on the basis of previously established physical laws that were confirmed by experience and mathematical calculation. As such, Leduc considered that Maupertuis's position was in between the Wolffian (and Kantian) concept of an entirely a priori metaphysics that was the necessary precondition of physical laws and the concept put forward by D'Alembert and Voltaire, who supported the view that physics was independent from a metaphysical foundation.[133]

In contrast to Maupertuis, Formey defended the unconditional power of ontological a priori principles in being able to account legitimately for secondary principles and the phenomena of all other sciences. According to Formey, this legitimacy was due to the epistemic status of these a priori principles, which was, as he claimed in relation to the Leibnizian principle of sufficient reason, as strong as that of the mathematical axioms. Maupertuis's and Formey's different perceptions of the degree of evidence required by metaphysical principles and how much they could be trusted implied that, after all, Maupertuis was not entirely in agreement with the concept of metaphysics as a foundational science, something that was proclaimed

---

132. See Maupertuis, 'Loix du mouvement', p.279 and 286.
133. See Christian Leduc, 'La métaphysique de la nature à l'Académie de Berlin', *Philosophiques* 42:1 (2015), p.11-30 (15).

at the Academy's renewal in 1746. Instead, he campaigned in favour of mathematics, which he wanted to endow with a new (higher) degree of usefulness by applying it to the inquiry into the proofs of God's existence. In this respect he claimed that proofs gained through mathematical calculation would be clearer and more certain than metaphysical ones:

> Voyons, si nous pourrons faire un usage plus heureux de cette science [la mathématique]. Les preuves de l'existence de Dieu qu'elle fournira, auront sur toutes les autres, l'avantage de l'evidence qui caracterise les verités mathématiques. Ceux qui n'ont pas assez de confiance dans les raisonnemens métaphysiques, trouveront plus de sûreté dans ce genre de preuves: & ceux qui ne font pas assez de cas des preuves populaires, trouveront dans celles-ci plus d'exactitude & d'élévation.[134]

Thus, Maupertuis openly rejected the ability of metaphysics to provide certain knowledge, and presented mathematics as a real alternative when dealing with questions concerning the existence of God. The last part of Maupertuis's 'Loix du mouvement' was also an attempt to demonstrate the laws of motion through calculation. In actual fact, Formey also recognised the superior power of mathematics in relation to finding evidence, and he transferred this power to metaphysics by claiming that the method of deriving subordinate propositions from their sources in metaphysics was equal to mathematical method[135] and that metaphysical principles, such as the one of sufficient reason, were axioms.[136] In contrast, as far as Maupertuis was concerned, such a comparison between mathematics and metaphysics was not admissible; he rejected those kinds of metaphysics that in his view only 'pretended' to be mathematically rooted but in reality were not.[137]

Formey's and Maupertuis's divergent views on metaphysics reveal that the programmatic description of metaphysics on which the Berlin Academy was founded according to its first yearbook was not put into practice in the same way by all its members. Nevertheless, the two men's respective positions on the proof of God's existence did not result from

---

134. See Maupertuis, 'Loix du mouvement', p.278.
135. See Formey, 'Preuves de l'existence', p.348.
136. See Formey, 'Examen de la preuve', p.370.
137. See Maupertuis, 'Loix du mouvement', p.278: 'Car il ne faut pas s'y tromper dans quelques Ouvrages, qui n'ont de mathématique que l'air & la forme, & qui au fond ne sont que de la Métaphysique la plus incertaine & la plus ténébreuse.'

a neat division between Wolffian metaphysics and Newtonian natural philosophy. On the contrary, the relationship between Maupertuis's position and that of Formey was much more complex, because Formey did not in essence reject the role of natural philosophy in accounting for God, and Maupertuis did not reject the necessity of metaphysical universal principles. Moreover, both of them were convinced that God's existence could be proved scientifically. However, according to the perception of their contemporaries, Formey's and Maupertuis's essays on the existence of God were symbols of two opposing schools of philosophy, not only with respect to their epistemological claims but also with respect to their effects on religion.

Newtonians against Wolffians: perception of the debate by two groups of contemporaries

The way in which Formey's correspondents reacted to his two essays on God's existence accounts for the opposing views of Maupertuis and Formey, Newtonianism and Wolffianism, and deism and Christian philosophy. Wolff and the *aléthophiles* in particular experimented with such opposing viewpoints. Wolff himself was very suspicious of Maupertuis's ideological position, suspecting that he would agree with the ideas of the famous materialist La Mettrie and, more importantly, that he had feigned his 1746 proof of God's existence.[138] In August 1748, a polemical review of Maupertuis's 'Loix du mouvement', in which Maupertuis was alleged to have mocked the proofs of God's existence discussed in the essay in the same manner as the so-called freethinkers, appeared in Gottsched's journal *Neuer Büchersaal*.[139] Moreover, the reviewer declared Maupertuis's principle of least action to be non-innovative and attributed it instead to Leibniz, whom Maupertuis was said to resent.[140] Manteuffel sent this article to Formey together with some subtle remarks on the harm that Maupertuis was causing to the Academy's reputation.[141] Seemingly, however, Formey

---

138. See Wolff to Manteuffel (8.9.1748), in *Briefwechsel zwischen Wolff und Manteuffel*, vol.3, p.465.
139. See 'I. Histoire de l'académie royale', p.114.
140. See 'I. Histoire de l'académie royale', p.116-17. In his 'Loix du mouvement' Maupertuis had, indeed, criticised Leibniz for his theory of the best of all worlds (see p.275).
141. See Manteuffel to Formey (9.9.1748), D, in which he communicated the article, and (10.9.1748), D for his remarks on Maupertuis.

replied to this attempt to denigrate Maupertuis by referring to the loyalty he owed to the Academy's president. Unfortunately, Formey's response to Manteuffel on 19 September 1748 has not survived, but it is clear from Manteuffel's reaction to this letter that Formey was not willing to openly contradict Maupertuis's essay out of a wish to preserve his own career, a point that both Manteuffel and Wolff understood. Manteuffel answered him:

> J'applaudis extrémement à Votre conduite, à l'égard de Votre President, dèsque Vous attachez, à l'étendue de ses lumieres, le sens limité, que Vous y attachez actuellement. Il seroit ridicule de risquer sa fortune, pour tacher de tirer un ami d'une erreur, dont on le sait coëffé, lors sur-tout que l'on prevoit, qu'au lieu de se corriger, il ne fera que se facher contre le correcteur.[142]

However, not all of Wolff's supporters held the same negative opinion on Maupertuis's essay and his philosophy in general. Formey's friend Emer de Vattel found that Maupertuis had strengthened the position of metaphysics in his text by showing that his mathematical laws could be traced back to metaphysical principles; as far as Vattel was concerned, Maupertuis was both a 'philosophe' and a 'géomètre'.[143] Nevertheless, Vattel's opinion appears exceptional.

In the confessional milieu of Formey's Calvinist correspondents, his own and Maupertuis's writings were also largely perceived as being opposed to one another. However, Formey's clerical correspondents were, in fact, concerned with the essays' effects on religion.[144] They criticised Maupertuis's essay for actually doing harm to the truth of God's existence, whereas they appreciated Formey's essays for restoring it. The common criticism that Genevan theologians and pastors levelled at Maupertuis was that he had destroyed the ordinary and easily accessible proofs of the existence of God, and replaced them with his complex and subtle metaphysical proof that would be

---

142. Manteuffel to Formey (26.9.1748), D. Manteuffel also forwarded Formey's answer to Wolff, who in turn commented on it by diminishing Maupertuis's scientific achievements and by expressing his understanding of Formey's conduct given his career situation; see Wolff to Manteuffel (26.9.1748), in *Briefwechsel zwischen Wolff und Manteuffel*, vol.3, p.488-89.
143. See Vattel to Formey (13.1.1749), in *Emer de Vattel à Jean Henri Samuel Formey*, p.96.
144. See Vernet to Formey (26.2.1750), in *Lettres de Genève*, p.259, and Peschier to Formey (4.8.1750), in *Lettres de Genève*, p.271-72.

4. The existence of God and the superiority of metaphysics

unintelligible to the majority of the general public.[145] This argument is particularly interesting because it could, equally, be applied to Formey's demonstration of Wolff's a posteriori proof in 1747. Indeed, the same people who criticised Maupertuis for corrupting the simple belief of the masses admonished Formey for not speaking to a public that was unsophisticated. However, they did so in a remarkably propitiatory vein. The theologian François de Roches even assured Formey that it was not important whether the unsophisticated understood his complex metaphysical defence of God, because neither would they understand the highly scientific confutation of God; however, in an academic setting, where there were more 'esprits subtiles', he considered Formey's essays to be very useful.[146]

In 1759 – more than ten years after his essays on God's existence and in the year of Maupertuis's death – Formey himself commented again on the link between metaphysics and the proofs of God's existence. In his journal *Nouvelle bibliothèque germanique*, he published anonymously an essay in which he reflected on the different methods of proving God's existence a posteriori. Formey had already written this piece in late 1754 or even 1755 as an entry for the 1755 prize essay competition run by the Academy of Leiden. However, because it was in French, it had not been included in the competition entries.[147] Formey finally published it under his name in the 1765 Academy yearbook.[148] The essay contained a reply to the criticism by the Genevans that scientific natural theology was inaccessible to the common people and, in particular, it defended Maupertuis's mathematico-metaphysical stance on this. Formey stressed there was a distinction between a scientific demonstration of the proof of God's existence and the promulgation of this proof via catechisms and theology:

---

145. See François de Roches to Formey (29.4.1749), in *Lettres de Genève*, p.227, Peschier to Formey (20.5.1749), in *Lettres de Genève*, p.230-31, and Vernet to Formey (25.5.1749), in *Lettres de Genève*, p.235-36.
146. See Roches to Formey (30.1.1750), in *Lettres de Genève*, p.257, and Peschier to Formey (19.12.1749), in *Lettres de Genève*, p.251-52.
147. See 'Discours sur ces questions: quel est le degré de certitude dont sont susceptibles les preuves tirées de la considération de cet univers pour demontrer l'existence d'une divinité? Et quelle est la meilleure maniere de faire usage de ces argumens a posteriori, pour établir cette importante vérité?', *Nouvelle bibliothèque germanique* 25 (1759), p.317-41.
148. 'Discours sur ces questions', in *Histoire de l'Académie royale des sciences et belles lettres de Berlin* (1765; Berlin, Haude & Spener, 1767), p.435-49. In the following, this version is quoted.

> Nous ne nous récrions point contre cette entreprise, comme quelques uns l'ont fait, en disant que la Démonstration de l'Existence de Dieu ne sauroit dépendre de calculs & de signes algébriques, qu'elle doit être à la portée de tout le monde, & qu'il seroit singulier qu'on fût obligé de faire main basse sur toutes les preuves ordinaires que les Catéchismes & les Cours de Théologie renferment pour y substituer un Principe tel que celui de la moindre Action, ou tout autre du même genre, qu'on voudroit ériger en Principe primitif à cet égard. Ces objections me paroissent peu concluantes.[149]

In general, Formey continued, even the most clear and concise philosophical demonstrations were unintelligible to the common people who were not familiar with the rules of reasoning; this was, however, not a reason for abandoning philosophical demonstrations altogether.[150] Therefore, Formey defended not only the mathematical metaphysics that Maupertuis adhered to in the face of criticism of its inaccessibility, but also his own position as a practising metaphysician; however, Formey also claimed that metaphysical common notions were universally intelligible.[151]

Although he came to Maupertuis's defence with regard to the complexity of his argument, Formey did, however, reject his mathematical metaphysics, just as he rejected physics and the physical mathematics in natural theology. In his view, the latter two generalised the marvels of nature either too much or too little.[152] In contrast, to find one single general law of the universe that could explain the cause of every effect, as Maupertuis's mathematico-metaphysical approach pretended to do, was simply above the finite intellectual capacities of human beings.[153]

By rejecting all these three approaches to a posteriori arguments for God's existence, Formey again emphasised the unique role of metaphysics in natural theology. In his view, all other proofs could only gain truth inasmuch as they were translated into metaphysical demonstration.[154] Thus, since the time of his two essays on God's existence, Formey's considerations as to the best way of proving God's

---

149. Formey, 'Discours sur ces questions', p.440.
150. See Formey, 'Discours sur ces questions', p.441.
151. See Formey, 'Discours sur ces questions', p.444.
152. See Formey, 'Discours sur ces questions', p.437-39.
153. See Formey, 'Discours sur ces questions', p.441-42.
154. See Formey, 'Discours sur ces questions', p.443.

existence had not, essentially, changed. On the contrary, in 1759, he rather uttered them with greater confidence.

It can be seen that, throughout his career at the Berlin Academy, Formey forged the image of a mutually fruitful relationship between science and religion in which the Christian notion of God was best defended by metaphysics and in which metaphysics obtained its sense and legitimacy through the service it rendered to the understanding of such a fundamental truth as the nature and existence of God. In his engagement with physico-theology he portrayed metaphysics as the indispensable link between the increasingly popular discipline of natural philosophy and theology. The Berlin Academy with its class of speculative philosophy that advertised the role of metaphysics as a foundational science was a good environment for such an undertaking, although in practice there existed tendencies to undermine the superior role of metaphysics among its members. Maupertuis and Euler in particular contributed to the detriment of the discipline by advertising mathematics for its higher degree of clarity and certainty.

The foundations of Formey's idea of mutual support between religion and metaphysics lay in his strong trust in the epistemic strength of basic or common notions and the demonstrative method. This trust in rational demonstration had its origins in Wolff's natural theology, which Formey propagated at the Academy, but had already been inherent in Descartes's assumption that God's existence was demonstrable in a rational manner. In this way, Formey had countered Bayle's scepticism in the early 1740s. Moreover, the concern with scepticism or pyrrhonism remained an important driving force for Formey's engagement with natural theology throughout his whole career.[155]

---

155. See Formey, 'Discours sur ces questions', p.449.

5. Pre-established harmony and fatalism

The question of how to prove the existence of God was only one crucial question of many in the answering of which Formey tried to accommodate both an increasingly natural philosophical worldview and traditional religious beliefs. Equally important in eighteenth-century Christian philosophy was the need to define human beings' role in God's Creation. It was crucial for human beings to know what determined their behaviour and thought, and not only to be able to judge the value of their actions, but also to be certain about how to reach salvation in the afterlife. Moreover, knowledge about their own capacities shaped people's image of God as the creator of those capacities. In early modern philosophy, these issues were addressed by theories about the order and interaction of things in the world in general and about the relationship between soul and body in particular.

In the scholastic tradition, a real mutual influence between soul and body had been assumed, whereas it was challenged in the seventeenth century because of Descartes's conceptualisation of a strict spirit–body dualism. To account for the relationship between the two completely distinct and ontologically different substances, Descartes's disciples conceived of only an ideal interaction between soul and body, and imagined God to constantly readjust the body's movements to the changing perceptions of the soul. This theory, which was referred to as occasionalism, was rejected by Leibniz, who agreed with the premise of Cartesian dualism but redefined the role played by God in the relationship between soul and body. Leibniz was convinced that all substances in the world were arranged in a causally interlinked order, and that from its 'birth' every single substance contained a template for all its future modifications. Thus, with regard to soul and body, he argued that both the soul's perceptions and the body's movements were caused by their respective internal dispositions that had been instilled in them by God at Creation. Likewise, from the outset, God had ensured that the soul's perceptions and the body's movements always corresponded to one another – soul and body were, therefore, in a pre-established harmony.[1]

Among theologians in particular, Leibniz's theory provoked fierce opposition; their most important objection to it was that it introduced fatalism. From a theological perspective, fatalism signified the absence of human as well as divine liberty, an absence that belonged to a world in which everything existed necessarily and by mechanical rules.[2] Theologians feared that, in a fatalistic world, people would have no incentive to work for their afterlife and, thus, would neglect their duties towards God. Moreover, God would have no power to intervene in the universe. This was why charges of fatalism often went hand in hand with accusations of Spinozism, materialism and atheism.[3] Leibniz was confronted with such criticism from Bayle, Clarke and others, and Christian Wolff also became deeply involved in the religious dispute about the fatalistic implications of pre-established harmony after he implemented Leibniz's theory in his own philosophical system.[4] In Wolff's disagreement with the Halle Pietists, which led to his expulsion from Prussia, the alleged fatalism of his philosophy was the key argument.[5] Although this debate about fatalism never reached a formal conclusion, it gradually lost its importance in the 1730s and 1740s.

Therefore, it came as a major surprise to the Wolffians that in 1741, just after Wolff was acquitted of the Pietists' accusations and allowed to

1. On Leibniz's theory of pre-established harmony and its philosophical context, see Gerd Fabian, *Beitrag zur Geschichte des Leib-Seele-Problems (Lehre von der prästabilierten Harmonie und vom psychophysischen Parallelismus in der Leibniz–Wolffschen Schule)* (Langensalza, 1925); Mario Casula, 'Die Lehre von der prästabilierten Harmonie in ihrer Entwicklung von Leibniz bis A. G. Baumgarten', in *Akten des II. internationalen Leibniz-Kongresses. Hannover 17.-22. Juli 1972*, ed. Internationaler Leibniz-Kongress, 4 vols (Wiesbaden, 1975), vol.3, p.397-414; *Causation in early modern philosophy: Cartesianism, occasionalism, and preestablished harmony*, ed. Steven Nadler (University Park, PA, 1993); David Scott, 'Leibniz and the two clocks', *Journal of the history of ideas* 58:3 (1997), p.445-63, and Marleen Rozemond, 'Leibniz on the union of body and soul', *Archiv für Geschichte der Philosophie* 79:2 (1997), p.150-78.
2. See Alessandro Zanconato, *La Dispute du fatalisme en France: 1730-1760* (Fasano and Paris, 2004), p.201-25.
3. See Zanconato, *La Dispute du fatalisme*, p.14.
4. See Casula, 'Die Lehre von der prästabilierten Harmonie', p.399-400.
5. See Bianco, 'Freiheit gegen Fatalismus'.

return to Halle by the king, Formey revived the dispute about fatalism. As a member of the Société des aléthophiles and promoter of Wolffian philosophy at the Collège français, he was probably the person from whom this had been least expected. Furthermore, Formey launched the revival of the dispute in a popular philosophical work that had the proclaimed aim of promoting Wolff's philosophy: his *Belle wolfienne*. In the second volume of his book, Formey replicated some of the Pietists' accusations against Wolff and enhanced them with criticism from other traditions. By reviving the accusation of fatalism, he thus openly doubted the compatibility between parts of Leibniz's and Wolff's philosophy and important religious and moral premises. Formey's doubts were inspired by Jean-Pierre de Crousaz's anti-Leibnizian campaign on the one side and by the Wolffians' own internal struggles to account for the theory of pre-established harmony on the other. However, it remains unclear why he chose to make his doubts public. He must have been aware of the risk of antagonising his Wolffian friends and potentially losing the support of the *aléthophiles*' network. In fact, although this incident did not cause a definite break between Formey and the Wolffians, Wolff and the *aléthophiles* were alienated by it.

It can be said that the content and intentions of the second volume of Formey's *Belle wolfienne* are very meaningful with respect to his position in relation to Wolff's philosophy as well as the elements of his own Christian philosophy. Furthermore, they illustrate the state of Wolffianism in mid-eighteenth-century Germany and further afield. After a brief introduction to *La Belle wolfienne*'s genre, this chapter will shed light on Formey's arguments against pre-established harmony and their sources. It will end by analysing the personal and broader debates that motivated Formey's criticism.

Popularising Wolff's philosophy: Formey's *Belle wolfienne*

Formey started publishing his *Belle wolfienne* in 1741, and it appeared in six consecutive volumes until 1753.[6] He himself classified his work

---

6. Formey, *La Belle wolfienne*, vol.1: *Avec deux lettres philosophiques, l'une sur l'immortalité de l'âme, l'autre sur l'harmonie préétablie* (The Hague, Le Vier, 1741); vol.2: *Avec un discours sur la morale des Chinois, traduit de Mr. Wolff* (The Hague, Le Vier, 1741); vol.3: *Contenant le reste de la Logique* (The Hague, Neaulme, 1743); vol.4: *Contenant l'Ontologie et la première partie de la Métaphysique* (The Hague, Neaulme, 1746); vol.5: *Contenant la Psychologie experimentale* (The Hague, Neaulme, 1753); vol.6: *Contenant l'abrégé de la Théologie naturelle* (The Hague, Neaulme, 1753).

as a philosophical novel,[7] and referred to the popular philosophical writings of Bernard de Fontenelle and Francesco Algarotti as his role models.[8] Like these authors, Formey used the genre of the *philosophie des dames*, which consisted of fictional dialogues between a lady and her teacher about a certain philosophical system, and were often meant to instruct female readers.[9] In Formey's plot, however, the roles of the lady and teacher are reversed. The female protagonist is the expert in Wolff's philosophy, whereas the first-person narrator Monsieur **, a young intellectual from Berlin, has barely read anything by Wolff until he goes on holiday to Charlottenburg. There he encounters the beautiful daughter of his host, Espérance, who is an ardent admirer of the philosopher. Primarily attracted by the beauty of the young woman, Monsieur ** asks her to engage in a 'cours de philosophie', in which she will instruct him and eventually convince him of Wolff's philosophy.[10] Monsieur **'s conversion to Wolffianism is quickly achieved,[11] and by reading Wolff he slowly becomes an equal partner in dialogue for the young lady philosopher.[12]

The first volume of *La Belle wolfienne* constituted an abridgement of Wolff's general introduction to philosophy that had appeared in his Latin *Logica*.[13] The dialogues between Espérance and Monsieur**, therefore, deal with the nature and purpose of philosophy, the advantages of the demonstrative method, and the basics of human reasoning and how it is rooted in the nature of the human soul. After

7. See Formey, 'Avertissement', in *Belle wolfienne*, vol.1, sig.*2r-v.
8. See Formey, *Belle wolfienne*, vol.1, p.18. Bernard Le Bovier de Fontenelle, *Entretiens sur la pluralité des mondes* (Paris, Blageart, 1686), and Francesco Algarotti, *Il Newtonianismo per le dame: ovvero, dialoghi sopra la luce, i colori e l'attrazione* (Naples [Venice], Pasquali, 1737).
9. See Ursula Pia Jauch, *Damenphilosophie & Männermoral, von Abbé de Gérard bis Marquis de Sade: ein Versuch über die lächelnde Vernunft*, 2nd edn (Vienna, 1991), and Concha Roldàn, 'Damenphilosophie und europäische querelle des femmes zur Zeit Wolffs', in *Christian Wolff und die europäische Aufklärung*, ed. J. Stolzenberg, O.-P. Rudolph and J. Ecole, vol.3, p.145-61. Even Wolff himself had apparently thought of writing such a *philosophie des dames*; see Jean Ecole, 'A propos du projet de Wolff d'écrire une "philosophie des dames"', *Studia leibnitiana* 15:1 (1983), p.46-57.
10. See Formey, *Belle wolfienne*, vol.1, p.16-17.
11. See Formey, *Belle wolfienne*, vol.1, p.56.
12. See Formey, *Belle wolfienne*, vol.1, p.86. For an analysis of *La Belle wolfienne*'s content from the perspective of literature, see Pott, *Reformierte Morallehren*, p.124-31.
13. Wolff, *Discursus praeliminaris*.

the critical intermezzo in *La Belle wolfienne*'s second volume, which is the topic of the present chapter, its third volume continues with the abridgement of Wolff's *Logica*. However, after the appearance of the third volume, Formey gave up his novelistic plot. Instead, the last three volumes present mere translations of Wolff's German *Metaphysik* (volumes 4 and 5) and his Latin *Theologia naturalis* (volume 6), to which Formey added only a few explanatory and critical notes. He justified this change in genre saying that he had encountered difficulties in transforming Wolff's abstract and complex metaphysics into an elegant prose style.[14]

The goal of Formey's *Belle wolfienne* as he conceived it in the beginning was to popularise Wolff's philosophy, that is to say, render it intelligible to non-professional readers. In Formey's view, most people in his day, even in Germany, ignored Wolff's philosophy because of its complexity and scope; hence, in his popular version of it, Formey tried to remove all the difficult and serious elements that had been contained in the original.[15] As such, like his sermons and translations of sermons that have been mentioned previously, Formey's *Belle wolfienne* was another contribution to the promotion of Wolffianism, something in which he engaged together with his Huguenot friends. Like Formey, his friend Jean Des Champs also published popular abridgements of Wolff's philosophy with the aim of rendering it more intelligible and less dry. In his *Cours abrégé de la philosophie wolffienne*, which appeared in two volumes in 1743 and 1747, he presented Wolff's logic, ontology and cosmology (first volume) and psychology (second volume) through fictional letters.[16]

Des Champs underlined the need to transform Wolff's academic philosophy into a popular genre if it was to be made accessible, in particular to a French audience. In general, understanding Wolff's writings required a certain degree of education and perseverance; Des Champs did not claim explicitly that French readers were not capable

---

14. See Formey, 'Préface', in *Belle wolfienne*, vol.4, sig.*2r.
15. See Formey, 'Avertissement', in *Belle wolfienne*, vol.1, sig.*2r.
16. Jean Des Champs, *Cours abrégé de la philosophie wolffienne, en forme de lettres*, vol.1: *Qui contient la Logique, l'Ontologie & la Cosmologie* (Amsterdam and Leipzig, Arkstee & Merkus, 1743); *Cours abrégé de la philosophie wolffienne, en forme de lettres*, vol.2:1: *Qui contient la Psychologie experimentale* (Amsterdam and Leipzig, Arkstee & Merkus, 1747), and *Cours abrégé de la philosophie wolffienne, en forme de lettres*, vol.2:2: *Qui contient la Psychologie raisonnée* (Amsterdam and Leipzig, Arkstee & Merkus, 1747).

of this, yet he believed they preferred less scientific writings as well as a lighter and more entertaining style:

> Il faut pourtant dire à l'honneur de Mr. *Wolff*, que tout homme capable de méditation & d'une attention soutenue, ne trouve point d'obscurités dans son *Système*, & qu'au contraire tout y paroit l'évidence même à un Esprit solide. Mais tel est en general le génie de la *Nation Françoise*: elle ne sauroit gouter ce qui est trop *scientifique* & destitué des agrémens du Stile: pour lui plaire, il faut toujours associer aux choses sublimes, ou profondes, les graces de l'élocution.[17]

In Des Champs's and Formey's view, the model for a successful French abridgement of Wolff's philosophy was Mme Du Châtelet's *Institutions de physique*, which appeared at the same time or shortly before the two men's own abridgements.[18] In her popular introduction to mechanics and geometry, Du Châtelet combined Newtonian physics with Leibnizian metaphysics, relying mostly on Wolff's works for the latter.[19] Hence, Des Champs and Formey praised her for having paved the way for Wolff's philosophy to become known in France as well as for the clarity, precision and elegance of her writing.[20] Nevertheless, Des Champs complained that her style was sometimes too flowery, which in his view could, potentially, alter the sense of the original philosophical content.[21] This shows that even eighteenth-century authors considered popular abridgements of school philosophy as an ambivalent undertaking because it was difficult to find a middle way

---

17. Des Champs, 'Epitre dedicatoire à leurs altesses royales Messeigneurs les princes Henri et Ferdinand freres du roi', in *Cours abrégé*, vol.1, sig.*4r-v (emphasis in the original). Compare to a later but similar statement by Emer de Vattel: Vattel to Formey (9.7.1751), in *Emer de Vattel à Jean Henri Samuel Formey*, p.129. Vattel, who translated Wolff's *Juris naturae et gentium* into French, attempted to remake Wolff's writing in a style that was less discouraging and more comprehensible for the common reader.
18. Emilie Le Tonnelier de Breteuil, marquise Du Châtelet, *Institutions de physique* (Paris, Prault, 1740). Formey could not have known this before the publication of the first volume of his *Belle wolfienne*; Des Champs claimed to have read it after he had finished the manuscript for his *Cours abrégé*.
19. See Andrea Reichenberger, *Emilie du Châtelets Institutions physiques: über die Rolle von Prinzipien und Hypothesen in der Physik* (Wiesbaden, 2016). For Wolff's influence on Du Châtelet's work, see particularly p.16-17, and for Wolff's appreciation of Du Châtelet, see p.69-71.
20. See Formey, 'Préface', in *Belle wolfienne*, vol.4, sig.*2r, and Des Champs, 'Avertissement de l'auteur', in *Cours abrégé*, vol.1, sig.*6v.
21. See Des Champs, 'Avertissement', in *Cours abrégé*, vol.1, sig.*6v-*7r.

between enticing a larger public to read them and being faithful to the original.

This ambivalence is also reflected in Wolff's own opinion of the French popular versions of his philosophy. As he wrote in a letter to Manteuffel in January 1741, he believed the advantage of his philosophy to be its strict demonstrative method, which was the only means by which to discover its truths. He was aware that most readers, in fact, did not have the intellectual capacity to comprehend this method and, therefore, had a pragmatic attitude towards the idea of softening or embellishing it. He approved of Formey's *Belle wolfienne* as a means of stimulating interest in his philosophy among people who would otherwise have completely ignored it.[22] Moreover, Wolff had a particular interest in disseminating his philosophy in France, where he believed the materialistic, deistic and sceptical attitudes that were propagated by English (Newtonian) philosophy were gaining increasing influence.[23] Consequently, Wolff was disappointed when he learned that, with its second volume, Formey's French abridgement of his philosophy had turned into a criticism of it. In particular, Wolff feared this would have a negative impact on the reception of his philosophy abroad.[24]

In addition to Wolff himself, Formey's Wolffian friends and readers were irritated by the exposition of criticism in the middle of his popular abridgement of their master's philosophy. Des Champs regarded Formey's procedure as dangerous because it could alienate readers that were not yet profoundly familiar with Wolff's philosophy.[25] Formey's friend Bocquet and the Dutch bookseller Prosper Marchand, who had facilitated the publication of *La Belle wolfienne* in The Hague, were particularly concerned about the absence of arguments in defence of Wolff in the book. Marchand advised Formey to invalidate

---

22. See Wolff to Manteuffel (27.1.1741), in *Briefwechsel zwischen Wolff und Manteuffel*, vol.1, p.401-402. In his letter, Wolff also referred to Des Champs's and Du Châtelet's views on the superficiality and lack of perseverance of the French reading public.
23. See Wolff to Manteuffel (7.6.1739 and 5.7.1739), in *Briefwechsel zwischen Wolff und Manteuffel*, vol.1, p.122 and 149-50.
24. See Wolff to Manteuffel (14.6.1741), in *Briefwechsel zwischen Wolff und Manteuffel*, vol.1, p.423. Compare with Wolff to Manteuffel (7.1.1743), p.488-89, in which Wolff suggested that Formey's critical second volume had been occasioned by the hostile atmosphere towards Wolff that dominated in Berlin.
25. See Des Champs, 'Avertissement', in *Cours abrégé*, vol.1, sig.[*8r-*9r].

the objections against Wolff that he had raised immediately.[26] The perception that Formey's criticism needed to be invalidated was also what drove the *aléthophiles*' reaction to it. A few months after the appearance of *La Belle wolfienne*'s second volume, Manteuffel published a thin booklet entitled *Lettre de Mr. P... jurisconsulte de Marbourg à Mlle Espérance de B.*, in which he took up Formey's prose and replied to criticism that had been raised.[27] In the 'Avis' to this writing, Manteuffel (who remained anonymous and simply presented himself as 'a friend of Mr Formey') justified its publication by saying he was trying to allay people's fears that Formey would end his work without disproving the criticism he had presented in its previous volume by doing so on Formey's behalf.

These concerns and countermeasures emphasise how much importance Wolff and the Wolffians attributed to popular philosophical writings such as Formey's *Belle wolfienne*. It appears they were mostly concerned with the circumstances in which Formey presented his criticism. With regard to the content of Formey's criticism, it contained almost nothing new, but repeated the arguments of previous controversies in relation to Wolff's philosophy.[28]

Formey's multivocal criticism of pre-established harmony and the *nexus rerum*

As Formey stated in 1741 at the beginning of the second volume of his *Belle wolfienne*, his intention was to collect all the arguments that had previously been raised against Wolff's philosophy and to add his own objections.[29] Thus, he wanted to present a multivocal criticism of Wolff, and this is reflected in the composite structure of

---

26. See Bocquet to Formey (26.5.1741), FF, and Marchand to Formey (19.9.1741), in Schillings, 'La correspondance entre Formey et Marchand', p.274.
27. [Ernst Christoph von Manteuffel], *Lettre de Mr. P... jurisconsulte de Marbourg à Mlle Espérance de B., contenant la suite du tome second de la Belle wolfienne* (n.p., n.n., 1741). In addition to the fictional letter to Formey's protagonist, the booklet included three pieces that defended pre-established harmony in particular: a passage from Fontenelle's appraisal of Leibniz's theory of pre-established harmony, a short treatise on the theory of pre-established harmony by Reinbeck, and a section of Leibniz's *Théodicée*.
28. This is also what Manteuffel thought about the content of Formey's criticism; see Manteuffel to Wolff (15.6.1741), in *Briefwechsel zwischen Wolff und Manteuffel*, vol.1, p.426-27.
29. See Formey, 'Avertissement', in *Belle wolfienne*, vol.2, sig.*2r-v.

5. Pre-established harmony and fatalism

the book. It consisted of three different types of criticism that relied on various sources and, therefore, differed in thematic focus, ideological standpoint and style. All of these criticisms were, however, variations on a single theme: to lay the blame for fatalistic consequences squarely on the different forms of causality inherent in Leibniz's and Wolff's philosophy.

Within the plot of *La Belle wolfienne*, Formey presents the criticism of Leibniz's and Wolff's philosophy as an argument between two opposing fictional characters whom he introduces in the second volume of his novel. The characters are two young university graduates who are invited to have lunch with Espérance, her sister and her mother as well as their visitor Monsieur **. Formey portrays the two young men as adversaries with respect to their attitude towards Wolffianism. Monsieur M… is a theologian from Halle, the centre of the Pietist opposition to Wolff. He is described as rather phlegmatic and having a tendency to mockery and, moreover, as showing a keen interest in the beautiful Espérance. Thus, Formey presents him as the natural enemy of the Wolffian party represented by the narrator, Monsieur **. In contrast, Monsieur P… is introduced as a lawyer from Marburg, the place where Wolff spent almost twenty years in exile. He is described as bright and lively and showing delight in Wolff's return to Halle University in 1740, making him a supporter of the Wolffian cause.[30] Formey, therefore, frames the difference of opinion about Leibniz's and Wolff's philosophy that develops at the lunch table in Charlottenburg as an argument between two young men who have been trained differently, whereas Espérance and Monsieur ** are just observers.

The discussion is, however, dominated by Monsieur M…, Wolff's critic, who presents his criticism in three different 'acts'. Short interventions by the other characters separate the acts from one another. The first act consists in a general attack against the alleged fatalism of Leibniz's and Wolff's philosophy from a religious point of view. The second and third acts comment on Wolff's arguments in relation to the Pietists' criticism of the *nexus rerum* as well as in relation to the theory of pre-established harmony.

The initial, more general criticism is contained in a polemical letter written by one of Monsieur M…'s correspondents, 'un Philosophe distingué, qui tient Tête au *Wolfianisme*',[31] who believes Leibniz's

30. See Formey, *Belle wolfienne*, vol.2, p.12.
31. See Formey, *Belle wolfienne*, vol.2, p.15.

philosophy to have a destructive effect on religion.[32] This letter is based on a real letter Formey received from Lausanne from his correspondent Jean-Pierre de Crousaz, who was a fierce opponent of Leibnizian and Wolffian philosophy. In *La Belle wolfienne*, Formey makes his anti-Wolffian character Monsieur M... read the letter out loud to the other characters. In this letter, Leibniz's concepts of substances (monads), causality and pre-established harmony are lumped together without distinction, and are portrayed as leading to a fatalistic world in which neither human beings nor God are free. First, Leibniz's philosophy is said to present a mechanical worldview according to which the human soul is linked to a bodily machine it is unable to control.[33] As the letter states, this has severe consequences for people's morality and religiosity; because human beings are exactly as God wants them to be in Creation and also because they act exactly as God wants them to, they cannot be either blamed or condemned for their actions by God,[34] nor can they beg God to ameliorate their situation.[35] Second, as the letter maintains, Leibniz's description of God's perfections and love of His creatures implies that God had no other choice but to create the world as it became and, thus, He could not be considered free.[36]

In the letter, these assumptions are contrasted with the Christian concept of a reciprocal love between God and His creatures that requires a free God who interacts with His free and active creatures. Only if God had created human beings out of free choice would His infinite benevolence become visible,[37] and only if human beings were free and active could they become happy by earning the gratitude of their Creator.[38] Furthermore, the alleged Leibnizian determinism is blamed for ridiculing events in the Bible, including the doctrine of the self-sacrifice of Christ.[39] The criticism of pre-established harmony contained in the letter read out by Monsieur M... concentrates, therefore, solely on the theory's assumed consequences, which are summarised under the concept of fatalism and portrayed as being harmful to religion. In contrast, questions with regard to the

32. See Formey, *Belle wolfienne*, vol.2, p.16.
33. See Formey, *Belle wolfienne*, vol.2, p.19.
34. See Formey, *Belle wolfienne*, vol.2, p.22.
35. See Formey, *Belle wolfienne*, vol.2, p.19-20.
36. See Formey, *Belle wolfienne*, vol.2, p.23.
37. See Formey, *Belle wolfienne*, vol.2, p.24.
38. See Formey, *Belle wolfienne*, vol.2, p.25.
39. See Formey, *Belle wolfienne*, vol.2, p.26-28.

metaphysical possibility of pre-established harmony are omitted. It is very likely that the religious and moral arguments of the letter written by Crousaz appealed to Formey in his role as a young pastor and, therefore, he replicated them in his *Belle wolfienne*.

Besides objecting to the implications of Leibniz's philosophy for religion and faith, Crousaz's letter also pursued a campaign against Leibnizianism and Wolffianism as a 'school of philosophy', all of which Formey also replicated in the plot of his *Belle wolfienne*. Probably the most violent statement of Crousaz's attack against Leibnizian and Wolffian philosophy was that Leibniz had, essentially, only copied Spinoza – the effective public incarnation of irreligion at this time – but had given Spinoza's ideas a more appealing (and perhaps seductive) cover.[40]

To oppose this attack, Wolff's partisan Monsieur P… refers to the defence that Wolff himself penned in 1724 against the attacks of his Pietist adversaries in Halle: the *De differentia nexus rerum sapientis, & fatalis necessitatis*.[41] In it, Wolff defended his notion of a causal interlinkage between all things in the universe – the *nexus rerum*[42] – as well as the theory of pre-established harmony against the accusations of fatalism and Spinozism. Like Crousaz, Wolff's Pietist adversaries associated the *nexus rerum* and pre-established harmony with a mechanical and deterministic worldview that curtailed freedom, and attacked it from a religious position.[43] In *La Belle wolfienne*, Formey's

---

40. See Formey, *Belle wolfienne*, vol.2, p.32.
41. Christian Wolff, *De differentia nexus rerum sapientis, & fatalis necessitatis, nec non systematis harmoniae praestabilatae & hypothesium spinosae luculenta commentatio, in qua simul genuina dei existentiam demonstrandi ratio expenditur et multa religionis naturalis capita illustrantur* (1724), ed. Jean Ecole, in *Christian Wolff: Gesammelte Werke*, ed. Jean Ecole *et al.*, section 2, vol.9 (Hildesheim, 1983). The German translation is 'Deutliche Erläuterung des Unterscheids unter einer weisen Verknüpfung der Dinge und einer unumgänglichen Nothwendigkeit/ desgleichen unter der Meinung von der vorherbestimmten Harmonie und den Lehrsätzen des Spinozens', in *Sammlung der Wolffischen Schutzschrifften, welche zu der Grundwissenschafft gehören*, ed. Gottlieb Friedrich Hagen (Halle, Renger, 1739), p.3-198.
42. Wolff defined the *nexus rerum* in his *Metaphysik*, §543. It included the causal linkage between things that succeeded each other in time as well as between things that coexisted in space. Casula, 'Die Lehre von der prästabilierten Harmonie', p.406, holds that Wolff's theory of the *nexus rerum* was a rudimentary version of Leibniz's theory of universal harmony.
43. In relation to the difference of opinion with Lange in particular, see Bianco, 'Freiheit gegen Fatalismus'; for an analysis of the broader controversy that

protagonist Monsieur M..., Wolff's critic, shows himself dissatisfied with Wolff's defensive arguments against these attacks, and raises several objections to Wolff's treatise.[44] This critical commentary on Wolff's *De differentia nexus rerum* constitutes the second and third part of the criticism of Leibniz's and Wolff's philosophy contained in *La Belle wolfienne*.

Most prominently, Monsieur M... destroys Wolff's defence against the accusation that his philosophy had the same implications as Spinoza's determinism. In his *Ethica*, Spinoza claimed that all things were determined because of God's necessary existence and that, hence, nothing in nature was contingent.[45] The criticism presented in *La Belle wolfienne* focused on the necessity of human beings' existence, which resulted from this kind of determinism. Formey first showed there was no difference between Spinoza's denial of possible existence and Wolff's distinction between possible and real existence. Unlike Spinoza, who held that every actually existing thing necessarily existed, Wolff was convinced that God granted existence only to certain things among many possible things. As far as Formey's protagonist (Monsieur M...) is concerned, however, Spinoza's and Wolff's opinions amount to the same thing.[46] Moreover, he states that, even if it were feasible to agree with Wolff's theory of possible existence, this would not account sufficiently for the world's contingency because God's decision to create the world was not completely arbitrary; even before its creation, the actually existing world must have contained a coercive reason that determined God to choose it instead of all the other possible worlds.[47] Finally, according to Monsieur M..., Wolff's argument that the world came into being contingently by divine decree does not rule out the determinism by which each element and every action in a causally linked order is characterised, a determinism that did not differ from Spinoza's:

---

    also includes the criticisms of Johann Franz Budde, Johann Georg Walch and Andreas Johannes Rüdiger, see Eric Watkins, 'From pre-established harmony to physical influx: Leibniz's reception in eighteenth-century Germany', *Perspectives on science* 6:1 (1998), p.136-203 (145-67).

44. See Formey, *Belle wolfienne*, vol.2, p.35.
45. See Baruch Spinoza, *The Collected works of Spinoza*, ed. Edwin Curley, 2 vols (Princeton, NJ, 1985), vol.1, *Ethics*, part 1, proposition 29, p.433-34.
46. See Formey, *Belle wolfienne*, vol.2, p.59.
47. See Formey, *Belle wolfienne*, vol.2, p.59-60.

5. Pre-established harmony and fatalism

> Mais, après tout, que la Nécessité absolue découle du Décret de Dieu, ou de l'Essence & de la Combinaison des Choses, n'est-ce pas pour nous la même chose? Nous nous trouvons dans une certaine Combinaison, dans une certaine Enchainure, où nous sommes déterminez nécessairement à telles ou telles Actions, à tels ou tels Etats: en serons-nous plus avancés, quand Monsieur Wolff nous aura appris, que tout cela est en soi contingent & hypothétique; & la Nature de nos Actions & de notre Sort ne demeure-t-elle pas la même que dans le Systême de Spinosa?[48]

The argument that Wolff's *nexus rerum* was genuinely deterministic regardless of its contingent existence via free divine decree was probably the most influential one. Not only was it the basis of much of Crousaz's polemics against Wolff, but it was also contained in the refutation that Johann Georg Walch penned against Wolff in 1724.[49] Formey himself also revived it in the last section of his commentary on Wolff's concept of the *nexus rerum*, in which he adopted the Pietists' argument that the predetermination of the world's order that was assumed in the theory of *nexus rerum* curtailed the existence of miracles.[50]

Formey concluded his critical commentary in relation to Wolff's defence of his *nexus rerum* by making his protagonist (Monsieur M...) repeat that Wolff had not succeeded in disproving the fatalistic implications of the causal interlinkage between all things in the world:

> En voilà, je pense, suffisamment, pour dégager ma Parole, & vous faire sentir, que le *Nexus Rerum* n'est pas aussi éloigné de la Fatalité, que Monsieur *Wolff* le prétend. Car, j'appelle *fatal* tout ce qui est inevitable, & doit éxister nécessairement, soit que la Raison de cette Nécessité se trouve dans l'Essence des Choses, ou dans la Nature du Plan, ou dans la Volonté du Premier-Etre. En effet, par rapport à moi, à mon Sort, à la Vertu, à la Religion, il est égal par quelle Voie la Liberté périsse: & je n'ai pas plus de Ressource & de Consolation dans la Nécessité hypothétique, que dans le *Fatalisme*.[51]

The above remark was an open denial of the compatibility between a determined order of the world and human liberty. This was not only

---

48. See Formey, *Belle wolfienne*, vol.2, p.61; compare also with p.68.
49. See Johann Georg Walch, *Bescheidene Antwort auf Herrn Christian Wolffens Anmerckungen über das Buddeische Bedenken dessen Philosophie betreffendt, welches selbst wieder beigefügt worden*, 2nd edn (Jena, Meyer, 1725), §7, p.28-29.
50. See Formey, *Belle wolfienne*, vol.2, p.68.
51. Formey, *Belle wolfienne*, vol.2, p.69 (emphasis in the original).

one of the foundations of Wolff's philosophical system but something that was also pertinent as far as orthodox Protestant religion was concerned. Thus, such a denial caused harm to the concept of divine prescience in general, a risk that Formey acknowledged in his *Belle wolfienne*. He made Monsieur M...'s Wolffian adversary, the young lawyer from Marburg, remark that, if God's prescience were to be retained, then a certain degree of necessity had to be allowed for: 'En attendant, souvenez-vous, que cette Nécessité, que vous fuïez avec tant d'Horreur, se trouve dans tous les Systêmes, où la Prescience de Dieu est admise.'[52] With this objection, Formey obliged his anti-Wolffian protagonist (Monsieur M...) to admit that he was deliberately ignoring the way divine prescience and liberty could coexist and state that his only aim was to avoid a system that was characterised by necessity.[53] Such a defence of complete human freedom has been associated traditionally with Socinian views[54] and, therefore, Formey's criticism of Wolff's alleged fatalism was, potentially, prone to heterodoxy; it was impossible to accuse Wolff of fatalism without also levelling the accusation at orthodox Protestant doctrine.

This indication of the similarities between Wolffian philosophy and orthodox Protestantism introduced the third part of the criticism in *La Belle wolfienne*, the part that dealt with the theory of pre-established harmony. By describing the entanglement between soul and body in particular, it was perceived that pre-established harmony constituted a special case of the *nexus rerum* or Leibniz's idea of universal harmony according to which all elements in the world were interlinked.[55] As mentioned above, this concept maintained that soul and body did not act directly on one another, although the perceptions of the soul always corresponded to the movements of the body and vice versa. Wolff adopted this idea of a psycho-physical parallelism because he considered it to be the most likely hypothesis to account for the relationship between soul and body. However, he never enthusiastically embraced it and, instead, constantly emphasised its irrelevance in relation to other crucial elements of his philosophy.[56] Nevertheless,

52. Formey, *Belle wolfienne*, vol.2, p.70.
53. See Formey, *Belle wolfienne*, vol.2, p.71.
54. See Sarah Mortimer, 'Human liberty and human nature in the works of Faustus Socinus and his readers', *Journal of the history of ideas* 70:2 (2009), p.191-211.
55. See Casula, 'Die Lehre von der prästabilierten Harmonie', p.401.
56. See Watkins, 'From pre-established harmony to physical influx', p.141-42, and Hans Poser, '"Da ich wider Vermuthen gantz natürlich auf die vorher bestimmte Harmonie des Herrn Leibnitz geführet ward, so habe ich dieselbe

Wolff's adversaries mainly used his arguments in relation to pre-established harmony to accuse him of fatalism. Therefore, Wolff's 1724 defensive treatise contained a second part in which he tried to defend Leibniz's theory of pre-established harmony against the accusation of Spinozism. Formey had already provided an account of pre-established harmony and Wolff's stance in relation to it in the appendix to the first volume of his *Belle wolfienne*, namely, in a 'Lettre philosophique sur l'harmonie préétablie'.[57] This short treatise was also based to some extent on the second part of Wolff's *De differentia nexus rerum*; however, it presented Wolff's arguments in a way that supported pre-established harmony. In contrast, in the second volume of *La Belle wolfienne*, Formey made use of the same arguments to defeat the idea of pre-established harmony.

With regard to the assumed fatalism of pre-established harmony, Formey concentrated on the fatalistic implications of the psycho-physical parallelism between soul and body inherent in this assumption and, thus, presented a slightly altered version of his earlier argument that the *nexus rerum* was genuinely deterministic, regardless of God's presumably free decree. More precisely, Formey obliged his protagonist (Monsieur M...) to accept that, as a result of God's decree, all thoughts and movements of human beings were foreseen by God, yet, he made Monsieur M... claim that pre-established harmony was different from God's prescience because it destroyed human liberty, which was understood as humans being able to determine their actions by themselves. According to this, in pre-established harmony, the soul lacked any liberty because it always had to perceive what the body felt, and every movement of the body was bound to happen, no matter whether the soul willed it.[58] In his *De differentia nexus rerum*, Wolff had overthrown this criticism by referring to a metaphor used by Isaac Jaquelot, according to which the body was compared with a servant whose actions had been preconceived by an artist (God) and, thus, they succeeded one another automatically. The commands of the servant's master, who represented the human soul, corresponded precisely to these preconceived actions. Wolff followed Jaquelot's

---

beybehalten"': Christian Wolffs Rezeption der prästabilierten Harmonie', in *Leibnizbilder im 18. und 19. Jahrhundert*, ed. Alexandra Lewendoski (Stuttgart, 2004), p.49-63.

57. Formey, *Belle wolfienne*, vol.1, 'Lettre philosophique sur l'harmonie préétablie à Mr. C...', p.161-90.

58. See Formey, *Belle wolfienne*, vol.2, p.76.

opinion and, as far as he was concerned, the lack of any real impact on the servant's/body's movements by the master/soul did not impede the soul's genuine liberty.[59] Formey had already quoted this metaphor in the 'Lettre philosophique sur l'harmonie préétablie' at the end of the first volume of *La Belle wolfienne*.[60] In its second volume he took it up again, yet criticised it as incorrect because it did not take people's awareness of their own situation into account. If humans did not know the movements of their bodily machines were predetermined by somebody else, they could believe it were them themselves who steered those movements through their will. However, if they were aware of a pre-established harmony, then the belief in their freedom could not persist: 'En un mot, si le Systême de l'*Harmonie préétablie* ne fait aucun Tort à la Liberté, il ne peut néanmoins qu'en ébranler la Persuasion dans ceux qui l'admettent. Du moins, il ne leur laisse aucun Moïen de s'en assurer, non plus qu'une Montre, qui auroit des Perceptions correspondantes à ses Mouvemens, ne pourroit se croire libre.'[61] Hence, according to Formey's viewpoint, the compatibility between pre-established harmony and liberty that Leibniz and Wolff postulated was simply not conceivable at this stage. However, as will become clear in the next chapter, he changed his opinion only a few years later when he engaged in the debate on free will.

In addition to this renewed statement concerning the fatalistic implications of pre-established harmony, Formey's criticism of this theory challenged the endeavour to conceive of the relationship between soul and body in general. He made his anti-Wolffian protagonist (Monsieur M...) state that all the different explanations of the relationship between soul and body neither differed on a phenomenological level nor affected human morality. This was an allusion to Wolff's own position concerning the different theories of the relationship between soul and body in general and pre-established harmony in particular. According to Wolff, all of these theories were based on the same empirically proven fact, namely, that soul and body interacted; however, none of them could prove with any certainty how this interaction functioned. Therefore, the theories were, in fact, nothing more than hypotheses and, thus, had no impact on practical

---

59. See Wolff, 'Deutliche Erläuterung des Unterscheids', §21, p.169-70.
60. See Formey, *Belle wolfienne*, vol.1, 'Lettre philosophique sur l'harmonie préétablie', p.187-88.
61. Formey, *Belle wolfienne*, vol.2, p.78.

philosophy that dealt with morality.[62] In his 'Lettre philosophique sur l'harmonie préétablie' in the first volume of *La Belle wolfienne*, Formey also emphasised the hypothetical character of pre-established harmony. Here, however, in defence of the theory, he argued that theologians had no right to attack it because it did not interfere with their field of expertise.[63] By contrast, in the second volume of *La Belle wolfienne*, Formey used Wolff's opinion on the hypothetical character of pre-established harmony to claim the failure of all three existing theories of the relationship between soul and body: the scholastic theory of philosophical influx; Cartesian occasionalism; and Leibniz's pre-established harmony. Furthermore, he pleaded for suspending research into the possible relationship between soul and body until the soul could be better known.[64]

Moreover, Formey also argued implicitly for the revival of the scholastic theory of physical influx that had been overthrown by Descartes and Leibniz because they believed it to violate the law of the conservation of motion or living forces in the universe. According to them, if two essentially different substances such as soul and body acted upon one another, out of necessity this would lead to an uneven distribution of forces in the universe, a phenomenon they wanted to circumvent by describing the relationship between soul and body to be equal and controlled by God. Formey now insinuated that it was possible the soul exercised precisely the amount of force on the body that was required not to violate the laws of the universe, even without God's involvement. He concluded that this would make Descartes's and Leibniz's objections against physical influx invalid. Furthermore, he questioned whether the law of the conservation of motion or living forces was true by referring to unspecified English philosophers who maintained neither this law nor Leibniz's concept of pre-established

---

62. See Wolff, *Metaphysik*, §845; *Ausführliche Nachricht von seinen eigenen Schriften, die er in deutscher Sprache von den verschiedenen Theilen der Welt-Weißheit heraus gegeben/ auf Verlangen ans Licht gestellet* (2nd edn, 1733), ed. Hans Werner Arndt, in *Christian Wolff: Gesammelte Werke*, ed. Jean Ecole *et al.*, 2nd edn, section 1, vol.9 (Hildesheim, 2016), §97; 'Deutliche Erläuterung des Unterscheids', §21, p.172-73. Bianco, 'Freiheit gegen Fatalismus', p.129-30, believes that these later comments on pre-established harmony by which Wolff curtailed the importance of the theory were a reaction to Lange's and other Pietists' criticism.
63. See Formey, *Belle wolfienne*, vol.1, 'Lettre philosophique sur l'harmonie préétablie', p.166-67.
64. See Formey, *Belle wolfienne*, vol.2, p.79.

harmony.[65] Formey, thus, also doubted the cosmological convictions on which Leibniz's theory of a psycho-physical parallelism relied.

Formey's suggestions concerning a possible revision of the traditional assumption of a real relationship between soul and body reflected developments in Germany, where the theory of physical influx had been reconsidered since 1720 and came to dominate the discourse on the relationship between soul and body in the second half of the eighteenth century.[66] Moreover, many of the philosophers, such as Johann Christoph Gottsched, Martin Knutzen and Johann Peter Reusch, who revised and embraced (altered) theories of physical influx in this period were disciples of Wolff. Their deliberations, like Formey's comments on physical influx in *La Belle wolfienne*, were most probably inspired by Wolff's own comments on the hypothetical character of theories of the relationship between soul and body as well as on the similarities between physical influx and pre-established harmony.[67] In fact, Gottsched's considerations with regard to physical influx raised similar issues to those Formey debated in his *Belle wolfienne* in the sense that Gottsched reassessed the metaphysical assumptions that Descartes and Leibniz had originally cited as the reason why they rejected this theory. Like Formey, Gottsched referred to the lack of knowledge on the true nature of soul and body, which according to him would simply forbid excluding the possibility of a real influence between these two entities. Moreover, he also questioned whether it was true that physical influx violated the law of the conservation of motion or living forces as Descartes and Leibniz had claimed.[68] These kinds of considerations led to the erosion of the theory of pre-established harmony from a metaphysical and natural philosophical point of view. Moreover, as Ursula Goldenbaum suggests, the renunciation of the theory of pre-established harmony by several of Wolff's German disciples resulted from their acceptance of the abiding Pietist criticism of it and, as such, was

---

65. See Formey, *Belle wolfienne*, vol.2, p.84.
66. See Watkins, 'From pre-established harmony to physical influx', p.167-83, and Falk Wunderlich, 'Meiers Verteidigung der prästabilierten Harmonie', in *Georg Friedrich Meier (1718-1777): Philosophie als 'wahre Weltweisheit'*, ed. Gideon Stiening and Frank Grunert (Berlin, 2015), p.113-22 (115-16).
67. See Bianco, 'Freiheit gegen Fatalismus', p.131. For a detailed analysis of Gottsched's and Knutzen's conceptualisations of physical influx see Eric Watkins, 'The development of physical influx in early eighteenth-century Germany: Gottsched, Knutzen, and Crusius', *The Review of metaphysics* 49:2 (1995), p.295-339.
68. See Watkins, 'The development of physical influx', p.301-302.

characteristic of the intellectual rapprochement between second-generation Pietists and Wolffians.[69]

Hence, the criticism of Wolff's philosophy presented in *La Belle wolfienne* combined the 'classical' arguments concerning its fatalistic implications with the rising misgivings about the epistemic foundations of pre-established harmony. It should be emphasised, therefore, that Formey's position in the debate on pre-established harmony and *nexus rerum* was motivated not only by his religious concerns but also by a natural philosophical interest in the sense that he denounced the theory's implications for morality and faith but also doubted its physical possibility. The question, however, is where his doubts came from and what drove him to present them in his popular abridgement of Wolff's philosophy.

The origins of Formey's criticism

Formey's doubts concerning pre-established harmony were raised in an epistolary debate with Jean-Pierre de Crousaz, in which Formey became familiar with the former's harsh criticism of Wolff's philosophy. Crousaz, who was a professor of philosophy and mathematics at the Academy of Lausanne, was a Cartesian scholar and inspired by Locke. Moreover, he was known for his stance against irreligion and immorality in the public sphere, and he had published refutations of Anthony Collins, Pierre Bayle, Alexander Pope, Leibniz and Wolff.[70] His criticism of the alleged fatalism of Leibnizian philosophy in particular dated back to the 1730s. In 1737 and 1738 he published refutations of Alexander Pope's *Essay on man*,[71] which he accused of

---

69. See Ursula Goldenbaum, 'Die öffentliche Debatte in der deutschen Aufklärung 1697-1796: Einleitung', in *Appell an das Publikum: die öffentliche Debatte in der deutschen Aufklärung 1697-1796*, ed. Ursula Goldenbaum, 2 vols (Berlin, 2004), vol.1, p.1-118 (57-58 and 67).
70. On Crousaz see Jacqueline de La Harpe, *Jean-Pierre de Crousaz et le conflit des idées au siècle des Lumières* (Geneva, 1955); on his refutations see particularly p.221-36. Moreover, for his role in the Swiss context, see Simone Zurbuchen, 'Die schweizerische Debatte über die Leibniz-Wolffsche Philosophie und ihre Bedeutung für Emer von Vattels philosophischen Werdegang', in *Reconceptualizing nature, science, and aesthetics: contribution à une nouvelle approche aux Lumières helvétiques*, ed. Patrick Coleman, Anne Hofman and Simone Zurbuchen (Geneva, 1998), p.91-113 (102-104).
71. Jean-Pierre de Crousaz, *Examen de l'essai de Mr. Pope sur l'homme* (Lausanne, Bousquet, 1737), and *Commentaire sur la traduction en vers de Mr. l'abbé Du Resnel de l'Essai de M. Pope sur l'homme* (Geneva, Pelissari, 1738).

being imbued with Leibnizian thought.[72] His criticism was embedded in a broader scholarly debate in Switzerland about the potential dangers of fatalism in general and of pre-established harmony in particular that had evolved in the learned journal entitled *Journal helvétique* in 1738.[73]

Formey's motivation for entering into correspondence with Crousaz in April 1738 was the latter's tireless fight against scepticism and irreligion. In Formey's first letter, he sought Crousaz's approval of and support for the publication of an abridgement of the comprehensive treatise against scepticism entitled *Examen du pyrrhonisme ancien et moderne* that Crousaz had written in 1733. The latter agreed with and approved of Formey's plans.[74] However, although Formey and Crousaz joined forces in the refutation of Pierre Bayle and scepticism in general, their opinions diverged considerably with respect to Leibniz's and Wolff's philosophy. From December 1739 onwards, in several letters to Formey, Crousaz elaborated his criticism of Leibniz's presumed fatalism and Wolff's incomprehensible methodology, and the danger they presented to religion.[75] By contrast, Formey showed his respect for Wolff's philosophy. In his supposedly third letter to Crousaz in November/at the beginning of December 1739, Formey admired and agreed with Wolff's ontology and logic, and did not judge the potentially alarming implications of his psychology, which Crousaz had apparently referred to as particularly dangerous in his previous letter:

> Quoique j'ai quelque prédilection pour le systême de Leibnitz & Wolff, Non juro [in?] verba Magistri surtout, je n'ai pas encore assés approfondi sa Psychologie pour juger, si elle renferme des principes dangereux. Je m'en suis tenu jusqu'à présent à la Logique, & à l'Ontologie, & je vous avouë que tout m'y a paru si lumineux, si bien lié, si solidement demontré, si different des autres Cours que j'avois lus auparavant, que j'en ai conçu une haute idée & du Philosophe, & de sa Philosophie.[76]

---

72. See La Harpe, *Jean-Pierre de Crousaz*, p.230-31, and Zurbuchen, 'Die schweizerische Debatte', p.95-96.
73. See Zurbuchen, 'Die schweizerische Debatte', p.106-108.
74. See Crousaz to Formey (3.11. (or 10.) 1739), FF.
75. See Crousaz to Formey (22.12.1739), FF.
76. Formey to Crousaz (n.d.), BCU Lausanne, Fonds Crousaz, IS 2024 III/233 (emphasis in the original).

5. Pre-established harmony and fatalism

However, as far as Crousaz was concerned, Leibniz's and Wolff's philosophy was as harmful to religion as Bayle's scepticism. He accused Wolff polemically of trying to attract readers by applying the same method as Bayle, namely, presenting coarse or provocative arguments.[77] Moreover, he considered the Leibnizian notion of human liberty in particular to be no different from Bayle's, describing this as a void concept that led to fatalism. Given Formey's predilection for Wolff's philosophy, Crousaz was slightly surprised that Formey agreed with Crousaz's refutation of Bayle, while simultaneously defending Wolff. Furthermore, Crousaz seems to have been worried that Formey's Wolffian bias could harm the evaluation of Bayle he made in his abridgement of Crousaz's *Examen du pyrrhonisme*.[78]

To alter Formey's opinion on Leibnizian and Wolffian philosophy, Crousaz continued to discredit it in his letters to Formey. In late August 1740, Formey received an almost twenty-page-long polemical pamphlet criticising the two German philosophers that had been written by Crousaz. This eventually became the previously cited letter by an anonymous philosopher that Monsieur M... reads out in *La Belle wolfienne*.[79] Consequently, the debate about the fatalistic consequences of the system of pre-established harmony that evolves at the lunch table in Espérance's home in Charlottenburg mirrored – at least in part – the epistolary difference of opinion that occurred between Crousaz and Formey precisely when the latter was in the process of writing his book in support of Wolff.[80]

---

77. See Crousaz to Formey, (s.d. [1740]), BCU Lausanne, Fonds Crousaz, IS 2024/XIII/A/7.
78. See, in particular, two letters by Crousaz to Formey (1.7.1740 and 24.8.1740), D.
79. The main part of the fictional letter in *La Belle wolfienne* was based on Crousaz's letter to Formey (n.d. [1740], BCU Lausanne, Fonds Crousaz, IS 2024 XIII/A/7, which was previously misdated to 1738. This letter reached Formey together with another letter from Crousaz (24.8.1740), D. The very first paragraph of the fictional letter (*Belle wolfienne*, vol.2, p.16-17) was copied from yet another letter: Crousaz to Formey (1.7.1740), D; in this letter, Crousaz announced that his long critical letter, which must have been written between December 1739 and April 1740, had already been posted.
80. Formey finished the manuscript of the first volume of *La Belle wolfienne* in summer 1740 (see Formey to Marchand, 9.8.1740, in Schillings, 'La correspondance entre Formey et Marchand', p.240) and that of the second volume in late 1740 (see Formey to Marchand, 18.2.1741, in Schillings, 'La correspondance entre Formey et Marchand', p.252). The publication date of the first volume in Holland was 1 November 1740 (before it had even arrived in Berlin; see Marchand to Formey, 20.12.[1740], in Schillings, 'La

This difference of opinion, however, seems to have been rather one-sided in the sense that Formey made no reply to Crousaz's criticism. On the contrary, by making Crousaz's criticism of Leibniz and Wolff public in his *Belle wolfienne*, it seems that Formey was expressing his support for the Swiss philosopher's position. Furthermore, in September 1741, after the publication of the second volume of *La Belle wolfienne* (and after the *aléthophiles* publicly criticised Formey for its content), Formey confessed to Crousaz that he had disabused himself of Wolffianism because of Crousaz's influence.[81] He even urged Crousaz to defend him against the *aléthophiles*' criticism of his *Belle wolfienne* by writing a refutation of Manteuffel's *Lettre du jurisconsulte*.[82] Crousaz did, indeed, pen a refutation of 300 pages; however, Marchand, *La Belle wolfienne*'s publisher, refused to insert it into the third volume of the work.[83]

The reason Formey seemed to adopt Crousaz's harsh criticism of Leibniz and Wolff without significant reservations lay in his lack of sufficient arguments to refute it. In 1740, when he received Crousaz's polemical letter criticising Leibniz and Wolff, it would appear he was not yet familiar with Wolff's treatises on psychology, in which the latter clarified his position concerning pre-established harmony and emphasised that it did not harm human liberty.[84] However, more importantly, Formey did not find an unequivocal defence of pre-established harmony among his Wolffian correspondents. In November 1740, he tried to discuss the potential failures and risks of Wolff's system with his Huguenot peer, the pastor Abraham Bocquet, as well as with Manteuffel, the patron of the Société des aléthophiles.

---

correspondance entre Formey et Marchand', p.245), whereas the second volume appeared in the spring of 1741 (see Marchand to Formey, 5.4.1741, in Schillings, 'La correspondance entre Formey et Marchand', p.259).

81. See Formey to Crousaz (29.9.1741), BCU Lausanne, Fonds Crousaz, IS 2024 XII/169.
82. See Crousaz to Formey (n.d.), BCU Lausanne, Fonds Crousaz, IS 2024 XIII/F/30.
83. See Marchand to Formey (19.6.1742), in Schillings, 'La correspondance entre Formey et Marchand', p.282. Crousaz later published his refutation as an independent treatise: Crousaz, *Réflexions sur l'ouvrage intitulé 'La Belle wolfienne' auxquelles on a joint plusieurs éclaircissemens sur le Traité de l'esprit humain* (Lausanne and Geneva, Bousquet, 1743).
84. This emerges from Formey's letter to Crousaz in late 1739, which is cited above (BCU Lausanne, Fonds Crousaz, IS 2024 III/233). However, Formey's 'Lettre philosophique sur l'harmonie pré-établie' in *La Belle wolfienne*'s first volume indicates he was aware of Wolff's position, which the latter had outlined in his rational psychology (see especially p.169).

Formey's aim in addressing these two different regular correspondents was, apparently, to collect arguments that he could insert into his *Belle wolfienne* to counter Crousaz's criticism of pre-established harmony.

Formey's Huguenot friend Bocquet, however, rather reinforced the doubts raised by Crousaz. Although he generally admired Wolff's philosophy, Bocquet admitted he considered Wolff's demonstration of human liberty to be unsatisfactory. Furthermore, he actually believed that the accusations levelled at Wolff by his Pietist adversary Joachim Lange were just, and that Wolff had not succeeded in disproving them. With this claim, Bocquet alluded to Wolff's and Lange's debate about fatalism during the 1720s, to which Wolff had contributed with his defence of the *nexus rerum* and pre-established harmony, and which had served Formey as a source for his *Belle wolfienne*:

> J'aime la philosophie de Wolff. Mais entre nous je ne me sens pas trop d'inclination pour le philosophe. Il y a longtems que je me suis apperçu que Lange avoit raison d'accuser Wolff de détruire la liberté. Mais je voudrois qu'il eût aussi renversé ses démonstrations: je vous avoue que plus je les examine et plus elles me persuadent. [...] Je me rappelle une objection qu'on lui [à Wolff] fait; dont il se tire assés mal: aprés quoi il continue la chaine de ses démonstrations, comme si le chainon qu'on lui dispute etoit aussi bon que les autres. C'est au § 498 de la metaphysique allemande. Il souhaite que la volonté ne se determine jamais sans motifs. On lui objecte qu'un homme qui doit choisir entre deux ducats qui lui paroissent parfaitement égaux, en choisira l'un quoiqu'il n'y ait pas plus de raison pour lui que pour l'autre. A cela Mr. Wolff répond qu'il y a plus de raison pour le ducat qui a eté choisi, qu'il etoit plus à la portée de celui qui devoit en prendre un. Qui ne voit que c'est là une supposition gratuite, et qui va contre la premiere supposition, puisque l'on suppose que les deux ducats paroissent à tous égards parfaitement égaux à celui qui doit en choisir un. Cependant Mr. Wolff pretend que cet exemple n'est pas une exception à la regle qu'il établit, et ne se fait aucun scrupule de passer outre.[85]

Unlike that of Crousaz, Bocquet's criticism focused not on the determinism that, presumably, resulted from the link between the soul and the mechanical body, but on Wolff's psychological considerations with regard to free will in the third chapter of his *Metaphysik*. More precisely, he criticised Wolff's proof of the impossibility of absolutely arbitrary choices. As will be shown in the next chapter, the

---

85. Bocquet to Formey (21.11.1740), FF.

assumption of arbitrary choices posed a crucial challenge to Leibniz's and Wolff's compatibilist theory of free will, because in the eighteenth century more and more philosophers believed it to be the only way of justifying human liberty. Furthermore, Bocquet's criticism of Wolff's explanation of human liberty was based on its logical failure. In contrast, Crousaz's criticism of Leibnizian philosophy was motivated by religious purposes and focused on the assumed consequences of its theories. Doubts concerning Wolff's concept of liberty were common for a Cartesian philosopher and self-proclaimed defender of religion such as Crousaz, but Bocquet's example shows that such doubts also existed among second-generation Prussian Huguenots, who were, generally, quite enthusiastic about Wolff's teachings. It is likely that Bocquet's doubts had at least as much influence on Formey as Crousaz's, and it was perhaps because of Bocquet's comments that Formey chose to discuss Wolff's *De differentia nexus rerum* in the second volume of *La Belle wolfienne*.

Formey expressed his doubts that the Wolffian *nexus rerum* might lead to fatalism to his Wolffian mentor Manteuffel,[86] and told him he would introduce this doubt and the critical issues linked to it into his *Belle wolfienne*.[87] Manteuffel's reaction to this was twofold. On the one hand, he seems to have been alarmed and tried to allay Formey's fears, immediately suggesting that Formey read Johann Jakob Köthen's pro-Wolffian text *Principia quaedam metaphysicae wolfianae* (1737).[88] Moreover, Manteuffel several times urged his friend Johann Gustav Reinbeck, the Wolffian theologian, to speak personally to Formey and to provide him with the necessary theological arguments with which to defend the *nexus rerum* against religious and moral criticism.[89] On the other hand – and this is interesting – Manteuffel did not, in principle, object to Formey's scheme of introducing the critical aspects of Wolff's philosophy into *La Belle wolfienne*, as long as they were discussed and rectified in turn, as Formey planned to do. Manteuffel even defended Formey's intentions against the publisher Ambrosius Haude, another member of the Société des aléthophiles, who considered Formey's projected work as dangerous for the Wolffian cause and feared he

---

86. See Manteuffel to Formey (30.11.1740), CV.
87. See Manteuffel to Reinbeck (24.1.1741), UBL, Ms 0344.
88. See Manteuffel to Formey (30.11.1740), CV.
89. See Manteuffel to Wolff (10.2.1741), in *Briefwechsel zwischen Wolff und Manteuffel*, vol.1, 407; see also the several letters from Manteuffel to Reinbeck between January and April 1741 in UBL, Ms 0344.

would not criticise Wolff in a positive way.[90] It can be said that Haude's fears were realised with the publication of *La Belle wolfienne*, and it is somehow ironic that it became Manteuffel's main accusation against Formey in the *Lettre du jurisconsulte*; however, this was most probably also a consequence of the *aléthophiles*' failure to answer Formey's doubts. Manteuffel prevented Formey from addressing his concerns about fatalism directly to Wolff, and Reinbeck, who was supposed to instruct Formey instead of Wolff, postponed this task for too long. As Manteuffel's letters to Reinbeck reveal, Reinbeck's answer to Formey had still not arrived by April 1741, when the second volume of *La Belle wolfienne* was just about to appear.[91] As a consequence, Manteuffel and the *aléthophiles* were only able to destroy Formey's doubts concerning pre-established harmony retroactively, namely, by publishing the *Lettre du jurisconsulte*.

The reason why Reinbeck took so long to rebut Formey's doubts in relation to the theories of the *nexus rerum* and pre-established harmony was most probably his own ambivalent position concerning these questions. In 1737, he published a treatise that dealt exclusively with the question of pre-established harmony,[92] in which he underlined its compatibility with religion and theological teachings, yet also uttered the reservations he had about the concept. On the one hand, Reinbeck argued that, compared with the theory of physical influx, pre-established harmony undoubtedly confirmed the existence of a Creator God[93] and was able to lift doubts concerning the immortality of the soul.[94] On the other hand, he singled out two crucial problems in the explanation of pre-established harmony that caused him to deny it. First, he challenged the idea that the sensations of the soul were produced from within the soul itself without any external

---

90. See Manteuffel to Reinbeck (24.1.1741), UBL, Ms 0344.
91. See Manteuffel to Reinbeck (9.4.1741), UBL, Ms 0344. Instead, Manteuffel arranged for Wolff to send him a reply addressing Formey's doubts.
92. Johann Gustav Reinbeck, *Erörterung der philosophischen Meynung von der sogenandten HARMONIA PRAESTABILITA*, [...] *aus Liebe zur Wahrheit und zur Verhütung fernerer verworrenen Streitigkeiten, nebst einem nöthigen Vorbericht herausgegeben* (Berlin, Haude, 1737). This treatise gave extra support to the expert report Reinbeck had written one year earlier for King Frederick William I's enquiry into Wolff's possible repatriation (*Bedencken über die der Wolffischen Philosophie von Joachim Langen in seinem kurtzen Abrisse beygemessenen Irrthümer, Commißionswegen aufgesetzt*, Berlin, n.n., 1736).
93. See Reinbeck, *Erörterung der philosophischen Meynung*, §XXVI, p.38-39.
94. See Reinbeck, *Erörterung der philosophischen Meynung*, §XXIX, p.44.

influence. Adherents of pre-established harmony have described this autonomous emergence of the soul's sensations as being the result of a causally linked sequence of sensations instilled in the soul at its creation. In Reinbeck's view, however, it was unlikely that the different subsequent sensations of the soul were directly causally linked to one another.[95] Second, Reinbeck found one of the assertions of pre-established harmony problematic: all bodily actions had to be imputed to God because the latter had instilled a mechanical order in the body at its creation. It followed from this that it was also possible to hold God responsible for the body's sinful behaviour.[96] Although Reinbeck was far from levelling the accusation that the theory of pre-established harmony was fatalistic, his reservations partly concerned similar aspects of the concept of fatality as those considered by Crousaz and the Pietists, namely, the absence of a direct connection between soul and body as well as the mechanical nature of the human body.

As for the *nexus rerum*, Reinbeck drafted an explanation of this theory in June 1741 that Manteuffel meant to insert into his *Lettre du jurisconsulte* to counter Formey's doubts. However, Manteuffel was not satisfied with Reinbeck's arguments in favour of the *nexus rerum* because he thought they would rather confirm Formey's doubts and distance him even further from Wolff's philosophy instead of confirming his belief in it. The contradictory element of Wolff's theory was highlighted in Reinbeck's draft, namely, that on the one hand the *nexus rerum* was defined as contingent and, on the other, its order was determined eternally by an omniscient and good God. As a theologian, Reinbeck portrayed the *nexus rerum* as an expression of God's wisdom, goodness, providence and perfections, all of which would be denied if it was assumed the world's order resulted from pure chance. In Manteuffel's view, this argument was true and would certainly gain Formey's approval. However, he believed that Reinbeck had failed to explain in what sense such a predetermined order affected the individual's moral responsibility.

To express his discomfort with Reinbeck's explanation, Manteuffel outlined the arguments he believed Formey would state in reply to it. Basically, he feared the latter would infer everything that happened in the world was an absolute necessity and, thus, would deny moral responsibility:

---

95. See Reinbeck, *Erörterung der philosophischen Meynung*, §XXXI, p.45-46.
96. See Reinbeck, *Erörterung der philosophischen Meynung*, §XXXII, p.46-47.

5. Pre-established harmony and fatalism

> S'il est vrai, comme il est; dira-t il [Formey]; que le <u>nexus rerum</u> est une complication, une suite d'evenemens prévus, fixez et determinez, de toute Eternité, par l'Etre Suprême infinement sage, bon, juste, et tout-puissant, il faut necessairement, que ce mème Etre-suprême ait prévu, fixé et determiné aussi toutes les ac[ti]ons morales, toutes les Volontez et Vellëitez des hommes; l'usage, bon ou mauvais, qu'ils font de leur Raison, et leur liberté, les raisons, les occasions mème, qui les portent, ou induisent à agir; parceque tout cela fait necessairement partie de ces evenemens. Cela étant; dira-t il encore; toutes nos actions, commes tous les evenemens, sont des suites necessaires de ce que l'Etre-suprême a fixé et determiné de toute Eternité, et ne sauroient ètre [attri]buez ou imputez à l'Homme; à qui il est impossible de changer les determinations ou les Decrets de l'Etre Suprême.

To discourage Formey from conceiving of such an idea of human beings' lack of imputability, Manteuffel urged Reinbeck to explain further what kind of necessity was implied in the *nexus rerum* and if moral behaviour really was the result of absolute necessity:

> La question n'est pas, si cette necessité peut s'expliquer de maniere qu'elle paroisse compatible avec toutes les Perfections de l'Etre suprème? Ny si cette [ex]plication la rend consolante, ou non, pour des créatures raisonnables? [...] Mais il s'agit de savoir, si cette necessité absoluë a lieu, ou non, dans nos actions morales? Et si la doctrine du <u>nexus rerum</u> l'implique, ou ne l'implique pas?[97]

Thus, Manteuffel's objections to Reinbeck's explanation of the *nexus rerum* revolved around the same concerns Reinbeck had already expressed concerning the theory of pre-established harmony in 1737, namely, that it removed all (moral) responsibility from the individual and, instead, passed it on to the omniscient supreme being. Given Manteuffel's purpose of refuting Formey's criticism in *La Belle wolfienne*, he could not tolerate these concerns and, therefore, urged Reinbeck to rework his explanation of the *nexus rerum* before he inserted it into his *Lettre du jurisconsulte*.

However, the *Lettre du jurisconsulte* also lacked strong positive proof that the *nexus rerum* and pre-established harmony allowed for the contingency of the world and human beings' moral responsibility.[98] Instead, it contained an explanation of all the negative

---

97. Manteuffel to Reinbeck (29.6.1741), UBL, Ms 0344 (emphasis in the original).
98. The only instance in which this was positively stated was in a quotation from Wolff's cosmology; see [Manteuffel], *Lettre du jurisconsulte*, p.24-25.

consequences that would be implied if the assumption that the *nexus rerum* and pre-established harmony curtailed contingency were true; God would be devoid of any power and wisdom and humans' behaviour would be that of brutes who were guided by instinct instead of reason. Moreover, the history of the world would appear senseless, and humans would be unable to receive grace.[99] In addition to this negative proof, the *Lettre du jurisconsulte* employed mostly formal and ad hominem arguments against Wolff's and Leibniz's fictional critics in *La Belle wolfienne*. It accused them of deliberately misinterpreting the work of Leibniz, Wolff and their disciples,[100] of having confusing and ridiculous ideas[101] and of reading Wolff's profound treatises in a very superficial and biased way.[102]

Therefore, the various answers by which the *aléthophiles* tried to counter Formey's arguments in relation to the fatalistic implications of Leibniz's and Wolff's philosophy underline how delicate the matter was and, most importantly, that the Wolffians' opinions were not unanimous. Formey's criticism of the *nexus rerum* and pre-established harmony in *La Belle wolfienne*, which had initially also been provoked by Crousaz, reflected the Wolffians' own difficulties with regard to demonstrating convincingly the compatibility between predetermined order and liberty. Moreover, these difficulties caused Reinbeck to hesitate in answering Formey's doubts, hesitations that might have confirmed the latter in his decision to publish the criticisms made by Crousaz and the Pietists.

In point of fact, Formey's apparent agreement with the criticisms made by Crousaz and others disappeared only shortly after the publication of the second volume of his *Belle wolfienne*. In the autumn of 1743, Formey wrote a critical review of Crousaz's *De l'esprit humain*, in which Crousaz pursued the aim of destroying the basics of Leibniz's metaphysics.[103] In Formey's review of this treatise, which appeared in the 1746 issue of his journal *Nouvelle bibliothèque germanique*, he objected to Crousaz's criticism of Leibniz's alleged fatalism.[104] With an almost

---

99. See [Manteuffel], *Lettre du jurisconsulte*, p.32-33.
100. See [Manteuffel], *Lettre du jurisconsulte*, p.17 and 20.
101. See [Manteuffel], *Lettre du jurisconsulte*, p.22.
102. See [Manteuffel], *Lettre du jurisconsulte*, p.26-27.
103. Jean-Pierre de Crousaz, *De l'esprit humain, substance differente du corps, active, libre, immortelle: vérités que la raison démontre, et que la révélation met au-dessus de tout doute* (Basle, Christ, 1741). In a letter to Formey (21.12.1741), FF, Crousaz had announced that his treatise would turn Leibniz's philosophy upside down.
104. 'Article VI. De l'esprit humain', *Nouvelle bibliothèque germanique* 1:2 (1746),

polemical tone, he presented Crousaz's criticism as confusing, unfair and lacking serious judgement.[105] However, content-wise, Formey's attempt to defend Leibniz's and Wolff's philosophy against Crousaz proved to be more difficult. Although Formey claimed the Wolffians had succeeded in ridding their philosophy of the accusations of fatalism,[106] he insinuated they had done less well in proving their philosophy did not curtail either God's or human beings' freedom.[107] Nevertheless, Formey tried hard to refute Crousaz's criticisms with regard to these issues.

First, Formey objected to Crousaz's opinion that human liberty consisted of the possibility of making completely arbitrary choices without being influenced by any motive. In contrast, Formey held that the Leibnizian theory of liberty argued that individuals' perception of the best option always influenced their choices, and, thus, those choices were determined to a certain extent.[108] Second, Formey criticised Crousaz's deliberations on God's freedom, which he considered to be self-contradictory. Crousaz claimed that God's choices were absolutely self-determined and, therefore, free, and also that they resulted from His perfections and His aim of pleasing His creatures. In Formey's view, these claims contained two opposing definitions of God's liberty, and, moreover, the latter claim corresponded to Leibniz's theory of liberty. To say God's choices were a result of His perfections was, in fact, acknowledging they were determined by motives.[109] Finally, Formey refuted Crousaz's charge against Leibniz, according to which the latter had depicted God as the author of sin. Formey countered that Leibnizianism was the only philosophical system able to weaken the impression of a maleficent God because it believed God to have chosen the best of all worlds.[110] In sum, his review of Crousaz's *De l'esprit humain* denigrated most of Crousaz's criticisms that Formey had introduced into his *Belle wolfienne* two years earlier. It is, thus, clear that the Swiss philosopher's apparently successful influence on

---

p.325-36. A letter from Jacques Pérard to Formey (27.11.1743), FF, suggests the article was written in the autumn of 1743.
105. See 'Article VI', p.327 and also 336, in which Formey presents his overall opinion of the work: 'je soupçonne qu'il [Crousaz] est parvenu à cette Epoque d'années, où l'Imagination reprend la place du Jugement.'
106. See 'Article VI', p.328.
107. See 'Article VI', p.329.
108. See 'Article VI', p.330-33.
109. See 'Article VI', p.333-35.
110. See 'Article VI', p.335-36.

him was not as profound and stable as it appeared to be, or as Crousaz might have wished. At the beginning of 1745, the epistolary exchange between Formey and Crousaz was finally interrupted. In his last letter, Crousaz accused Formey of being a pyrrhonian, and insinuated that the latter's image as a Christian philosopher that he conveyed through his moral discourses would suffer from his unorthodox views on the relationship between soul and body.[111]

This alteration in Formey's opinion with regard to Leibniz's and Wolff's alleged fatalism seems to have been sparked mostly by the young philosopher Emer de Vattel from Neufchâtel, who in the Swiss debate about pre-established harmony took a pro-Leibnizian position and published a defence of Leibniz's philosophy against Crousaz's criticisms in 1741.[112] In general, Vattel maintained that Crousaz's criticism was biased and unfounded, and that it imputed unjustified consequences to Leibniz's thought instead of engaging with its logic.[113] Moreover, according to Vattel, it was absurd to accuse Leibniz of irreligion because there was nothing in any of his writings to suggest he was against religion; on the contrary, it was Leibniz who provided the best means of dealing with heretics and sceptics.[114] As for the alleged fatality implied in pre-established harmony, Vattel disproved all of Crousaz's many claims concerning the assumed lack of human and divine freedom in Leibniz's system. In particular, he believed that Crousaz was wrong to attribute the possibility of completely arbitrary choices to God, instead of providing for the likelihood that God was driven by the best possible choice.[115] Furthermore, Vattel considered Crousaz's accusation that pre-established harmony made God the only active and responsible being in the world to be unjustified.[116] Closely linked to this was his accusation that the mechanical entanglement of the world assumed in pre-established harmony would curtail human liberty, an accusation that, according to Vattel, would fall apart if Crousaz would only embrace the correct notion of entanglement.[117]

111. See Crousaz to Formey (8.1.1745), D.
112. Emer de Vattel, *Défense du système leibnitien contre les objections et les imputations de Mr. de Crousaz* (Leiden, Luzac, 1741). In the book's second part, Vattel engaged critically with Crousaz's two refutations of Alexander Pope's *Essay on man* written in 1737 and 1738. See Zurbuchen, 'Die schweizerische Debatte', p.96.
113. See Vattel, *Défense du système leibnitien*, 'Préface', sig.**5v and sig.***r-v.
114. See Vattel, *Défense du système leibnitien*, 'Préface', sig.**7v and sig.***3r.
115. See Vattel, *Défense du système leibnitien*, p.320-22.
116. See Vattel, *Défense du système leibnitien*, p.326-29.
117. See Vattel, *Défense du système leibnitien*, p.330-31.

5. Pre-established harmony and fatalism

Formey read Vattel's work at the end of 1741, when he was still convinced of the chimeric character of Leibniz's notion of liberty. As he reported to Crousaz at the time, he was certain that Vattel would not be able to clarify this notion to Leibniz's advantage.[118] However, Formey changed his mind with regard to Vattel's defence of Leibniz and also in relation to pre-established harmony, most likely because of the two men's personal encounter. Since May 1742, Vattel had been a *pensionnaire* in Formey's house in Berlin, and the intimate correspondence that developed between them after Vattel's stay there suggests the two men formed a very close relationship and discovered a common intellectual standpoint. Eventually, Formey wrote a very positive review of Vattel's *Défense du système leibnitien* for the *Nouvelle bibliothèque germanique* that appeared just one issue after the one in which he discussed Crousaz's *De l'esprit humain* in a negative fashion.[119] It is, thus, very likely that Formey drew on Vattel's work to finally contradict Crousaz's arguments concerning the assumed fatality of Leibnizian pre-established harmony. Moreover, it is likely that, after having been publicly reprimanded for his attack on Wolffianism in the *Lettre du jurisconsulte*, Formey realised how much he had alienated his patron Manteuffel. His criticism of Crousaz and his return to a pro-Wolffian tone in his works were probably also a means to atone for the critical second volume of *La Belle wolfienne*.

Nevertheless, although Formey eventually renounced the charge of fatalism that had been made against Leibniz and Wolff, he continued to have epistemic doubts concerning the theory of pre-established harmony. This becomes evident in his discussion of a new theory of the relationship between soul and body that had been developed in 1759 by Johann Jakob Hentsch, a German professor of mathematics. Formey reviewed the latter's theory, which he presented in an article in the *Acta eruditorum*, in the 1764 Academy yearbook.[120] According to Hentsch's renewed theory of physical influx, there was an *'in distans'*

---

118. Formey to Crousaz (5.12.1741), BCU Lausanne, Fonds Crousaz, IS 2024 XIII/F/57.
119. 'Article VIII. Défense du système leibnitien', *Nouvelle bibliothèque germanique* 2:1 (1746), p.85-102. Formey also made a very positive reference to Vattel's work on the very first page of the preface to the fourth volume of his *Belle wolfienne*.
120. Formey, 'Nouvelles considérations sur l'union des deux substances dans l'homme, ou sur le commerce de l'âme et du corps', in *Histoire de l'Académie royale des sciences et belles lettres de Berlin* (1764; Berlin, Haude & Spener, 1766), p.364-73. Given the time between the publication of Hentsch's article in the *Acta eruditorum* and the date Formey discussed it, it is difficult to pinpoint when

influence between soul and body. Although Formey assessed the theory negatively,[121] he agreed with Hentsch's criticism of pre-established harmony. Formey insinuated that the sole ideal influence between soul and body assumed in this theory was almost inconceivable. How was it possible for bodily states to find an expression in the mind and vice versa if there was no mutual physical contact between soul and body?[122] Hence, at this point, Formey's biggest concerns with the theory of pre-established harmony were the shortcomings in explaining the psycho-physiological interplay that it displayed. In contrast, he claimed confidently that the argument proposing fatalism to be the result of pre-established harmony was untenable and easy to overthrow; liberty was contained in the essence of the soul and, as such, was not affected by the relationship between soul and body.[123] This last claim was a result of Formey studying Wolff's psychology and Leibniz's theory of free will, as will be shown in the next chapter.

Formey actually wrote it. However, a letter from Hentsch to Formey (2.4.1763), D, suggests that Hentsch sent his article to Formey for review in 1763.
121. See Formey, 'Nouvelles considérations', p.373.
122. See Formey, 'Nouvelles considérations', p.368-69.
123. See Formey, 'Nouvelles considérations', p.367.

6. The debate on free will

Formey did not solve the problem of the compatibility between a pre-established causal world order and the contingency of divine and human actions with the second volume of *La Belle wolfienne* in 1741. An important episode in his preoccupation with this problem was his engagement in the centuries-old debate on free will, a debate that was linked intimately to the debate on pre-established harmony and had similarly important implications for morality and religion. In his translation of Wolff's *Metaphysik*, Formey himself stressed the utmost importance of proving human liberty so that the rules of moral behaviour could be established.[1] However, in terms of religion and the notion of God, human liberty played an ambiguous role. Although it was a prerequisite for humans being responsible for their actions, human liberty seemed to be incompatible with divine nature, and with God's omnipotence and omniscience in particular. However, without humans being free, God would be responsible for the evil existing in the world.[2]

Christian philosophy in the mid-eighteenth century had to deal precisely with these ambiguities because the traditional Protestant doctrines of predestination and human sinfulness had become less rigorous and, thus, had lost their capacity to guide people's behaviour unequivocally. Formey's solution in the debate on free will consisted of a compromise between (divine) determination of the world and human freedom, a position that is commonly referred to as a compatibilist approach to liberty. It corresponded to orthodox Reformed doctrine of the seventeenth century, according to which God's will was free and, therefore, the things he willed, that is to say, His creatures, were

1. See Formey, *Belle wolfienne*, vol.5, p.310, n.159.
2. See Leibniz, *Théodicée*, §1, p.106.

contingent.³ In early modern Europe, Leibniz had been one of the most prominent defenders of this approach, and Formey drew very much on the former's works for his 'Réflexions sur la liberté', which he presented at the Academy in December 1747 and which was published in 1750.⁴

However, among Formey's contemporaries, Leibniz and his compatibilist approach to free will encountered harsh criticism, just as his theory of pre-established harmony had also done. Because Formey developed his approval of the Leibnizian theory of free will in the context of the Berlin Academy, this chapter will turn away from the theological criticism of Leibniz's and Wolff's philosophy that was discussed in the previous one. It will focus instead on the reactions of the academicians in Berlin who judged this philosophy from a metaphysical perspective. Although they – like Crousaz – also employed the concept of fatalism to dismiss the Leibnizian theory of free will, they were more concerned with the epistemological problems that questions related to the human soul posed. In fact, there was a tendency among them to be sceptical with regard to the provability of free will. Formey's 'Réflexions sur la liberté' echoed not only the theological and moral concerns linked to free will but also these epistemological uncertainties, trying to eradicate them. In this respect, Formey made use of Wolff's epistemological premises concerning the enquiry into the nature of the human soul. It is, therefore, necessary to first contextualise Formey's theory of free will in relation to the epistemological discourse on the emerging science of the mind before analysing the debate on free will that was taking place at the Berlin Academy.

An empirical science of the soul

As James Harris has stated with regard to the British context, in the eighteenth century, the question of free will was linked strongly to

---

3. See Andreas Beck, 'God, Creation, and providence in post-Reformation Reformed theology', in *The Oxford handbook of early modern theology, 1600-1800*, ed. Ulrich L. Lehner, Richard A. Muller and A. G. Roeber (Oxford, 2016), p.195-212 (201-202).
4. Formey, 'Réflexions sur la liberté', in *Histoire de l'Académie royale des sciences et belles lettres de Berlin* (1748; Berlin, Haude & Spener, 1750), p.334-55. Although the discourse was held on 14 December 1747 at the Academy's assembly, it appeared only in the 1748 yearbook.

concepts of an empirical science of the soul.[5] In relation to this, John Locke's *Essay concerning human understanding* was the most influential text because it was usually considered as having laid the foundations of 'an experimental philosophy of the human mind'.[6] The case of Formey and his immediate context shows that this can equally be said in relation to the debate on the European continent. However, in Germany in the first half of the eighteenth century, the epistemological debate was also much influenced by Wolff's metaphysics.

The particularity of Wolff's approach was that he divided the investigation of the human mind into two epistemologically different parts: empirical and rational psychology. The first was contained in the third chapter of his *Metaphysik* (1719) and the latter in the fifth, whereas in his later Latin oeuvre he developed each of the two approaches in a single treatise.[7] In his empirical psychology, Wolff established certain notions in relation to the mental faculties on the basis of experience, whereas in his rational psychology he tried to define the nature or essence of the soul in which these mental faculties were rooted.[8] The two approaches were intrinsically interconnected because the empirical approach validated the a priori principles that were established by the rational approach, and the rational approach generalised the observations of the soul obtained through the empirical approach. In addition, however, both approaches were self-contained systems of knowledge: rational psychology was able to form hypotheses with regard to other aspects of the soul that could not be perceived via experience,[9] and empirical psychology was not

---

5. See James A. Harris, *Of liberty and necessity: the free will debate in eighteenth-century British philosophy* (Oxford, 2005), p.18.
6. See Harris, *Of liberty and necessity*, p.3.
7. Christian Wolff, *Psychologia empirica, methodo scientifica pertractata, qua ea, quae de anima humana indubia experientiae fide constant, continentur* (2nd edn, 1738), ed. Jean Ecole, in *Christian Wolff: Gesammelte Werke*, ed. Jean Ecole *et al.*, section 2, vol.5 (Hildesheim, 1968), and *Psychologia rationalis, methodo scientifica pertractata, qua ea, quae de anima humana indubia experientiae fide innotescunt, per essentiam et naturam animae explicantur* (2nd edn, 1740), ed. Jean Ecole, in *Christian Wolff: Gesammelte Werke*, ed. Jean Ecole *et al.*, 2nd edn, section 2, vol.6 (Hildesheim, 1994).
8. See Wolff, *Metaphysik*, §191 and 727.
9. See Jean Ecole, 'Des rapports de l'expérience et de la raison dans l'analyse de l'âme ou la *Psychologia empirica* de Christian Wolff', *Giornale di metafisica* 4-5 (1966), p.589-617 (593), and Jean-Paul Paccioni, 'Wolff est-il "le vrai inventeur de la psychologie rationelle"? L'experience, l'existence actuelle et la rationalité dans le projet wolffien de psychologie', in *Die Psychologie Christian*

only an accumulation of observations but also contained notions and principles that could be deduced from these observations.[10]

According to Fernando Vidal, Wolff's empirical psychology in particular helped to establish a discipline that investigated the effects or faculties of the soul only insofar as they were observable through the body, that is, modern, 'scientific' psychology that was dissociated from metaphysics.[11] As such, Wolff's empirical psychology had a huge impact on the methodological discussions among German philosophers such as Gottlieb Friedrich Hagen and Johann Gottlob Krüger, who, during the second half of the eighteenth century, reflected on quantification and experimentation in psychology.[12] Wolff's empirical approach also allowed his disciples to introduce physiological observations taken from medicine, an approach that was very influential among the so-called 'psycho-physicians' during the 1740s and 1750s at the University of Halle, particularly Johann August Unzer.[13]

Wolff's empirical psychology also made its impression on some of the educated Prussian Huguenots. Both Jean Des Champs and Formey translated his work in the 1740s. Des Champs provided a relatively free translation of the Latin version of Wolff's empirical and rational psychology, and published it in 1747 as the second part

---

Wolffs: systematische und historische Untersuchungen, ed. Oliver-Pierre Rudolph and Jean-François Goubet (Tübingen, 2004), p.75-98 (95-96).

10. See Paola Rumore, 'Empirical psychology', in *Handbuch Christian Wolff*, ed. R. Theis and A. Aichele, p.175-96 (181). The two approaches to psychology also had to function independently from one another because psychology constituted the basis of practical philosophy (morals and politics) in Wolff's philosophical system. As Wolff alleged in his *Discursus praeliminaris*, §112, rational psychology was vulnerable to criticisms because it used a method that was often questioned, whereas empirical psychology was unshakeable because it relied on experience. Therefore, to protect his practical philosophy against attacks, he founded it on empirical psychology.
11. See Fernando Vidal, *Les Sciences de l'âme, XVI*-XVIII* siècle* (Paris, 2006), p.23. Ecole, 'Des rapports de l'expérience et de la raison', p.595, similarly evaluates Wolff's empirical psychology.
12. See Fernando Vidal, 'Le discours de la méthode dans la psychologie des Lumières', *L'Homme et la société* 167-69 (2008), p.53-82.
13. See *Vernünftige Ärzte: Hallesche Psychomediziner und die Anfänge der Anthropologie in der deutschsprachigen Frühaufklärung*, ed. Carsten Zelle (Tübingen, 2001), and Carsten Zelle, 'Johann August Unzers Gedanken vom Träumen (1746) im Kontext der Anthropologie der "vernünftigen Ärzte" in Halle', in *Zwischen Empirisierung und Konstruktionsleistung: Anthropologie im 18. Jahrhundert*, ed. Jörn Garber and Heinz Thoma (Tübingen, 2004), p.19-30.

of his *Cours abrégé de la philosophie wolffienne*.[14] Formey translated the German version of the empirical psychology, that is to say, the third chapter of the *Metaphysik*, and published it in the fifth volume of his *Belle wolfienne*.[15] Des Champs's and Formey's publications were preceded by an anonymous translation of the Latin version of the empirical psychology that had appeared in Amsterdam in 1745 under the title *Psychologie, ou Traité sur l'ame*.[16] Formey's translation in particular reveals his thorough engagement with Wolff's work because it also included some of Wolff's own later annotations to his *Metaphysik*, the *Anmerckungen*, as well as several comments by Formey himself, all of which were listed as footnotes.

In addition to translating it, Formey employed Wolff's empirical psychology as a source for several of his writings in the 1740s, notably for one of his first contributions to the Academy, the 'Essai sur les songes', in which he outlined a theory of dreaming that was uniquely based on the observation of the phenomena that accompanied the process of dreaming.[17] Less obviously but very likely, the article 'Entendement' that Formey wrote at this time for his *Dictionnaire philosophique*, and which later appeared in the *Encyclopédie*, probably resulted from Wolff's empirical psychology.[18] Ultimately, Formey's epistemological considerations in his 'Réflexions sur la liberté' betrayed the influence of Wolff's empirical psychology. Like Wolff, Formey emphasised the epistemological similarities between physics

14. Des Champs, *Cours abrégé*, vol.2:1 and vol.2:2.
15. As the correspondence with Jean Neaulme, the book's publisher, indicates, Formey submitted the manuscript of this volume in 1746 (Neaulme to Formey, 29.[8].1746, CV), although it was not published until 1753.
16. *Psychologie, ou Traité sur l'ame, contenant les connoissances, que nous en donne l'expérience, par M. Wolf* (Amsterdam, Mortier, 1745).
17. See Formey, 'Essai sur les songes'. Vis-à-vis Manteuffel, Formey even mentioned explicitly that his essay was indebted to Wolff's empirical psychology; see Formey to Manteuffel (27.1.1748), UBL, Ms 0347. For a more detailed account of Formey's Wolffian-inspired empirical approach to the process of dreaming in his 'Essai sur les songes', see my own 'The role of reason, experience, and physiology in J. H. S. Formey's *Essay on dreams*', in *The Experimental turn in eighteenth-century German philosophy*, ed. Karin de Boer and Tinca Prunea-Bretonnet (New York, 2021), p.158-80.
18. See 'Entendement, (Logique)', in *Encyclopédie*, vol.5 (Paris, Briasson et al., 1755), p.718. The article is reminiscent of Wolff's distinction between the clear and obscure notions that both exist in the human mind. Moreover, the article contains traces of Wolff's theory of perfectionability, because it holds that human understanding can be improved constantly.

and empirical psychology because the findings of both were based on observations and experiences. The difference was that physics dealt with bodies and psychology with a spirit, which was why the latter relied on inner instead of sensory experience.[19]

Formey also used inner experience as the empirical foundation of his proof of free will. More precisely, he argued that people's notion of their liberty relied on the 'sentiment de la pensée', by which he meant human beings' conscious perception of themselves and their ideas, that is to say, apperception and consciousness: 'La Pensée dans l'homme n'est autre chose que le témoignage intime, ou le sentiment qu'il a de ses idées par la reflexion. Ce témoignage le persuade qu'il existe, parce qu'il lui est impossible de concevoir qu'une même chose soit, & ne soit pas en même tems.'[20] In this statement, Formey referred first and foremost to Descartes's proof of human beings' existence through their self-consciousness (*cogito ergo sum*), and then applied it to the question of human liberty. Just as human beings were aware of their existence because they perceived that they were thinking, they reached certainty with regard to their liberty by reflecting on their actions: 'Le témoignage de ma pensée, bien loin de me disculper, m'accuse: il me convainc avec toute l'evidence possible, que je pouvois ne pas agir, ou agir d'une maniere diamétralement opposée.'[21]

It is likely that Formey's application of the Cartesian *cogito ergo sum* to the proof of human liberty was inspired by Wolff's proof of human beings' existence in general and the existence of the soul in particular, for which Wolff, likewise, had relied on Descartes.[22] Moreover, Wolff also stressed the certainty of the proof of human beings' existence, a certainty that would be transferred to all other proofs that relied on the same epistemic foundation, namely, consciousness.[23] Consequently,

---

19. See Formey, 'Réflexions sur la liberté', p.343. Compare with Wolff, *Discursus praeliminaris*, §111. See also Ecole, 'Des rapports de l'expérience et de la raison', p.594-96.
20. See Formey, 'Réflexions sur la liberté', p.340.
21. See Formey, 'Réflexions sur la liberté', p.341.
22. See Wolff, *Metaphysik*, §1 and 5, as well as *Psychologia empirica*, §11-14. For a detailed analysis of Wolff's appropriation of Descartes's *cogito*, see Werner Euler, 'Bewusstsein – Seele – Geist: Untersuchungen zur Transformation des Cartesischen "cogito" in der Psychologie Christian Wolffs', in *Die Psychologie Christian Wolffs*, ed. O.-P. Rudolph and J.-F. Goubet, p.11-50. Compare also with Crousaz, *De l'esprit humain*, p.106. Likewise, Crousaz compared the inner experience of liberty with Descartes's proof of existence.
23. See Wolff, *Psychologia empirica*, §16-17.

Wolff declared consciousness, which he called 'Bewusstsein', to be the main epistemic tool by which the soul was able to gain empirical knowledge about itself. He defined the soul as a thing that was conscious (*bewusst*) both of itself and of the things outside of itself,[24] and because the soul was only able to experience those of its faculties of which it was conscious, empirical psychology would only deal with those faculties.[25]

Typically, the defenders of liberty in the debate on free will throughout the eighteenth century declared inner experience or consciousness to be a certain proof of human liberty. By contrast, it was common among those who doubted or denied human liberty, such as Spinoza, Hobbes and Bayle, to argue against the probative force of inner experience.[26] Thus, when Formey stated in his 'Réflexions sur la liberté' that he had to defend inner experience against the objection that it led to mere illusions,[27] he targeted first and foremost those philosophers who embraced the determinateness of human actions. In addition to this, it appears likely that his defence of inner feeling was influenced by the doubts his friend Abraham Bocquet had uttered in 1740 with respect to the proof of human liberty. In the same letter in which Bocquet confessed he found Wolff's explanation of liberty unconvincing, he deplored the fact that his feeling of being free seemed to run contrary to reason: 'Il ne me reste en faveur de la liberté que la seule preuve de sentiment. Mais n'est il pas fâcheux que ce sentiment se trouve en opposition avec la raison. Qui des deux a le plus d'autorité?'[28] Bocquet's insinuation that inner feeling was not a sufficient proof might have motivated Formey to emphasise the authority of inner feeling with respect to the question of human liberty.

24. See Wolff, *Metaphysik*, §192.
25. See Wolff, *Metaphysik*, §193. In his *Belle wolfienne*, Formey used the term 'conscience' to translate Wolff's 'Bewusstsein', whereas the anonymous French translator of the empirical psychology chose the term 'sentiment'; see *Belle wolfienne*, vol.5, p.9-10, and *Psychologie, ou Traité sur l'ame*, p.42-43. In his 'Réflexions sur la liberté', p.341, Formey used the terms 'conscience' and 'sentiment' synonymously.
26. See Harris, *Of liberty and necessity*, p.9-10 and 81-82. For a mid-eighteenth-century engagement with Spinoza's and Bayle's arguments against liberty, see [Jacques André Naigeon and Claude Yvon], 'Liberté, (Morale)', in *Encyclopédie*, vol.9 (Neufchâtel, Faulche, 1765), p.462-71.
27. See Formey, 'Réflexions sur la liberté', p.339.
28. Bocquet to Formey (21.11.1740), FF (emphasis in the original), also quoted in chapter 5.

Thus, to strengthen his argument for liberty against any epistemological objection, Formey underlined first the probative force of consciousness or inner feeling by contrasting it with the epistemic vulnerability of sensory experience. Like Wolff, he argued the senses were subject to change and errors, whereas the cognitive perception of someone's inner state was constant and, thus, reliable.[29] Furthermore, Formey contrasted his experience-based proof of human liberty with the conjecture that a physical influence between soul and body existed. In his view, the observation that parts of someone's body moved when they wanted them to was insufficient for deducing the existence of free will. There was no secure knowledge about the principle according to which this apparent influence between soul and body functioned:

> Je demande donc, où est la preuve de sentiment, à laquelle tout homme, Païsan, ou Philosophe, qui voudra admettre l'influence réelle & physique de l'Ame sur le Corps puisse en appeller? Que sent-il? Qu'il veut, & que ses organes agissent, aprés qu'il a voulu. Mais oseroit-on dire que qui que ce soit voye & sente ce passage, ce nœud entre la determination de l'Ame sur le Corps. Je fais un mouvement, que j'avois conçu comme possible, avant que de le commencer. Je comprens, & je puis assurer, qu'il est une infinité de mouvemens, dont l'un n'est pas moins faisable que l'autre. Je sais de maniere à n'en pouvoir douter, que quand je veux marcher je marche, & que plusieurs mouvemens de mon corps répondent parfaitement aux déterminations de ma volonté. Mais je ne saurois aller plus loin, sans passer les bornes de l'experience. Elle garde un profond silence sur la maniere dont la chose se passe, elle ne me fait appercevoir en aucune maniere que ma volonté pousse mon bras. Quand je m'imagine donc qu'elle produit cet effet, de la même maniere que mes doits dirigent ma plume, je ne fais que m'embarasser d'une opinion trés confuse, qui a plutot l'air d'un instinct grossier que d'un raisonnement.[30]

By contrast, as Formey argued, the consciousness of being free to choose one thing instead of another was an immediate proof of human liberty that was beyond doubt.

---

29. See Formey, 'Réflexions sur la liberté', p.340 and 343. Compare with Wolff, *Metaphysik*, §326, in which he declared that experience could easily be confused with imagination or opinion, or could be held accountable for phenomena that, in reality, it did not contain.
30. Formey, 'Réflexions sur la liberté', p.342. Compare with Wolff, *Metaphysik*, §761.

This distinction between conjecture and empirical proof was an important element of Wolff's two epistemologically different psychologies. He assigned knowledge of the relationship between soul and body to the rational approach, because in his view such knowledge did not rely on experience but, instead, consisted of a priori hypotheses.[31] However, Wolff treated free will as empirical knowledge. He used this distinction to object in particular to the accusation that the theory of pre-established harmony curtailed human liberty. Because free will was an empirical truth, it could not be disproved by any hypothesis concerning the relationship between soul and body.[32] Formey drew on Wolff's psychology for his 'Réflexions sur la liberté' and, therefore, finally embraced the Wolffian solution to the assumed fatalistic implications of pre-established harmony that he had ignored in 1741 in the second volume of his *Belle wolfienne*. Finally and epistemologically, he dissociated discussions on the relationship between soul and body from discussions on the human will: 'Ainsi, qu'on admette ou qu'on rejette l'influence de l'ame sur le corps, les verités de sentiment, telles que la Liberté, n'en sauroient souffrir aucune atteinte.'[33] This was the position he also put forward in his above-mentioned review of Hentsch's renewed theory of physical influx in 1764.

Nevertheless, although Formey perceived empirical psychology to be a strong foundation of the proof of liberty against accusations of fatalism, other philosophers began to be aware of the limits of empirical psychology during the second half of the eighteenth century. The most compelling limit lay probably in the very nature of empirical knowledge, namely, that it was based on sense impressions, which made it vulnerable to some established sceptical attacks on the certainty of knowledge. In his 'Réflexions sur la liberté', Formey pointed to this issue and mentioned that some people doubted the proof of liberty because of the lack of clear knowledge on the nature and essence of soul and body. In Formey's eyes, this problem could be applied to all empirical proofs because they could rarely account for the principles that guided certain phenomena. This, however, did not deny the legitimacy of these proofs – a claim by which he partly contradicted his criticism of the physico-theological proofs of God's existence.[34] In the same vein, during the 1770s, the

---

31. See Wolff, *Metaphysik*, §529-30.
32. See Wolff, *Metaphysik*, §883-84, and *Anmerckungen*, §332.
33. See Formey, 'Réflexions sur la liberté', p.343.
34. See Formey, 'Réflexions sur la liberté', p.344.

German experimental philosophers Christian Gottfried Schütz and Johann Nicolaus Tetens, who, like Formey, were followers of Wolff's empirical psychology, outlined the problems that arose from utilising the empirical method of introspection without actually rejecting it. According to them, a method in which the soul itself became the observer of its own inner state was prone to illusions, hasty conclusions and incorrect generalisations.[35]

In addition, the second half of the eighteenth century saw the rise of an empirical science of the soul that neglected the method of introspection and, instead, relied on the observation of physiological phenomena. Charles Bonnet's sensualist study of the soul, the *Essai analytique sur les facultés de l'ame*, of 1760 was a great deal different from Wolff's empirical psychology that Formey had endorsed roughly ten years earlier. However, it seems that Formey also embraced Bonnet's new approach to the science of the soul because he reworked the *Essai analytique* into a popular version in which Bonnet's theories were presented in a dialogue between a master and his disciple.[36] The main way in which Bonnet's empirical science of the soul[37] differed from Wolff's was that the former assumed a physical influence between soul and body and, hence, considered the soul to act 'on and through its body'.[38] Moreover, Bonnet claimed that the spiritual soul was unable to gain clear knowledge about itself, although it was able to observe the effects it produced on the body.

> L'ame ne peut se connoître elle-même; elle ne connoit que par le ministere des sens: & comment des sens matériels lui donneroient-ils la perception d'elle-même? Elle ne connoit pas plus la matiere qu'elle ne se connoit elle-même; elle ne la voit qu'à travers un milieu; elle n'en juge que dans le rapport à ses sens. Nous n'appercevons donc des deux côtés que des effets, des résultats; & les principes, le comment, restent ensévelis dans une nuit profonde.[39]

---

35. See Vidal, 'Discours de la méthode dans la psychologie', p.63-70.
36. Bonnet, *Essai analytique*, and its abridgement: Formey, *Entretiens psychologiques, tirés de l'Essai analytique sur les facultés de l'ame* (Berlin, Pauli, 1769).
37. On the character of the empirical method Bonnet used in natural philosophy and metaphysics, see Marc J. Ratcliff, 'Une métaphysique de la méthode chez Charles Bonnet', in *Charles Bonnet: savant et philosophe (1720-1793)*, ed. René Sigrist *et al.* (Geneva, 1994), p.51-60.
38. See Bonnet, *Essai analytique*, p.xiii, and Formey, *Entretiens psychologiques*, p.7.
39. Bonnet, *Essai analytique*, p.xx, and Formey, *Entretiens psychologiques*, p.14.

As far as Wolff was concerned, he regarded the soul's effects as merely spiritual, and consciousness as being able to account for the meaning of these effects. The difference between Bonnet's and Wolff's empirical psychology emphasises the epistemological instability and changes that the science of the soul witnessed in the period during which Formey engaged with questions linked to volition and understanding. Although Formey himself remained firm in 1747 about the strength of consciousness as an empirical tool, this instability might explain why other of his contemporaries developed doubts concerning the provability of free will. However, before investigating the positions of his academic colleagues, it is time to analyse Formey's own assessment of free will.

Free will between absolute necessity and liberty of indifference

Although, in general, Formey's approach to the investigation of the soul in the 1740s reveals the strong influence of Wolff's empirical psychology, his explanation of free will contains several elements that were clearly borrowed from Leibniz. Like Leibniz's version, Formey's depiction of free will as a mental process offered a solution to the dichotomy between determination and contingency by developing the concept of a middle way between these two apparently mutually exclusive categories. Within the debate on free will, this compatibilist approach was positioned midway between necessitarian and absolute libertarian arguments[40] or, as Formey put it, between 'nécessité absolue' – the inevitable determination of human choices by existing motives – and 'liberté d'indifférence' – the absolute arbitrariness of human choices. Styled as a battle on two fronts, Formey's essay first presented arguments against the former before destroying the latter.

First, to counter the necessitarian vision of the absolute necessity of human choice, Formey developed the Aristotelian theory of the determination of the human will by non-binding motives that Leibniz had also adopted in his *Théodicée*.[41] This theory included the premise

40. For the terminology, see Harris, *Of liberty and necessity*, p.7. Harris' meaning of the term 'libertarianism' encompasses Leibniz's compatibilist stance, because in his view libertarian thought consisted of assuming that human actions were influenced by motives that did not curtail the freedom of those actions. However, Harris' notion of libertarianism does not include the opinion that choices result from pure chance. In the present study, the term 'absolute libertarianism' is used to describe this opinion.
41. See Leibniz, *Théodicée*, §45, p.157.

that everything that existed had to have a sufficient reason for doing so – a motive. However, likewise, it promoted the contingency of these motives. Formey described in detail the decision-making process of human beings as a mental effort that evolved between the two mental faculties of understanding and will: a decision emerged from understanding that offered several motives to the will. The will, however, was not constrained to act according to the motives offered and, consequently, could be considered free. According to Formey, this explanation was confirmed by the observation that people could change their mind and act against certain motives.[42]

In his 'Réflexions sur la liberté', Formey employed much effort to stress that the motives according to which judgement governed will were not determining. This was because his aim was to separate the Leibnizian theory of will from necessitarian, or even fatalistic, approaches. In the debate on free will, the idea that the human will was determined by motives was common to both necessitarian and certain libertarian philosophers. The crucial point that separated the two positions was, in fact, whether human beings were considered to be absolutely governed by such motives. A famous defender of necessitarian thought was a British deist and friend of John Locke, Anthony Collins, who in Formey's 'Réflexions sur la liberté' took the role of his (fictional) opponent.[43] Collins' argument for the determination of the will amounted to the claim that human beings were not able to suspend their volition – in other words, they were not able to not will.[44] In his *Philosophical inquiry concerning human liberty* of 1717, Collins stated that, in reality, there was no distinction between traditional libertarian and necessitarian arguments in the sense that they all assumed a certain determination of the will.[45] With this claim, Collins targeted in particular the English ecclesiastic and Boyle lecturer Samuel Clarke, who maintained a similar concept of free will to Leibniz. Like Leibniz, Clarke believed the will was determined by a judgement of the understanding, which in his view amounted to

---

42. See Formey, 'Réflexions sur la liberté', p.336. This explanation is the one that Manteuffel also provided in the *Lettre du jurisconsulte*, p.19-20, to counter Formey's doubts about the assumed fatality of pre-established harmony. Wolff has argued similarly in his *Metaphysik*, §516-18.
43. See Formey, 'Réflexions sur la liberté', p.335.
44. See Charles T. Wolfe, 'Determinism/Spinozism in the radical Enlightenment: the cases of Anthony Collins and Denis Diderot', *International review of eighteenth-century studies* 1 (2007), p.37-51 (39-47).
45. See Harris, *Of liberty and necessity*, p.55.

a moral necessity that was not contradictory to freedom.[46] In fact, Collins adopted this notion of moral necessity to claim the contrary, namely, the bondage of the will through motives.[47]

In his essay, Formey explained the difference between an absolute necessity on the one hand and a hypothetical necessity on the other, so that he could reject Collins and the necessitarians. In an ontological sense, the first characterised the essence of a thing and, hence, everything whose opposite was not possible. In contrast, the hypothetical necessity belonged to all aspects that conditioned a thing in addition to its essence and that were fully contingent. Formey's Leibnizian notion of free will was based on hypothetical necessity, more precisely, on a subform of it, moral necessity, which was defined as the motives that determined spiritual entities, as opposed to physical necessity, which referred to the effects produced by bodies.[48] This ontological distinction between different forms of necessity has its roots in scholasticism, yet was developed in detail by Wolff, who explained it with reference to his theories of essence and contradiction.[49] In his definition of the freedom of the will, which essentially followed Leibniz's approach, the concept of moral necessity in particular played a central role: it described the fact that human beings necessarily choose what they judge to be good instead of what they judge to be bad.[50] Leibniz, in his account of free will, used the concept of hypothetical necessity to make God's prescience compatible with the contingency of human actions.[51]

Upholding the notion of hypothetical or moral necessity was, however, a risky endeavour as far as Formey was concerned. Not only did Collins appropriate it from the libertarian Samuel Clarke to underpin his necessitarian claims, Clarke himself also referred to it so that he could accuse Leibniz of necessitarianism in their

---

46. See Samuel Clarke, *A Demonstration of the being and attributes of God and other writings*, ed. Ezio Vailati (Cambridge, 1998), p.73-74.
47. See Wolfe, 'Determinism/Spinozism in the radical Enlightenment', p.44-45, and Harris, *Of liberty and necessity*, p.55.
48. See Formey, 'Réflexions sur la liberté', p.337-38.
49. See Wolff, *Philosophia prima sive Ontologia, methodo scientifica pertractata, qua omnis cognitionis humanae principia continentur* (2nd edn, 1736), ed. Jean Ecole, in *Christian Wolff: Gesammelte Werke*, ed. Jean Ecole *et al.*, 4th edn, section 2, vol.3 (Hildesheim 2011), §315, 317, 318, and *Metaphysik*, §36 and 176.
50. See Wolff, *Metaphysik*, §521.
51. See Leibniz, *Théodicée*, §37, p.148-49.

famous correspondence.[52] However, it should be noted that on other occasions Clarke had defended a non-determining moral necessity. Most importantly, Wolff also declared the notion of moral necessity to be misleading, although he used the term in his *Metaphysik*. In his later annotations to this work, he dismissed the term 'moral necessity' because it could lead to the wrong impression that the human will was bound.[53] Formey was aware of this criticism because in his translation of Wolff's empirical psychology he reported Wolff's opinion on the meaning of moral necessity.[54] However, in his 'Réflexions sur la liberté', he remained faithful to this notion.

In the second part of his 'Réflexions sur la liberté', Formey turned his focus away from necessitarianism and, instead, attempted to harness absolute libertarianism, which maintained the existence of an absolute liberty or, as Formey and his contemporaries called it, a liberty of indifference. He defined absolute liberty as the possibility of making a decision without being influenced by any reason or external cause, a possibility that he considered to be out of the question.[55] With this opinion, Formey again followed in the footsteps of Leibniz, who in his *Théodicée* had stated that such an absolute liberty would mean that a choice emerged out of nothing because it was determined neither by God nor by the soul or the body.[56] As Formey argued, it ran contrary to reason and experience that things happened out of nothing.[57] Rather, Leibniz's principle of sufficient reason, which Formey strengthened by claiming it had been established as a legacy from Descartes, specified that an act of will was caused by a motive, and only if this were the case could an action take place.[58]

Nevertheless, as Formey acknowledged, acts of will existed that seemed to lack any motive and were, thus, presumably absolutely arbitrary, for example, when someone chooses an object out of a pile of identical objects. This was one of the main arguments of the

---

52. See Ezio Vailati, *Leibniz & Clarke: a study of their correspondence* (New York, 1997), p.103-104.
53. See Wolff, *Anmerckungen*, §167.
54. See Formey, *Belle wolfienne*, vol.5, p.316. Compare with 'Réflexions sur la liberté', p.339, in which Formey held Aristotle responsible for first having used the term 'necessity'.
55. See Formey, 'Réflexions sur la liberté', p.345.
56. See Leibniz, *Théodicée*, §320, p.510-11, quoted by Formey, 'Réflexions sur la liberté', p.345-46.
57. See Formey, 'Réflexions sur la liberté', p.346.
58. See Formey, 'Réflexions sur la liberté', p.347-48.

libertarians to try and prove their claim of an absolutely free will. In his correspondence with the libertarian Clarke, Leibniz went to great lengths to try and disprove it.[59] Consequently, Formey solved the problem of apparently uncaused volitions first and foremost by relying on Leibniz's theory of indiscernibles, according to which decisions were often determined by the many unperceived movements that exist inside and outside of us: 'Une infinité de petites perceptions, qui nous rendent quelque fois joyeux, chagrins; & différemment disposés, nous font quelquefois plus goûter une chose que l'autre, sans que nous puissions dire pourquoi. L'on ne doit donc pas trouver étrange que nous supposions en nous des motifs qui nous déterminent, sans que nous soyons capables d'en rendre raison.'[60] To confirm this claim, Formey referred to Leibniz's rejection of the famous paradox attributed to Jean Buridan, according to which an ass confronted with two identical piles of straw would starve to death because it could not decide between them.[61]

In his *Metaphysik*, Wolff also touched upon the problem of apparently unmotivated decisions by citing the example of a man who chose one of two coins that were exactly the same, and provided a solution to the problem that was in line with Leibniz's theory of indiscernibles. However, as mentioned above (see chapter 5), Formey's friend Abraham Bocquet, whose doubts concerning Wolff's theory of liberty had grown serious, did not find Wolff's solution convincing. The concerns of his Huguenot friend might have been a reason for Formey not to cite Wolff in countering the argument of arbitrary volition, although Wolff's enhanced version of Leibniz's claim against the liberty of indifference was featured in his text. Like Wolff, Formey argued that motives were based not always on clear and distinct perceptions but also on unclear and obscure notions that were conditioned by sensations and affections.[62] Finally, Formey also quoted Descartes, according to whom the appearance of arbitrariness that was attributed to some decisions resulted only from a defect of understanding. Therefore, in Descartes's view, arbitrary decisions

---

59. See Vailati, *Leibniz & Clarke*, p.92-101.
60. Formey, 'Réflexions sur la liberté', p.349. Compare with Leibniz, *Théodicée*, §46, p.158-59.
61. See Formey, 'Réflexions sur la liberté', p.350. Compare with Leibniz, *Théodicée*, §49, p.161-62.
62. See Formey, 'Réflexions sur la liberté', p.350. Compare with Wolff, *Metaphysik*, §502.

were, rather, a sign of imperfect and limited liberty than one of absolute liberty.[63] Hence, to reject the libertarian claim of the absolute liberty to act, Formey drew on a wide range of similar arguments, emphasising the importance he attached to the issue.

It was important for Formey to disprove the arbitrariness of human decisions because of his wish to uphold God's prescience. In his view, God would not be able to foresee human actions if they were absolutely free.[64] There were eighteenth-century theorists like the Anglican archbishop of Dublin William King and the German anti-Wolffian philosopher Christian August Crusius who believed liberty of indifference to be perfectly compatible with God's prescience. They usually argued that God's perfect intelligence enabled Him to know or foresee with certainty human actions without them being necessary or having a determining reason. Human beings simply ignored the precise functioning of this ability because of their limited knowledge of divine nature.[65] However, other contemporaries of Formey who adopted the theory of absolute liberty seem to have encountered problems in reconciling it with God's foreknowledge. This was the case for the majority of Calvinist theologians and pastors in Geneva, as a letter by the Genevan mathematician Gabriel Cramer suggests. He told Formey that they had embraced the liberty of indifference despite the difficulties they had in making it agree with divine prescience:

> Je vous dirai en confidence que la pluspart de nos théologiens sont pour la liberté d'indifférence, & fort embarassez par consequent à l'accorder avec la prévision divine. Nous avons toujours combattu ce sentiment, Mr. Calandrin & moi: aussi je m'assure que nous sommes regardez comme penchants au fatalism, car les hommes sont outrès dans les imputations qu'ils font à ceux qui pensent autrement qu'eux.

Cramer, who shared Formey's Leibnizian theory of liberty, therefore, praised the latter's 'Réflexions sur la liberté'.[66] A similar reaction to

---

63. See Formey, 'Réflexions sur la liberté', p.351.
64. See Formey, 'Réflexions sur la liberté', p.353.
65. See William King, 'Divine predestination and fore-knowledge, consistent with the freedom of mans will: a sermon preach'd at Christ-Church, Dublin, May 15, 1709', in *An Essay on the origin of evil*, translated by Edmund Law, 3rd edn (Cambridge, Thurlbourn, 1739), p.3-48 (40-41), and Christian August Crusius, *Entwurf der nothwendigen Vernunft-Wahrheiten, wiefern sie den zufälligen entgegen gesetzet werden*, 2nd edn (Leipzig, Gleditsch, 1753), §272-73, p.506-509.
66. See Gabriel Cramer to Formey (17.11.1750), in *Lettres de Genève*, p.285-86.

Formey's essay also came from the Genevan pastor Jean Peschier, who said that Formey's clear depictions had made him abandon his own belief in the liberty of indifference.[67] In the mid-eighteenth-century clerical milieu to which Formey belonged, Leibniz's theory of free will had, thus, the utmost relevance in the sense that it helped to correct some essential assumptions concerning dogma.

Moreover, Formey's defence of Leibniz's compatibilist theory of free will was also of great importance in his ongoing debate with critics of religion and freethinkers in the European Republic of Letters. In 1740, Voltaire published his *Métaphysique de Newton*, a popular philosophical treatise that dealt with major questions of natural theology, ontology and cosmology, and was largely critical of Leibniz's thought.[68] In Germany, which was a stronghold of Leibniz's philosophy, Voltaire's writing spawned much criticism, most famously from the Göttingen professor of philosophy Ludwig Martin Kahle, who penned a refutation of it in the very same year the *Métaphysique de Newton* was published.[69] This refutation was well received among the German and Huguenot Wolffians. Like Kahle, Wolff was outraged at what he considered to be Voltaire's aim, namely, to depict Newton as a metaphysician of the same calibre as Leibniz.[70] Furthermore, to give Kahle's refutation greater outreach, in particular in France, one of the Berlin Huguenots, François de Gautier de Saint-Blancard, who was a councillor at the French legal department in Berlin, translated it into French in 1744.[71] Formey, who maintained an epistolary exchange

67. See Peschier to Formey (27.10.1750), in *Lettres de Genève*, p.282.
68. The *Métaphysique de Newton* was first published by Jaques Desbordes in Amsterdam as an independent piece. From 1741 onwards it was published as an introduction to Voltaire's *Elémens de la philosophie de Newton* (Paris, Prault).
69. Ludwig Martin Kahle, *Vergleichung der Leibnitzischen und Neutonischen Metaphysik, wie auch verschiedener anderer philosophischer und mathematischer Lehren beyder Weltweisen angestellet und dem Herrn von Voltaire entgegen gesetzt* (Göttingen, Universitätsbuchhandlung, 1741). See Alexandra Lewendoski, 'Reaktionskette eines Leibnizverständnisses: Clarke, Newton, Voltaire, Kahle', in *Leibnizbilder im 18. und 19. Jahrhundert*, ed. Alexandra Lewendoski (Stuttgart, 2004), p.121-45 (139-44).
70. See Wolff to Mantueffel (27.1.1741), in *Briefwechsel zwischen Wolff und Manteuffel*, vol.1, p.402-403. Compare with Kahle, 'Vorrede', in *Vergleichung der Leibnitzischen und Neutonischen Metaphysik*.
71. Kahle, *Examen d'un livre intitulé La Metaphysique de Newton, ou Parallèle des sentimens de Newton & de Leibnitz par Mr. de Voltaire, traduit en françois par Mr. de Gautier Saint-Blancard* (The Hague, Gosse, 1744). This translation was already underway in 1741, as Formey reported in his 'Article XIII. Nouvelles litteraires',

with Kahle, not only knew Kahle's writing and the translation, he also placed favourable reviews of it in his *Bibliothèque germanique*.[72]

Formey's 'Réflexions sur la liberté' was part of this critical engagement with Voltaire's *Métaphysique de Newton* in Germany. In actual fact, some particular terms and phrases used by Voltaire reappeared in Formey's essay, which suggests that it had been provoked by a critical reading of Voltaire.[73] As mentioned above, Formey also quoted from the *Métaphysique de Newton* in his second essay on the existence of God (in its manuscript version), which he presented earlier in the same year as his 'Réflexions sur la liberté'. In the fourth chapter of Voltaire's work, which dealt with human liberty, he rejected Anthony Collins' necessitarianism with reference to Clarke, yet did not comment explicitly on Leibniz's theory of free will.[74] In preference, Voltaire presented his own two-sided theory of free will that allowed for both absolute arbitrariness and the determination of the will by motives. As far as Voltaire was concerned, the one at stake depended on the situation. On the one hand, there were situations of complete

---

in *Journal littéraire d'Allemagne, de Suisse et du Nord* 1:2 (1742), p.433-66 (466). Wolff himself, in his letter to Manteuffel (27.1.1741) in *Briefwechsel zwischen Wolff und Manteuffel*, vol.1, p.402-403, wished that Kahle's refutation could be translated so that Voltaire could read it. In his reply to Wolff (10.2.1741) in *Briefwechsel zwischen Wolff und Manteuffel*, vol.1, p.407-408, Manteuffel stated that he would translate it himself.

72. See 'Article VI. Vergleichung des Leibnitzischen und Neutonischen Metaphysik', *Journal littéraire d'Allemagne, de Suisse et du Nord* 1:2 (1742), p.373-95, and 'Article V. Vergleichung der Leibnizischen und Newtonischen Metaphysick [...] second extrait', *Nouvelle bibliothèque germanique* 1 (1746), p.84-107. Kahle thanked Formey for his favourable review in a letter to him (19.11.1742), CV, as well as for his support for the translation of Kahle's work (25.3.1744), CV.

73. For example: 'nous n'avons d'autre liberté, que celle de porter quelquefois de bon gré les fers auxquels la fatalité nous attache' (Voltaire, *Eléments de la philosophie de Newton*, p.213; compare with Formey, 'Réflexions sur la liberté', p.335); 'dictamen de mon entendement' (Voltaire, *Eléments de la philosophie de Newton*, p.215 and 216; compare with Formey, 'Réflexions sur la liberté', p.336); 'la liberté [spontanée] est à l'âme ce que la santé est au corps' (Voltaire, *Eléments de la philosophie de Newton*, p.216; compare with Formey, 'Réflexions sur la liberté', p.354).

74. See Robert L. Walters and William H. Barber, 'Introduction', in *The Complete works of Voltaire*, vol.15 (Oxford, 1992), p.1-180 (113-14), who emphasise that, with regard to human liberty, Voltaire's position did not differ much from Leibniz's and that it is striking he did not quote Leibniz. Voltaire's partiality for liberty of indifference was only temporary; during the course of his life, he tended increasingly towards a form of determinism.

indifference in which choices resulted not from intellectual judgement but solely from the exercise of the will. On the other hand, there were situations in which a human being's actions were determined by certain motives gained through understanding; Voltaire called the sort of freedom that was at play in these latter situations 'liberté de spontanéité'.[75] However, his German critics did not acknowledge that this notion of spontaneous liberty had, in fact, been partly in line with a notion of liberty in the Leibnizian sense. Kahle mainly focused on objecting to Voltaire's account of absolute liberty,[76] which is what Formey also did by disproving the liberty of indifference extensively in his 'Réflexions sur la liberté'.

Formey not only joined Kahle's rejection of Voltaire's notion of liberty of indifference, he also objected to Voltaire in relation to the crucial question of how to reconcile human liberty and divine prescience. Voltaire, by referring to the incomprehensibility of God's nature, claimed it was simply not possible to know whether God had foreseen human actions and, thus, declared – together with Newton – that the question was unanswerable:

> La difficulté d'accorder la liberté de nos actions avec la prescience éternelle de Dieu, n'arrêtait point Neuton, parce qu'il ne s'engageait pas dans ce labyrinthe; la liberté une fois établie, ce n'est pas à nous à déterminer comment Dieu prévoit ce que nous ferons librement. Nous ne savons pas de quelle manière Dieu voit actuellement ce qui se passe. Nous n'avons aucune idée de sa façon de voir, pourquoi en aurions-nous de sa façon de prévoir? Tous ses attributs nous doivent être également incompréhensibles.[77]

By contrast, Formey was convinced that the contingency of human actions and divine prescience were compatible and, what is more, that human beings could comprehend this compatibility. Formey accepted that human knowledge about God was limited; nevertheless, he viewed such limited knowledge as sufficient for recognising that God had foreseen all the things that had happened in the world. Most importantly, the knowledge of God's prescience did not interfere negatively with the certain knowledge of human liberty, because liberty lay as much in human nature as God's prescience lay in His:

---

75. See Voltaire, *Eléments de la philosophie de Newton*, p.214-16.
76. See Kahle, *Examen d'un livre intitulé La Metaphysique de Newton*, p.56-59.
77. Voltaire, *Eléments de la philosophie de Newton*, p.217.

> Il est bien surprenant que les Theologiens & les Philosophes ayent été pendant si long tems accrochés à la difficulté de concilier la contingence de nos actions avec la Prescience éternelle de Dieu, & que la pluspart l'ayent jugee insoluble. La souveraine intelligence de Dieu nous est incomprehensible, entant que nous n'en avons pas une pleine & entiere conception, qui puisse nous faire comprendre & embrasser parfaitement tout ce qui est en elle; mais l'imparfaite & mediocre connoissance que nous en avons, suffit pour nous autoriser à conclure qu'il a tout prévu [...] Ainsi la liberté étant une fois établie sur les preuves les plus convainquantes, il est certain que nous pouvons déterminer nos actions librement, non pas par la raison que Dieu les a prévües, mais parce que la Liberté est conforme à notre nature.[78]

In a very similar vein, Kahle had found an answer to this question: in his view, human actions happened in a certain way not because God had foreseen them but because men were forced to act in this way by using their liberty.[79]

It can be seen, therefore, that Formey's use of Leibniz's compatibilist theory of human liberty to reject both necessitarian arguments and the theory of liberty of indifference resulted from a complex web of conditions and aims. It was an attempt to solve the issue of the assumed fatalism of Leibniz's and Wolff's cosmology by defining liberty on a psychological level. This enabled Formey to correct his criticism of pre-established harmony for which he had earned the disapproval of his Wolffian friends in 1741. At the same time, his reflections on human liberty also resulted from the need to fight the opposite flaw to fatalism: the assumption that both the world and human actions were ruled by complete chance. Here, Voltaire's claims in the *Métaphysique de Newton* were certainly Formey's main target, and this also explains why Formey referred so explicitly and often to Leibniz in his essay instead of to Wolff, whose account of free will was only marginally different from Leibniz's – Voltaire, Leibniz's presumed critic, had to be beaten by citing the original. The reactions of Formey's Genevan correspondents to his 'Réflexions sur la liberté' and Bocquet's mistrust of Wolff's account of liberty alike emphasised that, crucially, both the curtailment of necessitarianism and the rejection of absolute libertarianism were needed to uphold religious doctrine.

---

78. Formey, 'Réflexions sur la liberté', p.352-53.
79. See Kahle, *Examen d'un livre intitulé La Metaphysique de Newton*, p.61-62.

The free will debate at the Berlin Academy

Formey's multifaceted defence of free will against both necessitarianism and absolute libertarianism was not only of relevance to confessional circles and the Wolffian Enlightenment, it also marked the beginning of a debate on free will at the Berlin Academy in which its members engaged for several decades. However, the subsequent contributions to this debate revealed the steady decline of the importance that Formey himself still attributed to the Leibnizian and Wolffian compatibilist account of free will. Moreover, Formey's positivist conviction that free will was a steadfast and provable truth appears exceptional compared with the epistemological uncertainties his academic colleagues betrayed with respect to the inquiry of the soul. Among them, the view grew stronger that there were no solutions to the question of whether the human being was free.

The importance of epistemological issues within the debate was already obvious in Antoine Achard's early considerations on human liberty that had been a direct trigger for Formey's 'Réflexions sur la liberté'. Achard, who was a Geneva-born preacher and philosopher of Huguenot descent,[80] presented a discourse on human liberty in one of the first sessions of the Société littéraire, the interim institution that existed between August 1743 and the eventual official inauguration of the renewed Academy in May 1746. Achard's discourse was supposed to be the introduction to a more substantial treatise on the subject, yet remained only an ephemeral piece.[81] He had conceived of his work as a discussion of several philosophers' opinions on this subject with the aim of leading him to the affirmation of human liberty and enabling him to refute the necessitarian claims of Bayle, Spinoza and Anthony Collins. According to the report of Achard's discourse that Formey wrote for the Academy's first yearbook, his focus lay on the refutation of Spinoza's pantheistic view, according to which all creatures were only modifications of a unique and infinite supreme being and, thus, necessarily existed. In Spinoza's system, the supreme all-embracing being was the only one that possessed active power and, therefore, the actions of its creations – both bodies and spirits – were necessary. In general, during the 1740s,

---

80. See Formey, 'Réflexions sur la liberté', p.334.
81. Antoine Achard, 'Sur la liberté', in *Histoire de l'Académie royale des sciences et des belles lettres de Berlin* (1745; Berlin, Haude, 1746), p.91-93. This is Formey's summary of Achard's oral presentation.

Spinoza's necessitarianism received a lot of opposition from the Berlin academicians who regarded it as fatalistic. In addition to Achard, the Academy's then secretary Philippe Joseph de Jariges commented on it in two successive essays in 1745 and 1746.[82] In his 'Réflexions sur la liberté', Formey joined in with the criticism of fatalism, yet his main target was Anthony Collins rather than Spinoza[83] and, unlike Achard, he refuted not only fatalism but also absolute liberty.

Formey seems to have disagreed with Achard on one crucial point: whether the processes that happened in the human soul were intelligible at all. As Achard had indicated to Formey, he had suspended his own research on human liberty because he had not been able to find a solution to the problem, only difficulties.[84] It might be, therefore, that Formey's attempt to demonstrate the evidence of the proof of human liberty through inner experience was a reaction to the doubts that Achard had faced. However, Achard was dissatisfied with the solution Formey presented in 1747. Following Locke, Achard claimed it was not possible to know the nature or essence of the soul, and that experience could teach only the effects that the soul had on the world. The most harmful consequence of Achard's doubts concerning the intelligibility of the human soul was, however, that it damaged his conviction that human beings were free. He stated that an empirical analysis of the issue, that is, through the observation of human actions, would reveal the determined character of such actions rather than their liberty.[85] Formey's self-confident demonstration of human liberty was in stark contrast to Achard's concerns; however, it

---

82. See Philippe Joseph de Jariges, 'Examen du Spinozisme et des objections de Monsieur Bayle sur ce système', in *Histoire de l'Académie royale des sciences et des belles lettres* (1745; Berlin, Haude, 1746), p.121-42, and 'Examen du Spinozisme et des objections de Monsieur Bayle sur ce système: seconde partie', in *Histoire de l'Académie royale des sciences et belles lettres* (1746; Berlin, Haude, 1748), p.295-316. Jariges even announced a third part of his treatise; however, it seems this was never achieved.
83. He mentioned Spinoza only twice; see 'Réflexions sur la liberté', p.336 and 344.
84. See Formey, 'Eloge de M. Achard', in *Nouveaux mémoires de l'Académie royale des sciences et belles-lettres* (1772; Berlin, Voss, 1774), p.58-68 (66). Other reasons for not finishing his study on human liberty were Achard's ill health and his feeling that his work would not contribute anything new to the debate.
85. This is based on the summary of a letter from Achard to Formey (2.2.1748) in Rolf Geissler, 'Antoine Achard (1696-1772), ein Prediger und Philosoph in Berlin', in *Schweizer im Berlin des 18. Jahrhunderts*, ed. M. Fontius and H. Holzhey, p.125-36 (135). According to Geissler, the letter has been preserved in the Autographa collection in the Biblioteka Jagiellońska in Krakow; however,

was only a brief intermezzo in the debate because misgivings similar to Achard's continued to exist among the academicians in Berlin.

A few years after Formey's contribution, the debate on liberty at the Academy was renewed by Johann Bernhard Merian, who joined the Academy in April 1750, the same year in which Formey's 'Réflexions sur la liberté' appeared in print. Merian was an eclectic philosopher from Basle who was influenced by British empiricism. He became a member of the Academy's philosophical class because of the patronage of his friend Jean II Bernoulli, who recommended him to the Academy's president, Maupertuis.[86] Merian's first contribution to the Academy in 1750, in which he showed a critical appreciation of Leibniz's and Wolff's theories of substance, ideas and apperception, was about the faculty of apperception.[87] With regard to the science of the soul, Merian argued for a merely empirical approach despite the limitations of the knowledge that could be gained through experience.[88] In his view, the faculties of the mind were intelligible only via a posteriori reasoning, that is, by analysing their effects on external objects.[89] This empirical approach to psychology also informed Merian's three essays on liberty. In the autumn of 1751 he presented two related essays that treated the matter from an

---

when I visited this archive in July 2014, Achard's letters in this collection were declared lost.

86. On Merian, see Friedrich Ancillon, 'Eloge de Jean Bernard Mérian, secrétaire perpétuel de l'Académie', in *Abhandlungen der königlichen preußischen Akademie der Wissenschaften zu Berlin* (1804-1811; Berlin, Realschulbuchhandlung, 1815), p.52-90; Jens Häseler, 'Johann Bernhard Merian: ein Schweizer an der Berliner Akademie', in *Schweizer im Berlin des 18. Jahrhunderts*, ed. M. Fontius and H. Holzhey, p.217-28, and Ulrich Dierse, 'Johann Bernhard Merian', in *Ueberweg Grundriss der Geschichte der Philosophie: die Philosophie des 18. Jahrhunderts*, vol.5: *Heiliges Römisches Reich Deutscher Nation, Schweiz, Nord- und Osteuropa*, ed. Helmut Holzhey and Vilem Mudroch (Basle, 2014), p.300-302.

87. Johann Bernhard Merian, 'Mémoire sur l'apperception de sa propre existence', and 'Mémoire sur l'apperception considérée relativement aux idées, ou Sur l'existence des idées dans l'âme', in *Histoire de l'Académie royale des sciences et belles lettres de Berlin* (1749; Berlin, Haude & Spener, 1751), p.416-41 and p.442-77. He presented these essays at the Academy on 11 June and 22 October 1750. For an analysis, see Udo Thiel, 'Between Wolff and Kant: Merian's theory of apperception', *Journal of the history of philosophy* 34:2 (1996), p.213-32.

88. See Merian, 'Mémoire sur l'apperception considérée relativement aux idées', p.444.

89. See Merian, 'Mémoire sur l'apperception de sa propre existence', p.417 and 418. On Merian's metaphysical empiricism, see Dumouchel, 'Hommes de nulle secte', p.747-48 and 751-52.

ontological perspective,[90] and in the 1753 Academy yearbook he published a single essay in which he upheld his notion of liberty against theories he presumed were fatalistic.[91] His empirical approach is most perceptible in his first two essays; for example, he argued that it was impossible to account for the principle of volition, but possible to account for changes in the universe that were provoked by the exercise of the will.[92]

By generally embracing an empirical approach to the soul, Merian, like Achard, doubted that the question of whether human beings were free could be answered and, therefore, he refrained from adopting a stance in the debate about it. Rather, he attempted to provide an ontological notion of liberty that enabled him to treat the question of free will on an abstract level. After having presented his two essays on liberty at the Academy, Merian wrote a letter to Bernoulli in Basle, stating that the essential question – namely, whether one could be conscious of being an active being – remained unsolved as far as he was concerned, and became ever more blurred the more he reflected on it.

> Je ne sçai si la Dissertation ontologique sur l'Action et la liberté, que je viens de lire à l'Academie à deux reprises savoir le 16ième Septembre et le 28ième Octobre, aura un sort pareil. Je risque extrêmement de la voir sifflée en Allemagne, ou les notions contraires à celles que j'adopte ont gagné le haut bout, et semblent ne souffrir point de contestation. Toujours je crois être assés sûr de mon fait, et avoir usé des précautions nécessaires. Mais le plus difficile de l'ouvrage reste à achever; c'est d'examiner si nous nous appercevons, que nous somes des êtres actifs. Plus je medite ce sujet, plus il me paroit et épineux, et delicat. [...] L'ontologie est une science trés comode, et les abstractions ne coutent guére; leur champs est vaste, et on taille en plein drap; mais c'est tout autre chose, lorsqu'il s'agit de les appliquer aux réalités.[93]

---

90. Merian, 'Dissertation ontologique sur l'action, la puissance et la liberté', and 'Seconde dissertation sur l'action, la puissance et la liberté', in *Histoire de l'Académie royale des sciences et belles lettres de Berlin* (1751; Berlin, Haude & Spener, 1753), p.459-85 and 486-516. He presented his essays on 16 September and 28 October 1751.
91. Merian, 'Examen d'une question concernant la liberté', in *Histoire de l'Académie royale des sciences et belles lettres de Berlin* (1753; Berlin, Haude & Spener, 1755), p.417-30. This essay was never presented orally at the Academy.
92. See Merian, 'Seconde dissertation', p.497.
93. See Merian to Jean II Bernoulli (30.11.1751), UBB, L Ia 711.

Merian's ontological approach, therefore, allowed him to conceive of a notion of liberty; however, this notion was weak because it could not be verified in reality. Unlike Formey, Merian was far from assuming strong evidence of inner experience.

In addition to these epistemological difficulties that were at large in relation to the question of liberty, Merian's methodological choice seems to have been motivated by his attempt to avoid being criticised by orthodox theologians. As he confessed in another letter to Bernoulli, his abstract claims concerning the issue of liberty were a means of absolving himself from all responsibility for the potential theological implications of his deliberations.[94] In this respect, Merian followed Locke, who in his account of liberty in his *Essay concerning human understanding*[95] did not settle clearly on a position in the debate because, as Harris believes, he did not want to delve into the metaphysical and theological problems that ran alongside the question of human freedom.[96]

In general, Merian's two ontological essays on liberty showed his critical engagement with Locke's account, through which he reached the position of liberty of indifference. In his first essay, Merian followed Locke's argument by establishing an ontological notion of liberty based on the theory of interaction of active and passive substances or states of being in the universe. According to this, a substance or state of being was passive when the reason for its existence lay outside of itself or when its existence was directly provoked by a previous state. In contrast, action signified a state that was independent of the states that preceded it and that was itself the source of a new sequence of states or substances.[97] The source or intrinsic principle of every action or active substance was the so-called power to act ('puissance d'agir'),[98] which included the possibility to both act and not act. For Merian, such a power to act was the only valid definition of liberty.[99] In his second essay, in which Merian applied his notion of liberty first to human volition and then to the universe as a whole, he did, however, deviate

---

94. See Merian to Jean II Bernoulli (8.8.1751), UBB, L Ia 711.
95. Locke's account of liberty is to be found in book 2, ch.21, 'Of power', in his *Essay concerning human understanding* (London, Basset & Mory, 1690).
96. See Harris, *Of liberty and necessity*, p.20-21.
97. See Merian, 'Dissertation ontologique', p.462.
98. See Merian, 'Dissertation ontologique', p.477-78.
99. See Merian, 'Dissertation ontologique', p.480.

somewhat from Locke's assumptions. Merian defined the will as being a truly active power, and thus equated volition with action. He then concluded that liberty was a power to will that enabled human beings to will and not to will what was offered to them.[100] As far as Merian was concerned, this was the true meaning of liberty of indifference. He specified that liberty of indifference did not mean that the understanding was faced by two completely equal impressions or motives – this was what Formey's Leibnizian concept of liberty of indifference contained – but it meant that a choice was not determined by the understanding at all. Yet, instead of referring to Leibniz or Formey at this point, Merian blamed Locke for never having truly penetrated the meaning of liberty of indifference.[101] More than that, he even accused Locke of necessitarianism because he held that the meaning of liberty was to do what one wanted. In Merian's view, to want something signified judging something to be good or bad, a capacity that was itself dependent on understanding and, thus, could not be considered free.[102]

Merian emphasised his vision of freedom as consisting of making choices that were not determined by any motive in his third essay on the subject in 1753, the 'Examen d'une question concernant la liberté'. However, in this work, he also stressed the difficulties of proving such a liberty of indifference. He stated clearly that, if it were possible to prove the existence of arbitrary choices, this would irrevocably demonstrate human and divine liberty; however, he refrained from providing such a proof and, instead, remained on the level of abstract considerations.[103] Notwithstanding his epistemological issues, Merian adopted a libertarian position with respect to human will that was somewhat stricter than Locke's in the sense that it did not allow for the determination of understanding. Likewise, his position ran contrary to Leibniz's theory of willing, which Merian associated with fatalism.[104] He rejected the Leibnizian and Wolffian notions of non-binding motives[105] as well as hypothetical

100. See Merian, 'Seconde dissertation', p. 496-97.
101. See Merian, 'Seconde dissertation', p.498.
102. See Merian, 'Seconde dissertation', p.501-502.
103. See Merian, 'Examen d'une question concernant la liberté', p.430.
104. Moreover, in his two essays 'Dissertation ontologique' and 'Seconde dissertation', Merian was polemical about the 'illustre auteur du nouveau système de la fatalité' (p.482 and 515), which was most likely a reference to Leibniz and his *Système nouveau de la nature* (1695).
105. See Merian, 'Seconde dissertation', p.503-507.

necessity and contingency[106] on which Formey's theory of the freedom of the will was based, and thus opposed Formey's position in the debate on free will.

Moreover, parts of Merian's two essays also clashed with fundamental theological assumptions. As far as Formey was concerned, this was probably untenable. Merian's ontological considerations with regard to divine freedom in particular amounted to almost heretical claims. Following the theory of active and passive powers, he doubted that God's omniscience could be considered an active power. However, because God's omnipotence had to be an active principle, and because passive and active powers could not exist in one being at the same time, Merian concluded that God could not be both omniscient and omnipotent:

> Il y a en Dieu des propriétés fondées sur la nécessité de son être, qui certainement ne peuvent pas être appellées des actions: prenons pour exemple la toute-science qui a de l'analogie avec notre science limitée […]. Dieu seroit-il plus actif par rapport à la science que nous ne le sommes par rapport à la notre? N'est-il point nécessité par sa propre nature à tout connoitre? & ne peut-on pas dire en quelque façon qu'il pâtit de sa nature? […] Toutes les raisons concevables donc, pour lesquelles l'action & la passion ne sauroient résider dans un sujet commun, recourant dans la substance divine, on seroit réduit à soutenir, que Dieu lui-même ne peut être tout-sage & tout-puissant à la fois.[107]

This statement implied that, if God's liberty was assumed to be contained in His omnipotence, His prescience had to be denied. Merian, however, did not state anything of this sort explicitly, but underlined again the mere abstract nature of his deliberations and his impartiality with regard to this question.

Merian was not the only member of the Academy who uttered his doubts concerning Leibnizian and elementary theological notions of liberty. The French philosopher André-Pierre Le Guay de Prémontval, who became a member of the Academy's class of speculative philosophy in June 1752,[108] also expressed his libertarian views by

---

106. See Merian, 'Dissertation ontologique', p.481-82, and 'Seconde dissertation', p.502.
107. Merian, 'Dissertation ontologique', p.476.
108. On Prémontval see Lloyd Strickland, 'Introduction: Prémontval's life and thought', in *The Philosophical writings of Prémontval*, ed. Lloyd Strickland (Lanham, MD, 2018), p.xiii-xxxii; on his conflict with Formey from 1759

rejecting Leibniz's theory of free will. However, he neglected to take the same precautionary measures as Merian, who engaged in an abstract academic debate. Instead, Prémontval's libertarian account was imbued with unorthodox claims concerning God's role in the universe. It is certainly for this reason that his three discourses on the subject of liberty, which he presented at the Academy in late 1753 and early 1754, were never published in the Academy yearbook. In 1754, therefore, Prémontval published them independently in a collection entitled *Pensées sur la liberté*.[109]

Prémontval not only disregarded God's existence in his enquiry concerning the possibility of human freedom – as he claimed, for analytical purposes[110] – he was also convinced that morality could persist independently of God's existence provided that one was free to carry out one's actions.[111] Moreover, he doubted that God was the creator of the world.[112] Most importantly, however, he rejected the compatibility of human liberty with a divinely determined order in the world. Prémontval held, like Formey, that human beings were convinced of their liberty through inner feeling; however, he believed this conviction had been contradicted by the notion of a God who had created and constantly conserved the world that has been propagated by both religious doctrine and Leibniz and his disciples:

> Mon cœur donc sent qu'il est libre: c'est tout ce que je puis dire. [...] Pour comble de scandale, c'est du sein de la religion, tant naturelle que révélée, c'est de l'idée d'un dieu créateur, conservateur, ordonateur de toutes choses, c'est de cette idée si sainte & si sublime que naissent les dificultés les plus insurmontables. Plus même l'idée de Dieu est relevée, telle sans contredit que celle qu'en donent notre grand

---

onwards, see Avi Lifschitz, 'From the corruption of French to the cultural distinctiveness of German: the controversy of Prémontval's *Préservatif* (1759)', *SVEC* 6 (2007), p.265-90.

109. See André-Pierre Le Guay de Prémontval, *Pensées sur la liberté, tirées d'un ouvrage manuscrit qui a pour titre: Protestations et déclarations philosophiques sur les principaux objets des connoissances humaines* (Berlin and Potsdam, Voss, 1754). See Strickland, 'Introduction', p.xvii-xviii, and Prémontval's letter to Johann David Michaelis (30.3.1754), in Johann David Michaelis, *Literarischer Briefwechsel*, ed. Johann Gottlieb Buhle, 3 vols (Leipzig, Weidmann, 1794-1796), vol.1, p.95.
110. See Prémontval, *Pensées sur la liberté*, p.79-80.
111. See Prémontval, *Pensées sur la liberté*, p.15 and 17.
112. See Prémontval, *Pensées sur la liberté*, p.75-76.

Leibniz & ses illustres disciples, vrais maîtres en métaphysique; plus le cruel fatalisme semble prêt à envahir & la philosophie & la religion.[113]

Formey was certainly shocked by this harsh attack against religious doctrine and Leibnizian philosophy that, in Prémontval's view, amounted to nothing less than fatalism.[114] However, it was Merian who criticised Prémontval's libertarianism, probably because it was much more radical than his own. Merian's third essay on liberty, the 'Examen d'une question concernant la liberté', contained several implicit references to Prémontval's text. For example, Prémontval held that a choice was only free if a human being was able to make the opposite choice under the same circumstances.[115] In his view, to prove the existence of liberty, the individual's choices had to vary. By contrast, if someone repeatedly made the same choice in the same circumstances,[116] he considered this to be a proof against liberty, a claim that Merian rejected in his 'Examen'.[117] Moreover, Prémontval believed that true liberty had to be contained in a human being's essence, and that it was not a gift from God. On the contrary, in Prémontval's view, human liberty was an imperfection, because it enabled human beings to choose what was bad.[118] Merian refuted this opinion in particular, not only for its lack of proof but also because it ran contrary to his conviction that liberty was a positive and active principle.[119]

Nevertheless, Merian and Prémontval shared the common position of liberty of indifference, according to which any kind of determining influence on the human soul was detrimental to the freedom of its choices. As far as Prémontval was concerned, and Merian and Formey too, volition was a mental process, and, for this to be free, it could not be determined by any external influence.[120] By contrast, unlike Formey (but like Merian), Prémontval considered freedom to consist only in the soul's capacity to modify itself by its own absolutely

---

113. Prémontval, *Pensées sur la liberté*, p.21-22.
114. Formey neither reviewed Prémontval's *Pensées sur la liberté* in his journals nor recommended the work to Berlin publishers; see Lifschitz, *Language and Enlightenment*, p.156.
115. See Prémontval, *Pensées sur la liberté*, p.9.
116. See Prémontval, *Pensées sur la liberté*, p.10-11.
117. See Merian, 'Examen d'une question concernant la liberté', p.429.
118. See Prémontval, *Pensées sur la liberté*, p.14 and 31-32.
119. See Merian, 'Examen d'une question concernant la liberté', p.417-19.
120. See Prémontval, *Pensées sur la liberté*, p.54.

active power.[121] At the same time, however, he realised it was not possible to apply such an ideal notion of liberty to reality, because this required the assumption that human beings were governed by pure chance. However, if the existence of free actions could serve to hold people responsible for their own actions – a condition that Prémontval clearly required – these actions could result neither from necessity nor from absolute chance. As a consequence, Prémontval admitted he was not able to solve the problem of human liberty. As far as Prémontval was concerned, unlike Formey, there was no middle way to be found between necessity and chance.[122] Thus, he finished his deliberations without drawing any conclusions.

Prémontval and Merian declared themselves incapable of positively confirming free will, and this seems to have been linked mainly to their rejection of the Leibnizian and Wolffian compatibilist theory of liberty on which Formey had based his unequivocal confirmation of free will. A similar observation can be made in the case of the Swiss philosopher Johann Georg Sulzer, who was a prominent defender of Leibniz's and Wolff's philosophy at the Berlin Academy,[123] yet did not embrace compatibilism with respect to human liberty. Sulzer, who joined the Academy shortly after Merian, that is, in October 1750, was particularly influenced by Wolff's empirical psychology. In fact, he extended Wolff's premises further and developed a 'physics of the soul'. This consisted of investigating the physiological processes that corresponded to the mental processes of the soul, and was similar to the experimentalist science of the soul that the so-called 'psycho-physicians' at the University of Halle practised.[124]

In 1759, Sulzer applied his 'physics of the soul' to a central issue in the debate concerning liberty, namely, how it was sometimes possible

---

121. See Prémontval, *Pensées sur la liberté*, p.54 and 77-79.
122. See Prémontval, *Pensées sur la liberté*, p.115-17.
123. See Elisabeth Décultot, 'Sulzer, ein Aufklärer? Anstatt einer Einleitung', in *Johann Georg Sulzer: Aufklärung im Umbruch*, ed. Elisabeth Décultot, Philipp Kampa and Jana Kittelmann (Berlin and Boston, MA, 2018), p.1-13 (4), and Frank Grunert and Gideon Stiening, 'Einleitung: Johann Georg Sulzer – Aufklärung zwischen Christian Wolff und David Hume', in *Johann Georg Sulzer (1720-1779): Aufklärung zwischen Christian Wolff und David Hume*, ed. Frank Grunert and Gideon Stiening (Berlin, 2011), p.11-18.
124. See Daniel Dumouchel, 'Johann Georg Sulzer: la psychologie comme "physique de l'âme"', in *Les Métaphysiques des Lumières*, ed. Pierre Girard, Christian Leduc and Mitia Rioux-Beaulne (Paris, 2016), p.171-90, and Stefanie Buchenau, 'Sulzers "Physik der Seele" zwischen Medizin und Philosophie', in *Aufklärung im Umbruch*, ed. E. Décultot, P. Kampa, and J. Kittelmann, p.36-50.

for an individual to act without any apparent motive or even against the most convincing motive.[125] As mentioned above, the observation of such apparently arbitrary actions was an argument in favour of the liberty of indifference, something that Formey had already disproved in 1747 with reference to Leibniz's theory of indiscernibles and Wolff's distinction between clear and obscure ideas. Sulzer's explanation of apparently arbitrary choices in 1759 also relied fundamentally on these considerations; however, he tried to justify them further by providing physiological explanations. With reference to Leibniz, Sulzer asserted that imperceptible forces existed that were capable of overruling the soul's capacity to act according to its will.[126] To explain the dominance of these forces but also their undetectable nature, he depicted their emergence as being through the processes of the nervous system.[127]

Nevertheless, Sulzer did not make use of all these thorough explanations to reject the account of the liberty of indifference that Merian and Prémontval had outlined in their respective essays. On the contrary, he claimed right at the beginning of his essay that he did not want to reopen the debate about liberty because he believed it to be futile:

> Mon intention n'est pas de renouveller les disputes sur la liberté; je les crois frivoles, du moins très inutiles. Car de quelque côté que tombât la victoire on n'y gagneroit jamais rien, vû que la decision ne peut rien changer dans la condition de l'homme. Libre ou non, il sera toujours ce que le concours des circonstances aura fait de lui. Mon seul dessein est de répandre quelques nouvelles lumieres sur la physique de l'ame.[128]

In Sulzer's view, theories concerning human liberty were disconnected from the physical state of human beings and, hence, amounted to mere speculation. Rather than engaging in such speculation, Sulzer wanted to research the observable facts alone.[129] Similarly

---

125. Johann Georg Sulzer, 'Explication d'un paradoxe psychologique: que non seulement l'homme agit & juge quelquefois sans motifs & sans raison apparentes, mais même malgré des motifs pressans & des raisons convainquantes', in *Histoire de l'Académie royale des sciences et belles lettres de Berlin* (1759; Berlin, Haude & Spener, 1766), p.433-50. Sulzer presented this at the Academy on 11 October 1759.
126. See Sulzer, 'Explication d'un paradoxe psychologique', p.439.
127. See Sulzer, 'Explication d'un paradoxe psychologique', p.443-45.
128. Sulzer, 'Explication d'un paradoxe psychologique', p.433-34.
129. See Buchenau, 'Sulzers "Physik der Seele"', p.39-40.

to Merian and Prémontval, his reluctance to choose a side in the debate on free will resulted from his epistemological convictions. His 'physics of the soul' betrayed his strong trust in empiricism in relation to psychological matters. However, unlike Formey, who believed that human liberty could be empirically proven, Sulzer did not extend the scope of his 'physics of the soul' to this matter. Moreover, Sulzer's claim reveals that he assumed a general determination of the world that would render the question of whether humans were free obsolete. Hence, although Sulzer was generally favourable to Leibniz's and Wolff's philosophy, he refused to demonstrate the compatibility of predetermination and contingency with respect to human liberty.

Sulzer was not the last to touch upon this particular question in relation to the debate on free will at the Berlin Academy. In 1770, another Wolffian philosopher, Nicolas de Béguelin, addressed the problem of how to reconcile liberty of indifference and divine prescience: against Leibniz's view, he believed that it was metaphysically possible that human beings make completely arbitrary choices. Yet, he admitted that, if this was true, it was difficult to conceive of God's ability to predict each of His creatures' choices. As a possible solution to this problem, Béguelin suggested that God might have endowed human beings with an instinct that guided their spontaneous decisions similar to that of animals.[130] It is true that the attempts among the academicians in Berlin to define human liberty as a liberty of indifference grew throughout the eighteenth century. However, concepts of a free will that was determined by non-binding motives as Formey had adopted it also continued to exist. As late as 1786, Jean de Castillon presented a view on human liberty that tried to combine the two different stances in the sense that he considered liberty to be the active faculty to choose between different motives or to reject them altogether and, consequently, to act without any motive.[131]

Among the various contributions to the question of human liberty, Formey's 'Réflexions sur la liberté' was unique because he embraced unconditionally the Leibnizian theory of liberty against all accusations of fatalism. As such, not only did Formey become

---

130. See Nicolas de Béguelin, 'Sur l'indifférence d'équilibre et le principe du choix', in *Nouveaux mémoires de l'Académie royale des sciences et belles-lettres* (1770; Berlin, Voss, 1772), p.247-57 (esp. 256-57).
131. Jean de Castillon, 'Recherches sur la liberté de l'homme', in *Mémoires de l'Académie royale des sciences et belles-lettres* (1786-1787; Berlin, Decker, 1792), p.517-33 (esp. 520 and 525).

the target of Merian's and Prémontval's anti-Leibnizian attacks, his thought also differed from the psycho-physiological demonstrations of the Wolffian Sulzer as well as Béguelin's considerations on the possibility of a liberty of indifference. Moreover, the debate among the Berlin academicians betrays the alteration in the concept of empirical knowledge of the soul during the second half of the eighteenth century. Although Formey, in a Wolffian manner, still held liberty to be provable empirically by inner feeling or consciousness, his colleagues were indebted to an empirical science of the soul that resembled the sensualist approach of Bonnet or the experimental psychology of the German psycho-physicians, both of which precluded the confirmation of free will. As far as Formey was concerned personally, his empirical engagement with the question of free will led him to reassess his own opinion on the assumed fatalistic implications of Leibniz's and Wolff's philosophy that he had criticised in his *Belle wolfienne*. Finally, for Formey to define the freedom of the will the way he did served his aim of confirming the compatibility of human liberty with divine prescience and, eventually, providence. By contrast, his colleagues mostly refrained from statements about this issue. In fact, in the 1750s a part of the Academy's members considered the existence of both human liberty and divine providence to be contradictory, which can be seen in the critical engagement with Leibniz's theory of optimism, expressed in the Academy's two prize contests of 1751 and 1755. This will be the subject of the next chapter.

7. Providence, moral duties and optimism

Formey's metaphysical notion of human liberty that included the compatibility of human free actions with (divine) predetermination went hand in hand with his concept of divine providence. In eighteenth-century Protestant theology and philosophy, the prevailing concept of providence was that of a general principle of order in the world that had been established and was preserved by God. This concept of providence, according to which God did not intervene actively in the world's order and 'concurred' with human beings' free actions, pertained to the Thomist tradition.[1] Through the rise of a mechanistic worldview in the seventeenth century, this tradition took hold in Protestantism, which had originally advanced an actualistic concept of providence according to which God intervened continuously and directly in the course of the world.[2]

However, despite the widespread acceptance in the eighteenth century of the definition of providence as a general principle of order, there were many aspects of providence that lacked specification or unanimous approval, for example, the question of God's purpose with regard to Creation and the role of providence in relation to salvation. With respect to moral philosophy, the question of the origin and meaning of evil in a provident world has been particularly important.

One influential attempt to answer these questions concerning providence and to account for the existence of evil in the world in particular was metaphysical optimism, which emerged at the end of the seventeenth and during the first half of the eighteenth century in France, Germany and England. According to optimist theories, God

---

1. See Ulrich L. Lehner, *Kants Vorsehungskonzept auf dem Hintergrund der deutschen Schulphilosophie und -theologie* (Leiden, 2007), p.8-9.
2. Lehner, *Kants Vorsehungskonzept*, p.12-13.

had created the best of all possible worlds because he was infinitely wise and good. The existing misery and evil in the world were a necessary part of this perfect world and, thus, were eventually to be considered as good too.[3] This theory of the best of all possible worlds was associated mostly with Leibniz, who advanced it as a demonstration of God's justice and goodness in his *Théodicée* in 1710. The foundation of Leibniz's optimism was his concept of perfection, according to which both human beings' and God's actions were prompted by striving for perfection, a concept that Wolff adopted from Leibniz, just as he did with his optimistic account of providence.[4]

However, optimism did not flourish only in the German lands. In the final decades of the seventeenth century, the French Oratorian priest and disciple of Descartes Nicolas Malebranche had already developed an optimist theory of the world's order and divine actions in his *Traité de la nature et de la grace*.[5] In England, in 1733 and 1734, the poet Alexander Pope published an optimist account in verse, his *Essay on man*; under the dictum 'Whatever is, is right', he described the world as devoid of evil.[6] Pope and Leibniz in particular were often associated with one another by eighteenth-century readers, and their ideas eventually conflated.[7]

Despite this multiple emergence of optimist accounts of divine providence in the whole of Europe, the concept was very controversial among philosophers and theologians throughout the eighteenth century. Whereas it received stronger and longer-lasting support

---

3. For the development and reception of the concept of optimism in seventeenth- and eighteenth-century Europe, see Luca Fonnesu, 'Der Optimismus und seine Kritiker im Zeitalter der Aufklärung', *Studia Leibnitiana* 26:2 (1994), p.131-62; Stefan Lorenz, *De mundo optimo: Studien zu Leibniz' Theodizee und ihrer Rezeption in Deutschland (1710-1791)* (Stuttgart, 1997); Hernan D. Caro, 'The best of all possible worlds? Leibniz's optimism and its critics 1710-1755', doctoral dissertation, Humboldt University Berlin, 2014; Paul Rateau, *Leibniz et le meilleur des mondes possibles* (Paris, 2015); Lloyd Strickland, 'Staying optimistic! The trials and tribulations of Leibnizian optimism', in *Leibniz's legacy and impact*, ed. Julia Weckend and Lloyd Strickland (New York, 2019), p.53-86.
4. See Clemens Schwaiger, 'Ethik', in *Handbuch Christian Wolff*, ed. R. Theis and A. Aichele, p.253-68 (256-57).
5. See Nicolas Malebranche, *Traité de la nature et de la grace* (Amsterdam, Elsevier, 1680). For its interpretation, see Lorenz, *De mundo optimo*, p.28-48.
6. See Alexander Pope, *An Essay on man: in epistles to a friend* (London, Wilford, 1733-1734). For Pope's optimism and the debate it unleashed in France, see Zanconato, *La Dispute du fatalisme*.
7. See Strickland, 'Staying optimistic!', p.64.

in Germany, which was mainly because of the spread of Leibniz's optimism through Wolff's *Metaphysik*,[8] it had gained a predominantly negative reputation in France since the 1730s. After the Lisbon earthquake of 1755, the criticism of optimism reached a peak because the enormous pain and misery this natural disaster caused led people to believe that optimist attempts to explain evil by God's goodness were simply absurd. As a consequence, optimism became the target of polemics and mockery, most famously in Voltaire's poem about the Lisbon earthquake and his satirical novel *Candide, ou De l'optimisme*.[9] However, Voltaire's polemics were only the culmination of the long decline of the theory of optimism. In 1753, the Berlin Academy organised a prize essay competition for submissions in 1755; the question was to compare Pope's dictum that everything was good with the theory of optimism and to evaluate the truth of the latter.[10] Among the German scholarly public, this question was considered largely as a deliberate challenge to Leibniz's theory of the best of all possible worlds and as another example of the Academy's assumed hostility towards Leibniz's philosophy in general.[11] Actually, the competition was preceded in 1751 and 1752 by the so-called 'König affair' at the Berlin Academy, in which Maupertuis and the mathematician Samuel König argued over the question of who had been the inventor of the principle of least action – Leibniz or Maupertuis – and which

8. See Strickland, 'Staying optimistic!', p.60.
9. See *Poème sur le désastre de Lisbonne* (1756), ed. David Adams and Haydn T. Mason, in *The Complete works of Voltaire*, vol.45A (Oxford, 2009), p.269-358, and *Candide, ou De l'optimisme* (1759), ed. René Pomeau, in *The Complete works of Voltaire*, vol.48 (Oxford, 1980).
10. See *Registres de l'Académie juin 1746-août 1786*, ed. Berlin-Brandenburgische Akademie der Wissenschaften, 7 June 1753, https://akademieregistres.bbaw.de/data/protokolle/0304-1753_06_07.xml (last accessed 24 July 2023): 'On demande l'Examen du Systéme de Pope, contenu dans la Proposition: Tout est bien. Il s'agit: 1. de déterminer le vrai sens de cette Proposition conformément à l'hypothese de son Auteur. 2. de la comparer avec le Système de l'Optimisme, ou du choix du meilleur, pour en marquer les rapports et les différences. 3. enfin d'alléguer les raisons qu'on croira les plus propres à confirmer ou à détruire ce Système.'
11. See Harnack, *Geschichte der Königlich Preussischen Akademie*, vol.1:1, p.403-404, who claimed that the aim of the prize question was to denigrate Leibniz's philosophy. For a modern account of the criticism of the prize question of 1755 that challenges the truth of Harnack's claim, see Lorenz, *De mundo optimo*, p.167-69.

provoked a confrontation between Leibnizians and anti-Leibnizians.[12] Finally, just a few months before the Lisbon earthquake in 1755, the Academy awarded the prize of its essay competition to an anti-Leibnizian essay by the German jurist Adolf Friedrich Reinhard, who rejected the theory of the best of all possible worlds on metaphysical grounds as well as for its moral implications.[13] The award further fuelled the public debate; most famously, the German writers Gotthold Ephraim Lessing and Moses Mendelssohn penned an essay of protest against the Academy's decision.[14] Formey also participated in the debate on optimism with a critical review of Reinhard's essay[15] (although he had, apparently, voted for it in the selection process at the Academy).[16]

Moreover, in 1759 Formey published a defence of Leibnizian and Popeian optimism by an author who gained increased renown in the 1750s: Rousseau. In 1756, in a private letter to Voltaire, Rousseau had criticised the latter's pessimistic and voluntarist depiction of providence in the poem about the Lisbon earthquake, and had

12. The 'König affair' led to strong reactions from the German scholarly public; see Ursula Goldenbaum, 'Das Publikum als Garant der Freiheit der Gelehrtenrepublik: die öffentliche Debatte über den "Jugement de l'Académie royale des sciences et belles lettres sur une lettre prétendue de M. de Leibnitz" 1752-1753', in *Appell an das Publikum*, vol.2, p.509-652.
13. See Adolf Friedrich Reinhard, 'Le système de Mr. Pope sur la perfection du monde, comparé à celui de Mr. Leibnitz, avec un examen de l'optimisme, pour satisfaire au problème proposé par l'Académie royale des sciences et belles-lettres de Berlin pour le prix de l'année 1755', in *Dissertation qui a remporté le prix proposé par l'Académie royale des sciences et belles-lettres de Prusse, sur l'optimisme, avec les pièces qui ont concouru* (Berlin, Haude & Spener, 1755), p.3-48.
14. See Marion Hellwig, *Alles ist gut: Untersuchungen zur Geschichte einer Theodizee-Formel im 18. Jahrhundert in Deutschland, England und Frankreich* (Würzburg, 2008), p.297-309.
15. See 'Article II. Dissertation qui a remporté le Prix [...] sur l'OPTIMISME', *Nouvelle bibliothèque germanique* 18 (1756), p.22-32. A collection of several pieces related to this debate, which appeared in European learned journals, Formey's piece included, was published in 1759: *Sammlung der Streitschriften über die Lehre von der besten Welt, und verschiedene damit verknüpfte wichtige Wahrheiten, welche zwischen dem Verfasser der im Jahr 1755 von der Akademie zu Berlin gekrönten Schrift vom Optimismo, und einigen berühmten Gelehrten gewechselt worden*, ed. Christian Ziegra (Rostock and Wismar, Berger & Boedner, 1759). A German translation of Formey's review can be found on p.8-19.
16. See Winter, *Die Registres der Berliner Akademie*, p.57. Based on a contemporary account by Sulzer, Winter maintains that Formey voted for Reinhard's anti-optimist essay to please Maupertuis.

confessed his own belief in universal providence and the immortality of the soul. Formey published this letter that later became known as Rousseau's *Lettre sur la providence* without the two correspondents' knowledge in one of his journals.[17] Although he disagreed with several of Rousseau's claims (for example that particular providence and the doctrine of eternal suffering do not exist), there can be no doubt that Formey essentially supported Rousseau's plea for optimism and his attack against Voltaire's pessimism.[18] In addition to his criticism of Reinhard's winning prize essay of 1755, the publication of Rousseau's *Lettre sur la providence* was hence a means to keep the debate on optimism alive in Berlin after the Lisbon earthquake.

However, this strategy of promoting and popularising the theory of optimism had already become tangible in Formey's oeuvre earlier on. Optimism was a central element of Formey's moral philosophy, which he promoted via his *Philosophe chrétien* and his sermons to a popular audience. Moreover, he also used optimism to defend providence in his apologetic writings against the *philosophes*. Most importantly, however, Formey tried to promote his optimist concept of providence via one of the Berlin Academy's essay competitions. Four years before the controversial essay competition in 1755, the theme of which was Pope's optimism, the Academy had already asked the European learned public to explain the role of providence in moral philosophy, a question that led participants to engage with optimist theories of providence. Although the 1751 prize essay competition provoked less public controversy than the one of 1755, the theme of which was optimism, it was still the subject of an internal

17. Formey inserted the 'Lettre de M. Jean Jacques Rousseau à M. de Voltaire' in his 'Lettre XLIII. A Mr. le P. G. le F. du 23 octobre 1759' and 'Lettre XLIV. A Mr. le P. G. le F. du 30 octobre 1759', in *Lettres sur l'état présent des sciences et des mœurs* 2 (July-December 1759) (Berlin, Haude & Spener, 1760), p.257-88. For a modern edition of the text, see *Lettre de J.-J. Rousseau à Monsieur de Voltaire*, ed. Henri Gouhier, in *Jean-Jacques Rousseau: œuvres complètes*, vol.4 (Paris, 1969), p.1058-67. In the following, the eighteenth-century publication of the letter by Formey is cited. On the genesis and publication history of Rousseau's *Lettre sur la providence*, see George R. Havens, 'Voltaire, Rousseau and the "Lettre sur la providence"', *Publications of the Modern Language Association of America* 59:1 (1944), p.109-30. On Rousseau's concept of providence as it becomes tangible in his *Lettre sur la providence* and other writings, see Victor Gourevitch, 'Rousseau on providence', *The Review of metaphysics* 53:3 (2000), p.565-611.
18. See 'Lettre XLIV', p.280 and 281-82. In his *Souvenirs*, vol.2, p.119, Formey stressed that he had published Rousseau's letter because he liked it a lot and that he wanted it to become publicly known.

debate at the Academy. This debate and Formey's public endorsement of the winning essay are crucial for understanding his concept of providence and its implications for moral philosophy. Moreover, Formey's engagement with this prize essay competition illustrates the clash between his optimist concept of providence and the opinions of his French colleagues at the Academy and abroad, Maupertuis and D'Alembert in particular. To also contextualise Formey's concept of optimistic providence within his confessional milieu, the present chapter compares the debate at the Academy with a debate about optimism that Formey had at about the same time with another Huguenot theologian, the pastor in London David-Renaud Boullier.

The Berlin Academy's 1751 prize essay competition on the theme of providence

In 1749, it was the turn of the Academy's class of speculative philosophy to suggest a question for the institution's annual prize essay competition for submissions in 1751. Its members opted for a moral philosophical topic that dealt with the impact providence could have on moral behaviour and the consequences thereof. The initiative for this question lay with Formey's German colleague Philip Heinius;[19] however, it was mainly Formey who defended it against the criticism that it subsequently received. The question, which was released to the European learned public via academic journals in the summer of 1749, presented the existence of divine providence explicitly as a certainty:

> Les Evènemens de la bonne & de la mauvaise Fortune, dépendant incontestablement de la volonté, ou du moins de la permission de Dieu, à l'égard duquel ce que nous appelons Fortune n'est qu'un vain nom, dénué de réalité; On demande, si ces Evènemens obligent les hommes à la pratique de certains devoirs, & quelle est la nature & l'étendue de ces devoirs?[20]

The claim of divine providence contained in the question resulted from the rejection of fate and chance, two concepts that were expressed by the French term *fortune*. In the mid-eighteenth century, the term *fortune*, which was derived from the roman goddess Fortuna who was

19. See Formey, *Souvenirs*, vol.2, p.361.
20. See 'Prix proposé par l'Académie royale des sciences et belles-lettres de Prusse, pour l'année 1751', *Nouvelle bibliothèque germanique* 5 (1748), p.230-31.

known for her capricious behaviour towards men, denominated all things, good and bad, that happened by chance (French *hasard*) and were, therefore, unpredictable.[21] In the *Encyclopédie*, this meaning was associated with the concept of fatality,[22] that is, the hidden cause of all unpredictable events that entailed either pleasure or pain.[23] Unlike chance, fatality (and hence *fortune*) implied that events had a determining cause, although this cause remained unknown to human beings; chance, by contrast, implied the absence of any cause whatsoever. By using the term *fortune*, the prize essay question therefore rejected the existence of both chance and unknown destiny and instead assumed that every pleasure and pain had a determining cause – God's will – and that this cause was intelligible to human beings.[24] Moreover, the question insinuated that the knowledge of this cause provided individuals with certain rules of behaviour.

This explicit position concerning the role of providence in moral philosophy, which was disseminated to the whole of learned Europe through the Academy's prize essay question, immediately sparked all kinds of criticism, mainly among the institution's own members. One strand of criticism concerned the very concept of providence that was expressed in the prize question, namely, a providence that was compatible with human free agency. This was the mainstream concept of eighteenth-century theology; however, it was rejected by both deists and atheists. The mathematician and external member of the Academy Jean D'Alembert, who claimed to account for the opinion of all 'gens de lettres de Paris', considered such a concept of

21. See 'Fortune, s.f.', in *Dictionnaire universel françois et latin*, 5 vols (Paris, Delaulne et al., 1721), vol.2, p.1939-43 (1941).
22. See D'Alembert, 'Fortune, s.m. (Morale)', in *Encyclopédie*, vol.7 (Paris, Briasson et al., 1757), p.205-206.
23. See André Morellet, 'Fatalité, (Métaph.)', in *Encyclopédie*, vol.6 (Paris, Briasson et al., 1756), p.422-29 (429).
24. Initially, the rejection of fate and chance in favour of providence had been stated less explicitly. When the class of speculative philosophy presented the proposed prize essay question to the Academy's assembly on 3 July 1749, the question did not as yet contain the statement that 'fortune' did not exist: 'Les Evenemens de la bonne et de la mauvaise Fortune, dependant uniquement de la Volonté, ou du moins de la permission de Dieu; On demande, si ces Evenemens obligent les hommes à la pratique de ce [*sic*] certains devoirs, et quelle est la nature et l'etendue de ces devoirs?' See *Registres de l'Académie*, 3 July 1749, https://akademieregistres.bbaw.de/data/protokolle/0136-1749_07_03.xml (last accessed 24 July 2023). Hence, the rejection of fortune and the emphasis on providence were only highlighted on the publication of the prize question.

providence paradoxical. In a letter to Formey in September 1749, he complained that the problem posed by the Academy was impossible to solve because the assumption that the world was governed by divine will would contradict the execution of moral duties:

> D'un côté, la question du bien & du mal moral suppose, ce me semble, la liberté; de l'autre la volonté divine, maîtresse absolue de tous les événemens, semble rendre tout nécessaire; c'est pourquoi il me paroît que votre question bien entendue se réduit à celle-ci: *attendu qu'il est fort douteux que nous soyons libres, on demande si nous le sommes?* En un mot, la dépendance où nous sommes de la volonté divine, formant une objection très forte, & peut-être insoluble contre la liberté & la question du bien & du mal, il me semble que cette dépendance ne devoit pas servir de donnée pour traiter cette question: c'est tourner le dos où l'on veut aller.[25]

In D'Alembert's view, a distinction between morally right or wrong actions required that human beings act freely, a requirement that, for him, did not exist in a necessary order that relied on God's will. Hence, with regard to human freedom, D'Alembert asserted the idea of liberty of indifference, according to which human beings' decisions were absolutely undetermined. Whereas D'Alembert claimed the concurrence of human liberty and providence to be contradictory in his letter to Formey, he portrayed them as coexistent a few years later in the article 'Fortuit' of the *Encyclopédie*. In this article he considered this coexistence to be a truth that human beings were unable to comprehend, and criticised the philosophers who tried to explain it philosophically.[26] This criticism probably also included Formey, whose compatibilist stance on human freedom was precisely an attempt to reconcile human beings' free actions with God's providence by using metaphysical demonstration. As stated above (see chapter 6), he professed that people's decisions and, thus, their actions were determined by moral motives that resulted from their God-given nature. Because Creation and, therefore, human nature, were based on God's free will, according to compatibilist theory, human actions were to be considered free or contingent.

Because of his different concept of human liberty, Formey did not accept D'Alembert's complaints about the assumed contradiction

---

25. D'Alembert to Formey (19.9.1749), printed in Formey, *Souvenirs*, vol.2, p.364 (emphasis in the original).
26. See D'Alembert, 'Fortuit, (Métaphys.)', in *Encyclopédie*, vol.7 (Paris, Briasson *et al.*, 1757), p.204-205.

7. Providence, moral duties and optimism

inherent in the prize essay question. Instead, he clarified that it was about the individual's moral duties in a provident world.[27] As Formey explained in more detail in a letter to Maupertuis, his notion of providence consisted in the existence of a universal interlinkage of all things:

> Il faut developer le veritable Systeme de l'enchainement universel de toutes choses, duquel résulte la vraye notion de l'Univers, et qui prouve qu'il y a des rélations, qui font de chaque individu une espece de centre, auquel tout se rapporte tandis que lui-même se rapporte à tout; d'où naissent des devoirs de gratitude et d'acquiescement, suivant que les choses fortuites qui nous arrivent sont avantageuses ou contraires &c.[28]

This definition corresponded to the Protestant view, according to which divine providence was a general principle of order in the world, but was also informed by the Leibnizian and Wolffian concepts of universal harmony and the *nexus rerum*. However, Formey's description of the individual's role within this system did not contain any trace of human free agency. Rather, he attributed a somewhat passive role to the individual by claiming that they simply had to be grateful for good fortune and to acquiesce to hardship. Formey had argued similarly in 1736 in his sermon *La Nature et la source du vrai contentement*, which he republished in 1750 in his *Philosophe chrétien*. Here, by referring to Scripture,[29] Formey urged his listeners to resign themselves to misery, rather than protesting against it: first, God's purposes were, ultimately, unintelligible to human beings anyway; and, second, God took care of the good outcome of everything.[30] Therefore, Formey's description of divine providence, which he exhibited in his letter to Maupertuis, relied predominantly on religious doctrine.

Nevertheless, at other times, Formey focused more strongly on a concept of providence based on natural law. In his moral philosophical essay *Sur les vicissitudes de la vie*, which he published in his *Philosophe chrétien* in 1750, and which had, therefore, probably originally been a sermon, Formey further developed the idea of providence that he

---

27. See D'Alembert to Formey (12.11.1749), CV.
28. Formey to Maupertuis (22.8.1749), Staatsbibliothek Berlin, Nachlass 218.
29. See Isaiah 55.8: '"For my thoughts are not your thoughts, neither are your ways my ways," declares the Lord.'
30. See Formey, *Sermons sur divers textes de l'écriture sainte*, p.41, and *Philosophe chrétien*, 1st edn, vol.1, p.239.

had advanced in his letter to Maupertuis: the existence of a universal interlinkage of everything in nature that meant that all happenings were determined. He added that this order had been instilled by God, and that people's impression that chance existed in the world resulted only from their ignorance of this order.[31] However, in contrast to his letter to Maupertuis and his essay on contentment, Formey's essay on the vicissitudes of life highlighted the role of human agency as well as that of divine agency within this order. More precisely, Formey distinguished between three types of events in human life and society that differed according to their cause: first, there were global events, such as birth and death, that were solely ruled by God in His function as a first cause; second, there were events that depended solely on human beings' active force and their capacity to influence the things surrounding them; finally, there were 'mixed events', the existence of which human beings were not able to influence yet, but to which they could adapt their personal needs.[32]

The result of this acknowledgement of a certain degree of human agency in providence was the possibility of inferring human duties. According to Formey's *Sur les vicissitudes de la vie*, one's general duty was to recognise and study one's position within the interlinked order so that one could evaluate the influence one had on other elements within that order and, therefore, make use of one's influence effectively.[33] Based on this general rule, Formey developed a number of particular duties for the individual to respect that reflected a certain degree of human self-determination: one should have and follow a plan in one's life; one should instruct oneself in the elements of one's professional vocation; one should act in accordance with the circumstances that providence provided; and, finally, one should develop one's capacity for self-governance, thereby controlling one's passions.[34] Formey added one last fundamental duty, which related only to religion, to all these worldly duties, namely, that one should always work for one's salvation.[35] Such a division between duties derived from natural law and those derived from religion corresponded to the general characteristics of Formey's sermons and moral philosophical essays, as was shown earlier (see chapter 3). With respect to his

---

31. See Formey, *Philosophe chrétien*, 1st edn, vol.1, p.18.
32. See Formey, *Philosophe chrétien*, 1st edn, vol.1, p.3-5.
33. See Formey, *Philosophe chrétien*, 1st edn, vol.1, p.19-20.
34. See Formey, *Philosophe chrétien*, 1st edn, vol.1, p.20-28.
35. See Formey, *Philosophe chrétien*, 1st edn, vol.1, p.29-30.

concept of providence, this double-sided approach emphasised that Formey considered providence to be intelligible through both natural reason and revelation, a view that he also maintained in *La Nature et la source du vrai contentement*, in which, however, he also emphasised that the revealed notion of providence was the most evident.[36]

Formey's conviction that providence was explicable by both reason and revelation clashed fundamentally with D'Alembert's views. After Formey's clarification about the concept of providence that underlay the prize essay question, D'Alembert made it clear in a second letter in autumn 1749 that he considered providence, that is, the 'physical and moral government of the world', to be a merely religious doctrine. As such, it remained enigmatic in D'Alembert's view and, therefore, was not a convenient subject for an academic prize essay competition that required evidence-based and clear notions rather than just vague explanations. According to D'Alembert, the only way to approach the topic from a philosophical point of view was to explain providence in terms of metaphysical optimism, which was a theory D'Alembert actually rejected. In his view, it was simply not possible to prove convincingly that the world in which everybody lived was the best of all possible worlds; only revelation was able to confirm this theory:

> Je crois d'ailleurs qu'a en juger par nos foibles lumieres, ce systême [Formey's notion of providence] est sujet à de grandes objections, si on le considere du côté purement Philosophique. Il tient à *l'optimisme*, & l'optimisme quoy qu'il presente au premier abord une idée magnifique, n'est pas sans de grandes difficultés. En un mot, on ne fera jamais voir (par les seuls principes de la Philosophie) que le monde est mieux tel qu'il est que s'il ny avoit aucun desordre Physique ny moral; si tous les climats etoient agreables, tous les hommes justes, vertueux, sans peine desprit ny de corps. Il faut avoir recours pour cela à la revelation, & je conclus delà que votre question peut faire la matiére d'un tres beau sermon, mais non, selon moy, d'un ouvrage purement metaphysique.[37]

D'Alembert's critical stance in relation to metaphysical optimism was exemplary with regard to the French attitude concerning this theory, which was marked by the Jesuits' criticism of Leibniz's *Théodicée* in the *Mémoires de Trévoux* during the first half of the eighteenth century.[38] In

---

36. See Formey, *Sermons sur divers textes de l'écriture sainte*, p.40-41, and *Philosophe chrétien*, 1st edn, vol.1, p.238-39.
37. D'Alembert to Formey (12.11.1749), CV (emphasis in the original).
38. See Rateau, *Leibniz et le meilleur des mondes*, p.353-92. He emphasises that the

his article 'Optimisme' in the *Encyclopédie*, D'Alembert repeated some of the major Jesuit criticisms, namely, that this theory curtailed divine liberty and that it portrayed evil as a component of good. However, the central criticism contained in his article was – as in his letter to Formey – that optimism was interwoven with revealed doctrine: D'Alembert maintained that, to justify its claim that the world was the best of all possible worlds, optimism relied on the biblical notion of God's highest wisdom and intelligence as well as the unintelligibility of God's purposes. As far as D'Alembert was concerned, resorting to revelation undermined the whole theory of optimism, and it became an empty metaphysical concept.[39] Not only D'Alembert, but Maupertuis too was critical about optimism. In his above-mentioned academic essay 'Les Loix du mouvement' (see chapter 4) on the physico-theological proof of God's existence that was published in 1746, Maupertuis doubted the success of Leibniz's and Malebranche's attempts to reconcile evil and imperfection with God's wisdom and power.[40] With regard to Pope's denial of the existence of evil in the world, Maupertuis rejected this idea because of its lack of proof; in his view, it relied merely on religious dogma.[41]

In his dispute with Formey about the prize essay question, Maupertuis, however, seems to have been most concerned with the question's effect on the Academy's public reputation. Shortly after the question was released to the public in 1749, Maupertuis informed Formey that he had already received several complaints about it, including the way it was formulated, from both French and German scholars. He called for more precision in posing prize essay questions because the Academy was judged by the questions it asked and the essays it decided to reward.[42] Formey, who did not want to be held

---

encyclopédistes, D'Alembert and Diderot in particular, adopted their negative attitude towards optimism and their principal arguments against it from the Jesuits' refutations, despite the ideological differences between the two groups (p.385).

39. See D'Alembert, 'Optimisme, s.m. (Phil.)', in *Encyclopédie*, vol.11 (Neufchâtel, Faulche, 1765), p.517. D'Alembert referred to Romans 11.33. Compare also with D'Alembert's criticism of optimism in his 'Discours préliminaire des éditeurs', in *Encyclopédie*, vol.1 (Paris, Briasson *et al.*, 1751), p.i-xlv (xxviii). Here, he portrays optimism as an example of Leibniz's flawed attempts to establish metaphysical systems; he claims that the main problem of the system of optimism was that it attempted to explain everything.
40. See Maupertuis, 'Loix du mouvement', p.275-76.
41. See Maupertuis, 'Loix du mouvement', p.276.
42. See Maupertuis to Formey (21.8.1749 and 24.8.1749), CV.

responsible for this situation and incur the wrath of his president, absolved himself of all responsibility for the choice of the question (and pointed to the fact that he had proposed other potential questions in his class). Nevertheless, because the question corresponded to his theological and philosophical beliefs, he defended not only the soundness of the topic, but also its diverse and interesting nature.[43]

Maupertuis's concerns about the Academy's reputation were shared by Merian, who joined the Academy after the prize essay question had been released and became a member of the awarding jury.[44] Like D'Alembert, Merian also criticised the incomprehensibility of the question, which he imputed mainly to Formey's inability to state his intentions with regard to it clearly enough. In his letters to his friend Jean II Bernoulli, Merian complained about the poor quality of the essays that had been sent in, which in his view testified that the participants had not understood the question.[45] To safeguard the Academy's scientific reputation, Merian even opted for a postponement of the award and a reformulation of the question; however, his academic colleagues on the awarding jury, Heinius and Sulzer, were against such a course of action because they feared it would make the Academy appear in a worse light than if it selected one of the pieces that had already been submitted.[46] Moreover, as Merian confessed to Maupertuis, his colleagues were also convinced that the topic would not result in any new answers, even if the question were reformulated.[47] Hence, it seems that Heinius and Sulzer, although they supported the prize essay question's content, acknowledged that it was directed at a rather narrow set of answers, the very same criticism that D'Alembert had put forward in his letters to Formey in 1749.

Eventually, the Academy awarded the prize to the piece that Merian had preferred and that, in his view, did at least maintain the institution's good reputation because it was by a renowned German senior scholar. However, Merian insisted that during the public announcement of the award the Academy should state clearly that it had not been entirely happy with any of the contributions it had

---

43. See Formey to Maupertuis (22.8.1749), Staatsbibliothek Berlin, Nachlass 218.
44. As well as Merian, the jury consisted of Heinius and Sulzer; see *Registres de l'Académie*, 7 January 1751, https://akademieregistres.bbaw.de/data/protokolle/0199-1751_01_07.xml (last accessed 24 July 2023).
45. See Merian to Jean II Bernoulli (17.4.1751), UBB, L Ia 711.
46. See Merian to Jean II Bernoulli (15.6.1751), UBB, L Ia 711.
47. See Merian to Maupertuis (17.5.1751), Archives de l'Académie des sciences et de l'Institut de France, Fonds Maupertuis 43 J, no.121.03.

received.[48] In standing firm on this issue, he was probably trying to prevent the content and quality of the prize essay, which he considered to be mediocre, from reflecting on the public image of the Academy's exalted intellectual position and scientific excellence. However, despite all the scientific doubts that some of the Academy's members had with regard to the prize essay question on providence, there is no evidence of it actually having been controversial among European scholars. On the contrary, the high number of entries in the competition – Merian reported to Bernoulli that the Academy had received over seventy essays – suggests that the question more than met the interest of the scholarly public.

The 'real' theory of fortune: Formey and the winning essay

The winning essay, which was officially awarded the prize at the Academy's public assembly on 27 May 1751,[49] corroborated the rejection of chance postulated in the question and highlighted human agency in providence. Hence, it corresponded to Formey's intentions with regard to the subject. The essay was written by Abraham Gotthelf Kästner, who was a professor of mathematics in Leipzig and an admirer of Maupertuis, and who had maintained a correspondence with the Academy's president since 1745. For his part, Maupertuis seems to have esteemed Kästner's mathematical skills and even offered him a position as an ordinary member at the Academy in 1750, something that Kästner, however, declined.[50] The essay not only revealed Kästner's aim of pleasing Maupertuis – it contained several references to Maupertuis's life and works – but relied generally on a natural philosophical and mathematical worldview that Kästner tried to apply to the traditional Protestant concept of providence. Moreover, his essay also contained implicit references to core concepts of Leibnizian and Wolffian philosophy, mainly to metaphysical optimism. In fact, Kästner was a Wolffian who also embraced certain of Newton's ideas.[51] As such, he, like

---

48. See Merian to Jean II Bernoulli (15.6.1751), UBB, L Ia 711.
49. See *Registres de l'Académie*, 27 May 1751, https://akademieregistres.bbaw.de/data/protokolle/0216-1751_05_27.xml (last accessed 24 July 2023).
50. See Kästner to Maupertuis (25.4.1750), in *Maupertuis et ses correspondants: lettres inédites du grand Frédéric, du prince Henri de Prusse, de Labeaumelle*, ed. Achille Le Sueur (1896; Geneva, 1971), p.284-86.
51. See Ahnert, 'Newton in the German-speaking lands', p.44.

Formey, seems to have been a bridge between the anti-Wolffian and Wolffian circles in mid-eighteenth-century Germany. He was a protégé of the *aléthophile* Gottsched and, apparently, frequented Manteuffel's Wolffian gatherings in Leipzig and enjoyed the personal esteem of Wolff.[52]

Formey himself was not involved in the selection of Kästner's essay by the Academy; he could not be a member of the awarding jury in 1751 because of sickness.[53] However, he demonstrated his strong approval of the chosen essay via specific publications in the aftermath of the competition: Formey not only printed a French translation of Kästner's entire essay in his journal *Nouvelle bibliothèque germanique*,[54] he had also published it independently under a different title in 1751. As well as helping the wide diffusion of Kästner's theory of providence, the latter publication also revealed Formey's aim of defending his own position in the debate about the question that had been asked. In fact, the Academy published Kästner's original Latin essay together with Kästner's own French translation of it in a collected volume that contained both the prize essay and all the others that had received a commendation in the competition.[55] This was common practice with regard to prize competitions. A further French version of Kästner's essay was, therefore, not absolutely necessary. Formey justified his republication of it by stating he had made a completely new translation; this, however, was not true. He only corrected a few words in Kästner's own translation and reprinted it under the new title *La Vraye Théorie de la fortune*.[56] In point of fact, Formey used his apparently new translation as a means of spreading

---

52. See Bronisch, *Mäzen der Aufklärung*, p.144-45; Wolff esteemed Kästner particularly for his translation of Cadwaller Colden's *Explication of the first causes of action in matter, and, of the cause of gravitation* (New York, Parker, 1745); see Wolff to Manteuffel (12.2.1748), in *Briefwechsel zwischen Wolff und Manteuffel*, vol.3, p.345-46.
53. See Merian to Jean II Bernoulli (17.4.1751), UBB, L Ia 711.
54. See 'Article IX. Piece qui a remporté le Prix sur le sujet des Evenemens fortuits', *Nouvelle bibliothèque germanique* 10 (1752), p.168-204.
55. See *Piece qui a remporté le prix sur le sujet des evenemens fortuits, proposé par l'Academie royale des sciences et belles lettres de Berlin pour l'année 1751, avec les pieces qui ont concouru* (Berlin, Haude & Spener, 1751).
56. See [Formey], *La Vraye Théorie de la fortune, avec les conséquences qui en résultent* (Berlin, Haude & Spener, 1751). In the dedication, he justified the publication of his own translation in addition to the official one with a reference to stylistic questions; according to him, Kästner, as a non-native French speaker, had not rendered the French good enough to ensure the essay's comprehensibility.

his own opinion on the topic, which he transmitted mainly through the publication's paratext. The choice of the title – the 'true' theory of fortune – already constituted a claim in defence of the subject of the prize question. It expressed the idea that arbitrary fate, as contained in the concept of fortune, did not exist in reality, exactly as Formey had promoted. Moreover, in his dedication in the *Vraye théorie de la fortune* Formey claimed that Kästner's writing proved his own position, namely, that the prize question had been neither trivial nor useless, as some people had argued in 1749; this constituted a hidden polemic against D'Alembert and Maupertuis.[57]

As far as the content of Kästner's winning essay was concerned, it seems to have complied with Formey's own convictions about the nature and role of providence. First and foremost, Kästner fully embraced the concept of providence that was claimed in the question: he assumed the universe had been created and continued to be governed by an omnipotent and good supreme being, and, therefore, all apparently fortuitous events fulfilled a purpose conceived by God. The recognition of such providence was the most powerful motivation for certain moral virtues to emerge.[58] In particular, Kästner posed a physico-theological notion of providence. With reference to Maupertuis's *Essai de cosmologie* (that is to say, the extended version of his earlier 'Loix du mouvement'), he described the universe as a complex interconnected system in which every detail required God's intervention and, thus, revealed His providence.[59] Rousseau, whose *Lettre sur la providence* Formey published eight years later, also considered the universe as a system in which every effect had a cause, yet he did not claim God to be the coordinator of the whole. Nevertheless, Formey supported this account of providence too.[60]

Second, Kästner assigned a certain degree of self-determination to humans within this system by claiming that they could conceive of and execute their own plans, but that the outcome of these plans depended on providence alone.[61] Behind this claim stood the concept of human beings having free agency within the limits of their dispositions, which had been instilled in them by God. As such, every

---

57. See [Formey], 'Dédicace', in *Vraye théorie*, sig.A3r-v.
58. See [Formey], *Vraye théorie*, p.10-12.
59. See [Formey], *Vraye théorie*, p.26-27.
60. See Formey, 'Lettre XLIII', p.269-74, with Formey's supporting comment on p.270.
61. See [Formey], *Vraye théorie*, p.14.

free individual automatically fulfilled a certain purpose in Creation as a whole:

> Tant que nous nous servirons de nos facultés conformément à nos lumieres, nous ne travaillerons jamais en vain, quand même les choses ne tourneroient pas de la maniere que nous les souhaitons; nous remplissons les vüés de la Providence. Dieu n'exige pas que nous travaillons à la journée comme des mercenaires; il veut que nous agissions d'une maniere proportionnée aux inclinations & aux forces qu'il a mises en nous. C'est à lui de faire tourner nos actions au bien de l'Univers. Il ne convient pas de croire que, semblable à un Ouvrier mal-habile, Dieu ait fait de nous des roües inutiles à sa machine.[62]

This depiction resembled Formey's claim in his moral philosophical essay about the vicissitudes of life, according to which people should base their behaviour on the recognition of their role in the interlinked order of the world that had been established by God. The idea inherent in Kästner's and Formey's claims, namely, that human beings were an indispensable and purposeful part of God's Creation, also corresponded to Wolff's teleological concept of providence.[63] Wolff described God as a being who, like humans, acted purposefully, and, because He, unlike humans, was omniscient, He was able to make sure His purposes were always fulfilled.[64] God knew and oversaw eternally all the effects that resulted from the essence and nature of beings and, therefore, He had created them only for the sake of executing His purposes through them.[65] As far as Wolff was concerned, God's overall purpose with the world was to reveal His perfection.[66] According to Kästner, unlike the belief in pure chance, one's conviction that one served a purpose in God's Creation constituted one's motive for acting at all, and gave meaning to the potential miseries one had to endure.[67] Similarly to Wolff, Kästner argued that most of the blessings (fortunate events) and afflictions (unfortunate events) by which God either rewarded virtue or punished

---

62. [Formey], *Vraye théorie*, p.14-15.
63. See Lehner, *Kants Vorsehungskonzept*, p.59-66.
64. See Wolff, *Metaphysik*, §1026.
65. See Wolff, *Metaphysik*, §1028 and 1032.
66. See Wolff, *Metaphysik*, §1045, and *Venünfftige Gedancken von den Absichten der natürlichen Dinge* (2nd edn, 1726), ed. Hans Werner Arndt, in *Christian Wolff: Gesammelte Werke*, ed. Jean Ecole *et al.*, section 1, vol.7 (Hildesheim, 1980), §2.
67. See [Formey], *Vraye théorie*, p.16.

vice were the natural results of people's actions that they themselves, however, were not able to foresee.[68]

In the second part of Kästner's essay, which was entitled *Nouvelles reflexions sur les evenemens fortuits*, he tried to answer the main point of the prize question, namely, which human duties resulted from either fortunate or unfortunate events. After having denied the existence of fortuitous events in favour of providence in the first part of his essay, in the second part Kästner used the term 'fortuitous' to describe events to which the individual had not contributed actively. Depending on whether these events were favourable to the individual's objectives, they had to be considered as fortunate or unfortunate. In relation to fortunate events, Kästner first claimed that the individual's duty in the light of these was simply to praise God.[69] Later in his essay, he specified that everything fortunate the individual experienced was an invitation by providence to exercise good deeds such as helping needy people and protecting good people. Likewise, he suggested that such good deeds would be rewarded by providence with more fortunate events in the future.[70] Therefore, in his considerations on the implications of fortunate events for the individual, Kästner relied mainly on Christian doctrines such as thankfulness and charity.

With regard to the experience of unfortunate events, however, Kästner's claims deviated from traditional Christian explanations: he outlined how, with the help of reflection and reason, human beings could deduce rules of moral behaviour from the unfortunate events that happened to them. More precisely, Kästner argued that, because human beings were able to discover God's will via experience, they were, therefore, able to adjust their moral behaviour a posteriori in the light of certain events. This argument was based on the core conviction of physico-theology, namely, that the laws human beings could recognise in the order of nature corresponded to God's purposes and will,[71] a conviction also upheld by Wolff.[72] Kästner maintained that, if one's endeavours were not followed by success, it was a sign that they ran contrary to the laws of nature and, thus, one needed to

---

68. See [Formey], *Vraye théorie*, p.29-30. Compare with Wolff, *Metaphysik*, §1002.
69. See [Formey], *Vraye théorie*, p.40-41.
70. See [Formey], *Vraye théorie*, p.58-59.
71. See [Formey], *Vraye théorie*, p.46.
72. See Wolff, *Metaphysik*, §1007-1008.

change one's behaviour to align with God's purposes.[73] To ascertain what type of behaviour corresponded to God's purposes, Kästner suggested that individuals apply a method of trial and error and calculate the risks they took by trying out different courses of action.[74] Kästner illustrated his idea with the example of the many ships that had sunk in the tropical sea in the past because of sailors ignoring the existence and functioning of the trade winds. Since they had been able to understand these geographical laws – after many bad experiences – sailors had been able to avoid the unfortunate outcome of their previous journeys in this area of the world.[75] Translated into moral philosophy, Kästner maintained, therefore, that the experience of unfortunate events was part of a process of individual learning at the end of which the individual might become virtuous. His description of this process suggested that individuals were able to shape their behaviour actively, a premise that was also inherent in religious ideas of reward and punishment. The particularity of Kästner's essay was, however, that he translated religion's doctrines of morality into a physico-theological concept of providence and combined it with mathematical science.

With these reflections on how individuals should react when confronted by unfortunate events in their life, Kästner touched upon one of the most important theological questions with respect to providence, namely, the origin and apparently unjust distribution of evil in the world. Why was it that the virtuous often had to suffer, whereas the immoral seemed to live a happy life? This question was also addressed in Formey's *Sur les vicissitudes de la vie*. He presented both a religious and a metaphysical answer, considering them to be equal. According to the religious explanation, which in his view was more intelligible to the majority of people, the seesaw of ups and downs in life lasted only for the duration of an individual's time on earth, and was meant to lead him or her to a stable existence in eternity.[76] Therefore, as Formey claimed, to focus on the fulfilment of pleasures in the present would be fruitless because there was no doubt these

---

73. See [Formey], *Vraye théorie*, p.47. Compare with p.17, in which Kästner has already anticipated the basics of his theory by claiming that human beings should always align their plans and wishes according to the laws God has instilled in them. If human beings' wishes are not fulfilled, this means they were not reasonable.
74. See [Formey], *Vraye théorie*, p.43-44 and 49.
75. See [Formey], *Vraye theorie*, p.42-43.
76. See Formey, *Philosophe chrétien*, 1st edn, vol.1, p.8-9.

pleasures would vanish at some point. In his view, eternal pleasure and peace could only be reached through respect for religion and the exercise of piety.[77] Kästner concurred with the distinction between the inconsistent and vicissitudinous nature of earthly experiences and the stability of eternal happiness.[78] He, too, argued that human beings had to follow the instructions of revelation to reach salvation, despite the fact that the nature of eternal life was completely unknown to them.[79] The motive of human beings for obeying divine orders should be their trust in God's goodness and wisdom.[80]

As well as being in agreement with regard to the religiously inspired explanation of evil, likewise, both Kästner and Formey developed metaphysical explanations of the origin of evil that drew on different elements of optimism. Formey's *Sur les vicissitudes de la vie* blended Wolff's early explanation of evil with Pope's theory of a perfect Creation. Formey closely followed Wolff's argument in his *Metaphysik* that God had not willed but enabled evil in the world. Because the capacity for evil was inherent in imperfect and limited human nature, God had enabled evil by creating human beings.[81] Similarly to Wolff, Formey claimed that the vicissitudes of life resulted solely from the individual's own active force, which was subject to desires and passions instead of wisdom and reason.[82] Like Wolff, Formey maintained that God necessarily had to create humans with all these weaknesses because, otherwise, the world would be a different one and not reflect God's wisdom.[83] Moreover, by quoting a passage from Pope's *Essay on man*,[84] Formey emphasised from a holistic perspective that, because everything in nature was good, humans, too, were good despite their imperfections.[85] Rousseau,

---

77. See Formey, *Philosophe chrétien*, 1st edn, vol.1, p.29-30.
78. See [Formey], *Vraye théorie*, p.35-36.
79. See [Formey], *Vraye théorie*, p.32-33.
80. See [Formey], *Vraye théorie*, p.34.
81. See Wolff, *Metaphysik*, §1056-58. In his later *Theologia naturalis: pars posterior*, Wolff, however, adopted Leibniz's more complex account of evil according to which there were three different types. Because Formey's *Sur les vicissitudes de la vie* contained only Wolff's earlier, more simple, explanation of evil, this showed that he had relied on Wolff's *Metaphysik*.
82. See Formey, *Philosophe chrétien*, 1st edn, vol.1, p.4; compare also with p.17.
83. See Formey, *Philosophe chrétien*, 1st edn, vol.1, p.6-7.
84. In the French translation by Jean-François Du Resnel Du Bellay, *Les Principes de la morale et du goût, en deux poëmes, traduits de l'anglois de M. du Pope* (Paris, Briasson, 1737), p.84.
85. See Formey, *Philosophe chrétien*, 1st edn, vol.1, p.7.

in his defence of optimism against Voltaire, saw the origin of both moral and physical evil in human beings. However, unlike Formey, he considered moral evil to be caused by the perfection and the initial corruption of human beings. As for such physical evils as the Lisbon earthquake, he justified them with human beings' intervention in the order of nature.[86]

Like Formey, Kästner held that the actual world was the best of all possible worlds, and that the seesaw of fortunate and unfortunate events in life reflected the nature of the best world.[87] However, instead of inferring the positive aspect of evil – in a Popeian vein – from the perfection of every element of the whole, Kästner deduced it – as did Leibniz and Wolff – from the overall perfection of the world: he explained that nothing that happened, misfortune included, could ever be disadvantageous for the individual because God made sure that it served the perfection of the whole.[88] Leibniz and Kästner were in agreement that this claim resulted from the rejection of the anthropocentric idea that the whole of Creation had to serve the happiness of humans alone.[89] Moreover, Kästner stressed that, although humans were unable to predict their future, they could be confident that the best would always happen.[90] As such, he underlined the hope and the confidence in God that sprang from an optimist concept of providence.[91]

The Leibnizian imprint on Kästner's essay is also evident in his attempt to portray the existence of evil in the provident world as a proof of God's holiness and justice. However, the way in which he developed this proof appeared innovative and emphasised again his support for physico-theology: Kästner compared the discipline of history, that is, the description of God's providence in the governance of intelligent beings, with physico-theology, the description of God's governance of nature. According to him, the latter was able to prove God's wisdom, His power and parts of His goodness, whereas the former demonstrated God's justice and holiness.[92] Based on this

---

86. See Formey, 'Lettre XLIII', p.263-64.
87. See [Formey], *Vraye théorie*, p.52-53.
88. See [Formey], *Vraye theorie*, p.19-20. Compare with Wolff, *Metaphysik*, §1060.
89. Compare with Leibniz, *Théodicée*, §118, according to which the happiness of intelligent creatures was an important but not the unique purpose of God, as well as §194.
90. See [Formey], *Vraye théorie*, p.56.
91. Compare with Leibniz, *Théodicée*, §58.
92. See [Formey], *Vraye théorie*, p.61-62.

comparison, he suggested that the apparent injustice in the distribution of good and evil among people should be regarded as a sign that God ruled men by fair rules, just as natural catastrophes were considered as belonging to the order of nature:

> C'est donc l'arrangement des choses matérielles dans la Nature, qui prouve un Créateur sage, puissant & bon; & ce sont les événemens qui arrivent dans le Monde des Esprits qui nous engagent à adorer le même Créateur comme saint & juste. Nous voyons des Monstres, des Tremblemens de Terre, & d'autres ravages Physiques, sans en conclurre pour cela qu'il n'y a point d'Ordre dans la Nature. Nous envisagerons du même œil le Bonheur apparent des Méchans, & les maux auxquels sont exposés les Gens de bien: ils ne nous empêcheront pas de croire que Dieu gouverne les Etres intelligens suivant les régles de la plus parfaite équité.[93]

With these considerations, Kästner turned a common criticism of the concept of a universal providence upside down, namely, that the existence of physical evil would prove God's lack of either power or goodness. Diderot, in the fifteenth of his *Pensées philosophiques*, had put precisely this argument in the mouth of the atheist: as far as he was concerned, God could only exist if this world really was the best of all possible worlds, which was obviously not the case. In Diderot's depiction, the optimist attempt to explain the existence of evil by portraying it as a necessary part of a perfect world was futile.[94] Formey, who published his refutation of Diderot's *Pensées philosophiques* in 1749, refrained from defending optimism on this occasion. He merely alleged that Diderot's arguments were repetitions that had been proved wrong many times before.[95] One year later, however, Formey resorted to metaphysical optimism to object to Diderot's denial of providence in the latter's *Lettre sur les aveugles*.

The debate between Formey and Boullier about Leibnizian optimism

In 1750, Formey published a refutation of Diderot's materialist and atheistic *Lettre sur les aveugles*, which had appeared the previous

---

93. [Formey], *Vraye théorie*, p.63-64.
94. See Denis Diderot, *Pensées philosophiques* (1746), ed. Robert Niklaus, in *Diderot: œuvres complètes*, vol.2 (Paris, 1975), p.1-61 (22-23).
95. See Formey, *Pensées raisonnables*, p.55.

year and because of which Diderot was detained for three months in the French state prison of Vincennes. Formey's refutation, which was entitled *Lettre de M. Gervaise Holmes*, took up the storyline of a central passage of Diderot's work, namely, the fictional dialogue between the blind mathematician Saunderson from Cambridge and the pastor Gervaise Holmes at the former's deathbed.[96] Diderot used this dialogue to challenge the physico-theological attempts to prove God's existence via the marvels of nature and to expose instead his materialist vision of the universe that precluded any type of teleological order and, thus, of providence.[97] Although Formey endorsed the criticism of the physico-theological argument for God's existence,[98] as he had already done in 1747 in his academic essays on God, he opposed Diderot's conclusion that there was no provident God at all. Hence, to defend religion against Diderot's atheist claims, Formey substituted Diderot's fictional discussion between Saunderson and the pastor Holmes with an account of metaphysical optimism. More precisely, to refute Diderot's insinuation that Saunderson's congenital (therefore, not self-inflicted) handicap was a sign of an imperfect order of nature and an unjust God,[99] Formey held that imperfections were also part of the best order God had created, and that by no means did they contradict God's goodness, wisdom and perfection.[100] A basic element of Leibniz's theodicy resonated in this argument, namely, that metaphysical

---

96. See Denis Diderot, *Lettre sur les aveugles, à l'usage de ceux qui voyent*, ed. Yvon Belaval and Robert Niklaus, in *Diderot: œuvres complètes*, vol.4 (Paris, 1978), p.1-107 (48-53).
97. See Diderot, *Lettre sur les aveugles*, p.49-51, and compare with Colas Duflo, 'La fin du finalisme: les deux natures – Holmes et Saunderson', *Recherches sur Diderot et sur l'Encyclopédie* 28 (2000), p.107-31; and Laura Duprey, 'Philosopher dans les ténèbres: la critique des causes finales dans la *Lettre sur les aveugles*', in *L'Aveugle et le philosophe, ou Comment la cécité donne à penser*, ed. Marion Chottin (Paris, 2009), p.107-25.
98. See Formey, *Gervaise Holmes*, p.44-48. Here, Formey used the same arguments against the physico-theological proof as in his earlier academic essays on God's existence. Thus, he did not – like Diderot – reject the existence of an order in nature but criticised those who inferred God's existence from this order without grounding it in universal metaphysical principles.
99. See Diderot, *Lettre sur les aveugles*, p.51. As Duflo points out, 'La fin du finalisme', p.122-23, as far as Diderot was concerned, this insinuation was a means of destroying the idea of a teleological divine order in favour of the materialist theory of the world being the product of fortuitous happenings.
100. See Formey, *Gervaise Holmes*, p.36-37.

evil, that is, any kind of imperfection, was part of the order of nature.[101] However, Formey provided an additional explanation for Saunderson's suffering that was not faithful to Leibniz: according to Formey, Saunderson's congenital blindness was a necessary exception to God's best plan, and resulted from a collision between the laws of nature that governed God's Creation; it was not a sign of God's lack of love for him.[102] In fact, this assumption almost contradicted the Leibnizian (and Malebranchean) idea that evil was intrinsic to the diverse, variegated and beautiful order of the world instead of being an exception to it.[103] It is not quite clear where Formey's view came from, but it is interesting that a similar explanation of evil was attributed to Leibniz by Adolf Friedrich Reinhard, who won the Berlin Academy's prize essay competition on the theme of optimism in 1755.[104]

As well as contradicting Diderot's atheist argument in relation to the imperfect order in the world, Formey also underlined the difference between his optimistic explanation of suffering in the world and two crucial religious doctrines: first, the voluntarist concept of God, according to which He ruled by absolute decree over His creatures and, thus, decided arbitrarily on their condition; and second, the concept that eternal punishment was inescapable:

> Je ne vous parlerai point avec quelques Théologiens du droit absolu de Dieu sur ses Créatures, en vertu duquel il en dispose à son gré, & s'en jouë, pour ainsi dire, comme d'une menuë poussiere. Ce ne sont pas-là mes idées; & je ne fermerai jamais la bouche à personne par cette réponse. Si vous vous trouviez dans un Plan, qui vous entrainât inévitablement dans une éternité de malheur, je croirois avoir fort mauvaise grace de vous dire: Ce Plan est l'Ouvrage des perfections

---

101. See Leibniz, *Théodicée*, §241. Leibniz had distinguished between three types of evil: metaphysical, physical and moral; see *Théodicée* §21. Wolff dealt with these different kinds of evil in detail only in 1737 in his *Theologia naturalis: pars posterior*, §282-92.
102. See Formey, *Gervaise Holmes*, p.37.
103. See Paul Rateau, 'The problem of evil and the justice of God', in *The Oxford handbook of Leibniz*, ed. Maria Rosa Antognazza (New York, 2018), p.100-15 (111).
104. In his 'Système de Mr. Pope', p.15, Reinhard maintained that, according to Leibniz, evil resulted from the inevitable collision of conflicting individual rules of perfection. Caro suggests this was a misinterpretation of Leibniz, 'The best of all possible worlds?', p.106-107.

divines; son Auteur est votre Maître; vous n'avez à prendre que le parti de la soumission.[105]

These claims were probably directed against Diderot's anti-clericalism; they sounded like a self-defence by which Formey wanted to stress his open-mindedness with respect to theological matters as compared to more orthodox clerics. However, Formey's statement also reveals his indebtedness to Leibniz, whose fundamental aim in the *Théodicée* was to strengthen God's goodness in accordance with His omnipotence. This, in turn, would inspire the individual's love for God.[106] This aim included rejecting the theory of God's absolute decree, which appeared in orthodox Reformed theories of predestination. In Leibniz's view, if God had absolute decree, it would curtail His justice and goodness and, consequently, destroy the individual's trust in Him.[107] Leibniz's account of salvation was also very positive, because he believed that God's fundamental (antecedent) aim was to save His creatures, even if, due to various different circumstances – their sins in particular – He could not eventually save all of them.[108] Leibniz rejected in particular the possibility that human beings were predestined for damnation.[109] Nevertheless, he never abjured the Christian doctrine of eternal punishment and, instead, tried to reconcile it with his view that, generally, the good in the world exceeded the evil.[110] These central claims of Leibnizian optimism contained a remarkably comforting consequence for human beings, something that Formey stressed in his fictional reply to Saunderson's suffering: he made the pastor Holmes claim that not only had Saunderson received various compensations for his suffering in his present life but, more importantly, he could also count on more rewards to come in eternal

---

105. Formey, *Gervaise Holmes*, p.38.
106. See Leibniz, *Théodicée*, §6.
107. See Leibniz, *Théodicée*, §176-78. Here, Leibniz argued mainly against supralapsarian thought. He defended Calvin, who, although supporting the doctrine of God's absolute decree, admitted this was incited by just reasons (§79).
108. See Leibniz, *Théodicée*, §80.
109. See Leibniz, *Théodicée* §23 and §81.
110. See Lloyd Strickland, 'Leibniz on eternal punishment', *British journal for the history of philosophy* 17:2 (2009), p.307-31, and Robert Merrihew Adams, 'Justice, happiness, and perfection in Leibniz's City of God', in *New essays on Leibniz's Theodicy*, ed. Larry M. Jorgensen and Samuel Newlands (Oxford, 2014), p.197-217. In 1708, Leibniz defended the doctrine of eternal punishment against its denial by the Socinian Ernst Soner, a defence to which he also referred in his *Théodicée*, §266.

life.[111] Therefore, metaphysical optimism enabled Formey to counter Diderot's pessimistic account of Saunderson's destiny with the image of a benevolent providence. A couple of years later, after the Lisbon earthquake had caused thousands of people to suffer, Rousseau took a similar position towards Voltaire to the one Formey had taken towards Diderot: he objected to Voltaire's account of God's cruel voluntarism by stressing God's unconditional benevolence and the comforting character of optimism.[112] This must have given satisfaction to Formey, which explains why he published Rousseau's *Lettre sur la providence* in 1759. Nevertheless, unlike Rousseau who considered God's existence and His providence as truths that relied on feeling and belief alone, Formey was convinced of their rational provability.[113] In his *Lettre de M. Gervaise Holmes*, Formey opposed atheism and materialism with metaphysical theories instead of revealed doctrine. As such, the work is an example of the rationalist apologetics characteristic of an eighteenth-century Christian philosopher.

However, this kind of rational Christian apologetics and Formey's defence of optimism in particular did not encounter unanimous approval from all Christian philosophers of the Reformed confession. This became most obvious in the argument that Formey's *Lettre de M. Gervaise Holmes* caused between him and another theologian-philosopher, David-Renaud Boullier. A second-generation Huguenot pastor born in Utrecht but who had lived in London since 1746, Boullier was a Cartesian and more orthodox Calvinist.[114] Like Formey, he believed that natural and revealed truths were not contradictory to one another, and that revealed religion was superior to natural religion.[115] Moreover, Boullier and Formey seemed to share the same negative opinion on contemporary attempts to defend religion by

---

111. See Formey, *Gervaise Holmes*, p.39.
112. See Formey, 'Lettre XLIII', p.261-62.
113. See Formey, 'Lettre XLIII', p.282-83. Compare with 'Lettre XLIV', p.276-78, where Rousseau tries to justify his belief in optimism with common sense experience and the observation of the course of nature whereas Formey deduces it from religion.
114. On Boullier's 'enlightened orthodoxy', see Graham Gargett, 'David-Renaud Boullier et l'orthodoxie éclairée', in *Refuge et désert*, ed. H. Bost and C. Lauriol, p.157-71.
115. See David-Renaud Boullier, *Lettres sur les vrais principes de la religion, où l'on examine un livre intitulé La religion essentielle à l'homme: on y a joint une defense des pensées de Pascal contre la critique de Mr. de Voltaire, et trois lettres relatives à la philosophie de ce poëte*, 2 vols (Amsterdam, Catuffe, 1741), vol.1, p.157-59.

'purging' it from dogmatic content, because they both believed that such attempts strengthened the arguments of the enemies of religion rather than destroyed them. Boullier made this claim to object to the 'essential religion' propagated by the Genevan woman philosopher Marie Huber,[116] whereas Formey, as shown above (see chapter 3), supported it against the *Instruction chrétienne* written by the liberal Genevan theologian Jacob Vernet. Finally, both Boullier and Formey regularly polemicised against the *philosophes*,[117] which is also why Boullier, in his critical review of Formey's refutation of the *Lettre sur les aveugles*, generally honoured the latter's apologetic efforts and attested to him having good Christian views.[118] The bone of contention between the two Huguenot philosophers, which caused Boullier's criticism of Formey's *Lettre de M. Gervaise Holmes*, was Leibnizian optimism.

In his critical review of Formey's writing, which appeared in March 1752 in the *Journal des sçavans*, Boullier attacked both the metaphysical foundation of the theory of the best of all possible worlds and its potential for contradicting religious doctrine. In so doing, he also criticised aspects that had not been mentioned explicitly in the *Lettre de M. Gervaise Holmes*. First and foremost, Boullier doubted that there was one absolutely perfect world among the infinite number of all possible worlds, as well as that the universe was a self-sustaining machine that had been set in motion for ever by God and did not need any further divine intervention; therefore, every individual suffering necessarily resulted from God's initial plan.[119] In Boullier's view, such a concept of divine providence disclosed a certain anthropomorphism in the sense that it attributed a human rationale to God.[120]

In addition to these fundamental objections to the idea of the best of all possible worlds, Boullier set particular Christian doctrines in

---

116. See Marie Huber, *La Religion essentielle à l'homme, distinguée de ce qui n'en est que l'accessoire* (Amsterdam, Wetsteins & Smith, 1738). For Boullier's rejection of Huber's theory of essential religion, see in particular *Lettres sur les vrais principes de la religion*, vol.1, p.8 and 63.
117. See Graham Gargett, 'David Boullier: pasteur du Refuge, adversaire des philosophes et défenseur de l'orthodoxie protestante', in *La Vie intellectuelle aux refuges protestants*, ed. J. Häseler and A. McKenna, p.305-37.
118. See 'Lettre de Mr. Gervaise Holmes', *Journal des sçavans* 160 (1752), p.516-44 (516 and 519).
119. See 'Lettre de Mr. Gervaise Holmes', p.520-21.
120. See 'Lettre de Mr. Gervaise Holmes', p.521-22.

opposition to the theory of optimism. First, by quoting Saint Paul,[121] he upheld the doctrine of God's absolute decree that Formey had rejected in the *Lettre de M. Gervaise Holmes*. More precisely, Boullier emphasised that God, as Creator, possessed sovereign liberty that allowed Him to distribute His grace freely and without disclosing His motives to humans. The difference between Formey and Boullier in conceiving of God's role in suffering arose from the opposing intellectualist and voluntarist conceptions of God's governance of the universe, the first attributing God's decisions to His wisdom and the latter attributing it to His free will. Both men agreed that Saunderson was not to blame for his congenital blindness, but for different reasons. On the one hand, Formey believed the blindness to be caused by a particular divine motivation that relied on God's wisdom and love for His creatures.[122] On the other hand, however, Boullier claimed the only reason for Saunderson's blindness was God's ability to instil it in him. As far as Boullier was concerned, suffering, therefore, resulted from God's omnipotence alone, although he tried to hedge his voluntarist account by highlighting that God's absolute liberty did not mean He acted capriciously or without respecting the perfections of His Creation.[123] Second, Boullier tried to denigrate optimism by confronting it with the biblical doctrine of the eternal punishment of sinners. He criticised Formey's positive account of salvation, according to which Saunderson would be recompensed for his earthly suffering in paradise, for not taking into account that there was at least one part of mankind, namely, all the impenitent sinners, who were to expect eternal suffering. As Boullier argued, if the optimist accepted the dogma of eternal punishment, of necessity, he had to acknowledge that God's perfect plan also included endless suffering.[124] Boullier's considerations pointed to the ambivalence that was contained in Leibniz's optimism with respect to the Christian doctrine of salvation.[125] Moreover, they also reflected the Calvinist debate about this doctrine, in which the reconcilability of God's

---

121. Romans 9.20 and 11.35.
122. See Formey, *Gervaise Holmes*, p.37: 'un Etre qui sait ce qu'il fait, & qui bien loin de vous maltraiter sans nécessité, n'a jamais cessé de vous aimer, et d'être votre tendre Pere'.
123. See 'Lettre de Mr. Gervaise Holmes', p.522.
124. See 'Lettre de Mr. Gervaise Holmes', p.523.
125. Twenty years later, during 1772-1773, this ambivalence inherent in Leibniz's theory incited a debate between the two German Leibnizian scholars Johann August Eberhard and Gotthold Ephraim Lessing about whether Leibniz really

7. Providence, moral duties and optimism

goodness with his allocation of punishments had been discussed since the beginning of the eighteenth century.[126] In this debate, Boullier himself criticised attempts to elevate God's goodness above all His other attributes.[127] It seems that in his critical review of the *Lettre de M. Gervaise Holmes*, Boullier's aim was to elicit from Formey a statement on this controversial question. However, Formey, who in 1739 had already defended the doctrine of eternal punishment in reply to Marie Huber's famous rejection of it,[128] did not take a stance on this.[129] Instead, in his (first) reply to Boullier's criticism, he slightly twisted the latter's argument and blamed him for maintaining that God's plan, inevitably, led *all* people into eternal suffering,[130] a claim

---

    believed in the doctrine of eternal punishment. See Adams, 'Justice, happiness, and perfection', p.208-209.

126. See Pierre-Olivier Léchot, 'Les peines de l'enfer sont-elles éternelles? Note à propos d'une controverse au sein du protestantisme de langue française durant les Lumières', *Etudes théologiques et religieuses* 89:2 (2014), p.199-224.

127. Boullier maintained this position against Marie Huber in his *Lettres sur les vrais principes de la religion*, vol.1, p.119-21. On Boullier's defence of eternal punishment in his sermons, see Gargett, 'David-Renaud Boullier et l'orthodoxie éclairée', p.166-70.

128. See Marie Huber, *Le Sisteme des anciens et des modernes, concilié par l'exposition des sentimens differens de quelques théologiens sur l'état des âmes séparées des corps, en quatorze lettres, nouvelle édition, augmentée par des notes & quelques pièces nouvelles* (Amsterdam, Wetsteins & Smith, 1733). For a modern edition and introduction to this work, see *Marie Huber: un purgatoire protestant? Essai sur l'état des âmes séparées des corps*, ed. Yves Krumenacker (Geneva, 2016). Formey's two letters about eternal punishment appeared as 'Article III. Lettre de M** à M*** sur l'eternité des peines', *Bibliothèque germanique* 45 (1739), p.85-101, and 'Article VII. Seconde lettre de Mr. F. à Mr. *** sur l'eternité des peines', *Bibliothèque germanique* 46 (1739), p.125-57. He republished them in 1754 as 'Deux lettres sur l'éternité des peines', in *Mélanges philosophiques*, vol.2, p.215-64.

129. In November 1755, Formey's Huguenot friend and Wolffian philosopher Emer de Vattel claimed that the doctrine of eternal punishment had been abandoned almost everywhere. He believed that Formey's endorsement of it in his 'Deux lettres sur l'éternité des peines' had been motivated by his aim of pleasing somebody; see Vattel to Formey (8.11.1755), in *Emer de Vattel à Jean Henri Samuel Formey*, p.159.

130. Instead of quoting Boullier correctly by writing 'qui entraîne pour une partie des Créatures une éternité de malheur' ('Lettre de Mr. Gervaise Holmes', p.523), Formey wrote 'qui entraînat inévitablement les hommes dans le malheur' ('Article IX. Remarques sur l'article concernant la Lettre de M. Gervaise Holmes, qui a été inséré dans le *Journal des savans*', *Bibliothèque impartiale* 5:3, 1752, p.443-46, 445).

that ran contrary to both biblical dogma and metaphysical optimism, and against which Boullier fiercely defended himself.[131]

In general, Formey's reply to Boullier's criticism, which appeared in the May/June 1752 issue of his own journal *Bibliothèque impartiale*, was very short. He justified this by saying that his adversary's impoliteness had precluded any serious discussion on content.[132] However, Formey's few content-related utterances suggest that he conceived of Boullier's criticism as an attempt to substitute his philosophical concept of providence with religious doctrine. He disagreed in particular with Boullier's recourse to Scripture to explain divine Creation and providence rather than employing metaphysical notions.[133] In contrast, Boullier, who in July 1752 again used the *Journal des sçavans* to defend himself publicly against Formey's accusation, emphasised that he considered metaphysics and Christian dogma to be compatible; he maintained that his voluntarist notion of God's free distribution of grace was as much a general metaphysical notion as it was biblical content.[134] Boullier's comment stressed that the debate between the two men was not only a debate between philosophy and religion, as Formey had tried to suggest in his earlier statement, but also a debate between two different schools of metaphysics: Boullier's defence of voluntarism was most likely inspired by Descartes, whereas Formey's intellectualism was Leibnizian.[135]

Following Boullier's relatively short reply to Formey in the *Journal des sçavans*, the debate between the two men continued in two private letters, which Formey, after Boullier's death, published in 1761 in the *Journal encyclopédique*.[136] In these two letters, the initial debate between the two men on the origins of Saunderson's blindness or imperfections in the world, in which Boullier had pitted his voluntarism against Formey's optimism and intellectualism, eventually turned into the question of God's liberty to create more generally. Since the first half

---

131. See 'Réponse à l'article IX de la *Bibliothèque impartiale*, mois de mai & de juin 1752', *Journal des sçavans* 162 (1752), p.513-17 (515).
132. See 'Article IX. Remarques sur l'article concernant la Lettre de M. Gervaise Holmes', p.446.
133. See 'Article IX. Remarques sur l'article concernant la Lettre de M. Gervaise Holmes', p.445.
134. See 'Réponse à l'article IX de la *Bibliothèque impartiale*', p.515.
135. On Descartes's theological voluntarism see Schneewind, *The Invention of autonomy*, p.184-85, and Lorenz, *De mundo optimo*, p.29-31.
136. See 'Lettre de Mr. Formey à l'auteur de ce journal au sujet de l'éloge historique de Mr. Boullier', *Journal encyclopédique* 3 (1761), p.122-38.

of the eighteenth century, orthodox theologians of all confessions had primarily founded their opposition to optimism on the argument that Leibniz's theory of God having chosen the best of all possible worlds curtailed His liberty. In Germany, this argument had first been raised in 1712 in the refutation of the *Théodicée* by the Lutheran theologian Johann Franz Budde,[137] and in France it had been disseminated since 1721 by the Jesuits via the *Mémoires de Trévoux*.[138] Moreover, this argument was still used in 1755 by Reinhard in his winning essay in the Academy's prize competition, the theme of which was optimism.[139] In his letter to Boullier, Formey refuted the argument by repeating Leibniz's claim that optimism did not destroy God's liberty because His motive of always choosing the best did not constitute any kind of external constraint or physical necessity.[140] As a consequence, Formey was able to state that the biblical voluntarist account of divine liberty and the Leibnizian one were compatible. Boullier countered that he was not willing to renew the debate about God's freedom to create and, instead, simply reiterated his adherence to the voluntarist tradition.[141] With regard to God's free distribution of grace in particular, Boullier held that only the biblical account of it (in Romans) was intelligible through the use of common sense, whereas Formey's (Leibnizian) account was not, and, moreover, that the two different accounts were not compatible with one another.[142]

Finally, Formey also addressed the question of the compatibility between optimism and the doctrine of eternal punishment, which Boullier had challenged. Formey argued that only an optimistic concept of divine providence would indicate that the reason for

---

137. See Lorenz, *De mundo optimo*, p.115-16.
138. According to Rateau, *Leibniz et le meilleur des mondes*, p.368, the argument had already appeared in 1721 in a review of Des Maizeaux's *Recueil de diverses pieces sur la philosophie, la religion naturelle, l'histoire, les mathematiques etc.* before it was developed in Castel's influential criticism of the *Théodicée* in 1737 (p.381).
139. See Reinhard, 'Le système de Mr. Pope', p.37-40.
140. See 'Lettre de Mr. Formey à l'auteur de ce journal', p.130. Compare with Leibniz, *Théodicée*, §230, and Wolff, *Metaphysik*, §987.
141. See 'Lettre de Mr. Formey à l'auteur de ce journal', p.134. Boullier referred to Saint Augustine, *De natura boni contra Manichaeos* (*c*.495 AD), and François de Salignac de La Mothe Fénelon, *Œuvres philosophiques, premiere partie: demonstration de l'existence de Dieu, tirée de l'art de la nature. Seconde partie: demonstration de l'existence de Dieu, et de ses attributs, tirée des preuves purement intellectuelles, et de l'idée de l'infini mesme* (Paris, Delaulne, 1718) as examples of the voluntarist tradition.
142. See 'Lettre de Mr. Formey à l'auteur de ce journal', p.135.

suffering was attributed not to God as the author of providence but, rather, to His creatures. This claim was based on the Leibnizian and Wolffian assumption that, essentially, moral evil was a fact of human nature and was only enabled by God, an assumption that Formey had already put forward in his essay on the vicissitudes of life.[143] Boullier rejected Formey's attempt to bring optimism in line with the doctrine of eternal suffering. He despised human attempts to establish hypotheses for God's behaviour and, thus, revealed a very negative view on natural theology more broadly. More importantly, with regard to optimism in particular, Boullier declared that the hypothesis of a divine plan that determined an individual's good and bad behaviour was an error that 'undermined the foundations of religion'.[144] Basically, Boullier was suggesting that Formey held heterodox views.

On both sides, the debate between the two Huguenot theologians has been fashioned to a large extent as a dispute about the relationship between reason and faith. Formey, in his replies to Boullier, highlighted his aim of reconciling the metaphysical explanation of providence provided by Leibnizian optimism with biblical doctrine, whereas Boullier constantly put a stronger emphasis on doctrine and tried to force Formey into the role of a heterodox who concurred with atheists and freethinkers. This last accusation in particular was linked to Formey's Wolffian rejection of the physico-theological proof of God's existence, which was the second major point along with optimism that Boullier criticised in his review of the *Lettre de M. Gervaise Holmes*.[145] Formey and Boullier's debate was, therefore, another demonstration of the heterogeneity that marked the apologetic mission of eighteenth-century Huguenot theologians and philosophers in the sense that their stances with regard to orthodoxy varied a great deal. Moreover, within the wide spectrum of positions, it could well be that a person changed roles from one context to another. In his debate with Boullier, the accusation of heterodoxy was levelled at Formey, whereas he himself levelled it against the Genevan theologian Jacob Vernet four years later when he criticised the latter's *Instruction chrétienne*.

However, the differences between Formey and Boullier were caused not only by their different positions in relation to orthodoxy, but also by the ideological division between Leibnizian and Cartesian

---

143. See 'Lettre de Mr. Formey à l'auteur de ce journal', p.130.
144. See 'Lettre de Mr. Formey à l'auteur de ce journal', p.135.
145. See 'Lettre de Mr. Gervaise Holmes', p.524-25.

philosophy. Boullier stressed constantly how dangerous and unintelligible he considered Leibniz's metaphysics to be,[146] while Formey accused him of being excessively passionate about Descartes's philosophy.[147] Moreover, Boullier in particular equated certain philosophical theories with national philosophies. For example, he considered the *Lettre de M. Gervaise Holmes* to show disdain for French and English philosophers because of the criticism of both the Cartesian and the physico-theological proof of God's existence.[148] By contrast, he believed that Leibniz's metaphysics had been exclusively embraced by German scholars because of a certain national zeal.[149] However, although Formey's contributions did indeed reveal his indebtedness to Leibnizian and Wolffian philosophy, he denied that he adhered to any particular philosophical school.[150] It is true that some of Formey's explanations show he did not rely completely on Leibniz's philosophy, for example, with respect to his above-mentioned definition of imperfection that seemed to rather contradict Leibniz's assumptions, as well as with respect to his concept of infinity.[151] However, not only was Formey more unfaithful to Leibniz than his opponent claimed but, in addition, Boullier himself based his arguments against Leibniz not on the latter's works but on Fontenelle's *Eloge de Leibnitz*.[152] Such a detachment from the original writings of the author whose theories the two men were discussing seems to have been common in the debates on Leibnizian optimism in the mid-eighteenth century; in France and in Britain in particular,

---

146. See 'Lettre de Mr. Gervaise Holmes', p.525-26, and 'Lettre de Mr. Formey à l'auteur de ce journal', p.138. Boullier had also shown his hostility towards Leibnizian philosophy elsewhere, as in his *Essai philosophique sur l'ame des bêtes ou l'on traite de son existence & de sa nature* (Amsterdam, Chauguion, 1728), p.270-81, in which he refuted the theory of pre-established harmony and defended occasionalism.
147. See 'Lettre de Mr. Formey à l'auteur de ce journal', p.123.
148. See 'Lettre de Mr. Formey à l'auteur de ce journal', p.133.
149. See 'Lettre de Mr. Gervaise Holmes', p.525-26, and 'Lettre de Mr. Formey à l'auteur de ce journal', p.138.
150. See 'Lettre de Mr. Formey à l'auteur de ce journal', p.130.
151. With regard to Formey's notion of the infinity of possible worlds that had been claimed by Leibniz (*Théodicée*, §225), he first stated it was not something he had maintained, and then presented a strange definition of Leibniz's notion of infinite, according to which it meant indefinite and not assignable; see 'Lettre de Mr. Formey à l'auteur de ce journal', p.129-30.
152. See 'Réponse à l'article IX de la *Bibliothèque impartiale*', p.514-15.

Leibniz's *Théodicée* appears to have been read relatively little, although it was discussed a great deal.[153]

The debate between Formey and Boullier, therefore, illustrates how the European reception of optimism merged with debates about the connection between metaphysical theories and revealed doctrine in attempting to explain divine providence. In his reception of Leibniz's *Théodicée*, Boullier carried on the accusations of heterodoxy already levelled at the work by its early Catholic and Lutheran critics in France and Germany, whereas Formey, moulded by his Wolffian education, was convinced of the alignment between optimism and orthodoxy. As his diverse moral philosophical essays show, Formey drew on optimism and the idea of the *nexus rerum* to explain divine providence in general and the cause of life's vicissitudes and evil in particular. Unlike voluntarist theories of providence, optimism allowed God's will to be intelligible to human beings to a certain degree, and also depicted the individual's happiness as a central purpose of Creation. That such an optimist concept of providence was independent of confession was also emphasised by the congruency of Formey's optimist account of providence with that of the Lutheran Kästner and by the similarities between Formey's Reformed and Rousseau's natural theological positions on the topic.

Formey's active endorsement of Kästner's winning essay in the Academy's 1751 prize competition was not only an expression of their general congruency in opinion, it was also a means by which Formey could take up his position against D'Alembert's and Maupertuis's reservations about the possibility of making providence intelligible to human beings by treating it philosophically. Therefore, the internal debate about the 1751 prize essay competition can be considered as another example of the clashes that existed at the Academy between Leibnizian–Wolffian positions on the one side and anti-Leibnizian and anti-Wolffian stances on the other. By insisting on the logic of the prize essay question, Formey succeeded in translating his religious and Wolffian view of the compatibility between providence and human self-determination, which he usually portrayed in his popular moral philosophy, into the context of the Academy.

To put the topic of providence on the Berlin Academy's agenda in the early 1750s was only Formey's first step in his undertaking to make Berlin a centre of the renewed debate on this topic. It was

---

153. See Rateau, *Leibniz et le meilleur des mondes*, p.363, and Strickland, 'Staying optimistic!', p.68.

followed by his rejection of the winning essay in the 1755 prize competition on optimism and his promotion of Rousseau's *Lettre sur la providence* in 1759. Formey guided the debate by using the tools he had at his disposal as a journalist and publisher: he translated, republished, reviewed and annotated the texts of other authors in order to introduce (controversial) arguments as well as to disseminate his own position.

8. Natural law, morality and science

Formey's optimist concept of providence drew on central elements of Leibnizian and Wolffian moral philosophy. Another important element that was present in Wolff's works in particular was natural law.[1] Sparked by the post-Reformation confessional conflicts, processes of state building and the growth of international trade, theories of natural law rose to be the dominating political vocabulary during the seventeenth century, mostly in Protestant countries. Natural law was at the centre of attempts to form a moral–legal theory that was independent from confession and applicable to humanity at large.[2] As far as the Huguenots in the diaspora are concerned, the engagement with natural law theories became an important tradition that involved Huguenot writers like Bayle, Jean Barbeyrac and Jean-Jacques Burlamaqui.[3] As one of the foundations of moral philosophy, it touched upon two important questions in particular:

1. On the history of early modern natural law see Knud Haakonssen, *Natural law and moral philosophy: from Grotius to the Scottish Enlightenment* (New York, 1996); Tim J. Hochstrasser, *Natural law theories in the early Enlightenment* (Cambridge, 2000); and, with a particular focus on the German lands, Hunter, *Rival enlightenments*. For an overview of the modern moral theories linked to natural law that developed in the seventeenth and eighteenth centuries, see Schneewind, *The Invention of autonomy*.
2. See Knud Haakonssen, 'Early modern natural law', in *The Routledge companion to ethics*, ed. John Skorupski (London and New York, 2010), p.76-87 (77-78).
3. See Tim J. Hochstrasser, 'The claims of conscience: natural law theory, obligation and resistance in the Huguenot diaspora', in *New essays*, ed. J. C. Laursen, p.15-51, who links the Huguenots' interest in natural law with their experience of persecution by the French monarch that sparked debates about rights of conscience. Compare with Pott, *Reformierte Morallehren*, p.3, who also emphasises the role played by Calvinist Covenant theology in the development of the Huguenots' strong interest in natural law.

what role God and divine law played in relation to norms of behaviour; and how theories of knowledge were linked to ethics. Based on the assumption that the fundamental rules of conduct were engraved in human nature and recognisable by reason, natural-law-based moral philosophy was prone to diminish the role of divine guidance and stress the individual's autonomy instead. Moreover, it gave a prominent role to the use of understanding in general and to knowledge about human nature in particular. As such, it went hand in hand with the development of science during the early modern period.[4]

In the mid-eighteenth century, the question of how the progress of knowledge and science affected morals gained much importance. This was mainly due to Rousseau's famous *Discours sur les sciences et les arts*, with which he won the prize essay competition held by the Academy of Dijon in 1749. Having been asked whether the cultivation of science and art had helped to purify morals, Rousseau offered a harsh criticism of civilisation. He blamed the decline of morality in society on the progress of science, a claim that Formey largely rejected. The belief in the reasonableness and perfectibility of human nature was central to Formey's moral philosophy and, thus, the negative influence of science on human behaviour was, theoretically, inconceivable to him. Nevertheless, his answer to Rousseau's claim was not straightforward and probably even overlapped with the latter's view. In particular, Rousseau and Formey held similar views on the behaviour of contemporary practitioners of science and philosophy.

The present chapter will demonstrate the impact that the debate about the relationship between science and morals had on Formey, and how it related to Wolffian moral philosophy. Rousseau's *Discours sur les sciences et les arts* caused him to take a particular stance several times during the 1750s and, most importantly, it influenced his most comprehensive moral philosophical treatise, the *Principes de morale*, which appeared in the early 1760s. This bipartite and systematic treatise has to be seen as the theoretical and secular counterpart to his popular philosophical *Philosophe chrétien*, and it therefore belonged to the context of secular learning. Before analysing this treatise and tracing its connections with Wolff's natural-law-based moral philosophy, Formey's earlier arguments against Rousseau's *Discours*

---

4. See Schneewind, *The Invention of autonomy*, p.7. Schneewind stressed that, although the emergence of new science was important in supporting modern moral philosophy, it was not the initial reason that had given rise to it.

sur les sciences et les arts will be outlined. In the context of this debate, a moral philosophy based on natural law was useful as far as Formey was concerned because it fulfilled the purpose of opposing criticism of intellectual improvement and science. However, in a confessional context, its overly strong focus on reason needed to be complemented by considerations on divine law. The final section of this chapter will, thus, illustrate how Formey interpolated Wolff's rationalist and secular moral philosophy with key elements of Calvinist ethics.

Formey on Rousseau's *Discours sur les sciences et les arts*

Rousseau's answer to the 1749 prize essay question set by the Academy of Dijon, that is, whether the development of the sciences had contributed to the purification of morals, rendered the Genevan philosopher, *encyclopédiste* and friend of Diderot instantly famous, because his treatise was the first effective and widely discussed challenge to the optimistic view on scientific progress that had determined seventeenth- and eighteenth-century culture. Rousseau's essential assumption, which he also exposed in all his subsequent works, was that human beings were only morally good in their natural state, and that their increasing depravity in society corresponded with the progress of the arts and sciences. As a consequence, Rousseau defended the argument that the progress of the sciences had caused moral decline, an argument that the majority of his contemporaries in France and Germany – Formey included – conceived of as paradoxical in the sense of being contrary to the common opinion of the benefits of scientific progress and the excitement about constant human enlightenment.[5] The public debate that this sparked was

---

5. See Michèle Crogiez, 'Paradoxe', in *Dictionnaire de Jean-Jacques Rousseau*, ed. Raymond Trousson and Frédéric Eigeldinger (Paris, 1996), p.683-85 (683). For the history of the reception of Rousseau's writings, in Germany in particular, see Raymond Trousson, 'Jean-Jacques Rousseau et son œuvre dans la presse périodique allemande de 1750 à 1800 (I)', *Dix-huitième siècle* 1:1 (1969), p.289-310; Ludwig Tente, *Die Polemik um den ersten Discours von Rousseau in Frankreich und Deutschland*, 3 vols (Kiel, 1974); Jacques Mounier, 'La réception de J. J. Rousseau en Allemagne au XVIIIe siècle', in *Aufklärungen: Frankreich und Deutschland im 18. Jahrhundert*, ed. Gerhard Sauder and Jürgen Schlobach (Heidelberg, 1985), p.167-79; Raymond Trousson, *Jean-Jacques Rousseau jugé par ses contemporains: du 'Discours sur les sciences et les arts' aux 'Confessions'* (Paris, 2000); and, most recently, Simone Zurbuchen, 'Zur Wirkungsgeschichte der beiden Diskurse', in *Jean-Jacques Rousseau: die beiden Diskurse zur Zivilisationskritik*, ed. Johannes Rohbeck and Lieselotte Steinbrügge (Berlin, 2015), p.195-220.

so immense that in 1753 a German publisher issued a two-volume *Recueil de toutes les pièces qui ont été publiées à l'occasion du discours de M. J. J. Rousseau*, which contained some of the more famous objections to Rousseau, such as those by Stanislaus Leszczynski, the Polish king, and Friedrich Melchior, baron von Grimm, as well as his replies to them.[6] Moreover, Rousseau's *Discours sur les sciences et les arts* contained a harsh criticism of all the – as he called them – depraved men of letters and philosophers who destroyed the foundations of faith and virtue for the sake of personal fame,[7] a criticism that fell on fertile ground among Christian philosophers such as Formey, who regularly campaigned against the immorality of the *philosophes*.

Nevertheless, although Formey acknowledged the depravity of certain philosophers, essentially, he condemned Rousseau's attack against the arts and sciences. This attempt to combine acknowledgement and rejection is the main characteristic of Formey's reaction to Rousseau's controversial writing, and it becomes evident in at least three different instances: first, in a critical review of the *Discours sur les sciences et les arts* that appeared immediately after its publication; second, in his 'Examen philosophique de la liaison réelle qu'il y a entre les sciences et les mœurs', which he presented at one of the Academy's public assemblies in June 1754;[8] and, finally, in his *Principes de morale*, a comprehensive moral philosophical treatise that appeared in two parts in 1762 and 1765. In Formey's first reaction to Rousseau, which appeared in the 1751 January/February issue of his own journal *Bibliothèque impartiale*, he doubted the seriousness of

---

6. *Recueil de toutes les pièces qui ont été publiées à l'occasion du discours de M. J. J. Rousseau, sur cette question proposée par l'Académie de Dijon pour le prix de l'année 1750, si le rétablissement des sciences & des arts a contribué à épurer les mœurs*, 2 vols (Gotha, Mevius, 1753). Formey reviewed this anthology in 'Article XV. Recueil de toutes les pièces', *Nouvelle bibliothèque germanique* 13:1 (1753), p.213-20.
7. See Tom Furniss, 'Rousseau: enlightened critic of the Enlightenment?', in *The Enlightenment world*, ed. M. Fitzpatrick, p.596-609 (600).
8. See Formey, 'Examen philosophique', p.397-416. This text was also published in two further editions in 1755: as a brochure in Paris (published under the *fausse adresse* of 'Avignon') and in the appendix of the *Journal des sçavans* published in Amsterdam: *Journal des sçavans, combiné avec les Mémoires de Trévoux* 10 (March 1755), p.529-50, and 11 (May 1755), vol.1, p.539-50. Compare with Formey's own reference to these different editions in 'Article II. Histoire de l'Académie royale des sciences, & c. année MDCCLIII. Troisième extrait', *Nouvelle bibliothèque germanique* 17:2 (1755), p.275-301 (276). The version of the 'Examen philosophique' that appeared in the Academy yearbook is cited in what follows.

8. Natural law, morality and science

Rousseau's argument.[9] Immediately afterwards, however, he specified the conundrum that Rousseau's *Discours sur les sciences et les arts* had posed to philosophers such as him who venerated the progress of science: how to reconcile the obvious depravity of a large number of people, particularly learned men, with the assumption of an intrinsic link between truth and virtue.[10] One solution to this conundrum, which, in its essence, Formey kept throughout his other writings in reply to the *Discours sur les sciences et les arts*, was to ascribe the relatively widespread immorality of learned men to an abuse of science. He argued that it was not the fault of the sciences if some 'so-called' philosophers were immoral, just as it was not the fault of food and liquor if immoral people ruined their health by consuming them in abundance.[11]

In 1754, Formey continued this opinion and elaborated on it in his second, much more extensive, engagement with the problem raised by Rousseau's *Discours sur les sciences et les arts*. In this, he advanced the peculiar argument that there was no causal relationship between the sciences and moral behaviour;[12] he alleged that the sciences had neither a good nor a bad effect on moral behaviour, or at least their influence was so small it was not worth considering.[13] Formey explained what he had already suggested by the comparison between the abuse of science and the abuse of food and liquor in his review article: in his view, human beings were born with the seeds of their particular moral behaviour and knowledge, and the sciences were able neither to develop nor to change these seeds; rather, they would merely help

---

9. See 'Article VI. Discours, qui a remporté le prix de l'Académie de Dijon', *Bibliothèque impartiale* 3:1 (1751), p.250-60 (250); compare with p.253, in which Formey suggests Rousseau established his argument only to attract the attention of the Academy.
10. See 'Article VI. Discours, qui a remporté le prix', p.251.
11. See 'Article VI. Discours, qui a remporté le prix', p.251.
12. In his 'Examen philosophique', Formey himself underlined the peculiarity of his argument as compared with the responses Rousseau's *Discours sur les sciences et les arts* had received so far from its critics, almost all of which relied on the assumption that morals and the sciences had a reciprocal influence. See Formey, 'Examen philosophique', p.397-98. In modern scholarship, Alexander Schmidt has highlighted the particularity of Formey's argument by describing it as sceptical. In his view, this seemed rather alien with respect to the largely anti-sceptical and Christian position concerning morality that is usually assumed as far as Formey is concerned; see Schmidt, 'Scholarship, morals and government', p.254-55.
13. See Formey, 'Examen philosophique', p.398.

the natural dispositions to manifest themselves in behaviour.[14] This is why the extent of knowledge did not change anything with regard to whether an individual was virtuous or immoral.[15] Formey tried to prove his argument through an account of three different historical states of human civilization, in each of which the sciences had only an accidental effect on the changes in morals,[16] as well as by attributing a faulty conception and practice of science to past and contemporary philosophers.[17] Finally, in Formey's view, even the correct practice of science had no impact whatsoever on the conduct of the people. He was particularly concerned with the behaviour of scientists, and claimed they were no different from other human beings, that is, there were some who were genuinely good and others who were genuinely bad; the practice of science only reinforced either one or the other of these inherent capacities.[18] Despite this general rejection of the claim that science had the ability to deprave human beings, Formey did, however, admit that a couple of aspects linked to the practice of science made scholars prone to immoral behaviour: the sedentary and unhealthy *vie de cabinet* caused negative humour and caprice; and the search for glory led to jealousy and perfidy.[19]

Such a statement, which amounted to an acknowledgement of Rousseau's observation of the depraved behaviour of contemporary philosophers, led the critics of the 'Examen philosophique' to blame Formey for supporting Rousseau instead of refuting him. The fiercest criticism of Formey's 'Examen philosophique' came from the French publicist and regular critic of Voltaire and the *encyclopédistes* Elie Fréron, who in his periodical *L'Année littéraire* accused Formey of having 'nothing but false reasoning and contradictory statements'.[20] Fréron tried to prove that several of Formey's depictions ran contrary to his main argument that the sciences did not affect morality and, therefore, agreed with Rousseau's opinion.[21] In particular, he denounced Formey's depiction of the life of scholars because it

---

14. See Formey, 'Examen philosophique', p.401-402; compare with p.411, in which he expressed this through a metaphor.
15. See Formey, 'Examen philosophique', p.403.
16. See Formey, 'Examen philosophique', p.398-405.
17. See Formey, 'Examen philosophique', p.405-407.
18. See Formey, 'Examen philosophique', p.410-11.
19. See Formey, 'Examen philosophique', p.411.
20. See 'Examen philosophique', *L'Année littéraire* 5 (1755), p.58-67 (59).
21. See 'Examen philosophique', *L'Année littéraire*, p.63.

supported Rousseau's argument.[22] The *Mémoires de Trévoux*, which was published by French Jesuits, also found Formey's solution to the question of the influence of science on morality unconvincing, and underlined its similarities with Rousseau's argument.[23] Moreover, both critical reviews emphasised that Formey's argument with regard to the accidental effect the sciences had on morality was misleading, because this had actually not been contested by Rousseau. On the contrary, as both reviewers made clear, Rousseau had denied that the sciences were genuinely corruptive, and maintained that their negative effect on morality resulted from their abuse by human beings.[24]

Formey, who replied to the criticism levelled by the French periodicals in an article in his *Nouvelle bibliothèque germanique*,[25] justified his emphasis on the accidental effect the sciences had on morality by referring to his aim of clarifying the problem raised by Rousseau. In his view, the people who had discussed this problem so far had shaped the idea of an immediate, almost physical influence that the sciences had on morality, an idea Formey wanted to destroy. Moreover, he emphasised that whether the sciences affected morality absolutely or accidentally was not central to his own argument.[26] Instead, he maintained that his proof of the non-determining effect the sciences had on morality was an a priori proof, because he had demonstrated that human nature precluded the fact that the human mind and heart were changed by the sciences. He set his a priori proof in opposition to the empirical proof that relied on the observation of the development of the sciences. In his view, this led only to arbitrary claims.[27] Nevertheless, Formey admitted to some extent that his argument

22. See 'Examen philosophique', *L'Année littéraire*, p.65.
23. See 'Article LXXVIII. Examen philosophique', *Mémoires pour l'histoire des sciences et beaux-arts* (July 1755, issue 2), p.1733-56 (1735). Regarding the claim that Formey and Rousseau held similar positions with regard to accusing the Republic of Letters and the sciences, see, for example, p.1745 and 1756.
24. See 'Article LXXVIII. Examen philosophique', p.1740-41, and 'Examen philosophique', *L'Année littéraire*, p.62.
25. See 'Article II. Histoire de l'Académie', p.275-301; the major part of this review (p.276-99) is dedicated to Formey's 'Examen philosophique'.
26. See 'Article II. Histoire de l'Académie', p.293-94.
27. See 'Article II. Histoire de l'Académie', p.295. Compare with Formey's review of the collection of the contributions to the debate about Rousseau's *Discours sur les sciences et les arts*: 'Article XV. Recueil de toutes les pièces', p.215. Here, he stated that it was impossible to give a clear answer to the question of whether the sciences had contributed to the purification of morals if such an answer was based on the observation of facts alone.

could hardly restore the reputation of the sciences. As there were generally more bad people than good people, there were also more genuinely immoral than virtuous learned men; as a consequence, the knowledge acquired by learned men caused an excess of poor moral conduct among them. He specified his argument in relation to the accidental impact the sciences had on morals by claiming that the sciences did indeed fuel more vice than virtue on an individual level, although they had a beneficial effect on society as a whole.[28]

Formey did not only hedge his argument about the absent link between sciences and morality in the light of the criticism it received in the periodical press; he had already leaned towards a reevaluation of this issue in the last part of his 'Examen philosophique'. Here, he argued that, theoretically, every science contained a moral aspect that could have a positive effect on society in the sense that it would help to deduce moral duties from the discovery of God's existence and perfections. As such, the effect of the sciences on morals was, however, only indirect, and it seems to have been linked mainly to one scientific discipline in particular, namely, physico-theology.[29] Moreover, Formey claimed the scientific endeavours that succeeded in encouraging such a natural theological virtue remained few in number.[30]

Formey argued similarly with respect to the discipline of moral philosophy, which he portrayed as the only science that could possibly have a direct link with morality because its subject was the regulation of moral behaviour.[31] However, as with existing physico-theological works, Formey bemoaned the lack of robustness and the uselessness of the discipline of moral philosophy in eighteenth-century Europe. In his view, the moral philosophy of his day lacked a scientific nature because it neither possessed a comprehensive theory nor provided clear principles that could determine human conduct successfully. Because of these insufficiencies, people's behaviour remained governed by their propensities and positive law. The only place on earth where, according to Formey, moral philosophy was exercised and used in a beneficial way for human conduct was China.[32] Compared with Chinese moral philosophy and virtue, all ancient and even Christian

---

28. See 'Article II. Histoire de l'Académie', p.296-98.
29. See Formey, 'Examen philosophique', p.412.
30. See Formey, 'Examen philosophique', p.413.
31. See Formey, 'Examen philosophique', p.413.
32. See Formey, 'Examen philosophique', p.414.

moral philosophies were ineffective.[33] This reference to the Chinese role model reveals Formey's indebtedness to Wolff, whose moral philosophy regularly drew on the example of the virtuous character of the Chinese to underline his claim that human beings had a natural and reason-based obligation to act virtuously, most famously in his *Oratio de Sinarum philosophia practica*.[34]

Formey was familiar with this speech on Chinese practical philosophy, which had been the immediate reason for Wolff's expulsion from Prussia in 1721, because he translated it into French and published it as an appendix to the second volume of his *Belle wolfienne* in 1741.[35] Wolff's moral philosophy was, in general, an important source for Formey's own writings, for example, his above-mentioned sermons on perfection that he republished under the title *Essai sur la perfection* in 1751, or his academic essay 'De la conscience' of the same year.[36] Formey's most comprehensive engagement with Wolff's moral philosophy was, however, his bipartite *Principes de morale*. This appeared in 1762 and 1765, and has to be considered as Formey's third reaction to Rousseau's *Discours sur les sciences et les arts*, along with his review and his 'Examen philosophique'.[37] The *Principes de*

---

33. See Formey, 'Examen philosophique', p.415. Compare with Pott, *Reformierte Morallehren*, p.202-203, who argues that Formey believed every moral philosophy was ineffective unless it was founded in religion. This interpretation, however, distorts Formey's argument, which did not oppose Christian to 'reasonable' moral philosophy but was rather concerned with the rationality of moral philosophy in general. Moreover, Pott neglects Formey's claim that even Christian moral philosophies were not sufficiently rational, which he regretted ('Examen philosophique', p.415-16).
34. See Christian Wolff, *Oratio de Sinarum philosophia practica / Rede über die praktische Philosophie der Chinesen* (1721/1726), ed. Michael Albrecht (Hamburg, 1985). For the interpretation of this work, see Albrecht, 'Die Tugend und die Chinesen', esp. p.244-46.
35. See Formey, 'Discours sur la morale des Chinois', in *Belle wolfienne*, vol.2, p.1-76.
36. See Formey, 'De la conscience', in *Histoire de l'Académie royale des sciences et belles lettres de Berlin* (1751; Berlin, Haude & Spener, 1753), p.3-29.
37. Formey, *Principes de morale déduits de l'usage des facultés de l'entendement humain*, 2 vols (Leiden, E. Luzac, 1762) (referred to subsequently as *Morale intellectuelle*), and *Principes de morale appliqués aux déterminations de la volonté*, 2 vols (Leiden, E. Luzac, 1765) (referred to subsequently as *Morale pratique*). The definitions of 'morale intellectuelle' and 'morale pratique' are based on Formey's own wording; see *Morale intellectuelle*, vol.1, p.xii. The *Principes de morale* relied on Wolff's *Philosophia moralis sive Ethica, methodo scientifica pertractata* (1750-1753), ed. Jean Ecole *et al.*, 5 vols, in *Christian Wolff: Gesammelte Werke*, ed. Jean Ecole

morale not only fulfilled the desideratum that Formey outlined at the end of the 'Examen philosophique', that is, a truly effective moral science, but it also contained a further answer to the problem of how to reconcile the observation of the depravity of learned men with a positive depiction of the role of learning.

Formey's scientific moral philosophy

Formey's *Principes de morale* was a comprehensive moral philosophical treatise that he considered to be of a superior scientific quality as compared with his other moral philosophical publications. This was why he listed all his memberships of different European academies on its title page, something he had not done in his previous publications because he considered them not sufficiently 'philosophical'. In his view, these previous publications were simple applications of logic to morality and social life, whereas his *Principes de morale* was an attempt at a more sophisticated approach.[38]

Formey's application of a sophisticated scientific or philosophical style to his *Principes de morale* can be attributed to the demonstrative method he claimed to apply,[39] as well as to the work's systematic character. Like Wolff, Formey classified moral philosophy as the culmination of a complex philosophical system that had its foundations in ontology and advanced through psychology, natural theology and cosmology, which, in turn, were the foundations of universal practical philosophy, natural law and, finally, moral philosophy.[40] By emphasising the fact that moral philosophy was rooted in theoretical philosophy, Formey portrayed his *Principes de morale* as a counter-example to other moral philosophies, which, in his view, were a

---

et al., section 2, vol.12-16 (Hildesheim, 1970-1973) (referred to subsequently as *Ethica*).

38. See Formey, *Morale intellectuelle*, vol.1, p.iv-vi.
39. See Formey, *Morale intellectuelle*, vol.1, p.xvi. Compare with Wolff, *Ethica*, vol.1, §4.
40. See Formey, *Morale intellectuelle*, vol.1, p.xix-xxi. Compare with Wolff, *Ethica*, vol.1, §9. Since the beginning of his career, Wolff had considered moral philosophy to be the ultimate goal of his philosophical work. See Winfried Lenders, 'Nachwort Philosophia moralis sive Ethica', in Wolff, *Ethica*, vol.5, p.i-xxii (ii-iii); Klara Joesten, *Christian Wolffs Grundlegung der praktischen Philosophie* (Leipzig, 1931), p.iv-v; Clemens Schwaiger, *Das Problem des Glücks im Denken Christian Wolffs: eine quellen-, begriffs- und entwicklungsgeschichtliche Studie zu Schlüsselbegriffen seiner Ethik* (Stuttgart-Bad Cannstatt, 1995), p.23-26.

collection of disordered and vague notions and popular opinions.[41] This portrayal confirmed his criticism of the contemporary insufficiency of the discipline of moral philosophy that he had used as the conclusion to his 'Examen philosophique'. Unlike popular moral philosophies, the purpose of his scientific moral philosophy was to provide universal principles of morality from which particular moral rules could be inferred.[42] Hence, the book was directed not at a popular readership but at people who had the intellectual capacity to study the different disciplines on which the principles of morality relied and who were able to instruct others in good moral behaviour.[43] Moreover, Formey recommended his book to those in society who were supposed to 'watch over the morals of the people', for example, pastors, fathers, teachers and judges, so they could adapt the laws they passed to become natural laws of human morality.[44]

Most importantly, however, the scientific and universal character of Formey's moral principles arose from the Leibnizian and Wolffian concept of a natural-law-based moral philosophy in which they were grounded. Like Wolff, Formey defined moral philosophy as a practical science that taught people how to become happy by regulating their free actions in accordance with the law of nature.[45] Leibniz's and Wolff's approach to natural law is commonly referred to as rationalist or intellectualist, because they maintained human beings were able to deduce innate laws of behaviour through the use of reason in an almost autonomous fashion. As such, their approach was not only opposed to traditional voluntarist moral theories that rooted morality in divine revelation but also to the new voluntarism of Hobbes, Pufendorf and Thomasius, who argued that morality was the result of positive laws imposed on human beings by God or a civil legislator.[46]

41. See Formey, *Morale intellectuelle*, vol.1, p.xxiii.
42. See Formey, *Morale intellectuelle*, vol.1, p.xviii.
43. See Formey, *Morale intellectuelle*, vol.1, p.xxv-xxvi. Compare with Wolff, *Ethica*, vol.1, §11.
44. See Formey, *Morale intellectuelle*, vol.1, p.xxx. However, in his 'Examen philosophique', p.416, Formey had made a plea for moral philosophical manuals that were accessible to everyone.
45. See Formey, *Morale intellectuelle*, vol.1, p.xiii. Compare with Wolff, *Ethica*, vol.1, §1.
46. For the different theories of natural law in Germany at the beginning of the eighteenth century, see Knud Haakonssen, 'German natural law', in *The Cambridge history of eighteenth-century political thought*, ed. Mark Goldie and Robert Wokler (Cambridge, 2006), p.251-90 (252), and Schneewind, *The Invention of autonomy*, p.8-9.

Wolff inferred the fundamental moral law according to which the individual should act from the basic characteristic of human nature – perfectibility.[47] Because, ultimately, all of a human being's actions served the pursuit of perfection,[48] the individual was, naturally, obligated to render their own and others' condition more perfect and to omit everything that made it less so. By following this fundamental premise, a human being's actions were automatically morally good.[49] Therefore, given the ontological foundation of the moral law of perfection, it had to be considered innate and universally applicable. Consequently, Wolff stressed that human beings required neither any further particular law nor any external legislator, God included.[50] Instead, he considered human reason to be people's only guide to virtue because it revealed the law of nature to them;[51] hence, if human beings gave in to their intelligent judgements, they were acting virtuously automatically.[52]

In his moral philosophical essays and sermons, Formey regularly referred to Leibnizian and Wolffian notions of natural law. For example, in his *Essai sur la perfection*, he adopted Wolff's ontological principle of perfection almost word for word.[53] In his academic essay

---

47. Perfectibility was the key notion of Wolff's entire philosophy. He defined this as the congruency of the actions of a thing with its overall purpose that was, in turn, underpinned by the harmonious collaboration of all the single components/actions of the thing in its striving to attain this congruency (see Wolff, *Metaphysik*, §152). See Dieter Hüning, 'Christian Wolffs "allgemeine Regel der menschlichen Handlungen"', *Jahrbuch für Recht und Ethik / Annual review of law and ethics* 12 (2004), p.91-113 (94-95). The inspiration for this principle came from Leibniz; see Schwaiger, 'Ethik', p.255-58.
48. See Wolff, *Vernünfftige Gedancken von der Menschen Thun und Lassen, zu Beförderung ihrer Glückseeligkeit* (4th edn, 1733), ed. Hans Werner Arndt, in *Christian Wolff: Gesammelte Werke*, ed. Jean Ecole et al., section 1, vol.4 (Hildesheim, 1976) (referred to subsequently as *Ethik*), §40.
49. See Wolff, *Ethik*, §12. On the particularity of Wolff's notion of human beings' natural obligation to be virtuous, see Dieter Hüning, 'Christian Wolffs Begriff der natürlichen Verbindlichkeit als Bindeglied zwischen Psychologie und Moralphilosophie', in *Die Psychologie Christian Wolffs: systematische und historische Untersuchungen*, ed. O.-P. Rudolph and J.-F. Goubet, p.143-67, and also his 'Christian Wolffs "allgemeine Regel"', p.96-102. For a focus on the implications of Wolff's notion of natural obligation for moral education, see Grote, *The Emergence of modern aesthetic theory*, p.23-28.
50. See Wolff, *Ethik*, §19-20.
51. See Wolff, *Ethik*, §23, and *Ethica*, vol.1, §259.
52. See Wolff, *Ethik*, §24.
53. See Formey, *Essai sur la perfection*, p.17-18: 'Nous ne commençons donc à connoître la perfection d'une chose, que quand, instruits du but auquel elle

'De la conscience', he stressed that the norms of morality were innate and, thus, not dependent on the existence of God.[54]

In his *Principes de morale*, Formey highlighted the strong link between understanding and morality that arose from the Wolffian notion of innate moral law. He explained that human beings could gradually reach perfection by executing their natural faculties adequately according to the purpose of these faculties. From this, he concluded that moral philosophy had to teach human beings what their natural faculties were and how to apply them in the best possible way.[55] As in Wolff's account, human understanding played a central role in this process because, as Formey claimed, the perfection of human beings' faculties depended proportionally on the perfection of their understanding or intellect.[56] To put it succinctly, because virtue was correlated with distinct knowledge, the main goal of Formey's moral philosophical treatise was to explain the use of the intellect to help individuals discover their duties:

> Mon grand but dans ces deux Ouvrages [the two parts of the *Principes de morale*], qui, à proprement parler, n'en sont qu'un, c'est de convaincre les hommes qu'ils ne parviendront jamais à posseder des vertus solides qu'après avoir acquis des lumieres distinctes; & cela de maniere que leur succès au premier de ces égards demeure toujours proportionnel à celui qu'ils ont eu préalablement au second.[57]

In practice, such an intellectualist moral philosophy had to go far beyond the presentation of rules of conduct and, instead, introduce psychological knowledge to a large extent. This extension of moral philosophy into the realm of psychology and theories of understanding is also apparent in the tradition that Formey claimed for his publication – he cited Malebranche, Locke and the German mathematician and physicist Ehrenfried Walther von Tschirnhaus,

---

tend, nous en examinons les pieces ou parties, & nous reconnoissons qu'elles se rapportent effectivement à ce but, qu'elles y tendent de concert' (also in Formey, *L'Idée, les règles et le modèle*, p.9).

54. See Formey, 'De la conscience', p.22. One of his first contributions to the Academy in 1745 had already been a presentation of Wolff's natural law; see Formey, 'Sur la loi naturelle', in *Histoire de l'Académie royale des sciences et des belles lettres* (1745; Berlin, Haude, 1746), p.102-103.
55. See Formey, *Morale intellectuelle*, vol.1, p.xiv.
56. See Formey, *Morale intellectuelle*, vol.1, p.xv.
57. Formey, *Morale pratique*, vol.1, p.xi. Compare with *Morale intellectuelle*, vol.1, p.xvi-xvii.

who had developed a theory of understanding in his 1687 *Medicina mentis*, as his role models.[58]

However, as a comparison with Wolff's philosophical oeuvre reveals, the almost unique source of Formey's publication – not only conceptually – was the two first volumes of Wolff's five-volume Latin *Ethica*. One reason why Formey avoided acknowledging openly that his moral philosophical treatise was based on this work might have been the increasing difficulty of publishing works related to Wolffian philosophy outside Germany from the mid-eighteenth century onwards.[59] The *Ethica* – Wolff's last major work before his death – was published between 1750 and 1753, but it received little public attention.[60] Formey received the single volumes from Wolff personally, and subsequently as he finished them, and reviewed them in his *Nouvelle bibliothèque germanique* between 1750 and 1753.[61] In Wolff's *Ethica*, the first two volumes constituted a general instruction as to how human beings could adapt their actions to the law of nature by making correct use of their intellectual faculties and their will. The last three volumes depicted the natural duties that resulted from a knowledge of natural law and that were divided into duties to oneself, to God and to others.[62] This was a common tripartition in eighteenth-century moral philosophical textbooks, and was used across philosophical and confessional divisions.[63] Wolff considered his *Ethica* to be an applied practical philosophy in the same way that politics and economics were also applied practical philosophies. Its theoretical foundations lay in natural law, and Wolff developed this in a separate treatise, the abridgement of which Formey translated into French.[64]

---

58. See Formey, *Morale intellectuelle*, vol.1, p.viii.
59. See Vattel to Formey (14.11.1754), in *Emer de Vattel à Jean Henri Samuel Formey*, p.155. Vattel reported that he was not able to find a publisher for his abridgement of Wolff's natural law in the Netherlands, Switzerland or France only because Wolff's name appeared in the title.
60. See Lenders, 'Nachwort Philosophia moralis sive Ethica', p.xviii-xix.
61. See Wolff to Formey (29.5.1751; 23.10.1751; 12.6.1753), CV. Formey's reviews of the *Ethica* appeared in *Nouvelle bibliothèque germanique* 7:2 (1750), p.337-46, *Nouvelle bibliothèque germanique* 10:1 (1752), p.120-32, *Nouvelle bibliothèque germanique* 11:1 (1752) p.97-103, *Nouvelle bibliothèque germanique* 12:1 (1753), p.38-48, and *Nouvelle bibliothèque germanique* 13:2 (1753), p.322-35.
62. See Lenders, 'Nachwort Philosophia moralis sive Ethica', p.xiv-xvi.
63. See Knud Haakonssen, 'Academic teaching, social morality, and the science of morals in eighteenth-century Britain', *Jahrbuch für Recht und Ethik / Annual review of law and ethics* 13 (2005), p.137-48 (139).
64. See Lenders, 'Nachwort Philosophia moralis sive Ethica', p.xii. Formey, *Principes*

Formey copied in its entirety the chapter division of the *Ethica*'s first two volumes for his *Principes de morale*, although he dispensed with Wolff's rigid paragraph structure and interpolated descriptions of his own experiences and other – very often Francophone – contemporary authors' ideas. For example, when he discussed the intellectual virtue of profoundness and solidity in science, he digressed to contemplate the usefulness and feasibility of the Parisian *Encyclopédie* and include an anecdotal account of his personal collaboration in this enterprise that incorporated long quotations from his correspondence.[65] In the examples of the arguments he cited, he often referred to his correspondents or colleagues at the Academy.[66] Moreover, in the second part of the *Principes de morale*, Formey engaged constantly with Rousseau's theory of education, which had just appeared in 1762 with the publication of the *Emile*. As early as 1763 and 1764, Formey expressed his disagreement with Rousseau's new pedagogics in two refutations entitled *Anti-Emile* and *Emile chrétien*. In the *Morale pratique*, which appeared in 1765, he criticised particularly Rousseau's claim that children must first be physically educated before appealing to their intellect and teaching them to have morals.[67]

Despite these digressions and practical examples, Formey was relatively faithful in his translation of the main points of Wolff's treatise. The first part of the *Principes de morale*, the so-called *Morale intellectuelle*, contained, in the first volume, a theory of the soul that systematically divided the different mental faculties and then developed so-called 'intellectual virtues', that is, ways of perfectly using human understanding, in the second. While the first volume corresponded to the first chapter of the first volume of Wolff's

---

du droit de la nature et des gens: extrait du grand ouvrage latin de Mr. de Wolff, 2 vols (Amsterdam, Rey, 1758). On the genesis of this book and its role with respect to the tradition of Reformed moral philosophy, see Pott, *Reformierte Morallehren*, p.98-107.

65. See Formey, *Morale intellectuelle*, vol.2, p.332-45.
66. See, for example, Formey, *Morale intellectuelle*, vol.1, p.24, for a reference to the excellent eyesight of the Academy's physicist Johann Nathanael Lieberkühn, or *Morale intellectuelle*, vol.2, p.412, for a reference to Charles Bonnet's discovery that reproduction by aphids was possible.
67. See Formey, *Morale pratique*, vol.1, p.22 and 135-36. Likewise, Formey referred to Rousseau's *Emile* on p.89, 123, 257-58, 336, 370-71 and 392. In the latter two instances he even showed that he agreed to some extent with some of Rousseau's claims.

Ethica, the second volume corresponded to chapters 2 to 4 of the first volume of Wolff's *Ethica*. Intellectual virtues were defined as habits of good practice of understanding. As such, they included the ability to distinguish between right and wrong and being certain or uncertain, as well as between probable and improbable in the study of a thing.[68] There were general ('formal') virtues such as intelligence, soundness and profoundness, which were linked to the way in which understanding functioned, as well as particular ('material') virtues such as science, wisdom, caution and art, which were bound to the objects of the knowledge that was acquired through understanding.[69] By leading to the perfection of human understanding, these virtues were an indispensable prerequisite for moral virtues.[70]

The second part of Formey's *Principes de morale*, the *Morale pratique*, built upon its first part and dealt with the regulation of the will by human understanding. Despite its informal title – *Morale pratique* – it consisted of general principles of action rather than mere descriptions of practical moral duties.[71] It aimed to show how the will could be enhanced and corrected by applying to it the distinct notions of good and bad, which could be gained through the methods presented in the *Morale intellectuelle*.[72] The human will was the immediate origin of moral behaviour in the sense that it was determined by the aim of enabling the good and avoiding the bad.[73] Formey bemoaned that most people's notions of good and bad were, however, corrupted by sensory experiences and, therefore, his *Morale pratique* aimed to demonstrate how to distinguish between real and false notions of good and bad.[74] By following the different chapters of the second volume of Wolff's *Ethica*, Formey first explained what the perfection of the will consisted in and how its possible imperfections could be remedied. Thereafter, he explained the psychological origin of the passions and the means by which

68. See Formey, *Morale intellectuelle*, vol.2, p.1. Compare with Wolff, *Ethica*, vol.1, §142.
69. See Formey, *Morale intellectuelle*, vol.2, p.3. Compare with Wolff, *Ethica*, vol.1, §143.
70. See Formey, *Morale intellectuelle*, vol.2, p.8-9. Compare with Wolff, *Ethica*, vol.1, §149.
71. See Formey, *Morale pratique*, vol.1, p.xxii.
72. See Formey, *Morale pratique*, vol.1, p.2.
73. See Formey, *Morale pratique*, vol.1, p.3.
74. See Formey, *Morale pratique*, vol.1, p.6 and 15.

they could be excited or calmed in a way such that they contributed to human beings' perfection and happiness.[75] Contrary to the Stoic approach, Formey argued that the oppression of the passions was not necessary to become virtuous and happy, nor was it possible.[76] He defined the passions as agitations of the soul that arose from a person's perception of good and bad; their strength depended on how strongly something was perceived to be good or bad.[77] To avoid the abuse of the passions, which was the source of vice,[78] the soul had to be trained to become passionate only about things that were genuinely good or bad.[79] Although Formey did not explicitly state it, it is clear that such a regulation of the passions involved the human intellect. In fact, Wolff claimed in his *Ethica* that to distinguish between apparently and really good objects was a completely intellectual task.[80] In most eighteenth-century moral philosophies, the passions or sentiments played a central role in motivating human behaviour and moral judgements,[81] and considerations on how to regulate or govern the passions in order to reach happiness and virtue were always part of such theories. Most prominently, Scottish sentimentalist philosophers of the beginning of the eighteenth century like the third earl of Shaftesbury and Francis Hutcheson believed human beings to have an inborn moral sense by which they evaluated the different affections and the morality of actions.[82] But in German moral thought and natural law theories, the passions also gained some ground in the wake of Christian Thomasius' antirationalism. One important opponent of Wolff's intellectualist natural law was the Göttingen professor of history and natural law Johann Jacob Schmauss, who considered human behaviour to be directly rooted in the emotions of fear and hope without any intervention of reason. In his view, the passions

---

75. See Formey, *Morale pratique*, vol.1, p.289.
76. See Formey, *Morale pratique*, vol.1, p.287.
77. See Formey, *Morale pratique*, vol.1, p.288.
78. See Formey, *Morale pratique*, vol.2, p.268.
79. See Formey, *Morale pratique*, vol.2, p.269-70.
80. See Wolff, *Ethica*, vol.2, §528.
81. See Thomas Ahnert, 'Pleasure, pain and punishment in the early Enlightenment: German and Scottish debates', *Jahrbuch für Recht und Ethik / Annual review of law and ethics* 12 (2004), p.173-88 (173-74).
82. For an overview of Scottish moral sense theories and their impact in Britain and on the continent, see Jacqueline Taylor, 'Moral sense and moral sentiment', in *The Routledge companion to eighteenth-century philosophy*, ed. A. Garrett, p.421-41.

were able to detect natural law and act according to it.[83] For Formey, however, this discussion seems not to have been relevant in the development of his moral philosophy.

There is no doubt that Formey's *Principes de morale*, with its psychologically founded considerations in relation to the human intellect, will and the passions, constituted the scientific moral philosophy the lack of which Formey had bemoaned in his 'Examen philosophique'. As such, the work further reversed Formey's initially strong claim about the non-existing link between sciences and moral conduct, a claim that he had already hedged in the light of the criticism that his 'Examen philosophique' had received in the French periodical press. Nevertheless, the *Principes de morale* contained not just a simple reversal of Rousseau's claim that the sciences caused moral decline. Wolff's intellectualist natural-law-based moral philosophy, on which Formey's *Principes de morale* was based, did not require an increase in understanding to automatically produce an increase in virtue. On the contrary, Wolff subjected the correlation between knowledge and morality, which was at the core of his theory of the innateness of morality, to a certain condition. This is explained more precisely in the first volume of his *Ethica*: 'The more one cultivates one's intellectual virtues, the more one enhances one's moral virtue, provided that one does it for the purpose of enhancing one's morality.'[84]

In his *Morale intellectuelle*, Formey underlined the importance of this condition which put the cultivation of science under the tutelage of morality:

> Il faut bien prendre garde que nous n'affirmons pas simplement que le degré des vertus morales répond toujours au degré des vertus intellectuelles; mais nous ajoutons pour condition, entant qu'on rapporte la culture des vertus intellectuelles à la culture des vertus morales. Cela fait une différence capitale. Le plus grand nombre de ceux qui étudient, ne pensent qu'à acquérir de la réputation, à parvenir aux Emplois, ou à remplir d'autres vuës humaines; il ne leur vient pas dans l'esprit que le premier but de toutes les études est de devenir meilleur.[85]

---

83. See Frank Grunert, 'Das Recht der Natur als Recht des Gefühls: zur Naturrechtslehre von Johann Jacob Schmauss', *Jahrbuch für Recht und Ethik / Annual review of law and ethics* 12 (2004), p.137-56 (esp. 144-45, 148 and 151).
84. Wolff, *Ethica*, vol.1, §159 (my translation from the Latin: 'Quo magis virtutes intellectuales perficiuntur, quatenus ad moralium culturam faciunt; eo magis virtutes morales perfici possunt').
85. Formey, *Morale intellectuelle*, vol.1, p.28-29.

Most importantly, Formey justified this limitation of the effect of intellectual virtues on moral virtues with an empirical observation of the bad behaviour of those who, supposedly, possessed the most intellectual virtues: learned men. By stating that the Republic of Letters was full of learned men who displayed neither decent behaviour nor virtues,[86] and who very often betrayed arrogance, pride and envy,[87] Formey again highlighted the same problems as Rousseau in his *Discours sur les sciences et les arts*.[88] Furthermore, Formey admitted this observation concurred with Rousseau's paradoxical view that the sciences harmed morality, and to avoid falling into the same paradox it was, therefore, necessary to subject the link between knowledge and virtue to a condition.[89] Finally, Formey repeated the argument he had already employed in his first reaction to the *Discours sur les sciences et les arts* in the *Bibliothèque impartiale* as well as in his 'Examen philosophique', namely, that true science or 'solid knowledge' contained nothing immoral per se. On the contrary, it was the abuse of science by the morally corrupt among its practitioners that had resulted in the negative image of science being harmful.[90] Compared with Formey's earlier reactions to Rousseau's criticism of the sciences, the achievement of the *Principes de morale* was, therefore, to solve the conundrum of how to reconcile the obvious depravity of a large part of society with his vision of a link between knowledge and virtue. Formey declared the enhancement of intellectual virtues – the practice of science included – to be indispensable for morality, provided that the

---

86. See Formey, *Morale intellectuelle*, vol.1, p.24.
87. See Formey, *Morale intellectuelle*, vol.1, p.27.
88. Wolff also justified his argument with a reference to the immorality of learned men as opposed to the goodness of uncivilized men (see the example in Wolff, *Ethica*, vol.1, §159). For more of Formey's criticism of the Republic of Letters, see *Morale intellectuelle*, vol.1, p.517-18. Compare with his 'Examen philosophique', p.405-406. Criticism of the conduct of learned men in the Republic of Letters was common at this time; see Alexander Schmidt, 'Sources of evil or seeds of the good? Rousseau and Kant on needs, the arts, and the sciences', in *Engaging with Rousseau: reaction and interpretation from the eighteenth century to the present*, ed. Avi Lifschitz (Cambridge, 2016), p.33-55 (43-44).
89. See Formey, *Morale intellectuelle*, vol.2, p.24 (without explicitly referring to Rousseau) and 27 (with an explicit reference to him).
90. See *Morale intellectuelle*, vol.1, p.25, 27 and 499-500. See also *Morale pratique*, vol.1, p.65-66, in which Formey elaborated in particular on the difference between the use and abuse of human understanding.

perfection of knowledge was pursued with the purpose of becoming virtuous.[91]

In its essence, this claim was not a complete contradiction of Rousseau's opinion. Rousseau not only denied that the sciences were corruptive per se but also conceded that they would have a potentially beneficial impact on society if they were conducted with the purpose of contributing to people's happiness instead of being used by scholars to build personal reputation.[92] Moreover, his *Discours sur les sciences et les arts* ended with a rudimentary account of the 'véritable philosophie', that is, the human capacity in general to reflect in the absence of passions. Through this 'véritable philosophie', everyone was able to discover their innate principles of virtue.[93] These considerations do not appear to be very different from Wolff's notion of the ontological foundation of moral duties and human beings' capacity to apprehend these via introspection. However, they seem to have gone unnoticed by most of his contemporaries and by Formey in particular. Moreover, since the appearance of Rousseau's *Discours sur l'origine de l'inégalité* in 1755, the significant difference between his and Wolff's perception of human perfectibility in natural law became obvious. Whereas Wolff considered perfectibility a positive thing and made it the fundamental element of human behaviour, Rousseau was ambiguous about it; as far as he was concerned, human perfectibility was, potentially, the origin of both inequality between men and moral depravity in civilised societies.[94] This difference in the notion of human perfectibility was also reflected in Formey's opposition towards Rousseau's pedagogical considerations. In his Wolffian *Principes de morale*, he pleaded for the perfection of knowledge through education to set free human beings' natural disposition to be virtuous. By contrast, Rousseau made it clear at the latest in his pedagogical treatise *Emile* that he considered the sole emphasis on the enhancement of knowledge to be contributing to the ills of current societies.

---

91. See Formey, *Morale intellectuelle*, vol.2, p.25. Compare with p.5 and 8-9, in which he also stated that, without intellectual virtues, moral virtues could not exist.
92. See Jean-Jacques Rousseau, *Discours sur les sciences et les arts* (1750), ed. François Bouchardy, in *Jean-Jacques Rousseau: œuvres complètes*, vol.3 (Paris 1964), p.1-30 (30).
93. See Rousseau, *Discours sur les sciences et les arts*, p.30.
94. On Rousseau's notion of perfectibility, see Henri Gouhier, 'La "perfectibilité" selon J.-J. Rousseau', *Revue de théologie et de philosophie* 110:4 (1978), p.321-39.

Divine and natural law in Formey's moral philosophy

With its plea for human beings' intellectual improvement, Formey's Wolffian moral philosophical treatise was a response to the challenge to scientific progress that had been provoked by Rousseau's answer to the Academy of Dijon's prize essay competition in the mid-eighteenth century; however, likewise, it diminished the role of religion in ethics. Because of its reliance on universally valid natural law, Wolffian moral philosophy was mainly secular. Wolff had underlined the secular character of his moral philosophy by arguing that atheists were also able to become naturally virtuous.[95] Nevertheless, he was convinced of the congruency of natural and divine law because both were given by God.[96] Furthermore, in his German *Ethik*, he even emphasised that natural virtue was inferior to both natural theological virtue (*Gottesseeligkeit*) and Christian virtue.[97] Whereas the first resulted only from human beings' natural striving for perfection, the latter two were, in addition, based on the aim of following God's will[98] and reaching salvation respectively.[99] It seems, however, that Wolff made the latter claims mainly to defend himself against accusations that his natural-law-based moral philosophy would undermine Christian moral theory.[100] Finally, in his *Ethica*, he avoided explicitly any considerations with regard to the role of Christian virtue and divine law because he attempted an exclusively philosophical approach, which implied that only those truths that could be deduced from

---

95. See Wolff, *Ethik*, §21-22 and 27 (for the universality of natural law); *Philosophia practica universalis, methodo scientifica pertractata*, vol.1 (1738), ed. Winfried Lenders, in *Christian Wolff: Gesammelte Werke*, ed. Jean Ecole et al., section 2, vol.10 (Hildesheim, 1971), §245; *Ethica*, vol.3, §91. Compare with Anton Bissinger, 'Zur metaphysischen Begründung der Wolffschen Ethik', in *Christian Wolff 1679-1754*, ed. W. Schneiders), p.148-60 (154 and 156).
96. See Wolff, *Ethik*, §29.
97. See Wolff, *Ethik*, §675-76.
98. See Wolff, *Ethik*, §673.
99. See Wolff, *Ethik*, §676. Compare with *Oratio de Sinarum philosophia practica*, p.27, in which Wolff also presented the three different stages of virtue without, however, judging one to be superior to the other two. See Albrecht, 'Die Tugend und die Chinesen', p.242-43. Albrecht stressed that the different stages of virtue only constituted different degrees of motivation to behave in a moral fashion.
100. See Wolff, *Ethik*, §677. Moreover, Wolff constantly emphasised that the purpose of his natural-law-based moral philosophy was to render service to religion / be a guide to grace. See Wolff, 'Vorrede zur Ethik', in *Ethik*, sig.):(7r, and also *Anmerckungen*, §428.

natural reason and experience as opposed to the truths of revelation would be examined.[101] How did this secular character of the model Formey used affect his own moral philosophy?

Importantly, Formey's adoption of such a secular moral philosophy could have been advantageous for the dissemination of his *Principes de morale* in France for two reasons. First, it was difficult for books with Protestant leanings to pass censorship in the Catholic country and, second, as his publisher Luzac in Holland never became tired of emphasising, non-theological books simply sold better. Luzac expected Formey's moral philosophy to be a success, and put a great deal of effort into improving Formey's manuscript to render it even more systematic and concise as well as secular.[102] Nevertheless, the book sold badly throughout Europe;[103] although the *Morale intellectuelle* was also translated into German, both parts of the *Principes de morale* appeared in one edition only.

Furthermore, Formey deviated from the secular approach to moral philosophy that Wolff had professed in his *Ethica* and, instead, introduced religion into his 'scientific' *Principes de morale*. He used the last chapter of his *Morale pratique* in particular to enhance Wolff's philosophical considerations by means of a decidedly Christian stance with regard to ethics. This last chapter dealt – as did its equivalent in Wolff's *Ethica* – with the purity of the soul, and served as a synthesis of the preceding considerations concerning the role of understanding, will and the passions in relation to morality. According to Wolff's definition, the soul was pure if it was devoid of taints that resulted from the lack of use or abuse of human beings' mental faculties.[104] The soul reached purity by not having any appetites and volitions that were contrary to human nature and, thus, to human perfection.[105] Formey added to this definition by saying that perfect purity could never be reached during an individual's earthly life,[106] and that, even here, a high degree of purity could only be achieved if an individual's behaviour was galvanised by their conviction of the soul's immortality

---

101. See Wolff, 'Praefatio', in *Ethica*, vol.2, sig.bv.
102. See Luzac to Formey (10.5.1760, 18.7.1761 and particularly 18.10.1763), in *Lettres d'Elie Luzac*, p.335, 348 and 356.
103. See Luzac to Formey (18.10.1763), in *Lettres d'Elie Luzac*, p.365-66.
104. See Formey, *Morale pratique*, vol.2, p.339. Compare with Wolff, *Ethica*, vol.2, §598-99.
105. See Formey, *Morale pratique*, vol.2, p.341. Compare with Wolff, *Ethica*, vol.2, §613 and 614.
106. See Formey, *Morale pratique*, vol.2, p.341.

as taught by Scripture.[107] Furthermore, Formey followed Wolff by declaring the purity of the soul to be a necessary prerequisite for moral uprightness and vice versa;[108] however, in addition, he stressed that this purity was also the prerequisite for salvation.[109]

Moreover, Formey held – like Wolff – that there was a natural obligation to purify the soul and claimed, therefore, that religion only assisted nature in the task of purification.[110] In general, Formey did not deviate from the core of Wolff's intellectualist natural-law-based moral philosophy, according to which human beings were capable of attaining a virtuous character (and, thus, a purified soul) by the proper use of understanding alone.[111] However, unlike Wolff's *Ethica*, the *Morale pratique* highlighted explicitly the complete congruency of this secular ethics with the teachings of 'true religion'.[112] As such, secular moral philosophy and religion gave one another reciprocal support:

> C'est à la Religion, je l'avoue, à soutenir l'homme dans cete carriere, & à seconder ses efforts; mais une saine Morale est de tous les moyens qui peuvent faire goûter à l'homme les préceptes de la Religion le plus naturel & le plus efficace; tout comme réciproquement la Religion est la grande source des motifs qui peuvent convaincre l'homme de l'importance & de l'utilité d'une saine Morale.[113]

Although this depiction revealed the equality between natural and divine law, other examples in the *Morale pratique* emphasised the superiority of divine law. For example, when Formey dealt with the wiseness or wickedness of human actions, he argued that natural law had only been sufficient to guide human beings before the Fall and that the introduction of divine law had been necessary to confirm natural law;[114] actions that were stimulated by the rules of Christian

---

107. See Formey, *Morale pratique*, vol.2, p.361.
108. See Formey, *Morale pratique*, vol.2, p.349. Compare with Wolff, *Ethica*, vol.2, §602-603.
109. See Formey, *Morale pratique*, vol.2, p. 346-47 and 349.
110. See Formey, *Morale pratique*, vol.2, p.349-50. Compare with Wolff, *Ethica*, vol.2, §604.
111. See Formey, *Morale pratique*, vol.2, p.339-40 and 352.
112. See Formey, *Morale pratique*, vol.2, p.362.
113. See Formey, *Morale pratique*, vol.2, p.356.
114. See Formey, *Morale pratique*, vol.1, p.157. Compare with Wolff, *Ethica*, vol.2, §115. Wolff only claimed that God had given natural law to humans in their natural state without further elaboration. In his essay/sermons on perfection,

ethics were, thus, superior, because Christian ethics contained a more helpful and discrete explanation of natural law.[115] This notion of an unbalanced relationship between Christian and secular ethics not only corresponded to Wolff's above-mentioned considerations in his *Ethik* but, more importantly, it was typical of Calvinist moral philosophies. Calvin's theology had already defined the relationship between natural and divine law along these lines.[116]

In the mid-eighteenth century, probably the most influential French Calvinist moral philosophy was Jacob Vernet's five-volume *Instruction chrétienne*, which was first published between 1751 and 1754 and then reappeared in a revised edition in 1756.[117] Its third and fourth volume in particular contained an account of Christian ethics that, like Wolff's *Ethica*, had the common structure of eighteenth-century moral philosophical textbooks: a theory of the foundation of morality was followed by an account of duties to God, to oneself and to others. Unlike Wolff's academic textbook, however, Vernet's work was directed at readers who had no academic education and used a didactical style that resembled a catechism.[118] Therefore, Vernet's work differed from Formey's Wolffian *Principes de morale* not only because of its confessional character but also because of

---

Formey presented a similar claim as in his *Morale pratique*; see Formey, *Essai sur la perfection*, p.86-88, and *L'Idée, les règles et le modèle*, p.19: 'Le Fils de Dieu est venu tracer la route de la perfection aux hommes, & sa Doctrine en est le divin modele. Mais cette perfection, c'est celle qui a son fondement dans la nature, [...], & qui etant alterée & comme effacée par les prodigieux egaremens des hommes, avoit besoin d'etre retablie dans sa pureté primitive. [...] La Religion Chrétienne bien comprise & bien expliquée n'est autre chose que le perfait [sic] rétablissement de la Loi naturelle. Mais ce qui lui donne une superiorité fort grande sur la Loi Naturelle, c'est la force des motifs qu'elle propose & par lesquels elle nous détermine à la pratique des Vertus & à la recherche de la Perfection.'

115. See Formey, *Morale pratique*, vol.1, p.169-70. Compare with Wolff, *Ethica*, vol.2, §133. Wolff only acknowledged that natural law and divine will were equal.
116. See Jennifer Herdt, 'Natural law in Protestant Christianity', in *The Cambridge companion to natural law ethics*, ed. Tom Angier (Cambridge, 2019), p.155-78 (165).
117. See Jacob Vernet, *Instruction chrétienne, divisée en cinq volumes*, 2nd edn, 5 vols (Geneva, Gosse, 1756); on the influence of the book, see Sorkin, *The Religious Enlightenment*, p.76, and Graham Gargett, 'Jacob Vernet and "the religious Enlightenment": "rational Calvinism", the pastors of Geneva and the French *philosophes*', *History of European ideas* 40:4 (2014), p.561-97 (572).
118. See Vernet, 'Avertissement sur cette seconde édition', in *Instruction chrétienne*, vol.1, p.vi.

its orientation towards a public of common people. As such, it was more similar to Formey's *Philosophe chrétien*. However, as mentioned above, Formey, who wrote a review of Vernet's *Instruction chrétienne* in 1756, found that it did not feature Christian dogma in enough depth (see chapter 3).

The *Instruction chrétienne* presented a voluntarist moral philosophy that declared God's will to be the first and principal motive for action.[119] According to this, paying homage to and obeying God was the main purpose of human behaviour and the fundamental moral principle.[120] However, Vernet's Christian ethics reflected a liberal theology; he not only stressed the reasonable nature of God's laws, which coincided with the free and rational nature of human beings, but also claimed that Christian ethics was founded on natural law. This claim correlated with his notion that Christian theology was based on natural theology.[121] In his view, the rules of conduct that men discovered through use of reason were as obligatory for behaviour as divine law because they corresponded to God's intentions.[122] Similar to Formey's depiction of the superiority of divine law, Vernet described divine law as a more helpful and authoritative version of natural law that refreshed people's knowledge of the latter as well as elucidating, expanding and strengthening it, and also purging it of potential errors.[123] In particular, the Christian dogmas of the immortality of the soul and the Last Judgement, which were only contained in Christian ethics, constituted an additional motive to be virtuous as compared with the effect of secular ethics.[124]

Moreover, Vernet's moral philosophy – like Formey's – was based on the assumption that human beings were inclined naturally to strive for perfection and happiness.[125] However, he stressed the role of perfectibility in Christian ethics in particular by claiming that the gospel required that human beings strive for perfection in the execution

---

119. See Vernet, *Instruction chrétienne*, vol.3, p.24.
120. See Vernet, *Instruction chrétienne*, vol.3, p.16 and 41.
121. See Vernet, *Instruction chrétienne*, vol.3, p.26, and vol.5, p.204. Compare also with David Sorkin, 'Geneva's "enlightened orthodoxy": the middle way of Jacob Vernet (1698-1789)', *Church history* 74:2 (2005), p.286-305 (291-92), and Gargett, 'Jacob Vernet and "the religious Enlightenment"', p.573.
122. See Vernet, *Instruction chrétienne*, vol.1, p.46-47.
123. See Vernet, *Instruction chrétienne*, vol.3, p.27.
124. See Vernet, *Instruction chrétienne*, vol.5, p.205.
125. See Vernet, *Instruction chrétienne*, vol.1, p.49, and vol.3, p.14.

of the duties of sanctification.[126] Like Formey, who maintained in his *Principes de morale* that perfection of the soul would not be attained during an individual's earthly life, Vernet also emphasised the impossibility of fulfilling divine laws to the most perfect degree because the Fall of man denied humans the possibility of becoming perfect. Moreover, he stressed that sanctification could be reached only by a sincere effort to attain perfection.[127] These considerations were central to the Calvinist concept of sanctification, according to which the good works of the Christian always remained imperfect, but were considered righteous by God once the believer had received grace.[128] Moreover, Wolff also stressed that human beings could never become perfect because only God was a perfect being.[129]

Despite the differences in genre and main source, Formey's and Vernet's moral philosophies certainly had fundamental similarities with regard to their portrayal of the relationship between natural and divine law as well as in relation to the notion of unreachable perfection. The difference between the two works was mainly the emphasis: the 'scientific' *Principes de morale* introduced divine law only into its margins; however, it was central to Vernet's catechism-like *Instruction chrétienne*. Moreover, Formey subtly altered the relationship between natural and divine law throughout his treatise in the sense that in one instance he stressed their equality, whereas in another he declared divine law to be superior to natural law. Although neither of these two possibilities was faithful to Wolff's *Ethica*, which Formey followed accurately in the rest of his *Principes de morale*, they corresponded to Wolff's opinion as he had uttered it elsewhere.

Formey's *Principes de morale*, therefore, reveals a multifaceted appropriation of Wolff's moral philosophy that illustrates his own particular needs and interests as a Huguenot philosopher. Although it reflected predominantly his aim to combat Rousseau by elaborating on the rational foundation of ethics, likewise, it had to fulfil Formey's religious purposes as a Christian philosopher. His attempt to establish a harmonious relationship between reason and faith within ethics was

---

126. See Vernet, *Instruction chrétienne*, vol.3, p.57-58. Formey had demonstrated the biblical requirement to strive for perfection in *L'Idée, les règles et le modèle / Essai sur la perfection* by referring to Jesus' exhortation to become as perfect as God (Matthew 5.48).
127. See Vernet, *Instruction chrétienne*, vol.3, p.60-61.
128. See McNutt, *Calvin meets Voltaire*, p.216-17.
129. See Wolff, *Ethik*, §44.

facilitated by the essential similarities between Wolff's philosophy and Calvinism. Most importantly, those similarities included the notion of the congruency of natural and divine law and the definition of natural law as the striving for perfection.[130]

With regard to Rousseau's philosophy, Formey put a great deal of effort into distinguishing his own position, and rather downplayed the existing similarities between his thought and that of Rousseau. As well as the criticism of the morality of the learned, which was articulated with great zeal by both of them, Rousseau and Formey also shared the fundamental assumptions that human beings were able to detect true virtue through introspection, and that science could, indeed, be beneficial for moral behaviour if conducted correctly. However, in his direct engagement with Rousseau's text, Formey did not affirm these latter two overlaps; he only partially admitted them when he himself was confronted with criticism of his 'Examen philosophique'. It is likely that this criticism also led to Formey's about-turn in argument from the 'Examen philosophique' to the *Principes de morale*. Whereas in the former he argued that science and morals were not linked to one another, he promoted an essentially positive link between intellectual improvement and morality in the latter.

Despite this about-turn in argument, there was considerable continuity between Formey's moral philosophical treatise and his earlier engagement with Rousseau's *Discours sur les sciences et les arts*. The *Principes de morale* not only carried on the criticism against Rousseau that had been uttered in the 'Examen philosophique', it also slightly diminished the positive link between science and morals in the light of Rousseau's argument. Most importantly, the *Principes de morale* also served as a remedy for the mediocre state of moral philosophy that Formey had bemoaned in his 1754 response to Rousseau. In his view, only a truly scientific moral philosophy was able to disprove Rousseau's claims. Formey's appropriation of Wolff's intellectualist natural law for moral philosophy, therefore, has to be viewed against the backdrop of the emerging challenge of intellectual improvement that had been fuelled by the European debate about Rousseau's *Discours sur les sciences et les arts*.

---

130. See Herdt, 'Natural law in Protestant Christianity', p.164-65.

Conclusion: religious Enlightenment between Calvinism and Wolffianism

The Christian philosophy of Samuel Formey consisted of a certain set of core beliefs that reveal the attempt to achieve a balance between human autonomy and divine determination. He believed in the purposefulness of God's creation in that he described divine providence as a sequence of events that were both chronologically and spatially interlinked. However, he did not accept the description of such a divinely organised order of the world as a valid proof of God's existence. Rather, he was convinced that God could only exist if the world's order was contingent, a truth that itself could only be proved metaphysically and not via the observation of nature alone. Moreover, Formey emphasised human beings' responsibility for their own actions and fate by arguing that, among the different possibilities that the divinely ordered world offered to them, they possessed freedom of choice. He was particularly critical about the idea that God had eternally predetermined the correlations between an individual's intelligent choices and their bodily movements, as if human beings functioned like machines. Nevertheless, Formey did not maintain that an individual's choices were arbitrary; he rather held they were determined by human beings' innate aim to become perfect. By following this natural obligation to become perfect, an individual could automatically become morally good and, eventually, reach salvation. Similarly, Formey contended that God's Creation was the result of His attempt to create the best of all possible worlds, and not a demonstration of His omnipotence, as voluntarist views asserted. Formey's Christian philosophy was, thus, of an explicitly optimist kind; it propagated trust in a good God and in human beings' capacity to become virtuous.

In a broader perspective, this kind of Christian philosophy demonstrates the evolution that Calvinist theology had undergone since the sixteenth century. Formey's anti-voluntarist and optimist views on divine providence imply that he rejected Calvin's theory of double predestination according to which certain people were predestined for salvation and others for damnation. Moreover, his conviction regarding human beings' predominantly rational nature and perfectibility reveals his adherence to a softened version of original sin. This theological stance was central to Arminianism, which had been condemned as a heresy in the first quarter of the seventeenth century at the Synod of Dort, and had also sparked religious dispute and persecution in the Berlin Refuge at the beginning of the eighteenth century. In Formey's time, however, such a position hardly incited fundamental controversy among his Calvinist co-confessionals; it had been incorporated into 'mainstream Calvinism' to a large extent. Compared with other 'religious Enlightenments', Formey's variant did not evolve from religious dissent.[1]

Nevertheless, some of Formey's claims caused theological disagreement among different Calvinist theologians and pastors, demonstrating the complexity of the issues at stake. Although Formey was as wary of determinism as the Swiss theologian Crousaz and the Prussian pastor Bocquet, he did not go so far as to embrace liberty of indifference as Crousaz and several Genevan pastors in the eighteenth century did. Crousaz in particular feared determinism or, as he called it, fatalism, because of its mechanistic implications for human nature that were associated with materialist philosophy and that ran contrary to the pillars of Christian morality. In contrast, Formey considered liberty of indifference to have at least as much of a negative impact on religion as determinism. The Dutch Huguenot Boullier rejected Formey's optimism as almost heterodox because it curtailed the traditional voluntarist definition of providence and the dogma of eternal punishment. In contrast, Formey considered his own position to be by no means offensive to revealed religion; on the contrary, he regarded it as the best way of opposing Diderot's pessimism about religion. Therefore, eighteenth-century Calvinists were not unanimous in their views on what was faithful to creed and, most importantly, what could counter the freethinkers' attacks

---

1. See for example *Enlightenment and religion: rational dissent in eighteenth-century Britain*, ed. Knud Haakonssen (Cambridge, 1996), and, with a focus on enthusiastic dissenters from Calvinism, Lionel Laborie, *Enlightening enthusiasm: prophecy and religious experience in early eighteenth-century England* (Manchester, 2016).

against religion in the most efficient way. In addition, categories such as orthodoxy and heterodoxy are not very useful in accounting for the different Calvinist positions of the eighteenth century because an objective definition of what was theologically orthodox did not exist; with respect to the complex theological problems linked to the relationship between human autonomy and divine determination, one author's orthodoxy was another's heterodoxy.

Moreover, the odd disagreements between Formey and his Calvinist peers resulted perhaps less from theological differences than from methodological issues and questions of philosophical taste. There was a broad consensus among Calvinist theologians in the eighteenth century about the harmonious relationship between reason and faith; however, it had slightly different implications for each of them. A common belief was that there were religious truths above natural reason, not contrary to it. As a consequence, certain theologians, particularly the Genevan Jacob Vernet, made a plea for an essential religion that omitted the truths above reason and highlighted religion's practical side.[2] Vernet, especially, disdained the theological speculations of scholastic metaphysics. In contrast, Formey considered approaches that undermined the rational explanation of religion's theological basis as potentially harmful to religion. His notion of the harmonious relationship between reason and faith was imbued with a strict rationalism, which he applied to theoretical and practical religion alike.

In Formey's view, human beings' extraordinary cognitive capacities were not only the prerequisite for their free will and natural morality. He also considered rationalist reasoning and self-consciousness as means by which human beings – as true philosophers – were able to deduce all these truths about themselves and about God's existence and attributes. As far as Formey was concerned, rationalist reasoning meant deducing truths from individual observations or certain generally valid axioms without letting sensations and passions interfere in this cognitive process. The method of rationalist reasoning could be applied to nearly everything, God's nature and biblical dogma included. In this sense, there were no truths above reason in Formey's view, only truths that could be apprehended more easily via divine revelation than via natural reason. Thus, he considered belief in divine revelation as an epistemological category on the

2. See Sorkin, *The Religious Enlightenment*, p.84, and Gargett, 'Jacob Vernet and "the religious Enlightenment"', p.567.

same level as natural reason; however, the former had the merit of being more straightforward and more comprehensible to the majority of people. This is what distinguished Formey's Christian philosophy from Vernet's notion of the compatibility between reason and faith, but also from deist rationalism. Formey never held that reason outplayed revelation, although some of his claims, such as the complete rationality of God's existence and the natural morality of human beings, were also promoted by deists.

Formey's rationalism was inspired by his reading of Christian Wolff. In general, the adherence of Formey and of most of the Prussian Huguenots to Wolffianism is what distinguished them from other parts of the Huguenot diaspora and Calvinist regions. Not only were Crousaz and Boullier hostile towards Leibniz's and Wolff's philosophical claims, the theologians and pastors in Geneva were also indifferent about Wolff's philosophy or had strong reservations about it.[3] As far as Formey's Wolffianism was concerned, it consisted mainly of his appropriation of Wolff's concept of a hierarchical system of knowledge. Like Wolff, Formey considered philosophy as one universal science, the subdisciplines of which built upon one another and, ultimately, were rooted in metaphysics. The rigour of the demonstrative method, the application of which Wolff had cultivated in all parts of philosophy, also constituted the backbone of most of Formey's truth claims. Additionally, he adopted several fundamental elements of Wolff's metaphysics and moral philosophy: the theories of the *nexus rerum* and the world's perfection, the rejection of the physico-theological proof of God's existence and the intellectualist approach to natural law.

Formey appropriated Wolff's philosophical claims mainly by translating and abridging the latter's writings, but also by reconstructing certain debates in which the latter was involved with his German theological opponents who accused him of irreligion or even atheism. Formey interlaced these debates with the debates that concerned him and his contemporaries, and in which he most often defended religion against freethinkers by applying Wolff's vindication that his rationalist philosophy was not contrary to revealed religion. Hence, in the context of Formey's religious apologetics against the *philosophes*, Wolff's philosophy changed meaning compared with its

---

3. See the remarks on Wolffianism in several letters that Formey received from Geneva: Peschier to Formey (20.2.1742 and 8.1.1751) and Cramer to Formey (30.12.1746), in *Lettres de Genève*, p.20, 291 and 168.

original context: it became a weapon against scepticism, materialism and irreligion alike, whereas it had been accused of fuelling precisely these phenomena by many German theologians in the first quarter of the eighteenth century. However, Formey did not embrace all of Wolff's positions fully and unconditionally. Instead, he took the internal evolution of Wolffian philosophy into account as well as other competing theories. Moreover, it is remarkable that he often drew on Leibniz's considerations on certain issues rather than Wolff's, although the latter had adopted and developed many of the former's theories. This might be due to the greater authority that Leibniz enjoyed internationally compared with Wolff.

Although Formey owed much to German philosophy, he was at least as much concerned with the philosophy of the French-speaking world. It is too narrow-minded to suggest that Formey exclusively embraced the ideas of the German *Aufklärung* because this enabled him to establish a moderate counterbalance to the new, often irreligious philosophy that was reaching all of Europe from France.[4] Not only is it difficult to distinguish neatly between the Calvinist and Leibnizian–Wolffian roots of Formey's Christian philosophy and, hence, impossible to locate his thinking squarely in either one of the two intellectual currents, Formey also tried explicitly to combine German philosophy with French philosophy, and French Huguenot philosophy in particular. In several of his academic treatises he was solicitous about depicting a philosophical legacy from Descartes through Leibniz to Wolff. Moreover, in the canon of essential writings of all disciplines that he published in several editions between 1746 and 1756, Formey presented a relatively international selection in which Calvinist texts were dominant in theology and philosophy, and French texts were dominant in literature. He named Wolff, Descartes, Gassendi and Newton as the most influential philosophers of recent centuries, but in logic and metaphysics he highlighted the works of Crousaz, Willem Jacob 's Gravesande, the marquis d'Argens, Malebranche, Locke, Leibniz, Francis Hutcheson, Etienne Bonnot de Condillac and D'Alembert.[5] Therefore, Formey's historical

---

4. This has been suggested by Krauss, 'Ein Akademiesekretär vor 200 Jahren', p.57-58; Fontius, 'Privilegierte Minderheiten', p.27, and Häseler, 'Samuel Formey, pasteur huguenot entre Lumières françaises et *Aufklärung*', p.247.
5. See Formey, *Conseils pour former une bibliothèque peu nombreuse, mais choisie*, 3rd edn (Berlin, Haude & Spener, 1755), p.13-16. See also Annett Volmer, 'Lektüre, Bildung, Wissenskanon: Jean-Henri-Samuel Formeys Ratschläge zum Aufbau

philosophical depictions reveal that the sources of his thought were not confined to Leibniz and Wolff alone.

Formey's Christian philosophy was marked by and coincided with major changes in philosophy that occurred during the course of the eighteenth century. He clearly continued the tradition of emphasising the compatibility between reason and faith that had been established by Leibniz and rationalist Calvinists such as Jaquelot at the end of the seventeenth and beginning of the eighteenth century. He fought the same enemies as them – scepticism about reason and growing irreligion; however, his was a response to a slightly different situation. By the mid-eighteenth century, the relatively vague fear of an assault against Christianity that had animated Leibniz and Jaquelot had become acute: deistic writings proliferated and atheism began to be openly embraced by some, particularly French authors. In Formey's view, however, the most striking difference was that all these views that posed danger to rationalism and religion alike began to leak into broader society. This was mainly due to the popularisation of philosophy through the use of new genres of writing such as the philosophical novel, poetry and pamphlets, which were written in the vernacular,[6] as well as the expansion of the periodical press. Philosophy in the eighteenth century was no longer an exclusive realm inhabited by a few elites at universities and in learned societies. As a result, subversive claims concerning religion, which had existed for a long time in philosophical writing, became very dangerous from the 1730s onwards. In 1764, in his refutation of Rousseau's *Emile*, the *Emile chrétien*, Formey compared the anti-religious writings of the seventeenth century, and the danger they posed, with those that had appeared in his own lifetime. The books of Spinoza, Hobbes and Vanini had been written in such a learned style they were accessible only to erudite men;[7] in contrast, the 'modern unbelievers' were using vulgar language, a pleasing style and fictional genres so their works would be read by those who in Formey's eyes should have been least exposed to their ideas, that is, women, young people and people of a lower social class.[8]

---

einer Privatbibliothek im 18. Jahrhundert', in *The Berlin Refuge 1680-1780*, ed. S. Pott, M. Mulsow and L. Danneberg, p.183-206, esp. 205-206.
6. See Van Damme, '"Philosophe"/Philosopher', p.157-58.
7. See Formey, *Emile chrétien*, vol.1, p.vi.
8. See Formey, *Emile chrétien*, vol.1, p.viii. Compare with similar claims in his 'Sur les rapports entre le savoir, l'esprit, le génie et le goût', in *Mémoires de l'Académie*

Formey's Christian philosophy was a reply to the expansion of philosophy beyond the realm of scholarly erudition in general and the spread of dangerous philosophy in particular. His strategy to counter this development seems to have been twofold: he tried to stabilise professional philosophy by adhering to strictly metaphysical deliberations in his academic lettres treatises, and, at the same time, he tried to disseminate the rationality of theological beliefs and dogma via popular philosophical writings, sermons and public debate. The difference between Formey's academic and popular writings often lay in the different emphasis he put on the notion of a perfect compatibility between reason and faith. In his academic treatises on God's existence or on free will, he did not bother to draw on revealed truths to make his point because metaphysics was sufficiently intelligible to an audience of trained philosophers. In contrast, Formey perceived the common reader as being unable to follow metaphysical deduction alone and, therefore, he often stressed the superior authority of revelation as a source of knowledge in his sermons and moral philosophical essays. With regard to the different audiences Formey addressed, it is thus possible to speak of a tendency to compartmentalise reason and faith in the sense that his arguments exclusively relied on natural reason when he spoke to professional philosophers, whereas he predominantly referred to revelation to justify his claims in front of popular audiences.

Formey's few attempts to reconcile popular and professional philosophical writing failed, as has become clear in the ambiguous reception of his so-called 'philosophical preaching'. Moreover, his attempt to make Wolff's rationalist Christian philosophy known to a broader public through embellished translations and abridgements also proved less successful; as two of his Huguenot correspondents insinuated, the prose style of the *Belle wolfienne* hardly made Wolff's philosophy more comprehensible to a reader previously unfamiliar with it.[9] From the 1760s at the latest, Formey seems to have become increasingly aware of the irreconcilability of professional and popular philosophy. He deliberately 'desecularised' his popular moral philosophical essays in the follow-up volumes of his *Philosophe chrétien* by reintroducing biblical dogma, and he published a 'scientific'

---

royale des sciences et belles-lettres (1788/1789; Berlin, Decker, 1793), p.371-93 (377-78).

9. See Paul-Emile Mauclerc to Formey (15.2.1741), FF, and Bocquet to Formey (13.3.1741), FF.

equivalent of his *Philosophe chrétien*, namely, his natural-law-based *Principes de morale*. Moreover, he gave up the prose style of his *Belle wolfienne* after the first three volumes and continued the series by merely translating Wolff's treatises. Formey's publication strategies and the reception of his diverse writings, therefore, show how difficult it was to put his ideal concept of philosophy as a universal science of human reason that was applicable to every subject and in every context into practice.

In the second half of the eighteenth century, not only did the realm of philosophical writing expand, but the two main foundations of Formey's philosophical method, rationalism and the systematic character of philosophy, also became increasingly eroded. First, the conviction that rationalism could support and enhance religious belief and morality began to be doubted and mocked, and this put rationalist Christian philosophers under pressure. With respect to Genevan pastors and theologians, Helena Rosenblatt suggests their response to this development was to turn to the sentimentalism promoted in Rousseau's novels and Shaftesbury's sentimentalist philosophy. As a result, reason was no longer predominant in their sermons.[10] In Berlin, in the generation that followed Formey's, feeling and passion were also reinstated within religion. In the history of the local Huguenot colony written by the pastors and scholars Jean-Pierre Erman and Frédéric Reclam in the 1780s and 1790s, it was claimed that religion was made for the heart and that reason was not able to enlighten anybody about anything concerning religious matters if it was not linked to feeling.[11] Formey, however, stuck to the rationalism that had been dominant from the late seventeenth to the mid-eighteenth century and that was the foundation of his Christian philosophy.

Second, the concept of a philosophical system in which every truth claim was deduced from certain basic principles was under attack. Around 1750, the 'anti-system debate', which had been fuelled by English experimental philosophy, culminated in France in the publications of Condillac and D'Alembert, who denounced the

---

10. See Helena Rosenblatt, 'The Christian Enlightenment', in *Enlightenment, reawakening and revolution*, ed. S. J. Brown and T. Tackett, p.283-301 (292-95).
11. See Jean-Pierre Erman and Pierre Chrétien Frédéric Reclam, *Mémoires pour servir à l'histoire des réfugiés françois dans les Etats du roi*, 9 vols (Berlin, Jasperd, 1782-1799), vol.3. p.104-105, quoted in Rosen Prest, *L'Historiographie des huguenots*, p.222.

hypothetical and abstract nature of philosophical systems.[12] Formey refuted Condillac's *Traité des systèmes*, which also criticised, among others, Leibniz and Wolff.[13] Since 1765, Merian, Formey's colleague at the Academy, had repeatedly made a plea against systematic metaphysics, which in his view had caused philosophical sectarianism and dogmatic enthusiasm among German philosophers.[14] Rather, Merian advocated the pursuit of an eclectic philosophy. His criticism was mainly targeted at Wolffianism, but also at Kantianism, which was in the ascendant in late-eighteenth-century Germany.[15] Although, during the later part of his career and after Wolff's death in particular, Formey denied ever having been a zealous partisan of Wolffianism, he never renounced the systematic philosophical method and trust in metaphysics as a fundamental science that he had adopted from Wolff.[16]

During Formey's lifetime, therefore, philosophy became less rationalist and more eclectic, yet it did not emancipate itself from theology. On the contrary, the notion of philosophy as a foundational discipline that engaged with religious questions continued to be widely accepted in the eighteenth century. The number of philosophers and writers who contested this notion and promoted the idea of an independent and secular philosophy remained relatively small, although they attracted much attention in European public debates. Most prominently, this was the case for *philosophes* like Diderot, D'Alembert and Voltaire whose opinions Formey regularly rejected by reflecting on the notion of the compatibility of natural and revealed truths in philosophy. Formey's confrontations with the *philosophes* have led past historians to view this notion as nothing more than an apologetic tool or a means to halt secularisation. This view obfuscated the fact that the compatibility of reason and faith was an established

---

12. See Peter R. Anstey, 'The principled Enlightenment: Condillac, D'Alembert and principle minimalism', in *Rethinking the Enlightenment: between history, philosophy, and politics*, ed. Geoff Boucher and Henry Martyn Lloyd (Lanham, MD, 2018), p.131-50.
13. See 'Article II. Traité des systemes', *Bibliothèque impartiale* 1:1 (1750), 2nd edn (Leiden, Luzac, 1753), p.30-45.
14. See Merian, 'Discours sur la métaphysique', p.467.
15. See Merian, 'Parallèle historique', esp. p.68 and 95. For Merian's defence of eclecticism at the Academy, see also Dumouchel, 'Hommes de nulle secte'.
16. See Formey, 'Discours préliminaire', in *Tableau du bonheur domestique*, p.xv-xvi. Compare with Merian's 'Eloge de Formey', p.59-60. Merian stressed that Formey had resisted becoming a fanatical Wolffian during his early career.

piece of knowledge with a long tradition in Western philosophy that informed most theories in eighteenth-century philosophy. As far as Formey was concerned, it was the self-evident foundation of his considerations in theoretical and practical philosophy as well as in his sermons.

Bibliography

Archival material

Archiv der Berlin-Brandenburgischen Akademie der Wissenschaften (BBAW), Berlin:
I. Historische Abteilung, PAW (1700-1811), Abt. IV, Nr. 12: 'Protokolle bei der Errichtung der neuen Akademie der Wissenschaften 1744-1746'.
I. Historische Abteilung, PAW (1700-1811), Ms C5, vol.1 (1747), I-M 345 ('Discours sur les preuves de l'existence de Dieu') and I-M 346 ('Discours sur les fins de la nature').

Archives de l'Académie des sciences et de l'Institut de France, Paris:
Fonds Maupertuis 43 J, no.121 (Johann Bernhard Merian to Pierre Louis Moreau de Maupertuis).

Biblioteka Jagiellońska, Krakow, Ms Berol.:
Fortunato Bartolomeo de Felice to Formey, CV.
Jean D'Alembert to Formey, CV.
Formey to Suzanne Bonnafous, CV.
Ludwig Martin Kahle to Formey, CV.
Ernst Christoph von Manteuffel to Formey, CV.
Pierre Louis Moreau de Maupertuis to Formey, CV.
Jean Neaulme to Formey, CV.
Johann Gustav Reinbeck to Formey, CV.
Christian Wolff to Formey, CV.

Bibliothèque cantonale et universitaire (BCU), Lausanne, Fonds Crousaz:
Jean-Pierre de Crousaz to Formey.
Formey to Jean-Pierre de Crousaz.

Geheimes Staatsarchiv – Preußischer Kulturbesitz (GStA PK), Berlin-Dahlem:
I. HA Rep. 122, Französisches Koloniedepartement, 7 a II, Nr. 1.
I. HA Rep. 244, Französisch-reformiertes (Ober-)Konsistorium, Nr. 82.

Staatsbibliothek zu Berlin –
Preußischer Kulturbesitz,
Nachlass 218:
Formey to Pierre Louis Moreau
de Maupertuis.
Staatsbibliothek zu Berlin –
Preußischer Kulturbesitz,
Nachlass Formey:
Abraham Bocquet to Formey, FF.
Georg Mathias Bose to Formey,
FF.
Théodore Cabrit to Formey, FF.
Alexandre-Auguste de Campagne
to Formey, FF.
Jacques de Campagne to Formey,
FF.
Balthasar Catel to Formey, FF.
Jean-Pierre de Crousaz to
Formey, D and FF.
Jean-Pierre Erman to Formey, D.
Fortunato Bartolomeo de Felice
to Formey, D and FF.

Jean-Laurent Garcin to Formey,
FF.
Johann Jakob Hentsch to Formey,
D.
Ernst Christoph von Manteuffel
to Formey, D and FF.
Paul-Emile Mauclerc to Formey,
FF.
Guillaume Pelet to Formey, FF.
Jacques Pérard to Formey, FF.

Universitätsbibliothek Basel (UBB):
L Ia 711 (Johann Bernhard
Merian to Jean II Bernoulli).
Universitätsbibliothek Leipzig
(UBL):
Ms 0344 (Ernst Christoph von
Manteuffel to Johann Gustav
Reinbeck).
Ms 0347 (Formey to Ernst
Christoph von Manteuffel).

Primary sources

'I. Histoire de l'Académie royale', *Neuer Büchersaal der schönen Wissenschaften und freyen Künste* 7:2 (1748), p.99-117.

Achard, Antoine, 'Le peu de fruit des prédications', in *Sermons*, 2 vols (Berlin, Decker, 1774), vol.2, p.153-78.

–, 'Sur la liberté', in *Histoire de l'Académie royale des sciences et des belles lettres de Berlin* (1745; Berlin, Haude, 1746), p.91-93.

Algarotti, Francesco, *Il Newtonianismo per le dame: ovvero, dialoghi sopra la luce, i colori e l'attrazione* (Naples [Venice], Pasquali, 1737).

Ancillon, Friedrich, 'Eloge de Jean Bernard Mérian, secrétaire perpétuel de l'Académie', in *Abhandlungen der königlichen preußischen Akademie der Wissenschaften zu Berlin* (1804-1811; Berlin, Realschulbuchhandlung, 1815), p.52-90.

'Article II. Dissertation qui a remporté le Prix [...] sur l'OPTIMISME', *Nouvelle bibliothèque germanique* 18 (1756), p.22-32.

'Article II. Histoire de l'Académie royale des sciences, & c. année MDCCLIII. Troisième extrait', *Nouvelle bibliothèque germanique* 17:2 (1755), p.275-301.

'Article II. Traité des systemes', *Bibliothèque impartiale* 1:1 (1750), 2nd edn (Leiden, Luzac, 1753), p.30-45.

'Article III. Lettre de M** à M*** sur l'eternité des peines', *Bibliothèque germanique* 45 (1739), p.85-101.

'Article V. Vergleichung der Leibnitzischen und Newtonischen Metaphysick […] second extrait', *Nouvelle bibliothèque germanique* 1 (1746), p.84-107.

'Article VI. De l'esprit humain', *Nouvelle bibliothèque germanique* 1:2 (1746), p.325-36.

'Article VI. Discours, qui a remporté le prix de l'Académie de Dijon', *Bibliothèque impartiale* 3:1 (1751), p.250-60.

'Article VI. Sermons sur le mystère de la naissance de J. Christ', *Bibliothèque germanique* 45 (1739), p.125-43.

'Article VI. Vergleichung des Leibnitzischen und Neutonischen Metaphysik', *Journal littéraire d'Allemagne, de Suisse et du Nord* 1:2 (1742), p.373-95.

'Article VII. Oratio dicta à Jacobo Verneti', *Nouvelle bibliothèque germanique* 21 (1757), p.97-111.

'Article VII. Seconde lettre de Mr. F. à Mr. *** sur l'eternité des peines', *Bibliothèque germanique* 46 (1739), p.125-57.

'Article VIII. Défense du systême leibnitien', *Nouvelle bibliothèque germanique* 2:1 (1746), p.85-102.

'Article VIII. Sermons sur divers textes de l'écriture sainte par Samuel Formey', *Bibliothèque germanique* 47 (1740), p.189-208.

'Article IX. Instruction chrétienne', *Nouvelle bibliothèque germanique* 18 (1756), p.153-82.

'Article IX. Piece qui a remporté le Prix sur le sujet des Evenemens fortuits', *Nouvelle bibliothèque germanique* 10 (1752), p.168-204.

'Article IX. Remarques sur l'article concernant la Lettre de M. Gervaise Holmes, qui a été inséré dans le *Journal des savans*', *Bibliothèque impartiale* 5:3 (1752), p.443-46.

'Article XIII. Nouvelles litteraires', *Journal littéraire d'Allemagne, de Suisse et du Nord* 1:2 (1742), p.433-66.

'Article XIV. Nouvelles litteraires', *Bibliothèque germanique* 5 (1723), p.203-41.

'Article XV. Recueil de toutes les pièces', *Nouvelle bibliothèque germanique* 13:1 (1753), p.213-20.

'Article XVI. Elementa', *Nouvelle bibliothèque germanique* 2 (1746), p.186-89.

'Article LXXVIII. Examen philosophique', *Mémoires pour l'histoire des sciences et beaux-arts* (July 1755, issue 2), p.1733-56.

Augustine of Hippo, *De natura boni contra Manichaeos* (c.495 AD).

Barbeyrac, Jean, 'Préface du traducteur telle qu'elle étoit dans la première édition MDCCVIII', in *Sermons sur diverses matieres importantes, par Mr Tillotson archevêque de Cantorberi, traduit de l'anglois par Jean Barbeyrac*, 6 vols (Amsterdam, Humbert, 1744), vol.2, p.v-xlviii.

Baudisson, abbé, *Essai sur l'union du christianisme avec la philosophie, ou l'on expose les progrès de la philosophie dans les siecles modernes, pour en conclure que les plus grands philosophes ont été soumis à la religion, & que la religion a* rendu les plus grands services à la philosophie (Paris, n.n., 1787).

Bayle, Pierre, *Continuation des pensées diverses, écrites à un docteur de Sorbonne à l'occasion de la comète qui parut au mois de decembre 1680, ou Réponse à plusieurs dificultez que Monsieur *** a proposées à l'auteur*, 2 vols (Rotterdam, Leers, 1705).

–, 'Simonides', in *Dictionnaire historique et critique*, 5th edn, 4 vols (Amsterdam, Compagnie des libraires, 1740), vol.4, p.208-15, *The ARTFL Project*, https://artfl-project.uchicago.edu/content/dictionnaire-de-bayle (last accessed 18 July 2023).

Beausobre, Isaac de, and Jacques Lenfant, *Le Nouveau Testament de notre seigneur Jesus-Christ, traduit en françois sur l'original grec, avec des notes literales pour éclaircir le texte*, 2 vols (Amsterdam, Humbert, 1718).

Béguelin, Nicolas de, 'Sur l'indifférence d'équilibre et le principe du choix', in *Nouveaux mémoires de l'Académie royale des sciences et belles-lettres* (1770; Berlin, Voss, 1772), p.247-57.

Bonnet, Charles, *Essai analytique sur les facultés de l'ame* (Copenhagen, Philibert, 1760).

Boullier, David-Renaud, *Essai philosophique sur l'ame des bêtes ou l'on traite de son existence & de sa nature* (Amsterdam, Chauguion, 1728).

–, *Lettres sur les vrais principes de la religion, où l'on examine un livre intitulé La religion essentielle à l'homme: on y a joint une defense des pensées de Pascal contre la critique de Mr. de Voltaire, et trois lettres relatives à la philosophie de ce poëte*, 2 vols (Amsterdam, Catuffe, 1741).

Boyle, Robert, *The Christian virtuoso: showing that by being addicted to experimental philosophy, a man is rather assisted, than indisposed to be a good Christian* (In the Savoy [London], n.n., 1690).

Brucker, Johann Jakob, *Historia critica philosophiae a mundi incunabulis ad nostram usque aetatem deducta*, 5 vols (Leipzig, Breitkopf, 1742-1744).

Castillon, Jean de, 'Recherches sur la liberté de l'homme', in *Mémoires de l'Académie royale des sciences et belles-lettres* (1786-1787; Berlin, Decker, 1792), p.517-33.

Clarke, Samuel, *A Demonstration of the being and attributes of God and other writings*, ed. Ezio Vailati (Cambridge, 1998).

–, *A Discourse concerning the being and attributes of God, the obligations of natural religion, and the truth and certainty of the Christian revelation* (London, Botham & Knapton, 1705).

–, *Traités de l'existence et des attributs de Dieu: des devoirs de la religion naturelle et des verités de la religion chrétienne, traduit de l'anglois par M. Ricotier* (1717), 2nd edn, 3 vols (Amsterdam, Bernard, 1727-1728).

Correspondance passive de Formey, Antoine-Claude Briasson et Nicolas-Charles-Joseph Trublet: lettres adressées à Jean-Henri-Samuel Formey (1739-1770), ed. Martin Fontius, Rolf Geissler and Jens Häseler (Paris, 1996).

Crousaz, Jean-Pierre de, *Commentaire sur la traduction en vers de Mr. l'abbé Du Resnel de l'Essai de M. Pope sur l'homme* (Geneva, Pelissari, 1738).

–, *De l'esprit humain, substance differente du corps, active, libre, immortelle: vérités que la raison démontre, et que la révélation met au-dessus de tout doute* (Basle, Christ, 1741).

–, *Examen de l'essai de Mr. Pope sur l'homme* (Lausanne, Bousquet, 1737).

–, *Examen du pyrrhonisme ancien et moderne* (The Hague, Hondt, 1733).

–, *Réflexions sur l'ouvrage intitulé 'La Belle wolfienne' auxquelles on a joint plusieurs éclaircissemens sur le Traité de l'esprit humain* (Lausanne and Geneva, Bousquet, 1743).

Crusius, Christian August, *Entwurf der nothwendigen Vernunft-Wahrheiten, wiefern sie den zufälligen entgegen gesetzet werden*, 2nd edn (Leipzig, Gleditsch, 1753).

D'Alembert, Jean, 'Fortuit, (Métaphys.)', in *Encyclopédie, ou Dictionnaire raisonné des sciences, des arts et des métiers, etc.*, ed. Denis Diderot and Jean D'Alembert, vol.7 (Paris, Briasson et al., 1757), p.204-205.

–, 'Fortune, s.m. (Morale)', in *Encyclopédie, ou Dictionnaire raisonné des sciences, des arts et des métiers, etc.*, ed. Denis Diderot and Jean D'Alembert, vol.7 (Paris, Briasson et al., 1757), p.205-206.

–, 'Optimisme, s.m. (Phil.)', in *Encyclopédie, ou Dictionnaire raisonné des sciences, des arts et des métiers, etc.*, ed. Denis Diderot and Jean D'Alembert, vol.11 (Neufchâtel, Faulche, 1765), p.517.

–, and Denis Diderot, 'Discours préliminaire des éditeurs', in *Encyclopédie, ou Dictionnaire raisonné des sciences, des arts et des métiers, etc.*, ed. Denis Diderot and Jean D'Alembert, vol.1 (Paris, Briasson et al., 1751), p.i-xlv.

–, 'Explication détaillée du système des connoissances humaines', in *Encyclopédie, ou Dictionnaire raisonné des sciences, des arts et des métiers, etc.*, ed. Denis Diderot and Jean D'Alembert, vol.1 (Paris, Briasson et al., 1751), p.xlvii-li.

d'Artis, Gabriel, *Lettre pastorale du plus ancien et plus légitime pasteur de l'eglise françoise de Berlin, à son troupeau, écrite de Londres, à l'occasion et au sujét de la traduction et des notes sur le Nouveau Testament, publiées par M.M. de Beausobre et Lenfant* (Amsterdam, Aux dépens de l'auteur, 1719).

Derham, William, *Physico-theology, or a Demonstration of the being and attributes of God from his works of Creation* (London, Innys, 1713).

Descartes, René, *Les Méditations métaphysiques touchant la première philosophie, nouvelle édition revûë & corigée*, 2 vols (Paris, Huart, 1724).

Des Champs, Jean, *Cinq sermons sur divers textes, expliqués selon la méthode du célèbre Mr. Wolff prononcés devant Sa Majesté la reine de Prusse* (Berlin, Haude, 1740).

–, *Cours abrégé de la philosophie wolffienne, en forme de lettres*, 2 vols (Amsterdam and Leipzig, Arkstee & Merkus, 1743-1747).

Diderot, Denis, *Lettre sur les aveugles, à l'usage de ceux qui voyent*, ed. Yvon Belaval and Robert Niklaus, in *Diderot: œuvres complètes*, vol.4 (Paris, 1978), p.1-107.

–, *Pensées philosophiques* (1746), ed. Robert Niklaus, in *Diderot: œuvres complètes*, vol.2 (Paris, 1975), p.1-61.

Du Châtelet, Emilie Le Tonnelier de Breteuil, marquise, *Institutions de physique* (Paris, Prault, 1740).

Du Resnel Du Bellay, Jean-François, *Les Principes de la morale et du goût, en deux poëmes, traduits de l'anglois de M. du Pope* (Paris, Briasson, 1737).

Emer de Vattel à Jean Henri Samuel Formey: correspondances autour du droit des gens, ed. André Bandelier (Paris, 2012).

Erman, Jean-Pierre, *Mémoire historique sur la fondation du Collège royal françois de Berlin* (Berlin, Starcke, 1789).

–, *Sermon pour le premier jubilé du centénaire de la fondation du Collège royal françois* (Berlin, Starcke, 1789).

–, and Pierre Chrétien Frédéric Reclam, *Mémoires pour servir à l'histoire des réfugiés françois dans les Etats du roi*, 9 vols (Berlin, Jasperd, 1782-1799).

'Examen philosophique', *L'Année littéraire* 5 (1755), p.58-67.

Fabricius, Johann Albert, *Hydrotheologie, oder Versuch durch aufmercksame Betrachtung der Wasser, die Menschen zur Liebe und Bewunderung ihres gütigsten, weisesten, mächtigsten Schöpfers zu ermuntern* (Hamburg, König & Richter, 1730).

Fénelon, François de Salignac de La Mothe, *Œuvres philosophiques, premiere partie: demonstration de l'existence de Dieu, tirée de l'art de la nature. Seconde partie: demonstration de l'existence de Dieu, et de ses attributs, tirée des preuves purement intellectuelles, et de l'idée de l'infini mesme* (Paris, Delaulne, 1718).

Fontenelle, Bernard Le Bovier de, 'De l'existence de Dieu', in *Œuvres diverses de M. de Fontenelle* (1714), 3rd edn, 3 vols (The Hague, Gosse & Neaulme, 1728), vol.1, p.363-68.

–, *Entretiens sur la pluralité des mondes* (Paris, Blageart, 1686).

Formey, Jean Henri Samuel, *Anti-Emile* (Berlin, Pauli, 1763).

–, *La Belle wolfienne*, 6 vols (The Hague, Le Vier (1-2) and Neaulme (3-6), 1741-1753).

–, *Conseils pour former une bibliothèque peu nombreuse, mais choisie*, 3rd edn (Berlin, Haude & Spener, 1755).

–, *Consolations raisonnables et religieuses* (Yverdon, [Felice], 1768).

–, 'De la conscience', in *Histoire de l'Académie royale des sciences et belles lettres de Berlin* (1751; Berlin, Haude & Spener, 1753), p.3-29.

–, 'Dialéle, (Logique)', in *Encyclopédie, ou Dictionnaire raisonné des sciences, des arts et des métiers, etc.*, ed. Denis Diderot and Jean D'Alembert, vol.4 (Paris, Briasson et al., 1754), p.935.

[–], 'Dieu, (Métaph. & Théol.)', in *Encyclopédie, ou Dictionnaire*

raisonné des sciences, des arts et des métiers, etc.*, ed. Denis Diderot and Jean D'Alembert, vol.4 (Paris, Briasson *et al.*, 1754), p.976-83.
–, *Discours moraux pour servir de suite au Philosophe chrétien*, 2 vols (Leiden, Jasperd, 1764-1765).
–, 'Discours préliminaire', in *Tableau du bonheur domestique, suivi de quelques discours sur des vérités intéressantes de la religion et de la morale* (Leiden, Jacqueau, 1766), p.i-lxxii.
–, 'Discours préliminaire sur la vraie piété', in *Le Philosophe chrétien, ou Discours moraux*, 2nd expanded edn, 3 vols (Leiden, E. Luzac, 1752-1755), vol.1, p.v-xxviii.
–, 'Discours sur ces questions: quel est le degré de certitude dont sont susceptibles les preuves tirées de la considération de cet univers pour demontrer l'existence d'une divinité? Et quelle est la meilleure maniere de faire usage de ces argumens a posteriori, pour établir cette importante vérité?', in *Histoire de l'Académie royale des sciences et belles lettres de Berlin* (1765; Berlin, Haude & Spener, 1767), p.435-49.
–, 'Discours sur l'esprit philosophique', in *Le Triomphe de l'évidence*, 2 vols (Berlin, Lange, 1756), vol.2, p.iii-xxiv.
–, *Elementa philosophiae seu medulla wolfiana in usum auditorum* (Berlin, Haude & Spener, 1746).
–, 'Eloge de M. Achard', in *Nouveaux mémoires de l'Académie royale des sciences et belles-lettres* (1772; Berlin, Voss, 1774), p.58-68.
–, 'Eloge de M. La Croze', in *Eloges des académiciens de Berlin et de divers autres savans*, 2 vols (Berlin, Bourdeaux, 1757), vol.2, p.63-79.
–, 'Eloge de Monsieur Pelloutier', in *Histoire de l'Académie royale des sciences et belles lettres de Berlin* (1757; Berlin, Haude & Spener, 1759), p.439-47.
–, 'Eloge du Grand-Chancelier de Jariges', in *Nouveaux mémoires de l'Académie royale des sciences et belles-lettres* (1771; Berlin, Voss, 1773), p.41-45.
–, *Emile chrétien, consacré à l'utilité publique*, 4 vols (Berlin, Neaulme, 1764).
[–], 'Entendement, (Logique)', in *Encyclopédie, ou Dictionnaire raisonné des sciences, des arts et des métiers, etc.*, ed. Denis Diderot and Jean D'Alembert, vol.5 (Paris, Briasson *et al.*, 1755), p.718.
–, *Entretiens psychologiques, tirés de l'Essai analytique sur les facultés de l'ame* (Berlin, Pauli, 1769).
[–], 'Epoque, (Logiq.)', in *Encyclopédie, ou Dictionnaire raisonné des sciences, des arts et des métiers, etc.*, ed. Denis Diderot and Jean D'Alembert, vol.5 (Paris, Briasson *et al.*, 1755), p.831-33.
–, *L'Esprit de Julie, ouvrage utile à la société et particulièrement à la jeunesse* (Berlin, Jasperd, 1762).
–, *Essai sur la perfection pour servir de suite au Système du vrai bonheur* (Utrecht [Paris], [Briasson], 1751).
–, 'Essai sur les songes', in *Histoire de l'Académie royale des sciences et belles lettres de Berlin* (1746; Berlin, Haude, 1748), p.317-34.

–, 'Examen de la preuve qu'on tire des fins de la nature, pour établir l'existence de Dieu', in *Histoire de l'Académie royale des sciences et belles lettres de Berlin* (1747; Berlin, Haude, 1749), p.365-84.

–, 'Examen philosophique de la liaison réelle qu'il y a entre les sciences et les mœurs', in *Histoire de l'Académie royale des sciences et belles lettres de Berlin* (1753; Berlin, Haude & Spener, 1755), p.397-416.

–, *Histoire abrégée de la philosophie* (Amsterdam, Schneider, 1760).

–, 'Histoire du renouvellement de l'Académie en MDCCXLIV', in *Histoire de l'Académie royale des sciences et des belles lettres de Berlin* (1745; Berlin, Haude, 1746), p.1-9.

–, *L'Idée, les règles et le modèle de la perfection en trois sermons sur St. Matth. Ch. V. v. 48* (Berlin, Jasperd, 1747).

–, *Lettre de M. Gervaise Holmes à l'auteur de la Lettre sur les aveugles* (Cambridge [Berlin], n.n., 1750).

–, 'Lettre de Mr. Formey à l'auteur de ce journal au sujet de l'éloge historique de Mr. Boullier', *Journal encyclopédique* 3 (1761), p.122-38.

–, *Lettres sur la prédication* (Berlin, Bourdeaux, 1753).

–, 'Lettre XLIII. A Mr. le P. G. le F. du 23 octobre 1759' and 'Lettre XLIV. A Mr. le P. G. le F. du 30 octobre 1759', in *Lettres sur l'état présent des sciences et des mœurs* 2 (July-December 1759) (Berlin, Haude & Spener, 1760), p.257-88.

–, *Mélanges philosophiques*, 2 vols (Leiden, E. Luzac, 1754).

–, 'Notice de mes ouvrages', in *Conseils pour former une bibliothèque peu nombreuse mais choisie*, 3rd edn (Berlin, Haude & Spener, 1755), p.104-22.

–, 'Nouvelles considérations sur l'union des deux substances dans l'homme, ou sur le commerce de l'âme et du corps', in *Histoire de l'Académie royale des sciences et belles lettres de Berlin* (1764; Berlin, Haude & Spener, 1766), p.364-73.

–, *Pensées raisonnables opposées aux Pensées philosophiques* (Berlin, Voss, 1749).

–, *Le Philosophe chrétien, ou Discours moraux*, 1st edn, 4 vols (Leiden, E. Luzac, 1750-1757).

–, *Le Philosophe chrétien, ou Discours moraux*, 2nd expanded edn, 3 vols (Leiden, E. Luzac, 1752-1755).

–, *Le Philosophe chrétien, ou Discours moraux*, 3rd edn, 4 vols (Leiden, E. Luzac, 1755-1758).

–, *Le Philosophe payen, ou Pensées de Pline, avec un commentaire littéraire et moral*, 3 vols (Leiden, E. Luzac, 1759).

[–], 'Préface', in *Histoire de l'Académie royale des sciences et des belles lettres de Berlin* (1745; Berlin, Haude, 1746), sig.[)(4]-)()(2v.

–, 'Les preuves de l'existence de Dieu, ramenées aux notions communes', in *Histoire de l'Académie royale des sciences et belles lettres de Berlin* (1747; Berlin, Haude, 1749), p.341-64.

–, *Principes de morale appliqués aux déterminations de la volonté*, 2 vols (Leiden, E. Luzac, 1765).

–, *Principes de morale déduits de l'usage des facultés de l'entendement humain*, 2 vols (Leiden, E. Luzac, 1762).

–, *Principes du droit de la nature et des gens: extrait du grand ouvrage latin de Mr. de Wolff*, 2 vols (Amsterdam, Rey, 1758).

–, *Recherches sur les elémens de la matière* (n.p., n.n., 1747).

–, 'Réflexions sur la liberté', in *Histoire de l'Académie royale des sciences et belles lettres de Berlin* (1748; Berlin, Haude & Spener, 1750), p.334-55.

–, *Sendschreiben an S. Eminenz den hochwürdigsten Herrn, Herrn Angelus Maria Quirini [...] in welchem erwiesen wird, daß D. Luther gelehrter und tugendhafter und folglich zur Besserung der Kirche tüchtiger gewesen sei, als die Kardinäle seiner Zeit* (Berlin, Voss, 1749).

–, *Sermons sur divers textes de l'écriture sainte* (Berlin, Michaelis, 1739).

–, *Souvenirs d'un citoyen*, 2 vols (Berlin, La Garde, 1789).

–, 'Sur la loi naturelle', in *Histoire de l'Académie royale des sciences et des belles lettres* (1745; Berlin, Haude, 1746), p.102-103.

–, 'Sur les rapports entre le savoir, l'esprit, le génie et le goût', in *Mémoires de l'Académie royale des sciences et belles-lettres* (1788/1789; Berlin, Decker, 1793), p.371-93.

–, *Systeme du vrai bonheur* (Utrecht [Paris], [Briasson], 1751).

–, *Le Triomphe de l'évidence*, 2 vols (Berlin, Lange, 1756).

[–], *La Vraye Théorie de la fortune, avec les conséquences qui en résultent* (Berlin, Haude & Spener, 1751).

'Fortune, s.f.', in *Dictionnaire universel françois et latin*, 5 vols (Paris, Delaulne *et al.*, 1721), vol.2, p.1939-43.

Frederick II of Prussia, *De la littérature allemande, des defauts qu'on peut lui reprocher, quelles en sont les causes, et par quels moyens on peut les corriger* (1780), in *Œuvres de Frédéric le Grand*, ed. Johann Preuss, vol.7 (Berlin, 1847), p.103-40, http://friedrich.uni-trier.de/fr/oeuvres/7/toc/ (last accessed 12 July 2023).

Freye Urtheile und Nachrichten zum Aufnehmen der Wissenschaften und der Historie überhaupt. XVI. Stück, Hamburg, Freytags, den 24. Februar 1747.

Freymüthige Nachrichten von neuen Büchern, und andern zur Gelehrtheit gehörigen Sachen 11 (1754).

Gedike, Friedrich, 'Über Berlin, von einem Fremden', *Berlinische Monatsschrift* 2 (1783), p.439-66.

–, 'Über Berlin, von einem Fremden', *Berlinische Monatsschrift* 3 (1784), p.268-81.

Gottsched, Johann Christoph, *Briefwechsel unter Einschluß des Briefwechsels von Luise Adelgunde Victorie Gottsched*, ed. Detlef Döring *et al.*, vol.6 (Berlin, 2012).

–, *Briefwechsel unter Einschluß des Briefwechsels von Luise Adelgunde Victorie Gottsched*, ed. Detlef Döring *et al.*, vol.7 (Berlin, 2013).

[–], *Grund-Riß einer Lehr-Arth ordentlich und erbaulich zu predigen nach dem Inhalt der Königlichen Preussischen allergnädigsten Cabinets-Ordre vom 7. Martii 1739 entworffen* (Berlin, Haude, 1740).

Huber, Marie, *La Religion essentielle à l'homme, distinguée de ce qui n'en est que l'accessoire* (Amsterdam, Wetsteins & Smith, 1738).

–, *Le Sisteme des anciens et des modernes, concilié par l'exposition des sentimens differens de quelques théologiens sur l'état des âmes séparées des corps, en quatorze lettres, nouvelle édition, augmentée par des notes & quelques pièces nouvelles* (Amsterdam, Wetsteins & Smith, 1733).

Jaquelot, Isaac, *Conformité de la foi avec la raison, ou Défense de la religion, contre les principales difficultez répandues dans le Dictionaire historique et critique de Mr. Bayle* (Amsterdam, Desbordes & Pain, 1705).

–, *Dissertations sur l'existence de Dieu, où l'on démontre cette verité par l'histoire universelle de la première antiquité du monde, par la refutation du systeme d'Epicure et de Spinosa, par les characteres de divinité qui se remarquent dans la religion des Juifs, et dans l'etablissement du christianisme* (The Hague, Foulque, 1697).

Jariges, Philippe Joseph de, 'Examen du Spinozisme et des objections de Monsieur Bayle sur ce système', in *Histoire de l'Académie royale des sciences et des belles lettres* (1745; Berlin, Haude, 1746), p.121-42.

–, 'Examen du Spinozisme et des objections de Monsieur Bayle sur ce système: seconde partie', in *Histoire de l'Académie royale des sciences et belles lettres* (1746; Berlin, Haude, 1748), p.295-316.

Journal des sçavans (July 1752).

Kahle, Ludwig Martin, *Examen d'un livre intitulé La Metaphysique de Newton, ou Parallèle des sentimens de Newton & de Leibnitz par Mr. de Voltaire, traduit en françois par Mr. de Gautier Saint-Blancard* (The Hague, Gosse, 1744).

–, *Vergleichung der Leibnitzischen und Neutonischen Metaphysik, wie auch verschiedener anderer philosophischer und mathematischer Lehren beyder Weltweisen angestellet und dem Herrn von Voltaire entgegen gesetzt* (Göttingen, Universitätsbuchhandlung, 1741).

King, William, 'Divine predestination and fore-knowledge, consistent with the freedom of mans will: a sermon preach'd at Christ-Church, Dublin, May 15, 1709', in *An Essay on the origin of evil*, translated by Edmund Law, 3rd edn (Cambridge, Thurlbourn, 1739), p.3-48.

Leibniz, Gottfried Wilhelm, *Essais de théodicée, sur la bonté de Dieu, la liberté de l'homme et l'origine du mal*, 2nd edn (Amsterdam, Mortier, 1714).

Lesser, Friedrich Christian, *Insecto-Theologia, oder Vernunfft- und schrifftmäßiger Versuch wie ein Mensch durch aufmercksame Betrachtung derer sonst wenig geachteten Insecten zu lebendiger Erkänntniß und Bewunderung der Allmacht, Weißheit, der Güte und Gerechtigkeit des grossen Gottes gelangen könnte* (Frankfurt am Main and Leipzig, Blochberger, 1738).

Le Sueur, Achille (ed.), *Maupertuis et ses correspondants: lettres inédites du grand Frédéric, du prince Henri de Prusse, de Labeaumelle* (1896; Geneva, 1971).

'Lettre de Mr. Gervaise Holmes', *Journal des sçavans* 160 (1752), p.516-44.

Lettres de Genève (1741-1793) à Jean Henri Samuel Formey, ed. André Bandelier and Frédéric Eigeldinger (Paris, 2010).

Lettres de l'Angleterre à Jean Henri Samuel Formey à Berlin: de Jean Des Champs, David Durand, Matthieu Maty et d'autres correspondants (1737-1788), ed. Uta Janssens and Jan Schillings (Paris, 2006).

Lettres d'Elie Luzac à Jean Henri Samuel Formey (1748-1770): regard sur les coulisses de la librairie hollandaise du XVIIIe siècle, ed. Hans Bots and Jan Schillings (Paris, 2001).

Locke, John, *An Essay concerning human understanding* (London, Basset & Mory, 1690).

[Ludovici, Carl Günther], 'Wahrheitliebende Gesellschafft', in *Grosses vollständiges Universal-Lexicon alles Wissenschafften und Künste, welche bisher durch menschlichen Verstand und Witz erfunden und verbessert worden*, ed. Johann Heinrich Zedler, 64 vols (Leipzig and Halle, Zedler, 1731-1754), vol.52 (1747), p.947-54.

Malebranche, Nicolas, *Traité de la nature et de la grace* (Amsterdam, Elsevier, 1680).

[Manteuffel, Ernst Christoph von], *Lettre de Mr. P... jurisconsulte de Marbourg à Mlle Espérance de B., contenant la suite du tome second de la Belle wolfienne* (n.p., n.n., 1741).

Maupertuis, Pierre Louis Moreau de, 'Des devoirs de l'académicien', in *Histoire de l'Académie royale des sciences et belles lettres de Berlin* (1753; Berlin, Haude & Spener, 1755), p.511-21.

–, *Essai de cosmologie* (n.p., n.n., 1751).

–, 'Les loix du mouvement et du repos déduites d'un principe metaphysique', in *Histoire de l'Académie royale des sciences et belles lettres de Berlin* (1746; Berlin, Haude, 1748), p.267-94.

Mengin, Ernst (ed.), *Das Recht der Französisch-Reformierten Kirche in Preußen: urkundliche Denkschrift* (Berlin, 1929).

Merian, Johann Bernhard, 'Discours sur la métaphysique', in *Histoire de l'Académie royale des sciences et belles lettres de Berlin* (1765; Berlin, Haude & Spener, 1767), p.450-74.

–, 'Dissertation ontologique sur l'action, la puissance et la liberté', in *Histoire de l'Académie royale des sciences et belles lettres de Berlin* (1751; Berlin, Haude & Spener, 1753), p.459-85.

–, 'Seconde dissertation sur l'action, la puissance et la liberté', in *Histoire de l'Académie royale des sciences et belles lettres de Berlin* (1751; Berlin, Haude & Spener, 1753), p.486-516.

–, 'Eloge de Monsieur Formey', in *Mémoires de l'Académie royale des sciences et belles-lettres* (1797; Berlin, Decker, 1800), p.49-82.

–, 'Examen d'une question concernant la liberté', in *Histoire de l'Académie royale des sciences et belles lettres de Berlin* (1753; Berlin, Haude & Spener, 1755), p.417-30.

–, 'Mémoire sur l'apperception de sa propre existence', in *Histoire de l'Académie royale des sciences et belles lettres de Berlin* (1749; Berlin, Haude & Spener, 1751), p.416-41.

–, 'Mémoire sur l'apperception considérée relativement aux idées, ou Sur l'existence des idées dans l'âme', in *Histoire de l'Académie royale des sciences et belles lettres de Berlin* (1749; Berlin, Haude & Spener, 1751), p.442-77.

–, 'Parallèle historique de nos deux philosophies nationales', in *Mémoires de l'Académie royale des sciences et belles-lettres* (1797; Berlin, Decker, 1800), p.53-96.

Michaelis, Johann David, *Literarischer Briefwechsel*, ed. Johann Gottlieb Buhle, 3 vols (Leipzig, Weidmann, 1794-1796).

Morellet, André, 'Fatalité, (Métaph.)', in *Encyclopédie, ou Dictionnaire raisonné des sciences, des arts et des métiers, etc.*, ed. Denis Diderot and Jean D'Alembert, vol.6 (Paris, Briasson et al., 1756), p.422-29.

[Naigeon, Jacques André, and Claude Yvon], 'Liberté, (Morale)', in *Encyclopédie, ou Dictionnaire raisonné des sciences, des arts et des métiers, etc.*, ed. Denis Diderot and Jean D'Alembert, vol.9 (Neufchâtel, Faulche, 1765), p.462-71.

Nieuwentijt, Bernard, *The Religious philosopher, or the Right way of contemplating the works of the creator*, 3 vols (London, Senex & Taylor, 1718-1719).

Nouvelles pieces sur les erreurs pretendues de la philosophie de Mons. Wolf. Contenant I. Memoire de Mons. Lange, contre cette philosophie. II. Reponse preliminaire d'un auteur anonime a ce memoire. III. Sommaire de la reponse de Mr. Wolf meme avec un avis au lecteur de l'histoire de ce nouveau differend (n.p., n.n., 1736).

Palissot de Montenoy, Charles, *Les Philosophes: comédie, en trois actes, en vers* (Paris, Duchesne, 1760).

Pelloutier, Simon, *Histoire des Celtes, et particulièrement des Gaulois et des Germains, depuis les tems fabuleux, jusqu'à la prise de Rome par les Gaulois*, 2 vols (The Hague, Beauregard, 1740-1750).

'Philosophe', in *Encyclopédie, ou Dictionnaire raisonné des sciences, des arts et des métiers, etc.*, ed. Denis Diderot and Jean D'Alembert, vol.12 (Neuchâtel, Faulche, 1765), p.509-11.

Piece qui a remporté le prix sur le sujet des evenemens fortuits, proposé par l'Academie royale des sciences et belles lettres de Berlin pour l'année 1751, avec les pieces qui ont concouru (Berlin, Haude & Spener, 1751).

Polignac, Melchior de, *Anti-Lucretius sive de deo et natura libri novem: opus posthumum*, 2 vols (Amsterdam, Rey, 1748).

Pope, Alexander, *An Essay on man: in epistles to a friend* (London, Wilford, 1733-1734).

Prémontval, André-Pierre Le Guay

de, *Pensées sur la liberté, tirées d'un ouvrage manuscrit qui a pour titre: Protestations et déclarations philosophiques sur les principaux objets des connoissances humaines* (Berlin and Potsdam, Voss, 1754).

'Prix proposé par l'Académie royale des sciences et belles-lettres de Prusse, pour l'année 1751', *Nouvelle bibliothèque germanique* 5 (1748), p.230-31.

Psychologie, ou Traité sur l'ame, contenant les connoissances, que nous en donne l'expérience, par M. Wolf (Amsterdam, Mortier, 1745).

Ray, John, *The Wisdom of God manifested in the works of the Creation* (London, Smith, 1691).

Recueil de nouvelles pieces philosophiques, concernant le different renouvellè entre Messieurs Joachim Lange […] et Chretien Wolf […]: seconde edition augmentee considerablement (n.p., n.n., 1737).

Recueil de toutes les pièces qui ont été publiées à l'occasion du discours de M. J. J. Rousseau, sur cette question proposée par l'Académie de Dijon pour le prix de l'année 1750, si le rétablissement des sciences & des arts a contribué à épurer les mœurs, 2 vols (Gotha, Mevius, 1753).

Registres de l'Académie juin 1746-août 1786, ed. Berlin-Brandenburgische Akademie der Wissenschaften, https://akademieregistres.bbaw.de/ (last accessed 24 July 2023).

Reinbeck, Johann Gustav, *Bedencken über die der Wolffischen Philosophie von Joachim Langen in seinem kurtzen Abrisse beygemessenen Irrthümer, Commißionswegen aufgesetzt* (Berlin, n.n., 1736).

–, *Erörterung der philosophischen Meynung von der sogenandten HARMONIA PRAESTABILITA, […] aus Liebe zur Wahrheit und zur Verhütung fernerer verworrenen Streitigkeiten, nebst einem nöthigen Vorbericht herausgegeben* (Berlin, Haude, 1737).

–, *Nouveau recueil de quatre sermons, prononcez par Monsieur Reinbeck […], traduits de l'allemand, avec un ajouté de quelques pieces interessantes* (Berlin and Leipzig, Haude, 1741).

–, *Recueil de cinq sermons, prononcez par Monsieur Jean Gustave Reinbeck […]; traduits par un anonyme, & par Mons. Jean Des-Champs* (Berlin, Haude, 1739).

–, *Sermons sur le mystere de la naissance de J.-C., prononcez le premier & le second jour de Noël 1737, […]; traduits par un anonyme, & Messrs. S. Formey & J. Perard, ministres de l'Eglise françoise* (Berlin and Leipzig, Haude, 1738).

Reinhard, Adolf Friedrich, 'Le système de Mr. Pope sur la perfection du monde, comparé à celui de Mr. Leibnitz, avec un examen de l'optimisme, pour satisfaire au problème proposé par l'Académie royale des sciences et belles-lettres de Berlin pour le prix de l'année 1755', in *Dissertation qui a remporté le prix proposé par l'Académie royale des sciences et belles-lettres de Prusse, sur l'optimisme, avec les pièces qui ont concouru* (Berlin, Haude & Spener, 1755), p.3-48.

'Réponse à l'article IX de la *Bibliothèque impartiale*, mois de mai & de juin 1752', *Journal des sçavans* 162 (1752), p.513-17.

Roques, Pierre, *Le Pasteur évangélique, ou Essais sur l'excellence et la nature du St. Ministère, sur ce qu'il exige de ceux qui en sont revêtus, & sur les sources du peu de progrès que fait, aujourd'hui, la prédication de l'Evangile* (Basle, König, 1723).

Rousseau, Jean-Jacques, *Discours sur les sciences et les arts* (1750), ed. François Bouchardy, in *Jean-Jacques Rousseau: œuvres complètes*, vol.3 (Paris 1964), p.1-30.

–, *Lettre de J.-J. Rousseau à Monsieur de Voltaire*, ed. Henri Gouhier, in *Jean-Jacques Rousseau: œuvres complètes*, vol.4 (Paris, 1969), p.1058-67.

Schillings, Jan, 'La correspondance entre Formey et Marchand (1736-1749)', *Lias* 39:2 (2012), p.231-320.

Spinoza, Baruch, *The Collected works of Spinoza*, ed. Edwin Curley, 2 vols (Princeton, NJ, 1985).

Stolzenberg, Jürgen, *et al.* (ed.), *Briefwechsel zwischen Christian Wolff und Ernst Christoph von Manteuffel 1738 bis 1748: historisch-kritische Edition in 3 Bänden*, 3 vols (Hildesheim, 2019).

Sulzer, Johann Georg, 'Explication d'un paradoxe psychologique: que non seulement l'homme agit & juge quelquefois sans motifs & sans raison apparentes, mais même malgré des motifs pressans & des raisons convainquantes', in *Histoire de l'Académie royale des sciences et belles lettres de Berlin* (1759; Berlin, Haude & Spener, 1766), p.433-50.

Vattel, Emer de, *Défense du système leibnitien contre les objections et les imputations de Mr. de Crousaz* (Leiden, Luzac, 1741).

Vernet, Jacob, *Instruction chrétienne, divisée en cinq volumes*, 2nd edn, 5 vols (Geneva, Gosse, 1756).

Voltaire, *Candide, ou De l'optimisme*, ed. René Pomeau, in *The Complete works of Voltaire*, vol.48 (Oxford, 1980).

–, *Eléments de la philosophie de Newton*, ed. Robert L. Walters and William H. Barber, in *The Complete works of Voltaire*, vol.15 (Oxford, 1992).

–, *Poème sur le désastre de Lisbonne*, ed. David Adams and Haydn T. Mason, in *The Complete works of Voltaire*, vol.45A (Oxford, 2009), p.269-358.

Walch, Johann Georg, *Bescheidene Antwort auf Herrn Christian Wolffens Anmerckungen über das Buddeische Bedenken dessen Philosophie betreffendt, welches selbst wieder beigefügt worden*, 2nd edn (Jena, Meyer, 1725).

–, 'Gott', in *Philosophisches Lexicon* (Leipzig, Gleditsch, 1726), p.1339-55.

Wolff, Christian, *Ausführliche Nachricht von seinen eigenen Schriften, die er in deutscher Sprache von den verschiedenen Theilen der Welt-Weißheit heraus gegeben/ auf Verlangen ans Licht gestellet* (2nd edn, 1733), ed. Hans

Werner Arndt, in *Christian Wolff: Gesammelte Werke*, ed. Jean Ecole et al., 2nd edn, section 1, vol.9 (Hildesheim, 2016).

–, *De differentia nexus rerum sapientis, & fatalis necessitatis, nec non systematis harmoniae praestabilatae & hypothesium spinosae luculenta commentatio, in qua simul genuina dei existentiam demonstrandi ratio expenditur et multa religionis naturalis capita illustrantur* (1724), ed. Jean Ecole, in *Christian Wolff: Gesammelte Werke*, ed. Jean Ecole et al., section 2, vol.9 (Hildesheim, 1983).

–, 'Deutliche Erläuterung des Unterscheids unter einer weisen Verknüpfung der Dinge und einer unumgänglichen Nothwendigkeit/ desgleichen unter der Meinung von der vorherbestimmten Harmonie und den Lehrsätzen des Spinozens', in *Sammlung der Wolffischen Schutzschrifften, welche zu der Grundwissenschafft gehören*, ed. Gottlieb Friedrich Hagen (Halle, Renger, 1739), p.3-198.

–, *Discursus praeliminaris de philosophia in genere / Einleitende Abhandlung über Philosophie im Allgemeinen: historisch-kritische Ausgabe* (1728), ed. Günter Gawlick and Lothar Kreimendahl (Stuttgart-Bad Cannstatt, 1996).

–, *Horae subsecivae marburgenses, quibus philosophia ad publicam privatamque utilitatem aptatur* (1729-1741), ed. Jean Ecole, 3 vols, in *Christian Wolff: Gesammelte Werke*, ed. Jean Ecole et al., section 2, vol.34:1-3 (Hildesheim, 1983).

–, *Oratio de Sinarum philosophia practica / Rede über die praktische Philosophie der Chinesen* (1721/1726), ed. Michael Albrecht (Hamburg, 1985).

–, *Philosophia moralis sive Ethica, methodo scientifica pertractata* (1750-1753), ed. Jean Ecole et al., 5 vols, in *Christian Wolff: Gesammelte Werke*, ed. Jean Ecole et al., section 2, vol.12-16 (Hildesheim, 1970-1973).

–, *Philosophia practica universalis, methodo scientifica pertractata*, vol.1 (1738), ed. Winfried Lenders, in *Christian Wolff: Gesammelte Werke*, ed. Jean Ecole et al., section 2, vol.10 (Hildesheim, 1971).

–, *Philosophia prima sive Ontologia, methodo scientifica pertractata, qua omnis cognitionis humanae principia continentur* (2nd edn, 1736), ed. Jean Ecole, in *Christian Wolff: Gesammelte Werke*, ed. Jean Ecole et al., 4th edn, section 2, vol.3 (Hildesheim 2011).

–, *Psychologia empirica, methodo scientifica pertractata, qua ea, quae de anima humana indubia experientiae fide constant, continentur* (2nd edn, 1738), ed. Jean Ecole, in *Christian Wolff: Gesammelte Werke*, ed. Jean Ecole et al., section 2, vol.5 (Hildesheim, 1968).

–, *Psychologia rationalis, methodo scientifica pertractata, qua ea, quae de anima humana indubia experientiae fide innotescunt, per essentiam et naturam animae explicantur* (2nd edn, 1740), ed. Jean Ecole, in *Christian Wolff: Gesammelte Werke*, ed. Jean Ecole et al., 2nd edn, section 2, vol.6 (Hildesheim, 1994).

–, *Theologia naturalis, methodo scientifica pertractata: pars prior, integrum systema complectens, qua existentia et attributa Dei a posteriori demonstrantur* (2nd edn, 1739), ed. Jean Ecole, in *Christian Wolff: Gesammelte Werke*, ed. Jean Ecole *et al.*, section 2, vol.7.1 (Hildesheim, 1978).

–, *Theologia naturalis, methodo scientifica pertractata: pars posterior qua existentia et attributa Dei ex notione entis perfectissimi et natura animae demonstrantur* (2nd edn, 1741), ed. Jean Ecole, in *Christian Wolff: Gesammelte Werke*, ed. Jean Ecole *et al.*, section 2, vol.8 (Hildesheim, 1980).

–, *Vernünfftige Gedancken von den Absichten der natürlichen Dinge* (2nd edn, 1726), ed. Hans Werner Arndt, in *Christian Wolff: Gesammelte Werke*, ed. Jean Ecole *et al.*, section 1, vol.7 (Hildesheim, 1980).

–, *Vernünfftige Gedancken von der Menschen Thun und Lassen, zu Beförderung ihrer Glückseeligkeit* (4th edn, 1733), ed. Hans Werner Arndt, in *Christian Wolff: Gesammelte Werke*, ed. Jean Ecole *et al.*, section 1, vol.4 (Hildesheim, 1976).

–, *Vernünfftige Gedancken von Gott, der Welt und der Seele des Menschen, auch allen Dingen überhaupt* (11th edn, 1751), ed. Charles A. Corr, in *Christian Wolff: Gesammelte Werke*, ed. Jean Ecole *et al.*, section 1, vol.2 (Hildesheim, 1983).

–, *Der Vernünfftigen Gedancken von Gott, der Welt und der Seele des Menschen, auch allen Dingen überhaupt, anderer Theil, bestehend in ausführlichen Anmerckungen* (4th edn, 1740), ed. Charles A. Corr, in *Christian Wolff: Gesammelte Werke*, ed. Jean Ecole *et al.*, section 1, vol.3 (Hildesheim, 1983).

–, 'Vorbericht von der Welt-Weisheit', in *Vernünfftige Gedancken von den Kräften des menschlichen Verstandes und ihrem richtigen Gebrauche in Erkäntniss der Wahrheit* (14th edn, 1754), ed. Hans Werner Arndt, in *Christian Wolff: Gesammelte Werke*, ed. Jean Ecole *et al.*, 4th edn, section 1, vol.1 (Hildesheim, 2006), p.115-22.

–, 'Wie fern man aus der Ordnung der Natur beweisen könne, daß ein Gott seye', in *Gesammelte kleine philosophische Schriften, welche meistens aus dem Lateinischen übersezt, vierter Theil* (1739), in *Christian Wolff: Gesammelte Werke*, ed. Jean Ecole *et al.*, section 1, vol.21:4 (Hildesheim, 1981), p.233-75.

Yvon, Claude, *Accord de la philosophie avec la religion, ou Histoire de la religion, divisée en XII époques* (Paris, Valade, 1782).

Ziegra, Christian (ed.), *Sammlung der Streitschriften über die Lehre von der besten Welt, und verschiedene damit verknüpfte wichtige Wahrheiten, welche zwischen dem Verfasser der im Jahr 1755 von der Akademie zu Berlin gekrönten Schrift vom Optimismo, und einigen berühmten Gelehrten gewechselt worden* (Rostock and Wismar, Berger & Boedner, 1759).

Secondary sources

Aarsleff, Hans, 'The Berlin Academy under Frederick the Great', *History of the human sciences* 2:2 (1989), p.193-207.

Adams, Robert Merrihew, 'Justice, happiness, and perfection in Leibniz's City of God', in *New essays on Leibniz's Theodicy*, ed. Larry M. Jorgensen and Samuel Newlands (Oxford, 2014), p.197-217.

–, *Leibniz: determinist, theist, idealist* (New York, 1994).

Ahnert, Thomas, 'Newtonianism in early Enlightenment Germany, c. 1720 to 1750: metaphysics and the critique of dogmatic philosophy', *Studies in history and philosophy of science* 35:3 (2004), p.471-91.

–, *The Moral culture of the Scottish Enlightenment, 1690-1805* (New Haven, CT, 2014).

–, 'Newton in the German-speaking lands', in *The Reception of Isaac Newton in Europe*, ed. Helmut Pulte and Scott Mandelbrote, 3 vols (London, 2019), vol.1, p.41-58.

–, 'Pleasure, pain and punishment in the early Enlightenment: German and Scottish debates', *Jahrbuch für Recht und Ethik / Annual review of law and ethics* 12 (2004), p.173-88.

–, *Religion and the origins of the German Enlightenment: faith and the reform of learning in the thought of Christian Thomasius* (Rochester, NY, 2006).

Albertan-Coppola, Sylviane, 'Présentation et état de recherche', *Dix-huitième siècle* 34 (2002), special issue: *Christianisme et Lumières*, ed. Sylviane Albertan-Coppola and Antony McKenna, p.5-9.

Albrecht, Michael, 'Einleitung', in *Die natürliche Theologie bei Christian Wolff*, ed. Michael Albrecht (Hamburg, 2011), p.9-16.

–, 'Die Tugend und die Chinesen: Antworten von Christian Wolff auf die Frage zum Verhältnis von Religion und Moral', in *Nuovi studi sul pensiero di Christian Wolff*, ed. Sonia Carboncini (Hildesheim, 1992), p.239-62.

Aner, Karl, *Die Theologie der Lessingzeit* (Hildesheim, 1964).

Anstey, Peter R., 'The principled Enlightenment: Condillac, D'Alembert and principle minimalism', in *Rethinking the Enlightenment: between history, philosophy, and politics*, ed. Geoff Boucher and Henry Martyn Lloyd (Lanham, MD, 2018), p.131-50.

Antognazza, Maria Rosa, 'Arguments for the existence of God: the continental European debate', in *The Cambridge history of eighteenth-century philosophy*, ed. Knud Haakonssen, 2 vols (Cambridge and New York, 2006), vol.2, p.731-48.

–, 'Faith and reason', in *The Oxford handbook on Leibniz*, ed. Maria Rosa Antognazza (Oxford and New York, 2018), p.717-34.

–, 'Reason, revelation and arguments for the deity', in *The Routledge companion to eighteenth-century philosophy*, ed. Aaron Garrett (London and New York, 2014), p.145-66.

Artigas-Menant, Geneviève, 'Perspectives', *Dix-huitième siècle* 34 (2002), special issue: *Christianisme et Lumières*, ed. Sylviane Albertan-Coppola and Antony McKenna, p.10-12.

Badinter, Elisabeth, *Les Passions intellectuelles*, 2 vols (Paris, 2010).

Bandelier, André, 'L'encyclopédisme avant l'*Encyclopédie*: attentes genevoises et projet de "Dictionnaire philosophique" de J. H. S. Formey', in *L'Encyclopédie d'Yverdon et sa résonance européenne: contextes, contenus, continuités*, ed. Jean-Daniel Candaux *et al.* (Geneva, 2005), p.55-68.

–, and Christian Sester, 'Science et religion chez quelques correspondants genevois de l'Académie de Berlin', in *L'Encyclopédie d'Yverdon et sa résonance européenne: contextes, contenus, continuités*, ed. Jean-Daniel Candaux *et al.* (Geneva, 2005), p.31-54.

Bartholmèss, Christian, *Histoire philosophique de l'Académie de Prusse depuis Leibniz jusqu'à Schelling, particul. sous Frédéric-le-Grand*, 2 vols (Paris, 1850).

Beck, Andreas, 'God, Creation, and providence in post-Reformation Reformed theology', in *The Oxford handbook of early modern theology, 1600-1800*, ed. Ulrich L. Lehner, Richard A. Muller and A. G. Roeber (Oxford, 2016), p.195-212.

Berkvens-Stevelinck, Christiane, 'Entre ferveur et scepticisme: une enquête huguenote', in *Scepticisme, clandestinité et libre pensée / Scepticism, clandestinity and free-thinking*, ed. Gianni Paganini, Miguel Benítez and James Dybikowski (Paris, 2002), p.195-212.

–, 'Prediger der französischen Kirche in Berlin', in *Franzosen in Berlin: über Religion und Aufklärung in Preußen – Studien zum Nachlass des Akademiesekretärs Samuel Formey*, ed. Martin Fontius and Jens Häseler (Basel, 2019), p.97-124.

Beutel, Albrecht, 'Causa Wolffiana: die Verteibung Christian Wolffs aus Preußen 1723 als Kulminationspunkt des theologisch-politischen Konflikts zwischen Halleschem Pietismus und Aufklärungsphilosophie', in *Reflektierte Religion: Beiträge zur Geschichte des Protestantismus*, ed. Albrecht Beutel (Tübingen, 2007), p.125-69.

–, 'Evangelische Predigt vom 16. bis 18. Jahrhundert', *TRE* 27 (1997), p.296-311.

Bianco, Bruno, 'Freiheit gegen Fatalismus: zu Joachim Langes Kritik an Wolff', in *Zentren der Aufklärung*, vol.1: *Halle: Aufklärung und Pietismus*, ed. Norbert Hinske (Heidelberg, 1989), p.111-55.

Birnstiel, Eckart, 'Asyl und Integration der Hugenotten in Brandenburg-Preußen', in *Hugenotten und deutsche Territorialstaaten: Immigrationspolitik und Integrationsprozesse*, ed. Guido

Braun and Susanne Lachenicht (Munich, 2007), p.139-54.

Bissinger, Anton, 'Zur metaphysischen Begründung der Wolffschen Ethik', in *Christian Wolff 1679-1754: Interpretationen zu seiner Philosophie und deren Wirkung*, ed. Werner Schneiders, 2nd edn (Hamburg, 1986), p.148-60.

Bödeker, Hans Erich, 'Journals and public opinion: the politicization of the German Enlightenment in the second half of the eighteenth century', in *The Transformation of political culture: England and Germany in the late eighteenth century*, ed. Eckart Hellmuth (London, 1990), p.423-45.

Böhm, Manuela, *Sprachenwechsel: Akkulturation und Mehrsprachigkeit der Brandenburger Hugenotten vom 17. bis 19. Jahrhundert* (Berlin and New York, 2010).

–, Jens Häseler and Robert Violet (ed.), *Hugenotten zwischen Migration und Integration: neue Forschungen zum Refuge in Berlin und Brandenburg* (Berlin, 2005).

Brogi, Stefano, *Teologia senza verità: Bayle contro i 'rationaux'* (Milan, 1998).

Bronisch, Johannes, *Mäzen der Aufklärung: Ernst Christoph von Manteuffel und das Netzwerk des Wolffianismus* (Berlin, 2010).

Brooke, John Hedley, *Science and religion: some historical perspectives* (Cambridge and New York, 1991).

Brun, Emmanuelle, 'L'apologétique conciliatrice française et le dialogue de l'Aufklärung chrétienne avec le "parti philosophique"', doctoral dissertation, Université Nice Sophia Antipolis, 2014.

Buchenau, Stefanie, 'Notions directrices et architechtonique de la métaphysique: la critique kantienne de Wolff en 1763', *Astérion* 9 (2011), https://doi.org/10.4000/asterion.2136 (last accessed 12 July 2023).

–, 'Sulzers "Physik der Seele" zwischen Medizin und Philosophie', in *Johann Georg Sulzer: Aufklärung im Umbruch*, ed. Elisabeth Décultot, Philipp Kampa and Jana Kittelmann (Berlin and Boston, MA, 2018), p.36-50.

–, 'Die Teleologie zwischen Physik und Theologie', in *Die natürliche Theologie bei Christian Wolff*, ed. Michael Albrecht (Hamburg, 2011), p.163-74.

Bulman, William J., 'Introduction: Enlightenment for the culture wars', in *God in the Enlightenment*, ed. William J. Bulman and Robert G. Ingram (Oxford, 2016), p.1-41.

Burson, Jeffrey D., *The Culture of enlightening: abbé Claude Yvon and the entangled emergence of the Enlightenment* (Notre Dame, IN, 2019).

–, *The Rise and fall of theological Enlightenment: Jean-Martin de Prades and ideological polarization in eighteenth-century France* (Notre Dame, IN, 2010).

Buschmann, Cornelia, 'Die philosophischen Preisfragen und Preisschriften der Berliner Akademie der Wissenschaften im 18. Jahrhundert', in *Aufklärung in Berlin*, ed. Wolfgang Förster (Berlin, 1989), p.165-228.

Calinger, Ronald S., 'The Newtonian–Wolffian controversy: 1740-1759', *Journal of the history of ideas* 30:3 (1969), p.319-30.

Candaux, Jean-Daniel, 'Roques', in *Dictionnaire des journalistes (1600-1789)*, http://dictionnaire-journalistes.gazettes18e.fr/journaliste/704-pierre-roques (last accessed 17 July 2023).

–, et al. (ed.), *L'Encyclopédie d'Yverdon et sa résonance européenne: contextes, contenus, continuités* (Geneva, 2005).

Caro, Hernan D, 'The best of all possible worlds? Leibniz's optimism and its critics 1710-1755', doctoral dissertation, Humboldt University Berlin, 2014.

Cassirer, Ernst, *Die Philosophie der Aufklärung*, in *Gesammelte Werke, Hamburger Ausgabe*, vol.15 (Hamburg, 2003).

Casula, Mario, 'Die Lehre von der prästabilierten Harmonie in ihrer Entwicklung von Leibniz bis A. G. Baumgarten', in *Akten des II. internationalen Leibniz-Kongresses. Hannover 17.-22. Juli 1972*, ed. Internationaler Leibniz-Kongress, 4 vols (Wiesbaden, 1975), vol.3, p.397-414.

–, 'Die theologia naturalis von Christian Wolff: Vernunft und Offenbarung', in *Christian Wolff 1679-1754: Interpretationen zu seiner Philosophie und deren Wirkung*, ed. Werner Schneiders, 2nd edn (Hamburg, 1986), p.129-38.

Collini, Stefan, Donald Winch and John Burrow, *That noble science of politics: a study in nineteenth-century intellectual history* (Cambridge, 1983).

Crogiez, Michèle, 'Paradoxe', in *Dictionnaire de Jean-Jacques Rousseau*, ed. Raymond Trousson and Frédéric Eigeldinger (Paris, 1996), p.683-85.

Curran, Mark, *Atheism, religion and Enlightenment in pre-revolutionary Europe* (Woodbridge, 2012).

Darnton, Robert, 'Epistemological angst: from encyclopedism to advertising', in *The Structure of knowledge: classifications of science and learning since the Renaissance*, ed. Tore Frängsmyr (Berkeley, CA, 2001), p.53-75.

Daston, Lorraine, and H. Otto Sibum, 'Introduction: scientific personae and their histories', *Science in context* 16:1-2 (2003), p.1-8.

Decker, Christian, *Vom Höfling zum städtischen Handwerker: soziale Beziehungen hugenottischer Eliten und 'gemeiner' Kolonisten in Preußen 1740 bis 1813* (Frankfurt am Main, 2012).

Décultot, Elisabeth, 'Sulzer, ein Aufklärer? Anstatt einer Einleitung', in *Johann Georg Sulzer: Aufklärung im Umbruch*, ed. Elisabeth Décultot, Philipp Kampa and Jana Kittelmann (Berlin and Boston, MA, 2018), p.1-13.

Devillairs, Laurence, 'La voie d'une apologétique rationaliste: de Descartes à Fénelon', in *Apologétique 1650-1802: la nature et la grâce*, ed. Nicolas Brucker (Bern, 2010), p.85-105.

Dieckmann, Herbert, *Le Philosophe: texts and interpretation* (St Louis, MO, 1948).

Dierse, Ulrich, 'Johann Bernhard Merian', in *Ueberweg Grundriss der Geschichte der Philosophie: die Philosophie des 18. Jahrhunderts*, vol.5: *Heiliges Römisches Reich Deutscher Nation, Schweiz, Nord- und Osteuropa*, ed. Helmut Holzhey and Vilem Mudroch (Basle, 2014), p.300-302.

Donato, Clorinda, 'Jean Henri Samuel Formey's contribution to the *Encyclopédie d'Yverdon*', in *Schweizer im Berlin des 18. Jahrhunderts*, ed. Martin Fontius and Helmut Holzhey (Berlin, 1996), p.87-98.

Döring, Detlef, 'Beiträge zur Geschichte der Gesellschaft der Alethophilen in Leipzig', in *Gelehrte Gesellschaften im mitteldeutschen Raum (1650-1820)*, ed. Detlef Döring and Kurt Nowak, vol.1 (Stuttgart, 2000), p.95-150.

Draper, John William, *History of the conflict between religion and science* (New York, 1875).

Duflo, Colas, 'La fin du finalisme: les deux natures – Holmes et Saunderson', *Recherches sur Diderot et sur l'Encyclopédie* 28 (2000), p.107-31.

Dumouchel, Daniel, '"Hommes de nulle secte": éclectisme et refus des systèmes chez Jean Bernard Mérian', *Dialogue: Canadian philosophical review / Revue canadienne de philosophie* 57:4 (2018), p.745-65.

–, 'Johann Georg Sulzer: la psychologie comme "physique de l'âme"', in *Les Métaphysiques des Lumières*, ed. Pierre Girard, Christian Leduc and Mitia Rioux-Beaulne (Paris, 2016), p.171-90.

Duprey, Laura, 'Philosopher dans les ténèbres: la critique des causes finales dans la *Lettre sur les aveugles*', in *L'Aveugle et le philosophe, ou Comment la cécité donne à penser*, ed. Marion Chottin (Paris, 2009), p.107-25.

Ecole, Jean, 'A propos du projet de Wolff d'écrire une "philosophie des dames"', *Studia leibnitiana* 15:1 (1983), p.46-57.

–, 'Des rapports de l'expérience et de la raison dans l'analyse de l'âme ou la *Psychologia empirica* de Christian Wolff', *Giornale di metafisica* 4-5 (1966), p.589-617.

–, 'Introduction de l'éditeur', in C. Wolff, *Theologia naturalis, methodo scientifica pertractata: pars prior, integrum systema complectens, qua existentia et attributa Dei a posteriori demonstrantur* (2nd edn, 1739), ed. Jean Ecole, in *Christian Wolff: Gesammelte Werke*, ed. Jean Ecole *et al.*, section 2, vol.7.1 (Hildesheim, 1978), p.v-cxvi.

–, 'Introduction de l'éditeur', in C. Wolff, *Theologia naturalis, methodo scientifica pertractata: pars posterior qua existentia et attributa Dei ex notione entis perfectissimi et natura animae demonstrantur* (2nd edn, 1741), ed. Jean Ecole, in *Christian Wolff: Gesammelte Werke*, ed. Jean Ecole *et al.*, section 2, vol.8 (Hildesheim, 1980), p.v-lxxix.

Eijnatten, Joris van, 'Reaching

audiences: sermons and oratory in Europe', in *The Cambridge history of Christianity*, ed. Stewart J. Brown and Timothy Tackett, vol.7: *Enlightenment, reawakening and revolution 1660-1815* (Cambridge, 2006), p.128-46.

Euler, Werner, 'Bewusstsein – Seele – Geist: Untersuchungen zur Transformation des Cartesischen "cogito" in der Psychologie Christian Wolffs', in *Die Psychologie Christian Wolffs: systematische und historische Untersuchungen*, ed. Oliver-Pierre Rudolph and Jean-François Goubet (Tübingen, 2004), p.11-50.

Fabian, Gerd, *Beitrag zur Geschichte des Leib-Seele-Problems (Lehre von der prästabilierten Harmonie und vom psychophysischen Parallelismus in der Leibniz–Wolffschen Schule)* (Langensalza, 1925).

Favaretti Camposampiero, Matteo, 'Der psychotheologische Weg: Wolffs Rechtfertigung der Gotteserkenntnis', in *Die natürliche Theologie bei Christian Wolff*, ed. Michael Albrecht (Hamburg, 2011), p.71-96.

Ferrari, Stefano (ed.), *Fortunato Bartolomeo de Felice: un intellettuale cosmopolita nell'Europa dei lumi* (Milan, 2017).

Ferret, Olivier, *La Fureur de nuire: échanges pamphlétaires entre philosophes et antiphilosophes (1750-1770)*, *SVEC* 2007:03.

Fleischmann, Wolfgang Bernard, 'Zum Anti-Lucretius des Kardinals de Polignac', *Romanische Forschungen* 77 (1965), p.42-63.

Fonnesu, Luca, 'Der Optimismus und seine Kritiker im Zeitalter der Aufklärung', *Studia Leibnitiana* 26:2 (1994), p.131-62.

Fontius, Martin, '"Libertas philosophandi" und "siècle de la philosophie": zum geistesgeschichtlichen Standort Formeys', in *Franzosen in Berlin: über Religion und Aufklärung in Preußen – Studien zum Nachlass des Akademiesekretärs Samuel Formey*, ed. Martin Fontius and Jens Häseler (Basel, 2019), p.125-252.

–, 'Privilegierte Minderheiten als Instrument königlicher Kulturpolitik?', in *Französische Kultur: Aufklärung in Preußen*, ed. Martin Fontius and Jean Mondot (Berlin, 2001), p.17-30.

–, 'Zwischen "libertas philosophandi" und "siècle de la philosophie": zum geistesgeschichtlichen Standort Formeys und der zweiten Generation der réfugiés', in *L'Allemagne et la France des Lumières / Deutsche und französische Aufklärung: mélanges offerts à Jochen Schlobach par ses élèves et amis*, ed. Michel Delon and Jean Mondot (Paris, 2003), p.45-68.

–, and Jens Häseler (ed.), *Franzosen in Berlin: über Religion und Aufklärung in Preußen – Studien zum Nachlass des Akademiesekretärs Samuel Formey* (Basel, 2019).

Ford, James Thomas, 'Preaching in the Reformed tradition', in *Preachers and people in the reformations and early modern period*, ed. Larissa Taylor (Leiden and Boston, MA, 2001), p.65-88.

Furniss, Tom, 'Rousseau: enlightened critic of the Enlightenment?', in *The Enlightenment world*, ed. Martin Fitzpatrick *et al.* (New York, 2004), p.596-609.

Gargett, Graham, 'David Boullier: pasteur du Refuge, adversaire des philosophes et défenseur de l'orthodoxie protestante', in *La Vie intellectuelle aux refuges protestants*, ed. Jens Häseler and Antony McKenna (Paris, 1999), p.305-37.

–, 'David-Renaud Boullier et l'orthodoxie éclairée', in *Refuge et désert: l'évolution théologique des huguenots de la révocation à la Révolution française*, ed. Hubert Bost and Claude Lauriol (Paris, 2003), p.157-71.

–, 'Jacob Vernet and "the religious Enlightenment": "rational Calvinism", the pastors of Geneva and the French *philosophes*', *History of European ideas* 40:4 (2014), p.561-97.

Geiger, Ludwig, *Berlin 1688-1840: Geschichte des geistigen Lebens der preußischen Hauptstadt*, 2 vols (Berlin, 1892).

Geissler, Rolf, 'Antoine Achard (1696-1772), ein Prediger und Philosoph in Berlin', in *Schweizer im Berlin des 18. Jahrhunderts*, ed. Martin Fontius and Helmut Holzhey (Berlin, 1996), p.125-36.

–, 'Der Beitrag Formeys zum Enzyklopädismus im 18. Jahrhundert', in *Franzosen in Berlin: über Religion und Aufklärung in Preußen – Studien zum Nachlass des Akademiesekretärs Samuel Formey*, ed. Martin Fontius and Jens Häseler (Basel, 2019), p.293-373.

–, 'Bibliographie des écrits de Jean Henri Samuel Formey', in *La Correspondance de Jean Henri Samuel Formey (1711-1797): inventaire alphabétique*, ed. Jens Häseler (Paris, 2003), p.419-73.

–, 'Formey journaliste: observations sur la collaboration au *Journal encyclopédique* et d'autres journaux européens', in *La Vie intellectuelle aux refuges protestants*, ed. Jens Häseler and Antony McKenna (Paris, 1999), p.137-56.

–, 'Die Hugenotten im literarischen Leben Berlins', in *Hugenotten in Berlin*, ed. Sibylle Badstübner-Gröger and Gottfried Bregulla (Berlin, 1988), p.363-91.

–, 'J.-H.-S. Formey critique des philosophes français: observations sur les rapports entre Wolffianisme et Lumières françaises', in *Transactions of the eighth international congress on the Enlightenment*, ed. H. T. Mason, 3 vols (1992), vol.1, p.507-11.

Goldenbaum, Ursula, 'Der "Berolinismus": die preußische Hauptstadt als ein Zentrum geistiger Kommunikation in Deutschland', in *Aufklärung in Berlin*, ed. Wolfgang Förster (Berlin, 1989), p.339-62.

–, 'Die öffentliche Debatte in der deutschen Aufklärung 1697-1796: Einleitung', in *Appell an das Publikum: die öffentliche Debatte in der deutschen Aufklärung 1697-1796*, ed. Ursula

Goldenbaum, 2 vols (Berlin, 2004), vol.1, p.1-118.

–, 'Das Publikum als Garant der Freiheit der Gelehrtenrepublik: die öffentliche Debatte über den "Jugement de l'Académie royale des sciences et belles lettres sur une lettre prétendue de M. de Leibnitz" 1752-1753', in *Appell an das Publikum: die öffentliche Debatte in der deutschen Aufklärung 1697-1796*, ed. Ursula Goldenbaum, 2 vols (Berlin, 2004), vol.2, p.509-652.

Goldgar, Anne, *Impolite learning: conduct and community in the Republic of Letters, 1680-1750* (New Haven, CT, and London, 1995).

Götze, Jannis, and Martin Meiske (ed.), *Jean Henri Samuel Formey: Wissensmultiplikator der Berliner Aufklärung* (Erlangen, 2016).

Gouhier, Henri, 'La "perfectibilité" selon J.-J. Rousseau', *Revue de théologie et de philosophie* 110:4 (1978), p.321-39.

Gourevitch, Victor, 'Rousseau on providence', *The Review of metaphysics* 53:3 (2000), p.565-611.

Grau, Conrad, 'Die Berliner Akademie der Wissenschaften und die Hugenotten', in *Hugenotten in Berlin*, ed. Sibylle Badstübner-Gröger and Gottfried Bregulla (Berlin, 1988), p.327-62.

–, 'Hugenotten in der Wissenschaft Brandenburg-Preußens Ende des 17. und im 18. Jahrhundert', *Zeitschrift für Geschichtswissenschaft* 34:6 (1986), p.508-22.

Große, Annelie, 'Dossier critique de l'article DIEU, (Métaph. & Théol.) (*Encyclopédie*, t.IV, p.976a-983a)' (2019), in *Edition Numérique Collaborative et CRitique de l'Encyclopédie (ENCCRE)*, http://enccre.academie-sciences.fr/encyclopedie/article/v4-2500-0/ (last accessed 18 July 2023).

–, '"Mother of all sciences" or mere speculation? The justification of metaphysics at the Berlin Academy between 1746 and 1765', in *The Berlin Academy in the reign of Frederick the Great: philosophy and science*, ed. Tinca Prunea-Bretonnet and Peter R. Anstey, Oxford University Studies in the Enlightenment (Liverpool, Liverpool University Press / Voltaire Foundation, 2022), p.39-69.

–, 'The role of reason, experience, and physiology in J. H. S. Formey's *Essay on dreams*', in *The Experimental turn in eighteenth-century German philosophy*, ed. Karin de Boer and Tinca Prunea-Bretonnet (New York, 2021), p.158-80.

–, 'Stranding in the *Encyclopédie*: the case of Samuel Formey's philosophical dictionary, 1742-1747', in *Stranded encyclopedias, 1700-2000: exploring unfinished, unpublished, unsuccessful encyclopedic projects*, ed. Linn Holmberg and Maria Simonsen (Cham, 2021), p.37-71.

Grote, Simon, *The Emergence of modern aesthetic theory: religion and morality in Enlightenment Germany and Scotland* (Cambridge, 2017).

–, 'Review-essay: religion and Enlightenment', *Journal of the history of ideas* 75:1 (2014), p.137-60.

Grunert, Frank, 'Das Recht der Natur als Recht des Gefühls: zur Naturrechtslehre von Johann Jacob Schmauss', *Jahrbuch für Recht und Ethik / Annual review of law and ethics* 12 (2004), p.137-56.

–, and Gideon Stiening, 'Einleitung: Johann Georg Sulzer – Aufklärung zwischen Christian Wolff und David Hume', in *Johann Georg Sulzer (1720-1779): Aufklärung zwischen Christian Wolff und David Hume*, ed. Frank Grunert and Gideon Stiening (Berlin, 2011), p.11-18.

Gumbrecht, Hans Ulrich, and Rolf Reichardt, 'Philosophe, Philosophie', in *Handbuch politisch-sozialer Grundbegriffe in Frankreich 1680-1820*, ed. Rolf Reichardt and Eberhard Schmitt, vol.3 (Munich, 1985), p.7-89.

Gusdorf, Georges, 'L'Europe protestante au siècle des Lumières', *Dix-huitième siècle* 17:1 (1985), p.13-40.

Haakonssen, Knud, 'Academic teaching, social morality, and the science of morals in eighteenth-century Britain', *Jahrbuch für Recht und Ethik / Annual review of law and ethics* 13 (2005), p.137-48.

–, 'Early modern natural law', in *The Routledge companion to ethics*, ed. John Skorupski (London and New York, 2010), p.76-87.

– (ed.), *Enlightenment and religion: rational dissent in eighteenth-century Britain* (Cambridge, 1996).

–, 'German natural law', in *The Cambridge history of eighteenth-century political thought*, ed. Mark Goldie and Robert Wokler (Cambridge, 2006), p.251-90.

–, 'The historiographical vagaries of Enlightenment and religion', in *Enlightenments and religions: 14th C. Th. Dimaras lecture (2009)* (Athens, 2010), p.91-136.

–, *Natural law and moral philosophy: from Grotius to the Scottish Enlightenment* (New York, 1996).

Haase, Erich, *Einführung in die Literatur des Refuge: der Beitrag der französischen Protestanten zur Entwicklung analytischer Denkformen am Ende des 17. Jahrhunderts* (Berlin, 1959).

Hammerstein, Notker, 'Vom Rang der Wissenschaften: zum Aufstieg der philosophischen Fakultät', in *Geschichte als Arsenal: ausgewählte Aufsätze zu Reich, Hof und Universitäten in der Frühen Neuzeit*, ed. Michael Maaser and Gerrit Walther (Göttingen, 2010), p.185-97.

Harnack, Adolf, *Geschichte der Königlich Preussischen Akademie der Wissenschaften zu Berlin*, 3 vols (Berlin, 1900).

Harris, James A., *Of liberty and necessity: the free will debate in eighteenth-century British philosophy* (Oxford, 2005).

Harrison, Peter, 'Myth 24: that religion has typically impeded the progress of science', in *Newton's apple and other myths about science*, ed. Ronald L. Numbers and Kostas Kampourakis (Cambridge and London, 2015), p.199-200.

–, 'Physico-theology and the mixed sciences: the role of theology in early modern natural philosophy', in *The Science of nature in the* seventeenth century: patterns of changes in early modern natural philosophy, ed. Peter R. Anstey and John A. Schuster (Dordrecht, 2005), p.165-83.

–, *The Territories of science and religion* (Chicago, IL, and London, 2015).

Hartweg, Frédéric, 'Frühaufklärung und Orthodoxie im Widerstreit: Dokumente aus der Frühphase der französisch-reformierten Kirche in Berlin', *Recherches germaniques* 16 (1986), p.225-48.

–, 'Le grand Beausobre: Aspekte des intellektuellen und kirchlichen Lebens der ersten Generation des Berliner Refuge', in *Geschichte als Aufgabe: Festschrift für Otto Büsch*, ed. Wilhelm Treue (Berlin, 1988), p.55-82.

–, 'Toleranz, Naturrecht und Aufklärung / Lumières im Berliner Refuge', in *Hugenotten und deutsche Territorialstaaten: Immigrationspolitik und Integrationsprozesse*, ed. Guido Braun and Susanne Lachenicht (Munich, 2007), p.211-29.

Häseler, Jens (ed.), *La Correspondance de Jean Henri Samuel Formey (1711-1797): inventaire alphabétique* (Paris, 2003).

–, 'Entre république des lettres et république des sciences: les correspondances "scientifiques" de Formey', *Dix-huitième siècle* 40:1 (2008), p.93-103.

–, 'Introduction à l'inventaire de la correspondance de Jean Henri Samuel Formey', in *La Correspondance de Jean Henri Samuel Formey (1711-1797): inventaire alphabétique*, ed. Jens Häseler (Paris, 2003), p.9-35.

–, 'Jean Henri Samuel Formey – l'homme à Berlin', in *Les Grands Intermédiaires culturels de la République des Lettres: études et réseaux de correspondances du XVIe au XVIIIe siècle*, ed. Christiane Berkvens-Stevelinck, Hans Bots and Jens Häseler (Paris, 2005), p.413-34.

–, 'Johann Bernhard Merian: ein Schweizer an der Berliner Akademie', in *Schweizer im Berlin des 18. Jahrhunderts*, ed. Martin Fontius and Helmut Holzhey (Berlin, 1996), p.217-28.

–, 'Journaux savants et l'Académie de Berlin: deux acteurs sur le marché de l'information scientifique en Prusse', *Archives internationales d'histoire de science* 63 (2013), p.199-214.

–, 'Samuel Formey, pasteur huguenot entre Lumières françaises et *Aufklärung*', *Dix-huitième siècle* 34 (2002), p.239-47.

–, 'Société anonyme [San]', in *Handbuch der Berliner Vereine und Gesellschaften 1786-1815*, ed. Uta Motschmann (Berlin, 2015), p.5-6.

–, and Albert Meier (ed.), *Gallophobie im 18. Jahrhundert* (Berlin, 2005).

Havens, George R., 'Voltaire, Rousseau and the "Lettre sur la providence"', *Publications of the Modern Language Association of America* 59:1 (1944), p.109-30.

Hellwig, Marion, *Alles ist gut: Untersuchungen zur Geschichte einer Theodizee-Formel im 18. Jahrhundert in Deutschland, England und Frankreich* (Würzburg, 2008).

Herdt, Jennifer, 'Natural law in Protestant Christianity', in *The Cambridge companion to natural law ethics*, ed. Tom Angier (Cambridge, 2019), p.155-78.

Heyd, Michael, *Between orthodoxy and the Enlightenment: Jean-Robert Chouet and the introduction of Cartesian science in the Academy of Geneva* (The Hague, 1982).

Hochstrasser, Tim J., 'The claims of conscience: natural law theory, obligation and resistance in the Huguenot diaspora', in *New essays on the political thought of the Huguenots of the Refuge*, ed. John Christian Laursen (Leiden, 1995), p.15-51.

–, 'The institutionalisation of philosophy in continental Europe', in *The Cambridge history of eighteenth-century philosophy*, ed. Knud Haakonssen, 2 vols (Cambridge and New York, 2006), vol.1, p.69-96.

–, *Natural law theories in the early Enlightenment* (Cambridge, 2000).

Hüning, Dieter, 'Christian Wolffs "allgemeine Regel der menschlichen Handlungen"', *Jahrbuch für Recht und Ethik / Annual review of law and ethics* 12 (2004), p.91-113.

–, 'Christian Wolffs Begriff der natürlichen Verbindlichkeit als Bindeglied zwischen Psychologie und Moralphilosophie', in *Die Psychologie Christian Wolffs: systematische und historische Untersuchungen*, ed. Oliver-Pierre Rudolph and Jean-François Goubet (Tübingen, 2004), p.143-67.

Hunter, Ian, 'The history of philosophy and the persona of the philosopher', *Modern intellectual history* 4:3 (2007), p.571-600.

–, 'Multiple enlightenments: rival Aufklärer at the University of Halle 1690-1730', in *The Enlightenment world*, ed. Martin Fitzpatrick *et al.* (New York, 2004), p.576-95.

–, *Rival enlightenments: civil and metaphysical philosophy in early modern Germany* (Cambridge and New York, 2001).

–, 'The university philosopher in early modern Germany', in *The Philosopher in early modern Europe: the nature of a contested identity*, ed. Conal Condren, Stephen Gaukroger and Ian Hunter (Cambridge and New York, 2006), p.35-65.

–, Stephen Gaukroger and Conal Condren, 'Introduction', in *The Philosopher in early modern Europe: the nature of a contested identity*, ed. Conal Condren, Stephen Gaukroger and Ian Hunter (Cambridge and New York, 2006), p.1-16.

Hunter, Michael, 'Science and heterodoxy: an early modern problem reconsidered', in *Reappraisals of the scientific revolution*, ed. David C. Lindberg and Robert S. Westman (Cambridge, 1990), p.437-60.

Hutton, Sarah, 'Intellectual history and the history of philosophy', *History of European ideas* 40:7 (2014), p.925-37.

Ihalainen, Pasi, 'The Enlightenment sermon: towards practical religion and a sacred national community', in *Preaching, sermons and cultural change in the long eighteenth century*, ed. Joris van Eijnatten (Leiden and Boston, MA, 2009), p.219-60.

Israel, Jonathan, *Democratic Enlightenment: philosophy, revolution, and human rights 1750-1790* (Oxford and New York, 2012).

–, *Enlightenment contested: philosophy, modernity, and the emancipation of man 1670-1752* (Oxford and New York, 2006).

–, *Radical Enlightenment: philosophy and the making of modernity 1650-1750* (Oxford, 2001).

Jacob, Margaret C., *The Secular Enlightenment* (Princeton, NJ, and Oxford, 2019).

Janssens-Knorsch, Uta, 'Jean Deschamps, Wolff-Übersetzer und "Aléthophile français" am Hofe Friedrichs des Großen', in *Christian Wolff 1679-1754: Interpretationen zu seiner Philosophie und deren Wirkung*, ed. Werner Schneiders, 2nd edn (Hamburg, 1986), p.254-65.

–, *The Life and 'Mémoires secrets' of Jean Des Champs, 1707-1767: journalist, minister, and man of feeling* (Amsterdam, 1990).

Jauch, Ursula Pia, *Damenphilosophie & Männermoral, von abbé de Gérard bis marquis de Sade: ein Versuch über die lächelnde Vernunft*, 2nd edn (Vienna, 1991).

Joesten, Klara, *Christian Wolffs Grundlegung der praktischen Philosophie* (Leipzig, 1931).

Kertscher, Hans-Joachim, *'Er brachte Licht und Ordnung in die Welt': Christian Wolff – eine Biographie* (Halle, 2018).

Knobloch, Eberhard, 'Leonhard Euler als Theoretiker', *Berichte und Abhandlungen der Berlin-Brandenburgischen Akademie der Wissenschaften* 13 (2007), p.241-60.

Kors, Alan Charles, *Atheism in France 1650-1729* (Princeton, NJ, 1990).

Krauss, Werner, 'Ein Akademiesekretär vor 200 Jahren: Samuel Formey', in *Studien zur deutschen und französischen Aufklärung*, ed. Werner Krauss (Berlin, 1963), p.53-62.

–, 'La correspondance de Formey', *Revue d'histoire littéraire de la France* 63 (1963), p.207-16.

Krumenacker, Yves (ed.), *Marie Huber: un purgatoire protestant? Essai sur l'état des âmes séparées des corps* (Geneva, 2016).

Kunisch, Johannes, *Friedrich der Grosse: der König und seine Zeit* (Munich, 2004).

Laborie, Lionel, *Enlightening enthusiasm: prophecy and religious experience in early eighteenth-century England* (Manchester, 2016).

Labrousse, Elisabeth, *Pierre Bayle*, 2 vols (Dordrecht, 1963-1964).

–, 'The political ideas of the Huguenot diaspora (Bayle and Jurieu)', in *Church, state, and society under the Bourbon kings*, ed. Richard M. Golden (Lawrence, KS, 1982), p.222-83.

Lachenicht, Susanne, 'Etude comparée de la création et

de la survie d'une identité huguenote en Angleterre et dans le Brandenbourg au XVIIIe siècle', in *L'Identité huguenote: faire mémoire et écrire l'histoire (XVIe-XXIe siècle)*, ed. Philip Benedict, Hugues Daussy and Pierre-Olivier Léchot (Geneva, 2014), p.279-94.

–, *Hugenotten in Europa und Nordamerika: Migration und Integration in der Frühen Neuzeit* (Frankfurt am Main, 2010).

La Harpe, Jacqueline de, *Jean-Pierre de Crousaz et le conflit des idées au siècle des Lumières* (Geneva, 1955).

Laursen, John Christian, 'Impostors and liars: clandestine manuscripts and the limits of freedom of the press in the Huguenot Netherlands', in *New essays on the political thought of the Huguenots of the Refuge*, ed. John Christian Laursen (Leiden, 1995), p.73-100.

–, 'Introduction', in *New essays on the political thought of the Huguenots of the Refuge*, ed. John Christian Laursen (Leiden, 1995), p.1-14.

–, 'Temporizing after Bayle: Isaac de Beausobre and the Manicheans', in *The Berlin Refuge 1680-1780: learning and science in European context*, ed. Sandra Pott, Martin Mulsow and Lutz Danneberg (Leiden and Boston, MA, 2003), p.89-110.

La Vopa, Anthony, 'A new intellectual history? Jonathan Israel's Enlightenment' (2009), in *Enlightenment past and present: essays in a social history of ideas*, Oxford University Studies in the Enlightenment (Liverpool, Liverpool University Press / Voltaire Foundation, 2022), p.99-125.

Léchot, Pierre-Olivier, 'Les peines de l'enfer sont-elles éternelles? Note à propos d'une controverse au sein du protestantisme de langue française durant les Lumières', *Etudes théologiques et religieuses* 89:2 (2014), p.199-224.

Leduc, Christian, 'La métaphysique de la nature à l'Académie de Berlin', *Philosophiques* 42:1 (2015), p.11-30.

Lehner, Ulrich L., *Kants Vorsehungskonzept auf dem Hintergrund der deutschen Schulphilosophie und -theologie* (Leiden, 2007).

Lenders, Winfried, 'Nachwort Philosophia moralis sive Ethica', in Wolff, *Philosophia moralis sive Ethica, methodo scientifica pertractata*, vol.5, ed. Jean Ecole et al., in *Christian Wolff: Gesammelte Werke*, ed. Jean Ecole et al., section 2, vol.16 (Hildesheim, 1973), p.i-xxii.

Le Ru, Véronique, 'De la science de Dieu à la superstition: un enchaînement de l'arbre encyclopédique qui donne à penser', *Recherches sur Diderot et sur l'Encyclopédie* 40-41 (2006), p.67-76, https://doi.org/10.4000/rde.346 (last accessed 12 July 2023).

Levitin, Dmitri, *Ancient wisdom in the age of the new science: histories of philosophy in England, c.1640-1700* (Cambridge, 2015).

Lewendoski, Alexandra,

'Reaktionskette eines Leibnizverständnisses: Clarke, Newton, Voltaire, Kahle', in *Leibnizbilder im 18. und 19. Jahrhundert*, ed. Alexandra Lewendoski (Stuttgart, 2004), p.121-45.

Lifschitz, Avi, 'From the corruption of French to the cultural distinctiveness of German: the controversy of Prémontval's *Préservatif* (1759)', *SVEC* 6 (2007), p.265-90.

–, *Language and Enlightenment: the Berlin debates of the eighteenth century* (Oxford and New York, 2012).

Longo, Mario, 'A "critical" history of philosophy and the early Enlightenment: Johann Jakob Brucker', in *Models of the history of philosophy*, vol.2: *From the Cartesian age to Brucker*, ed. Gregorio Piaia and Giovanni Santinello (Dordrecht, 2011), p.477-577.

Lorenz, Stefan, *De mundo optimo: Studien zu Leibniz' Theodizee und ihrer Rezeption in Deutschland (1710-1791)* (Stuttgart, 1997).

–, 'Theologischer Wolffianismus: das Beispiel Johann Gustav Reinbeck', in *Christian Wolff und die europäische Aufklärung*, ed. Jürgen Stolzenberg, Oliver-Pierre Rudolph and Jean Ecole, 5 vols (Hildesheim and New York, 2007-2010), vol.5, p.103-21.

Lugt, Mara van der, *Bayle, Jurieu, and the Dictionnaire historique et critique* (Oxford, 2016).

McKenna, Antony, 'Les critiques de Bayle au 18e siècle: l'exemple de Jean-Pierre de Crousaz', in *Aufklärung und Aufklärungskritik in Frankreich: Selbstdeutungen des 18. Jahrhunderts im Spiegel der Zeitgenossen*, ed. Johannes Rohbeck and Sonia Asval (Berlin, 2003), p.35-62.

–, 'Deus absconditus: quelques réflexions sur la crise du rationalisme chrétien entre 1670 et 1740', in *Apologétique 1680-1740: sauvetage ou naufrage de la théologie?*, ed. Maria Cristina Pitassi (Geneva, 1991), p.13-28.

–, 'Le dilemme de l'apologétique au XVIIIe siècle', in *Apologétique 1650-1802: la nature et la grâce*, ed. Nicolas Brucker (Bern, 2010), p.10-20.

McMahon, Darrin M., *Enemies of the Enlightenment: the French counter-Enlightenment and the making of modernity* (Oxford and New York, 2001).

–, and Samuel Moyn, 'Introduction: interim intellectual history', in *Rethinking modern European intellectual history*, ed. Darrin M. McMahon and Samuel Moyn (Oxford, 2014), p.3-12.

McNutt, Jennifer Powell, *Calvin meets Voltaire: the clergy of Geneva in the age of Enlightenment, 1685-1798* (Farnham, 2013).

Marcolungo, Fernando Luigi, 'Christian Wolff und der physiko-theologische Beweis', in *Die natürliche Theologie bei Christian Wolff*, ed. Michael Albrecht (Hamburg, 2011), p.147-61.

Marcu, Eva, 'Un encyclopédiste oublié: Formey', *Revue d'histoire littéraire de la France* 53:3 (1953), p.296-305.

–, 'Formey and the Enlightenment', doctoral dissertation, Columbia University, Ann Arbor, 1952.

Martin, Henri-Jean, 'La tradition perpétuée', in *Histoire de l'édition française: le livre triomphant 1660-1830*, ed. Henri-Jean Martin and Roger Chartier (Paris, 1984), p.175-85.

Marx, Jacques, 'Une liaison dangereuse au XVIIIe siècle: Voltaire et Jean-Henri Samuel Formey', *Neophilologus* 53:2 (1969), p.138-46.

Masseau, Didier, *Les Ennemis des philosophes: l'antiphilosophie au temps des Lumières* (Paris, 2000).

–, 'La position des apologistes conciliateurs', *Dix-huitième siècle* 34 (2002), p.121-30.

Matytsin, Anton, 'The Protestant critics of Bayle at the dawn of the Enlightenment', in *Scepticism in the eighteenth century: Enlightenment, Lumières, Aufklärung*, ed. Sébastien Charles and Plinio J. Smith (Dordrecht, 2013), p.63-76.

–, *The Specter of skepticism in the age of Enlightenment* (Baltimore, MD, 2016).

May, Louis-Philippe, 'Histoire et sources de l'*Encyclopédie*: d'après le registre de délibérations et de comptes des éditeurs et un mémoire inédit', *Revue de synthèse* 58 (1938), p.5-30.

Middell, Katharina, 'Hugenotten in Leipzig: Etappen der Konstruktion einer "hybriden" Identität', in *Réfugiés und Emigrés: Migration zwischen Frankreich und Deutschland im 18. Jahrhundert*, ed. Thomas Höpel and Katharina Middell (Leipzig, 1997), p.56-75.

Möller, Horst, *Aufklärung in Preussen: der Verleger, Publizist und Geschichtsschreiber Friedrich Nicolai* (Berlin, 1974).

–, 'Enlightened societies in the metropolis: the case of Berlin', in *The Transformation of political culture: England and Germany in the late eighteenth century*, ed. Eckart Hellmuth (London, 1990), p.219-33.

Mori, Gianluca, *Bayle philosophe* (Paris, 1999).

Mortimer, Sarah, 'Human liberty and human nature in the works of Faustus Socinus and his readers', *Journal of the history of ideas* 70:2 (2009), p.191-211.

Mounier, Jacques, 'La réception de J. J. Rousseau en Allemagne au XVIIIe siècle', in *Aufklärungen: Frankreich und Deutschland im 18. Jahrhundert*, ed. Gerhard Sauder and Jürgen Schlobach (Heidelberg, 1985), p.167-79.

Moureau, François, 'L'*Encyclopédie* d'après les correspondants de Formey', *Recherches sur Diderot et l'Encyclopédie* 3 (1987), p.125-45.

Müller, Hans Martin, 'Homiletik', *TRE* 15 (1986), p.526-65.

Mulligan, Lotte, 'Robert Boyle, the "Christian virtuoso" and the rhetoric of "reason"', in *Religion, reason and nature in early modern Europe*, ed. Robert Crocker (Dordrecht, 2001), p.97-116.

Mulsow, Martin, *Die drei Ringe: Toleranz und clandestine Gelehrsamkeit bei Mathurin Veyssière La*

Croze (1661-1739) (Tübingen, 2001).

Must, Nicholas, *Preaching a dual identity: Huguenot sermons and the shaping of confessional identity, 1629-1685* (Leiden and Boston, MA, 2017).

Nadler, Steven (ed.), *Causation in early modern philosophy: Cartesianism, occasionalism, and preestablished harmony* (University Park, PA, 1993).

Neis, Cordula, 'Formey's "Discours sur l'origine des sociétés et du langage et sur le système de la compensation" (1763) im Kontext der Berliner Debatte um den Sprachursprung', in *Jean Henri Samuel Formey: Wissensmultiplikator der Berliner Aufklärung*, ed. Jannis Götze and Martin Meiske (Erlangen, 2016), p.169-84.

Nuovo, Victor, *John Locke: the philosopher as Christian virtuoso* (Oxford, 2017).

Paccioni, Jean-Paul, 'Wolff est-il "le vrai inventeur de la psychologie rationelle"? L'experience, l'existence actuelle et la rationalité dans le projet wolffien de psychologie', in *Die Psychologie Christian Wolffs: systematische und historische Untersuchungen*, ed. Oliver-Pierre Rudolph and Jean-François Goubet (Tübingen, 2004), p.75-98.

Pagden, Anthony, *The Enlightenment and why it still matters* (New York, 2013).

Palladini, Fiammetta, *Die Berliner Hugenotten und der Fall Barbeyrac:*

Orthodoxe und 'Sozinianer' im Refuge (1685-1720) (Leiden, 2011).

Paul, Herman, 'What is a scholarly persona? Ten theses on virtues, skills, and desires', *History and theory* 53:3 (2014), p.348-71.

Pitassi, Maria-Cristina, '"Des explications de l'Ecriture plus raisonnables que dans les sermons": autour du Nouveau Testament de Jacques Lenfant et Isaac de Beausobre', in *Refuge et désert: l'évolution théologique des huguenots de la révocation à la Révolution française*, ed. Hubert Bost and Claude Lauriol (Paris, 2003), p.143-56.

Pocock, J. G. A., *Barbarism and religion*, vol.1: *The Enlightenments of Edward Gibbon, 1737-1764* (Cambridge, 1999).

–, *Barbarism and religion*, vol.5: *Religion: the first triumph* (Cambridge, 2011).

–, 'Clergy and commerce: the conservative Enlightenment in England', in *L'età dei Lumi: studi storici sul settecento europeo in onore di Franco Venturi*, ed. Raffaele Ajello, E. Cortese and V. Piano Moratari, 2 vols (Naples, 1985), vol.1, p.523-62.

–, 'The concept of language and the *métier d'historien*: some considerations on practice', in *The Languages of political theory in early modern Europe*, ed. Anthony Pagden (Cambridge, 1987), p.19-38.

Pohlmeyer, Werner, *250 Jahre Staatliches Französisches Gymnasium 1689-1939* (Berlin, 1939).

Popkin, Richard H., 'Pierre Bayle's place in 17th-century scepticism', in *Pierre Bayle: le philosophe de Rotterdam*, ed. Paul Dibon (Amsterdam, 1959), p.1-19.

Porter, Roy, and Mikuláš Teich (ed.), *The Enlightenment in national context* (Cambridge, 1981).

Poser, Hans, '"Da ich wider Vermuthen gantz natürlich auf die vorher bestimmte Harmonie des Herrn Leibnitz geführet ward, so habe ich dieselbe beybehalten": Christian Wolffs Rezeption der prästabilierten Harmonie', in *Leibnizbilder im 18. und 19. Jahrhundert*, ed. Alexandra Lewendoski (Stuttgart, 2004), p.49-63.

Pott, Sandra, '"Gentle, refined, cultivated, witty people": comments on the intellectual history of the Berlin Refuge and on relevant research', in *The Berlin Refuge 1680-1780: learning and science in European context*, ed. Sandra Pott, Martin Mulsow and Lutz Danneberg (Leiden and Boston, MA, 2003), p.3-24.

–, *Reformierte Morallehren und deutsche Literatur von Jean Barbeyrac bis Christoph Martin Wieland* (Tübingen, 2002).

–, Martin Mulsow, and Lutz Danneberg (ed.), *The Berlin Refuge 1680-1780: learning and science in European context* (Leiden and Boston, MA, 2003).

Ratcliff, Marc J., 'Une métaphysique de la méthode chez Charles Bonnet', in *Charles Bonnet: savant et philosophe (1720-1793)*, ed. René Sigrist *et al.* (Geneva, 1994), p.51-60.

Rateau, Paul, *Leibniz et le meilleur des mondes possibles* (Paris, 2015).

–, 'The problem of evil and the justice of God', in *The Oxford handbook of Leibniz*, ed. Maria Rosa Antognazza (New York, 2018), p.100-15.

–, 'Sur la conformité de la foi avec la raison: Leibniz contre Bayle', *Revue philosophique de la France et de l'étranger* 136:4 (2011), p.467-85.

Reichenberger, Andrea, *Emilie du Châtelets Institutions physiques: über die Rolle von Prinzipien und Hypothesen in der Physik* (Wiesbaden, 2016).

Rétat, Pierre, *Le 'Dictionnaire' de Bayle et la lutte philosophique au XVIIIe siècle* (Paris, 1971).

Roldàn, Concha, 'Damenphilosophie und europäische querelle des femmes zur Zeit Wolffs', in *Christian Wolff und die europäische Aufklärung*, ed. Jürgen Stolzenberg, Oliver-Pierre Rudolph and Jean Ecole, 5 vols (Hildesheim and New York, 2007-2010), vol.3, p.145-61.

Roosen, Franziska, *Soutenir notre Eglise: hugenottische Erziehungskonzepte und Bildungseinrichtungen im Berlin des 18. Jahrhunderts* (Bad Karlshafen, 2008).

Rosenblatt, Helena, 'The Christian Enlightenment', in *The Cambridge history of Christianity*, ed. Stewart J. Brown and Timothy Tackett, vol.7: *Enlightenment, reawakening and revolution 1660-1815* (Cambridge, 2006), p.283-301.

Rosen Prest, Viviane, *L'Historiographie des huguenots en Prusse au temps des Lumières: entre mémoire, histoire et légende – J. P. Erman et P. C. F. Reclam, Mémoires pour servir à l'histoire des réfugiés français dans les Etats du roi* (Paris, 2002).

Rozemond, Marleen, 'Leibniz on the union of body and soul', *Archiv für Geschichte der Philosophie* 79:2 (1997), p.150-78.

Rumore, Paola, 'Empirical psychology', in *Handbuch Christian Wolff*, ed. Robert Theis and Alexander Aichele (Wiesbaden, 2018), p.175-96.

Schillings, Jan, 'Elargissement de la République des Lettres vers les "pays du Nord": la *Bibliothèque germanique* et ses suites – profil thématique et géographique du journal', in *Journalisme et République des Lettres: l'élargissement vers les 'pays du Nord' au dix-huitième siècle*, ed. Christiane Berkvens-Stevelinck and Hans Bots (Amsterdam, 2009), p.15-82.

Schmidt, Alexander, 'Scholarship, morals and government: Jean-Henri-Samuel Formey's and Johann Gottfried Herder's responses to Rousseau's first discourse', *Modern intellectual history* 9:2 (2012), p.249-74.

–, 'Sources of evil or seeds of the good? Rousseau and Kant on needs, the arts, and the sciences', in *Engaging with Rousseau: reaction and interpretation from the eighteenth century to the present*, ed. Avi Lifschitz (Cambridge, 2016), p.33-55.

Schmidt-Biggemann, Wilhelm, 'Mutmaßungen über die Vorstellung vom Ende der Erbsünde', in *Deutschlands kulturelle Entfaltung: die Neubestimmung des Menschen*, ed. Bernhard Fabian, Wilhelm Schmidt-Biggemann and Rudolf Vierhaus (Hamburg, 1980), p.171-92.

Schneewind, J. B., *The Invention of autonomy: a history of modern moral philosophy* (Cambridge and New York, 1998).

Schneiders, Werner (ed.), *Christian Wolff 1679-1754: Interpretationen zu seiner Philosophie und deren Wirkung*, 2nd edn (Hamburg, 1986).

–, 'Deus est philosophus absolute summus: über Christian Wolffs Philosophie und Philosophiebegriff', in *Christian Wolff 1679-1754: Interpretationen zu seiner Philosophie und deren Wirkung*, ed. Werner Schneiders, 2nd edn (Hamburg, 1986), p.9-30.

–, 'Zwischen Welt und Weisheit: zur Verweltlichung der Philosophie in der Frühen Moderne', *Studia Leibnitiana* 15:1 (1983), p.2-18.

Schröder, Winfried, *Ursprünge des Atheismus: Untersuchungen zur Metaphysik- und Religionskritik des 17. und 18. Jahrhunderts* (Stuttgart-Bad Cannstatt, 1998).

Schubert, Anselm, *Das Ende der Sünde: Anthropologie und Erbsünde zwischen Reformation und Aufklärung* (Göttingen, 2002).

Schulze, G., *Festschrift zur Feier des 200jährigen Bestehens des kgl. Französischen Gymnasiums* (Berlin, 1890).

Schwab, Richard N., Walter E. Rex and John Lough (ed.), *Inventory of Diderot's Encyclopédie*, vol.6, SVEC 93 (1972).

Schwaiger, Clemens, 'Ethik', in *Handbuch Christian Wolff*, ed. Robert Theis and Alexander Aichele (Wiesbaden, 2018), p.253-68.

–, *Das Problem des Glücks im Denken Christian Wolffs: eine quellen-, begriffs- und entwicklungsgeschichtliche Studie zu Schlüsselbegriffen seiner Ethik* (Stuttgart-Bad Cannstatt, 1995).

Scott, David, 'Leibniz and the two clocks', *Journal of the history of ideas* 58:3 (1997), p.445-63.

Scribano, Emanuela, *L'Existence de Dieu: histoire de la preuve ontologique de Descartes à Kant* (Paris, 2002).

–, 'Ontological argument', in *The Cambridge Descartes lexicon*, ed. Lawrence Nolan (Cambridge, 2015), p.544-49.

Sheehan, Jonathan, 'Enlightenment, religion, and the enigma of secularization: a review essay', *The American historical review* 108:4 (2003), p.1061-80.

Skinner, Quentin, 'Meaning and understanding in the history of ideas (1969)', in *Visions of politics*, ed. Quentin Skinner, 3 vols (Cambridge, 2002), vol.1, p.57-89.

Sorkin, David, 'Geneva's "enlightened orthodoxy": the middle way of Jacob Vernet (1698-1789)', *Church history* 74:2 (2005), p.286-305.

–, *The Religious Enlightenment: Protestants, Jews, and Catholics from London to Vienna* (Princeton, NJ, 2008).

Sparn, Walter, 'Vernünftiges Christentum: über die geschichtliche Aufgabe der theologischen Aufklärung im 18. Jahrhundert in Deutschland', in *Wissenschaften im Zeitalter der Aufklärung*, ed. Rudolf Vierhaus (Göttingen, 1985), p.18-57.

Stam, Frans P., *The Controversy over the theology of Saumur, 1635-1650: disrupting debates among the Huguenots in complicated circumstances* (Amsterdam, 1988).

Stewart, M. A., 'Arguments for the existence of God: the British debate', in *The Cambridge history of eighteenth-century philosophy*, ed. Knud Haakonssen, 2 vols (Cambridge and New York, 2006), vol.2, p.711-30.

Stolzenberg, Jürgen, Oliver-Pierre Rudolph and Jean Ecole (ed.), *Christian Wolff und die europäische Aufklärung*, 5 vols (Hildesheim and New York, 2007-2010).

Strassberger, Andres, *Johann Christoph Gottsched und die 'philosophische' Predigt: Studien zur aufklärerischen Transformation der protestantischen Homiletik im Spannungsfeld von Theologie, Philosophie, Rhetorik und Politik* (Tübingen, 2010).

Strickland, Lloyd, 'Introduction: Prémontval's life and thought', in *The Philosophical writings of Prémontval*, ed. Lloyd Strickland (Lanham, MD, 2018), p.xiii-xxxii.

–, 'Leibniz on eternal punishment', *British journal for the history of philosophy* 17:2 (2009), p.307-31.

–, 'Staying optimistic! The trials

and tribulations of Leibnizian optimism', in *Leibniz's legacy and impact*, ed. Julia Weckend and Lloyd Strickland (New York, 2019), p.53-86.

Szyrwińska, Anna, 'Die Pietisten', in *Handbuch Christian Wolff*, ed. Robert Theis and Alexander Aichele (Wiesbaden, 2018), p.383-403.

Taylor, Jacqueline, 'Moral sense and moral sentiment', in *The Routledge companion to eighteenth-century philosophy*, ed. Aaron Garrett (London and New York, 2014), p.421-41.

Tente, Ludwig, *Die Polemik um den ersten Discours von Rousseau in Frankreich und Deutschland*, 3 vols (Kiel, 1974).

Terrall, Mary, *The Man who flattened the earth: Maupertuis and the sciences in the Enlightenment* (Chicago, IL, 2002).

Theis, Robert, 'Theologie', in *Handbuch Christian Wolff*, ed. Robert Theis and Alexander Aichele (Wiesbaden, 2018), p.219-50.

–, '"Ut & scias, & credas, quae simul sciri & credi possunt" Aspekte der Wolffschen Theologie', in *Die natürliche Theologie bei Christian Wolff*, ed. Michael Albrecht (Hamburg, 2011), p.17-39.

–, and Alexander Aichele (ed.), *Handbuch Christian Wolff* (Wiesbaden, 2018).

Thiel, Udo, 'Between Wolff and Kant: Merian's theory of apperception', *Journal of the history of philosophy* 34:2 (1996), p.213-32.

Thomson, Ann, *L'Ame des Lumières: le débat sur l'être humain entre religion et science: Angleterre-France (1690-1760)* (Seyssel, 2013).

–, 'Formey', in *Dictionnaire des journalistes (1600-1789)*, http://dictionnaire-journalistes.gazettes18e.fr/journaliste/310-jean-henri-formey (last accessed 11 July 2023).

–, 'L'histoire intellectuelle: quelles idées, quel contexte?', *Revue d'histoire moderne et contemporaine* 59:4bis (2012), p.47-64.

–, 'Informal networks', in *The Cambridge history of eighteenth-century philosophy*, ed. Knud Haakonssen, 2 vols (Cambridge and New York, 2006), vol.1, p.121-36.

–, 'Les premières "Boyle Lectures" et les verités au-dessus de la raison', *Revue de la Société d'études anglo-américaines des XVIIe et XVIIIe siècles* 68 (2011), p.97-110.

Tonelli, Giorgio, 'La disputa sul metodo matematico nella filosofia della prima metà del settecento e la genesi dello scritto kantiano sull'evidenza', in *Da Leibniz a Kant: saggi sul pensiero del settecento*, ed. Claudio Cesa (Naples, 1987), p.81-107.

Trousson, Raymond, 'Jean-Jacques Rousseau et son œuvre dans la presse périodique allemande de 1750 à 1800 (I)', *Dix-huitième siècle* 1:1 (1969), p.289-310.

–, *Jean-Jacques Rousseau jugé par ses contemporains: du 'Discours sur les sciences et les arts' aux 'Confessions'* (Paris, 2000).

Vailati, Ezio, *Leibniz & Clarke: a study of their correspondence* (New York, 1997).

Van Damme, Stéphane, '"Philosophe"/Philosopher', in *The Cambridge companion to the French Enlightenment*, ed. Daniel Brewer (Cambridge, 2014), p.153-66.

Van Kley, Dale K., 'The varieties of enlightened experience', in *God in the Enlightenment*, ed. William J. Bulman and Robert G. Ingram (Oxford, 2016), p.278-316.

Velder, Christian, *300 Jahre Französisches Gymnasium Berlin / 300 ans au Collège français* (Berlin, 1989).

Vermij, Riek, 'Nature in defence of Scripture: physico-theology and experimental philosophy in the work of Bernard Nieuwentijt', in *The Book of nature in early modern and modern history*, ed. Klaas van Berkel and Arjo Vanderjagt (Leuven, 2006), p.83-96.

Vidal, Fernando, 'Le discours de la méthode dans la psychologie des Lumières', *L'Homme et la société* 167-69 (2008), p.53-82.

–, *Les Sciences de l'âme, XVIe-XVIIIe siècle* (Paris, 2006).

Voisine, Jacques, 'J. Formey (1711-1797): vulgarisateur de l'œuvre de Rousseau en Allemagne', in *Mélanges d'histoire littéraire offerts à Daniel Mornet, professeur honoraire à la Sorbonne, par ses anciens collègues et ses disciples français* (Paris, 1951), p.141-53.

Volmer, Annett, 'Journalismus und Aufklärung: Jean Henri Samuel Formey und die Entwicklung der Zeitschrift zum Medium der Kritik', *Jahrbuch für Kommunikationsgeschichte* 9 (2007), p.101-29.

–, 'Lektüre, Bildung, Wissenskanon: Jean-Henri-Samuel Formeys Ratschläge zum Aufbau einer Privatbibliothek im 18. Jahrhundert', in *The Berlin Refuge 1680-1780: learning and science in European context*, ed. Sandra Pott, Martin Mulsow and Lutz Danneberg (Leiden and Boston, MA, 2003), p.183-206.

Walters, Robert L., and William H. Barber, 'Introduction', in *The Complete works of Voltaire*, vol.15 (Oxford, 1992), p.1-180.

Watkins, Eric, 'The development of physical influx in early eighteenth-century Germany: Gottsched, Knutzen, and Crusius', *The Review of metaphysics* 49:2 (1995), p.295-339.

–, 'From pre-established harmony to physical influx: Leibniz's reception in eighteenth-century Germany', *Perspectives on science* 6:1 (1998), p.136-203.

Weinberger, Jerry, 'Francis Bacon and the unity of knowledge: reason and revelation', in *Francis Bacon and the refiguring of early modern thought: essays to commemorate 'The Advancement of learning' (1605-2005)*, ed. Julie Robin Solomon and Catherine Gimelli Martin (Aldershot and Burlington, VT, 2005), p.109-27.

Whaley, Joachim, 'The Protestant Enlightenment in Germany', in *The Enlightenment in national context*, ed. Roy Porter and Mikuláš Teich (Cambridge, 1981), p.106-17.

Whatmore, Richard, *What is intellectual history?* (Cambridge, 2016).

Whelan, Ruth, 'Reason and belief: the Bayle-Jacquelot debate', *Rivista di storia della filosofia* 48:1 (1993), p.101-10.

Wilke, Jürgen, 'Rechtsstellung und Rechtsprechung der Hugenotten in Brandenburg-Preußen (1685-1809)', in *Die Hugenotten 1685-1985*, ed. Rudolf von Thadden and Michelle Magdelaine (Munich, 1985), p.100-14.

Winter, Agnes, 'Die Hugenotten und das höhere Bildungswesen in Brandenburg-Preußen', in *Im Spannungsfeld von Staat und Kirche: 'Minderheiten' und 'Erziehung' im deutsch-französischen Gesellschaftsvergleich, 16.-18. Jahrhundert*, ed. Heinz Schilling and Marie-Antoinette Gross (Berlin, 2003), p.271-95.

Winter, Eduard, *Die Registres der Berliner Akademie der Wissenschaften 1746-1766* (Berlin, 1957).

Wolfe, Charles T., 'Determinism/Spinozism in the radical Enlightenment: the cases of Anthony Collins and Denis Diderot', *International review of eighteenth-century studies* 1 (2007), p.37-51.

Wunderlich, Falk, 'Meiers Verteidigung der prästabilierten Harmonie', in *Georg Friedrich Meier (1718-1777): Philosophie als 'wahre Weltweisheit'*, ed. Gideon Stiening and Frank Grunert (Berlin, 2015), p.113-22.

Yardeni, Myriam, *Le Refuge huguenot: assimilation et culture* (Paris, 2002).

Young, B. W., *Religion and Enlightenment in eighteenth-century England: theological debate from Locke to Burke* (Oxford, 1998).

Zanconato, Alessandro, *La Dispute du fatalisme en France: 1730-1760* (Fasano and Paris, 2004).

Zelle, Carsten, 'Johann August Unzers Gedanken vom Träumen (1746) im Kontext der Anthropologie der "vernünftigen Ärzte" in Halle', in *Zwischen Empirisierung und Konstruktionsleistung: Anthropologie im 18. Jahrhundert*, ed. Jörn Garber and Heinz Thoma (Tübingen, 2004), p.19-30.

– (ed.), *Vernünftige Ärzte: Hallesche Psychomediziner und die Anfänge der Anthropologie in der deutschsprachigen Frühaufklärung* (Tübingen, 2001).

Zurbuchen, Simone, 'Die schweizerische Debatte über die Leibniz-Wolffsche Philosophie und ihre Bedeutung für Emer von Vattels philosophischen Werdegang', in *Reconceptualizing nature, science, and aesthetics: contribution à une nouvelle approche aux Lumières helvétiques*, ed. Patrick Coleman, Anne Hofman and Simone Zurbuchen (Geneva, 1998), p.91-113.

–, 'Zur Wirkungsgeschichte der beiden Diskurse', in *Jean-Jacques Rousseau: die beiden Diskurse zur Zivilisationskritik*, ed. Johannes Rohbeck and Lieselotte Steinbrügge (Berlin, 2015), p.195-220.

Index

Academy of Berlin, 6, 11, 16, 32-33, 55, 64, 69, 102, 108-10, 119, 134, 136, 138-41, 180, 183, 199, 201-202, 206, 208, 210, 246, 252, 263, 285n
- class of speculative philosophy, 109, 136-37, 145, 205, 218, 219n
- prize essay competitions, 224
  - 1747: on monadology, 133-34
  - 1751: on the impact of providence on moral behaviour, 33-34, 211, 217-21, 223-28, 246
  - 1755: on optimism, 211, 215-17, 236, 243, 247
  - 1763: on metaphysical vs. mathematical truths, 136
  - 1795: on the progress of metaphysics in Germany, 136
- Wolffian-Newtonian divide/ Wolffian-anti-Wolffian divide, 110, 131-35, 140-41, 246

Achard, Antoine, Calvinist pastor in Berlin, member of the Berlin Academy, 91, 199-202
- *Sur la liberté*, 199

Acta eruditorum, 177

aléthophiles, 71-72, 88-89, 133, 141, 149, 154, 168, 171, 174
- Société des aléthophiles, 65n, 67-69, 85, 149, 168, 170

Algarotti, Francesco, 17
- *Il Newtonianismo per le dame*, 150n

Amsterdam, 183, 195n

Anières, Paul Loriol d', Calvinist pastor in Berlin, 64

anti-philosophes, 20-21, 28, 50-51

apologetics, 21-23, 27, 98, 105, 217
- Christian, 4-5, 20, 37, 107, 280
- liberal, 105-106
- rationalist, 22, 238

apperception, 184, 201, *see also* consciousness; experience, inner

arbitrary choices/will, 169-70, 175-76, 192-93, 204, 209-10, 277, *see also* liberty, of indifference

Argens, Jean-Baptiste de Boyer, marquis d', French philosopher, member of the Berlin Academy, 17, 281

Arianism, 59

Arminianism/Arminian, 12, 59-60, 62-63, 81, 113, 278

Artis, Gabriel d', Calvinist pastor in Berlin, 60-61

atheism, 3n, 4, 18, 51, 68, 113, 115n, 117, 148, 238, 280, 282

Augustine of Hippo, 43, 243n

Bacon, Francis, 3, 4n, 129
- *Advancement and proficiencie of learning*, 39

Barbeyrac, Jean, Calvinist pastor in Berlin, 12n, 60, 76, 89, 90n, 91, 102, 249

Basle, 58, 89, 201-202

Baudisson, abbé de, French clergyman
- *Essai sur l'union du christianisme avec la philosophie*, 5

Bayle, Pierre, 3, 4n, 32, 43, 75, 110, 112-17, 148, 165-67, 185, 199, 249

325

Continuation des pensées diverses sur la comète, 114, 115n, 117n
Dictionnaire historique et critique, 75, 110, 113-15
his fideism, 3, 112
his scepticism, 3, 32, 110-12, 114, 121, 145, 167
Beausobre, Isaac de, Calvinist pastor in Berlin, 58, 60-64, 65n, 72, 81
and Jacques Lenfant: *Le Nouveau Testament de notre seigneur Jesus-Christ*, 61, 63
Béguelin, Nicolas, Swiss philosopher at the Berlin Academy, 17-18
Sur l'indifférence d'équilibre et le principe du choix, 210-11
Berlin Refuge/Huguenot colony, 12n, 18, 30, 56, 57n, 58-60, 63-66, 72, 76-78, 81, 92, 278, 284
Bernard, Jacques, Calvinist theologian in Leiden, 32, 113
Bernoulli, Jean II, Swiss mathematician in Basle, 201-203, 225-26, 227n
Bernoulli, Jean III, Swiss mathematician in Berlin, member of the Berlin Academy, 17
best of all possible worlds, theory of, 141n, 175, 214-16, 223-24, 233-34, 239, 243, 277, *see also* optimism
Bibliothèque germanique/Nouvelle Bibliothèque germanique, 62, 64, 87, 106, 143, 174, 177, 196, 227, 255, 262
Bibliothèque impartiale, 242, 252, 267
Bocquet, Abraham, Calvinist pastor in Prenzlau and Magdeburg, 71-72, 74-75, 96, 111n, 153, 168-70, 185, 193, 198, 278
body, human, 147-48, 160-63, 169, 172, 182, 188, *see also* soul-body-relationship
Bonnet, Charles, Swiss natural philosopher, 37, 188-89, 211, 263n
Essai analytique sur les facultés de l'ame, 37, 38n, 188
Bose, Georg Matthias, professor of physics in Wittenberg, 38
Boullier, David-Renaud, Calvinist pastor in London, 218, 238-46, 278, 280

Boyle, Robert, 3, 4, 109
The Christian virtuoso, 2-3
Boyle Lectures, 110, 112n, 118, 124, 190
Brucker, Johann Jakob, German theologian and historian in Augsburg, 40
Historia critica, 40, 61
Budde, Johann Franz, Lutheran theologian in Jena, 123n, 158n, 243
Burlamaqui, Jean-Jacques, Calvinist philosopher in Geneva, 249

Cabrit, Isaac Théodore, Calvinist pastor in Cottbus, 60n, 71
Calvin, Jean 25, 44, 95, 115, 237n, 272, 278
Campagne, Alexandre-Auguste de, French councillor in Berlin, 64
Campagne, Jacques de, lawyer in Prenzlau, 64, 65n
Cartesianism/Cartesian philosophy, 5, 57-59, 81, 110, 112-13, 116, 118-19, 121, 129, 147, 163, 165, 170, 184, 238, 244-45
Castillon, Jean de, Italian mathematician in Berlin, member of the Berlin Academy,
Recherches sur la liberté de l'homme, 210
Catel, Balthasar, Calvinist pastor in Halberstadt, 91
Catt, Henri, Calvinist writer in Berlin, member of the Berlin Academy, 17
Chauvin, Etienne, Calvinist pastor in Berlin, 62
Church, French Reformed, 6, 56, 60, 76, 79, 83, 92, 101
Church discipline (*Discipline ecclésiastique*), 59, 72-73, 78-79, 81, 95-96
confession of faith (*Confession de foi*), 59, 44, 78
Clarke, Samuel, 110, 112, 118, 148, 196
his theory of free will, 190-93
Collège français, 6, 56-57, 67, 76, 78-81, 83, 149

Collins, Anthony, 165, 196, 199-200
  his necessitarianism 190-91
common/first notions, 42, 119,
  130, 135n, 138, 144-45, *see also*
  principles, metaphysical or a priori
compatibility
  of reason and faith, *see* reason and faith, compatibility of
  of (pre)determination and liberty, 33, 159, 162, 174, 179, 197, 206, 210-11, 213, 246
Condillac, Etienne Bonnot de, French clergyman and philosopher, 281
  Traité des systèmes, 284-85
consciousness, 184-86, 189, 211, 279, *see also* apperception; experience, inner; introspection
contingency, 123, 126-27, 131, 158, 173-74, 179, 189-91, 197, 205, 210, *see also* Wolff, proof of God; God, proofs of His existence, cosmological proof
contradiction, principle of, 122, 191
corruption of human beings, 44-45, 117, 233, *see also* original sin
Cramer, Gabriel, mathematician in Geneva, 194, 280n
Crousaz, Jean Pierre de, professor of philosophy and mathematics in Lausanne, 32, 113, 117-18, 149, 156-57, 159, 165-70, 172, 174-77, 180, 278, 280-81
  Examen du pyrrhonisme ancien et moderne, 113-14, 116, 166-67
  De l'esprit humain, 174-75, 177, 184n
Crusius, Christian August, German philosopher in Leipzig, 194

D'Alembert, Jean, 25, 33, 111, 139, 218-20, 223, 225, 228, 281, 284-85
  on optimism, 223-24
  on providence, 220, 223, 246
deism, 4, 7, 18, 22, 24, 26, 76, 105, 141, 153, 190, 219, 280, 282
demonstration, method of/ demonstrative method, 41n, 46, 101-102, 144-45, 150, 153, 220, 258, 280

Derham, William, English theologian, 110, 124, 136
Descartes, René, 5, 6n, 115, 120, 129, 145, 147, 163-64, 184, 192-93, 214, 242, 245, 281
  his rationalism, 112, 120
  his ontological proof of God, 115, 118-20
Des Champs, Jean, Calvinist pastor and writer in Berlin and England, 65-66, 69-72, 87, 89, 153, 182
  Cinq sermons sur divers textes, expliqués selon la méthode du célèbre Mr. Wolff, 87-88, 101
  Cours abrégé de la philosophie wolffienne, 151-53, 183
Des Combles, Pierre, Calvinist pastor in Berlin, 64
Des Vignobles, Alphonse, Calvinist pastor in Berlin, 62
determinism, 33, 156, 158, 169, 196n, 278
Diderot, Denis, 7, 20n, 21, 33, 40, 76, 103, 111, 224n, 236-38, 251, 278, 285
  Pensées philosophiques, 37, 53, 104, 234
  Lettres sur les aveugles, 234-35
divine law, 27, 31, 250-51, 269, 271-75, *see also* natural law, relation to divine law
Du Châtelet, Emilie Le Tonnelier de Breteuil, marquise, 153n
  Institutions de physique, 152
Du Marsais, César Chesneau, French philosopher,
  Le Philosophe, 49-50, 52
duties, 30, 74n, 222, 230, 261-62
  moral, 220-21, 256, 264, 268
  pastoral, 62, 64, 72-76, 78, 81
  towards God, 90, 148, 262, 272

Eberhard, Johann August, German philosopher, 240n
Elisabeth Christine, queen consort of Prussia, 87
empirical method, 125, 136, 181-82, 187-89, 200-202, 211, 255, 267, *see also* experience; psychology, empirical

empiricism, 18, 50, 52, 115, 201, 210
Encyclopédie, 25, 40-43, 50, 104, 111, 114, 219, 263
  Art. 'Philosophe', 50-52
  Art. 'Dieu', *see* Formey, 'Dieu' (*Encyclopédie*)
  Art. 'Entendenment', *see* Formey, 'Entendement' (*Encyclopédie*)
  Art. 'Fatalité', 219n
  Art. 'Fortuit', 220
  Art. 'Fortune', 219n
  Art. 'Optimisme', 224
  Système des connoissances humaines, 39, 41-42
Encyclopédie d'Yverdon, 104
Erman, Jean-Pierre, Calvinist pastor in Berlin and professor at the Collège français, 79, 284
esprit philosophique, 20, 52-53
essential religion, 106-107, 239, 279
eternal punishment, doctrine of, 236-37, 240-41, 243-44, 278
ethics, 33, 250, 269-74, *see also* moral philosophy
  Christian, 251, 272-73
Euler, Leonhard, Swiss mathematician in Berlin, member of the Berlin Academy, 17-18, 131-34, 145
evil, 179, 213-15, 224, 231-34, 236-37, 244, 246
  origin of, 27, 213, 231-33, 244
experience, 2, 41-42, 98-99, 101, 138-39, 181, 182n, 184, 186-87, 192, 200-201, 230-31, 238n, 270, *see also* empirical method
  inner, 184-85, 200, 203, *see also* apperception; consciousness; introspection
  sensory, 41, 125, 184, 186, 264, *see also* senses; sensation

Fabricius, Johann Albert, professor of rhetoric and ethics in Hamburg, 124, 136
faith, 1, 23, 43-44, 51-52, 62, 69, 77, 89, 91, 101, 112, 157, 165, 252, *see also* Revelation/revealed religion; reason and faith
Fall, *see* original sin
fatalism 32, 68, 127, 148-49, 155-57, 159-62, 165-67, 169-71, 174-78, 180, 187, 194, 198, 200, 204, 207, 210-11, 278
Felice, Fortunato Bartolomeo de, Italian-Swiss writer and publisher, 104-105
Fénelon, François de Salignac de La Mothe, 5, 243n
Fontenelle, Bernard de, 112, 118, 150, 154n
  Eloge de Leibnitz, 245
  Entretiens sur la pluralités des mondes, 150n
Formey, Jean Henri Samuel,
  Anti-Emile, 7n, 263
  Consolations raisonnables et religieuses, 35, 36n, 104
  De la conscience, 257, 261
  'Dieu' (*Encyclopédie*), 110-12, 114-18
  Discours moraux, 35, 36n, 37, 105-107
  Discours sur ces questions: quel est le degré de certitude dont sont susceptibles les preuves tirées de la consideration de cet univers pour démontrer l'existence d'une divinité?, 143-45
  Discours sur l'esprit philosophique, 52-54
  Elementa philosophiae seu medulla wolfiana, 80
  Emile Chrétien, 7n, 37, 263, 282
  'Entendement' (*Encyclopédie*), 183
  Entretiens psychologiques, 188n
  Essai sur la perfection, 88-89, 94, 99, 257, 260, 272n, 274n
  Essai sur les songes, 135n, 183
  Examen de la preuve qu'on tire des fins de la nature, 119n, 121-23, 125n, 126-27, 135-36, 138n, 140n
  Examen philosophique de la liaison réelle qu'il y a entre les sciences et le mœurs, 7n, 252, 253n, 254, 255n, 256-59, 266-67, 275
  his correspondence, 8-9, 15, 18, 34, 36n, 53n, 100, 111n, 133, 142, 166, 177, 183n, 263
  his encyclopaedism, 110-14
  his preaching practice/sermons, 27, 58, 76-77, 83-86, 88, 92-93, 95-98, 101-102, 108

Histoire abégée de la philosophie, 39-42, 48, 53n, 114n
La Belle wolfienne, 63, 70, 130, 149-51, 152n, 153-65, 167-71, 173-77, 179, 183, 185n, 187, 192n, 211, 257, 283-84
La Vraye Théorie de la fortune, 227
Le Philosophe chrétien, 35-38, 45-47, 51, 53-55, 73-76, 83-84, 86, 95-100, 103-106, 108, 217, 221, 222n, 223n, 231n, 232n, 250, 273, 283-84
Le Philosophe payen, 47, 78n
Les preuves de l'existence de Dieu, ramenées aux notions communes, 119, 120n, 121-22, 130, 140n
Le Système du vrai bonheur, 36, 88
Le Triomphe de l'évidence, 114, 116-17
Lettre de M. Gervaise Holmes, 7n, 235-41, 244-45
Lettres sur la predication, 89n, 90-91, 94n, 102n
Mercure et Minerve, 71
Nouvelles considérations sur l'union des deux substances dans l'homme, 177n
Pensées raisonnables, 7n, 37, 53-54, 104, 234n
Principes de morale, 250, 252, 257-58, 261, 263-64, 266-68, 270, 272, 274-75, 284
  Morale intellectuelle (1st part), 257n, 258n, 259n, 261n, 262n, 263-64, 266, 267n, 268n, 270
  Morale pratique (2nd part), 257n, 261n, 263-64, 265n, 267n, 270-71, 272n
Recherches sur les elemens de la matière, 133
Réflexions sur la liberté, 180, 183-87, 190-94, 196-201, 210
Sendschreiben an S. Eminenz den hochwürdigsten Herrn, Herrn Angelus Maria Quirini, 38n
Sermons sur divers textes de l'écriture sainte, 77n, 78n, 84, 96n, 97n, 99n, 101n, 102n, 221n, 223n
Souvenirs d'un citoyen, 6n, 58n, 59n, 66n, 76, 217n, 218n, 220n
Forneret, Philippe, Calvinist pastor in Berlin, 58-60, 67n

fortune/*fortune*, 218-19, 221, 228
Frankfurt an der Oder, University of, 59
Frederick II, king of Prussia, 11, 16, 18, 36n, 56, 66, 67n, 68-70
  and the German Enlightenment, 11, 15-17
Frederick William, elector of Brandenburg-Prussia, 11
Frederick William I, king of Prussia, 36n, 66, 69, 77n, 86, 171n
free will, 27, 31, 33, 162, 169-70, 178-80, 184-87, 189-91, 193, 195-99, 202, 205-208, 210-11, 220, 240, 279, 283
Fréron, Elie, French writer and journalist, 254

Garcin, Jean-Laurent, Calvinist pastor in Holland, 37
Gedike, Friedrich, German writer and publisher in Berlin, description of Berlin, 15-18
Geneva/Genevans, 24-25, 36-37, 45n, 60, 96, 105-107, 142-43, 194-95, 198-99, 239, 244, 251, 272n, 278-80, 284
  Academy of, 58-59
God,
  as Creator, 46, 117, 147, 156, 158, 171, 206, 240
  His absolute decree, 236-37, 240, *see also* voluntarism
  His free will, 156, 161, 175, 179, 219-20, 240, *see also* liberty, divine
  His goodness/benevolence, 31, 117, 156, 172, 214-15, 232, 234-35, 237-38, 240-41, 277
  His incomprehensibility, 114-16, 128-29, 197, 221, 224
  His nature, 3, 116, 145, 279
  His omnipotence, 31, 117, 179, 205, 237, 240
  His omniscience, 117, 172, 179, 205, 229
  His perfections, 116, 129, 156, 172, 175, 229, 235-37, 256, 274
  His prescience, 160-61, 191, 194, 197-98

His purposes, 109, 122, 128-29, 213, 221, 224, 228, 229-31, 233n, 277
His similarity to human beings, 116, 120-21, 229
His wisdom, 116, 128-29, 172, 174, 224, 232-33, 235, 240, *see also* omniscience
proofs of His existence, 32, 102, 109, 111-12, 116, 118, 121, 135-36, 138-44, 235n, 277
  consensus omnium proof, 115-17
  cosmological/a posteriori proof, 118, 121-23, 126-27, 143-44
  historical proof, 112
  metaphysical proof, 111-12, 130, 142-43
  ontological proof, *see* Descartes, ontological proof
  physical proof, 112, 136
  physico-theological proof, 109, 121, 123-27, 130-31, 136, 138, 187, 224, 235n, 244-45, 280, *see also* physico-theology
  proof from design, *see* physico-theological proof
  teleological proof, *see* physico-theological proof
Göttingen, 195, 265
Gottsched, Johann Christoph, journalist and professor of metaphysics and logic in Leipzig, 69, 85, 88, 132-33, 141, 164, 227
  Grund-Riß einer Lehr-Arth ordentlich und erbaulich zu predigen, 86-87, 108
Gottsched, Luise Adelgunde, German writer in Leipzig, 69, 93
Gravesande, Willem Jacob 's, professor of astronomy and mathematics in Leiden, 281
Grimm, Friedrich Melchior, baron von, German writer and journalist in Paris, 252

Hagen, Gottlieb Friedrich, German philosopher, 157n, 182
Halle, 14, 134n, 148-49, 157
  University of, 15, 59, 68-69, 155, 182, 208

Haude, Ambrosius, bookseller in Berlin, 69, 170-71
Heinius, Philipp, German philosopher, member of the Berlin Academy, 218, 225
Hentsch, Johann Jakob, professor of mathematics in Helmstedt, 177-78, 187
heterodoxy, 12, 15, 23-24, 60, 68, 72, 76, 81, 107-108, 113, 160, 244, 246, 278-79
Hobbes, Thomas, 185, 259, 282
Holbach, Paul-Henri Thiry, baron d', 1n, 21
homiletics, *see* preaching
Huber, Marie, philosopher in Geneva, 239
  Le Sisteme des anciens et des modernes, 241
human understanding, 39, 106, 112, 115, 117, 128, 183n, 189-90, 193, 197, 204, 250, 261-64, 266, 267n, 270-71, *see also* reason, natural
Hume, David, 23
Hutcheson, Francis, Scottish moral philosopher, 265, 281

immorality, 4n, 104, 165, *see also* morality, decline of
  of pastors and believers, 90-91
  of philosophers, 50, 75, 252-54, 256, 267n
innateness,
  of knowledge about God, 115-16, 118-19, *see also* God, proofs of His existence, *consensus omnium* proof
  of morality, 259-61, 266, 268
intellectualism, 240, 242, 259-61, 265-66, 271, 275, 280
introspection, 188, 268, 275, *see also* consciousness; experience, inner

Jaquelot, Isaac, Calvinist pastor in The Hague, Basle and Berlin, 2-4, 32, 62n, 112-13, 118, 161, 282
  Conformité de la foi avec la raison, 3, 117
  Dissertations sur l'existence de Dieu, 112, 118

Jariges, Philippe Joseph de, German jurist in Berlin, member of the Berlin Academy, 134n
Examen du Spinozisme, 200
Jöcher, Christian Gottlieb, professor and librarian in Leipzig, 69
Journal des sçavans, 94, 239, 242
Journal encyclopédique, 242
Journal helvétique, 166

Kahle, Ludwig Martin, professor of philosophy in Göttingen, 195-98
Vergleichung der Leibnitzischen und Neutonischen Metaphysik, 195-96
Kant, Immanuel, 13
Kästner, Abraham Gotthelf, professor of mathematics in Leipzig, 226-34, 246
King, William, archbishop of Dublin, 194
Knutzen, Martin, professor of metaphysics in Königsberg, 164
König, Samuel, Swiss mathematician in Franeker, 215
Köthen, Johann Jakob, Lutheran theologian,
Principia quaedam metaphysicae wolfianae, 170
Krüger, Johann Gottlob, professor of medicine and philosophy in Helmstedt, 182

La Croze, Mathurin Veyssière de, French court librarian and professor of philosophy in Berlin, 57-58, 60-62, 64, 66n, 67
La Mettrie, Julien Offray de, 17, 69, 141
Lange, Joachim, professor of theology in Halle, 68, 70, 157n, 163n, 169
Lausanne, 35n, 59, 156
Academy of, 165
least action, principle of, 127, 131n, 138-39, 141, 215
Le Clerc, Jean, Calvinist theologian in Amsterdam, 32, 113
Leibniz, Gottfried Wilhelm, 2-4, 6, 13-14, 28, 32-33, 43, 72, 80, 98, 113, 119, 121-22, 126, 136, 138, 141, 147-49, 154n, 155-58, 161-68, 174-77, 180, 191-93, 195, 198, 201, 204, 206-11, 215, 224, 232n, 233, 235-37, 245, 259, 260n, 280-82, 285
his concept of universal harmony, 127, 157n, 160, 221
his principle of sufficient reason, *see* sufficient reason
his theory of liberty, 170, 175, 177-78, 180, 189-92, 195-96, 198, 204, 206
his theory of indiscernables, 193, 209
his theory of monads, 98, 133, 156
his theory of optimism, 211, 214, 240, 243 *see also* best of all possible worlds; optimism
his theory of pre-established harmony, *see* pre-established harmony
Théodicée, 3n, 44n, 113, 154n, 179n, 189, 192, 193n, 214, 223, 233n, 236n, 237, 243, 246
Leiden, 53, 103, 105n
Academy of, 143
Leipzig, 14, 58, 69, 85, 133, 226-27
Lenfant, Jacques, Calvinist pastor in Berlin, 58, 60-62, 72, 81
and Isaac de Beausobre: *Le Nouveau Testament de notre seigneur Jesus-Christ*, 61, 63
Lesser, Friedrich Christian, Lutheran theologian in Nordhausen, 124, 136
Lessing, Gotthold Ephraim, 216, 240n
Leszczynski, Stanislaus I, king of Poland, 252
libertarianism, 189-94, 198-99, 204-207
liberty, 117, 160, 174, 178, 193-94, 201-209, *see also* free will
absolute, 192, 194, 197, 200, 240, *see also* liberty of indifference
divine, 148, 175, 179, 204-205, 224, 240, 242-43
human, 33, 68, 100, 108, 148, 159, 161-62, 167-70, 175-76, 179, 184-87, 196-200, 204, 206-11, 213, 220, 228

of indifference, 33, 189, 192-95, 196n, 197, 203-204, 207, 209-11, 220, 278, *see also* libertarianism
Lieberkühn, Johann Nathanael, physicist, member of the Berlin Academy, 263n
Locke, John, 5, 23, 115, 165, 190, 200, 203-204, 261, 281
  Essay concerning human understanding, 181, 203
Ludovici, Carl Günther, professor of philosophy in Leipzig, 69
Luther, Martin, 38n, 44
Luzac, Elie, publisher in Leiden, 53, 94, 96, 103-105, 270

Malebranche, Nicolas, 6n, 214, 224, 261, 281
  Traité de la nature et de la grace, 214
Manteuffel, Ernst Christoph, Saxon diplomat in Prussia and patron of the sciences, 15, 66-70, 74, 80, 83n, 85, 86n, 87-88, 93, 100, 133-34, 135n, 141-42, 153, 168, 170-73, 177, 183n, 196n, 227
  Lettre de Mr. P... jurisconsulte de Marbourg, 154, 168, 171-74, 177, 190n
Marburg, 65, 155, 160
  University of, 87
Marchand, Prosper, bookseller in The Hague, 153, 168
materialism, 51, 148, 238, 281
mathematics, 40, 41n, 57, 69, 137, 140, 144-45, 231
mathematical metaphysics, 140, 143-44
Mauclerc, Paul-Emile, Calvinst pastor and journalist in Stettin, 62, 64
Maupertuis, Pierre Louis Moreau de, 16n, 17, 32, 110, 122, 131-32, 134-45, 201, 215, 216n, 218, 221-22, 224-26, 228, 246
  Discours sur les devoirs de l'académicien, 136
  Les Loix du mouvement, 135-36, 140-41, 224, 228
Melanchthon, Philipp, 48
Mémoires de Trévoux, 223, 243, 255

Mendelssohn, Moses, Jewish philosopher in Berlin, 216
Merian, Johann Bernhard, Swiss philosopher, member of the Berlin Academy, 16n, 17-18, 33, 201-11, 225-26, 285
  Discours sur la métaphysique, 136, 285n
  Dissertation ontologique sur l'action, la puissance et la liberté, 201-202, 204n
  Eloge de Monsieur Formey, 35, 63
  Examen d'une question concernant la liberté, 202, 204, 207
  his theory of liberty, 202-205, 207
  Seconde dissertation sur l'action, la puissance et la liberté, 201-202
metaphysics, 6, 14, 32, 81, 110, 112, 121-22, 130-33, 135-45, 151-52, 174, 181-82, 188n, 242, 245, 279-81, 283, 285
  as foundational science, 137, 139, 145, 285
morality/moral behaviour, 24, 33, 43, 47, 75, 85, 91, 94, 96, 98, 104, 106-108, 156, 162-63, 165, 173, 179, 206, 218, 230, 258-59, 261, 263-66, 270, 272, 275, 279-80, 284, *see also* ethics
  Christian, 106, 231, 257n, 259, 263n, 269, 278
  decline of, 90, 250-51, 266, *see also* immorality
  effect of sciences on, 250, 253-56, 266, 275
moral philosophy, 23, 33, 48-49, 90, 104-105, 107, 213, 217-19, 246, 249, 256-59, 261, 266, 270, 272-75, 280
  based on natural law, 249-51, 259-60, 266-67, 269, 271, 275, *see also* Wolff, his moral philosophy
motion, 239
  conservation of, 163-64
  laws of, 135, 138-40, *see also* least action

natural law, 14, 16, 23, 26, 31, 33, 57, 60, 88, 98, 221, 249, 258, 260, 261n, 262, 265-66, 268-69 *see also*

moral philosophy, based on natural law
  intellectualist approach to, 259, 265, 271, 275, 280, *see also* intellectualism
  relation to divine law/revelation, 99-100, 222, 269, 271-75
natural philosophy, 1, 3, 57, 109, 122, 128-29, 138, 141, 145, 188n
  Newtonian, 6, 125-26, 141
natural religion, 16, 46, 86, 105, 238
natural theology, 81, 90, 98, 110, 112, 114, 118-19, 121, 128-29, 143-45, 195, 244, 258, 273, *see also* Wolff, natural theology
nature, marvels of, 117, 124, 128, 144, 235, *see also* God, proofs of His existence, physico-theological proof
necessitarianism, 189-92, 196, 198-200, 204
necessity/necessary existence, 123, 148, 158, 160, 173, 191-92, 194, 199, 205, 208, 220
  absolute, 122, 127, 172, 159, 172-73, 189, 191
  of God, 122-23, 126-27, 158, 205
  hypothetical, 127, 159, 191, *see also* contingency
  moral, 191-92
  physical, 191, 243
Neuer Büchersaal, 132, 141
Newton, Isaac, 5, 17, 23, 109, 124-26, 131, 136, 195, 197, 226, 281, *see also* natural philosophy, Newtonian; physico-theology
nexus rerum, notion of, 98, 155, 157, 159-61, 165, 169-74, 221, 246, 280
Nicolai, Friedrich, publisher in Berlin, 17
Nieuwentijt, Bernard, Dutch physician, 124

occasionalism, 147, 163, 245n
optimism, 33, 93, 211, 213-18, 223-24, 226, 232-40, 242-47, 277-78, *see also* D'Alembert, on optimism; best of all possible worlds; Leibniz, his optimism
order of nature, 117-18, 123, 126-27, 129, 230, 233-36

original sin, dogma of, 43-48, 63, 107, 278-79
orthodoxy, 26, 88, 100, 160, 244, 246, 279
  Calvinist, 10, 12, 59-60, 63, 81, 179, 237
  enlightened, 24-25, 238n
  Lutheran, 48, 85

Palissot de Montenoy, Charles, French playwright,
  Les Philosophes: comédie, en trois actes, en vers, 50
Paris/Parisian, 39, 58, 104, 110, 112, 118, 137, 219, 252n, 263
passions, 50, 52, 117-18, 222, 232, 264-66, 268, 270, 279, 284
pelagianism, 59
Pelloutier, Simon, Calvinist theologian in Berlin, 58, 60, 62
Pérard, Jacques, Calvinist pastor in Stettin, 69-70
perfectibility, 88, 98-99, 183n, 250, 260, 268-69, 273, 278, *see also* Wolff, his principle of perfectibility
Peschier, Jean, Calvinist pastor in Geneva, 60n, 105, 107n, 195
philosophes, 5-6, 15, 18, 20-22, 27, 32, 34, 51, 53-54, 75-77, 104, 217, 239, 252, 280, 285
  concept of, 49-51
philosophy,
  academic, 55, 94, 151
  eclectic, 16, 40, 201, 285
  popular, 9, 31, 45, 47, 83, 103, 105, 107-108, 149, 150-54, 165, 195, 250, 282-83
  practical, 13, 14n, 80, 108, 182n, 257-58, 262, 286
physical influx, theory of, 163-64, 171, 177, 186-88
physico-theology, 23, 109-10, 118, 124, 128, 130, 145, 230, 233, 256, *see also* God, proofs of His existence, physico-theological proof
physics, 129, 139, 144, 152, 183-84, *see also* natural philosophy
Pietism/Pietists, 14, 32, 72, 85, 88, 163n, 165, 172
  their criticism of Wolff's

philosophy, 15, 68, 70, 87, 123, 148-49, 155, 157, 159, 163n, 164, 169, 174
Polignac, Melchior de, French Catholic cardinal, *Anti-Lucretius*, 98
Pope, Alexander, 165, 214-17, 224, 232-33
  Essay on man, 165, 176n, 214, 232
Prades, Jean-Martin de, French Catholic theologian, 17, 22-23
preaching, 58, 60, 78, 84, 95n
  Calvinist, 85, 87, 89-92, 95-96, 101-102
  Wolffian philosophical, 70, 85-87, 89, 92-93, 108, 283
predestination, 62, 179, 237, 278
pre-established harmony, 31-34, 148-49, 154-57, 160-69, 171-74, 176-80, 187, 190n, 198, 245n
Prémontval, André-Pierre Le Guay de, French mathematician and philosopher in Berlin, member of the Berlin Academy, 33, 205, 209-11
  Pensées sur la liberté, 206-208
principles,
  metaphysical or a priori, 125, 136-42, 181-82, 235n, *see also* common/first notions
  moral, 256, 259, 264, 268
providence, 33-34, 101, 213-14, 216-23, 226-31, 233-35, 242, 244, 246, 249
  divine, 27, 31, 108, 172, 211, 213-14, 218, 220-21, 228, 233, 238-39, 242-44, 246, 277-78
psychology, 80, 85, 151, 166, 168-69, 178, 182, 187, 211, 258, 261, 266, *see also* soul, science of the
  empirical, 135, 181-85, 187-89, 192, 201, 208, *see also* Wolff, his psychology
  rational, 168n, 181-82, *see also* Wolff, his psychology
Pufendorf, Samuel, 14, 60, 259

rationalism, 3, 28, 32, 41, 75, 108, 279, 280, 282, 284-85, *see also* Wolff, his rationalism
Cartesian, 5-6, 59, 110, 118-19, 121, *see also* Descartes, his rationalism
rational religion, 13-14, 23, 113
Ray, John, British theologian and natural philosopher, 124
reason, natural, 2-3, 4n, 13-14, 24-26, 29, 39-40, 42-45, 48, 51, 53, 63, 79, 86, 98, 106, 109, 117n, 118, 174, 185, 192, 230, 232, 250-51, 259-60, 265, 270, 273, 282-84, *see also* human understanding
  limitedness of, 61-62, 79, 106, 112-13, 128, *see also* truths above reason
reason and faith, 4, 23, 45n, 46, 49, 77-79, 99-100, 112, 122, 223, 244, 270, 279-80
  compatibility of, 2-4, 14, 33, 43, 47-48, 62n, 113, 280, 282-83, 285
  harmonious relationship of, 2-3, 10, 26-27, 30-31, 274, 279
Réclam, Frédéric, Calvinist pastor in Berlin, 284
Reinbeck, Johann Gustav, Lutheran preacher in Berlin, 67n, 69, 74, 85-87, 89, 108, 154n, 170-74
  Erörterung der philosophischen Meynung von der sogenandten HARMONIA PRAESTABILITA, 171-72
  Nouveau recueil de quatre sermons, 71n
  Recueil de cinq sermons, 70-71
  Sermons sur le mystere de la naissance de J.-C., 70, 87
Reinhard, Adolf Friedrich, jurist in Neustrelitz, 216-17, 236, 243
Reusch, Johann Peter, Lutheran theologian in Jena, 164
Revelation/revealed religion, 2-3, 25, 28, 31, 42-43, 45-46, 49, 51, 63, 70, 77-78, 86, 99-101, 104-106, 109, 112, 223-24, 232, 238, 246, 259, 270, 278-80, 283, *see also* faith; reason and faith
  superiority of, 46-48, 98-102, 238, 283
Roches, François de, Calvinist theologian in Geneva, 143

Roques, Pierre, Calvinist theologian in Basle, 89-90, 102
Le Pasteur evangélique, 89-91, 106
Rousseau, Jean-Jacques, 7, 9n, 33, 105, 216, 232, 238, 246, 252, 254-55, 266, 268-69, 274-75, 284
Discours sur les sciences et les arts, 250-53, 255n, 257, 267-68, 275
Discours sur l'origine de l'inégalité, 268
Emile, ou De l'éducation, 263, 268, 282
Lettre sur la providence, 216-17, 228, 238, 247
Rüdiger, Andreas Johannes, German philosopher, 158n

Sack, August Friedrich Wilhelm, court preacher in Berlin, 69
Saint-Blancard, François de Gautier de, French councillor in Berlin, 195
salvation, 24, 31, 44-46, 61, 102, 106, 147, 213, 222, 232, 237, 240, 269, 271, 277-78
Saumur, Academy of, 58, 59n
scepticism, 3, 69, 75, 121, 145, 153, 166, 176, 281-82, *see also* Bayle, his scepticism
Schmauss, Johann Jacob, professor of natural law in Göttingen, 265
Schütz, Christian Gottfried, professor of philosophy and rhetoric in Halle, 188
scholastics/scholasticism, 5, 57-58, 61, 107, 115, 137, 147, 163, 191, 279
sensations, 171-72, 193, 279
senses, 39, 118, 186-87, *see also* experience, sensory
sentimentalism, 265, 284
Shaftesbury, Anthony Ashley Cooper, third earl of, 265, 284
Soner, Ernst, German physician, 237n
Spalding, Johann Joachim, Lutheran preacher in Berlin, 95n
Die Bestimmung des Menschen, 88
Spinoza, Baruch de, 75, 157-59, 185, 199-200, 282
Ethica, 158
spinozism, 123, 127, 148, 157, 161

Société amusante, 65, 71
Société anonyme, 62, 65
Socinianism/Socinians, 12, 25, 59-61, 160, 237n
soul, 147-48, 156, 160-63, 171-72, 182, 184-85, 188-89, 192, 199-200, 202, 207-209, 263, 265, 270-71, 274
essence/nature of the, 120, 150, 178, 180-81, 187, 200
immortality of the, 46, 171, 217, 270, 273
science of the, 33, 181, 188-89, 201, 208, 211, *see also* psychology
soul-body-relation, 31-32, 98, 147-48, 160-63, 169, 172, 176-78, 186-88, *see also* occasionalism; physical influx; pre-established harmony
sufficient reason, principle of, 14, 93, 121-22, 126, 139-40, 190, 192
Sulzer, Johann Georg, Swiss philosopher in Berlin, member of the Berlin Academy, 17-18, 208, 210-11, 216n, 225
Explication d'un paradoxe psychologique, 209
his physics of the soul, 208, 210

teleology, 129, 229, *see also* God, proofs of His existence, physico-theological proof
Teller, Romanus, professor of theology in Leipzig, 69
Tetens, Johann Nicolaus, professor of physics in Bützow, 188
The Hague, 153
Thomasius, Christian, 14-15, 23-24, 259, 265
Tillotson, John, archbishop of Canterburry, 89
trinity, dogma of, 3, 14, 60, 107
truths above reason, 3, 14, 106, 279
Tschirnhaus, Ehrenfried Walther, German mathematician in Dresden,
Medicina mentis, 261-62
Turrettini, François, Calvinist theologian in Geneva, 58-59
Turrettini, Jean-Alphonse, Calvinist theologian in Geneva, 24, 59

Unzer, Johann August, German physician in Halle, 182
Utrecht, 238

Vattel, Emer de, Swiss natural lawyer and privy councillor in Dresden, 93, 142, 152n, 176-77, 241n, 262n
Défense du système leibnitien, 176-77
Vernet, Jacob, Calvinist theologian in Geneva, 36-37, 105-108, 279-80
Instruction chrétienne, 106-107, 239, 244, 272-74
virtue/virtues, 104, 229, 252-53, 256, 260-61, 265-69, 275
intellectual, 263-64, 266-67, 268n
moral, 228, 264, 266-67, 268n, see also morality
Voltaire, 7, 9n, 17, 20n, 21, 69, 76, 103, 105, 125, 139, 195, 216-17, 233, 238, 254, 285
Candide, ou De l'optimisme, 215
Métaphysique de Newton, 125, 195-98
Poème sur le désastre de Lisbonne, 215-16
voluntarism, 216, 236, 238, 240, 242-43, 246, 259, 273, 277-78, see also God, His absolute decree

Walch, Johann Georg, Lutheran theologian in Jena, 111, 158n, 159
Philosophisches Lexicon, 111-12, 115, 123n
Wittenberg, University of, 38
Wolff, Christian, 6, 8, 13-15, 18-19, 28, 32-33, 40, 47-48, 63-65, 67-72, 74, 80-81, 85, 87-88, 93-94, 100, 102, 110, 119-22, 126-27, 129-37, 141-42, 148-55, 157-69, 171-72, 174-77, 180-81, 183-87, 189, 191-92, 195, 198, 201, 208-11, 214, 227, 229, 232-33, 249, 257, 259, 262n, 265, 267n, 268, 271, 272n, 275, 280-85
Anmerckungen, 183
De differentia nexus rerum sapientis & fatalis necessitates, 157-58, 161, 170

Discursus praeliminaris de philosophia in genere, 41, 137, 150
Ethica, 262-66, 269-72, 274
Ethik, 269, 272
his concept of God, 119-20, 229-30, 232, 274
his concept of philosophy, 39-43, 280
his moral philosophy, 250-51, 257-61, 266, 269-71, 274, 280
his natural theology, 43, 63, 69, 80, 110, 118, 120, 129, 145, see also natural theology
his principle of perfectibility, 88, 98, 183n, 214, 260, 268, 274-75, 280, see also perfectibility
his proof of God, 120-23, 126-27, 143
his psychology, 135, 166, 168, 178, 181-83, 185, 187-89, 192, 208, see also psychology, empirical; psychology, rational
his rationalism, 13, 63, 69, 81, 251, 259, 280, 283, see also rationalism
his theory of liberty, 168-70, 185, 187, 193, 198
Horae subsecivae marburgenses, 87-88, 98-99, 123, 126-27
Logica, 150-51
Logik, 65
Metaphysik, 43, 120, 151, 169, 179, 181, 183, 192-93, 215, 232
Oratio de Sinarum philosophia practica, 257, 269n
on pre-established harmony, 149, 157, 160-61, 163-64, 169, 187
Ratio praelectionum, 123
Theologia naturalis, 63, 120, 151, 232n, 236n
women readers, 36, 150, 282

Yvon, Claude abbé de, French writer and journalist, 4
Accord de la philosophie avec la religion, 5